Children's
Literature
Review

Guide to Gale Literary Criticism Series

For criticism on	Consult these Gale series
Authors now living or who died after December 31, 1959	*CONTEMPORARY LITERARY CRITICISM (CLC)*
Authors who died between 1900 and 1959	*TWENTIETH-CENTURY LITERARY CRITICISM (TCLC)*
Authors who died between 1800 and 1899	*NINETEENTH-CENTURY LITERATURE CRITICISM (NCLC)*
Authors who died between 1400 and 1799	*LITERATURE CRITICISM FROM 1400 TO 1800 (LC)* *SHAKESPEAREAN CRITICISM (SC)*
Authors who died before 1400	*CLASSICAL AND MEDIEVAL LITERATURE CRITICISM (CMLC)*
Authors of books for children and young adults	*CHILDREN'S LITERATURE REVIEW (CLR)*
Dramatists	*DRAMA CRITICISM (DC)*
Poets	*POETRY CRITICISM (PC)*
Short story writers	*SHORT STORY CRITICISM (SSC)*
Black writers of the past two hundred years	*BLACK LITERATURE CRITICISM (BLC)*
Hispanic writers of the late nineteenth and twentieth centuries	*HISPANIC LITERATURE CRITICISM (HLC)*
Native North American writers and orators of the eighteenth, nineteenth, and twentieth centuries	*NATIVE NORTH AMERICAN LITERATURE (NNAL)*
Major authors from the Renaissance to the present	*WORLD LITERATURE CRITICISM, 1500 TO THE PRESENT (WLC)*

ISSN 0362-4145

volume 64

Children's Literature Review

Excerpts from Reviews,
Criticism, and Commentary
on Books for Children
and Young People

Jennifer Baise
Editor

Thomas Ligotti
Associate Editor

GALE GROUP

Detroit
New York
San Francisco
London
Boston
Woodbridge, CT

STAFF

Jennifer Baise, *Editor*

Thomas Ligotti, *Associate Editor*

Maria Franklin, *Permissions Manager*
Kimberly F. Smilay, *Permissions Specialist*
Kelly A. Quin, *Permissions Associates*
Sandy Gore, *Permissions Assistant*

Victoria B. Cariappa, *Research Manager*
Andrew Guy Malonis, Barbara McNeil, Gary J. Oudersluys, Maureen Richards,
Cheryl L. Warnock, *Research Specialists*
Patricia T. Ballard, Tamara C. Nott, Tracie A. Richardson, *Research Associates*
Phyllis Blackman, Timothy Lehnerer, *Research Assistant*

Mary Beth Trimper, *Production Director*
Stacy Melson, *Buyer*

Michael Logusz, *Graphic Artist*
Randy Bassett, *Image Database Supervisor*
Robert Duncan, *Imaging Specialists*
Pamela Reed, *Imaging Coordinator*

Contents

Preface   vii

Acknowledgments   xi

Preface

Literature for children and young adults has evolved into both a respected branch of creative writing and a successful industry. Currently, books for young readers are considered among the most popular segments of publishing. Criticism of juvenile literature is instrumental in recording the literary or artistic development of the creators of children's books as well as the trends and controversies that result from changing values or attitudes about young people and their literature. Designed to provide a permanent, accessible record of this ongoing scholarship, *Children's Literature Review (CLR)* presents parents, teachers, and librarians—those responsible for bringing children and books together—with the opportunity to make informed choices when selecting reading materials for the young. In addition, *CLR* provides researchers of children's literature with easy access to a wide variety of critical information from English-language sources in the field. Users will find balanced overviews of the careers of the authors and illustrators of the books that children and young adults are reading; these entries, which contain excerpts from published criticism in books and periodicals, assist users by sparking ideas for papers and assignments and suggesting supplementary and classroom reading. Ann L. Kalkhoff, president and editor of *Children's Book Review Service Inc.*, writes that "*CLR* has filled a gap in the field of children's books, and it is one series that will never lose its validity or importance."

Scope of the Series

Each volume of *CLR* profiles the careers of a selection of authors and illustrators of books for children and young adults from preschool through high school. Author lists in each volume reflect:

■ an international scope.

■ representation of authors of all eras.

■ the variety of genres covered by children's and/or YA literature: picture books, fiction, nonfiction, poetry, folklore, and drama.

Although the focus of the series is on authors new to *CLR*, entries will be updated as the need arises.

Organization of This Book

An entry consists of the following elements: author heading, author portrait, author introduction, excerpts of criticism (each preceded by a bibliographical citation), and illustrations, when available.

■ The **Author Heading** consists of the author's name followed by birth and death dates. The portion of the name outside the parentheses denotes the form under which the author is most frequently published. If the majority of the author's works for children were written under a pseudonym, the pseudonym will be listed in the author heading and the real name given on the first line of the author introduction. Also located at the beginning of the introduction are any other pseudonyms used by the author in writing for children and any name variations, including transliterated forms for authors whose languages use nonroman alphabets. Uncertainty as to a birth or death date is indicated by question marks.

■ An **Author Portrait** is included when available.

■ The **Author Introduction** contains information designed to introduce an author to *CLR* users by presenting an overview of the author's themes and styles, biographical facts that relate to the author's literary career or critical responses to the author's works, and information about major awards and prizes the author has received. The introduction begins by identifying the nationality of the author and by listing the genres in which s/he has written for children and young adults. Introductions also list a group of representative titles for which the author or illustrator being profiled is best known; this section, which begins with the words "major works include," follows the genre line of the introduction. For seminal figures, a listing of major works about the author follows when appropriate, highlighting important biographies about the author or illustrator that are not excerpted in the entry. The centered heading "Introduction" announces the body of the text.

- **Criticism** is located in three sections: **Author's Commentary** (when available), **General Commentary** (when available), and **Title Commentary** (commentary on specific titles).

  - The **Author's Commentary** presents background material written by the author or by an interviewer. This commentary may cover a specific work or several works. Author's commentary on more than one work appears after the author introduction, while commentary on an individual book follows the title entry heading.

  - The **General Commentary** consists of critical excerpts that consider more than one work by the author or illustrator being profiled. General commentary is preceded by the critic's name in boldface type or, in the case of unsigned criticism, by the title of the journal. *CLR* also features entries that emphasize general criticism on the oeuvre of an author or illustrator. When appropriate, a selection of reviews is included to supplement the general commentary.

  - The **Title Commentary** begins with the title entry headings, which precede the criticism on a title and cite publication information on the work being reviewed. Title headings list the title of the work as it appeared in its first English-language edition. The first English-language publication date of each work (unless otherwise noted) is listed in parentheses following the title. Differing U.S. and British titles follow the publication date within the parentheses. When a work is written by an individual other than the one being profiled, as is the case when illustrators are featured, the parenthetical material following the title cites the author of the work before listing its publication date.

    Entries in each title commentary section consist of critical excerpts on the author's individual works, arranged chronologically by publication date. The entries generally contain two to seven reviews per title, depending on the stature of the book and the amount of criticism it has generated. The editors select titles that reflect the entire scope of the author's literary contribution, covering each genre and subject. An effort is made to reprint criticism that represents the full range of each title's reception, from the year of its initial publication to current assessments. Thus, the reader is provided with a record of the author's critical history. Publication information (such as publisher names and book prices) and parenthetical numerical references (such as footnotes or page and line references to specific editions of works) have been deleted at the discretion of the editors to provide smoother reading of the text.

- Centered headings introduce each section, in which criticism is arranged chronologically; beginning with Volume 35, each excerpt is preceded by a boldface source heading for easier access by readers. Within the text, titles by authors being profiled are also highlighted in boldface type.

- Selected excerpts are preceded by **Explanatory Annotations,** which provide information on the critic or work of criticism to enhance the reader's understanding of the excerpt.

- A complete **Bibliographical Citation** designed to facilitate the location of the original book or article precedes each piece of criticism.

- Numerous **Illustrations** are featured in *CLR*. For entries on illustrators, an effort has been made to include illustrations that reflect the characteristics discussed in the criticism. Entries on authors who do not illustrate their own works may also include photographs and other illustrative material pertinent to their careers.

Special Features: Entries on Illustrators

Entries on authors who are also illustrators will occasionally feature commentary on selected works illustrated but not written by the author being profiled. These works are strongly associated with the illustrator and have received critical acclaim for their art. By including critical comment on works of this type, the editors wish to provide a more complete representation of the artist's career. Criticism on these works has been chosen to stress artistic, rather than literary, contributions. Title entry headings for works illustrated by the author being profiled are arranged chronologically within the entry by date of publication and include notes identifying the author of the illustrated work. In order to provide easier access for users, all titles illustrated by the subject of the entry are boldfaced.

CLR also includes entries on prominent illustrators who have contributed to the field of children's literature. These entries are designed to represent the development of the illustrator as an artist rather than as a literary stylist. The illustrator's section is organized like that of an author, with two exceptions: the introduction presents an overview of the illustrator's styles and techniques rather than outlining his or her literary background, and the commentary written by the illustrator on his or her works is called "illustrator's commentary" rather than "author's commentary." All titles of books containing illustrations by the artist being profiled are highlighted in boldface type.

Other Features: Acknowledgments, Indexes

■ The **Acknowledgments** section, which immediately follows the preface, lists the sources from which material has been reprinted in the volume. It does not, however, list every book or periodical consulted for the volume.

■ The **Cumulative Index to Authors** lists all of the authors who have appeared in *CLR* with cross-references to the biographical, autobiographical, and literary criticism series published by Gale Research. A full listing of the series titles appears before the first page of the indexes of this volume.

■ The **Cumulative Index to Nationalities** lists authors alphabetically under their respective nationalities. Author names are followed by the volume number(s) in which they appear.

■ The **Cumulative Index to Titles** lists titles covered in *CLR* followed by the volume and page number where criticism begins.

A Note to the Reader

CLR is one of several critical references sources in the Literature Criticism Series published by Gale Research. When writing papers, students who quote directly from any volume in the Literature Criticism Series may use the following general forms to footnote reprinted criticism. The first example pertains to material drawn from periodicals, the second to material reprinted from books.

[1]T. S. Eliot, "John Donne," *The Nation and the Athenaeum,* 33 (9 June 1923), 321-32; excerpted and reprinted in *Literature Criticism from 1400 to 1800,* Vol. 10, ed. James E. Person, Jr. (Detroit: Gale Research, 1989), pp. 28-9.

[1]Henry Brooke, *Leslie Brooke and Johnny Crow* (Frederick Warne, 1982); excerpted and reprinted in *Children's Literature Review,* Vol. 20, ed. Gerard J. Senick (Detroit: Gale Research, 1990), p. 47.

Suggestions Are Welcome

In response to various suggestions, several features have been added to *CLR* since the beginning of the series, including author entries on retellers of traditional literature as well as those who have been the first to record oral tales and other folklore; entries on prominent illustrators featuring commentary on their styles and techniques; entries on authors whose works are considered controversial; occasional entries devoted to criticism on a single work or a series of works; sections in author introductions that list major works by and about the author or illustrator being profiled; explanatory notes that provide information on the critic or work of criticism to enhance the usefulness of the excerpt; more extensive illustrative material, such as holographs of manuscript pages and photographs of people and places pertinent to the careers of the authors and artists; a cumulative nationality index for easy access to authors by nationality; and occasional guest essays written specifically for *CLR* by prominent critics on subjects of their choice.

Readers who wish to suggest authors to appear in future volumes, or who have other suggestions, are cordially invited to contact the editor. By mail: Editor, *Children's Literature Review,* Gale Research, 835 Penobscot Bldg., 645 Griswold St., Detroit, MI 48226-4094; by telephone: (800) 347-GALE; by fax: (313) 961-6599; by E-mail: CYA@Gale.com.

Acknowledgments

The editors wish to thank the copyright holders of the criticism included in this volume and the permissions managers of many book and magazine publishing companies for assisting us in securing reproduction rights. We are also grateful to the staffs of the Detroit Public Library, the Library of Congress, the University of Detroit Mercy Library, Wayne State University Purdy/Kresge Library Complex, and the University of Michigan Libraries for making their resources available to us. Following is a list of the copyright holders who have granted us permission to reproduce material in this volume of *CLR*. Every effort has been made to trace copyright, but if omissions have been made, please let us know.

COPYRIGHTED ESSAYS IN *CLR*, VOLUME 64, WERE REPRODUCED FROM THE FOLLOWING PERIODICALS:

The Book Report, v. 16, March/April, 1998, p. 36. © copyright 1998 by Linworth Publishing, Inc., Worthington, Ohio. Reproduced by permission.—*Book World-The Washington Post,* March 27, 1994 for a review of *Small Gods, and Others* by Gregory Feeley. © 1994, Washington Post Book World Service/Washington Post Writers Group. Reproduced by permission of the author.—*Booklist,* v. 76, 1980; v. 85, September 1, 1988; v. 85, May 1, 1989; v. 86, March 15, 1990; v. 87, May 1, 1991; v. 87, June 1, 1991; v. 88, September 1, 1991; v. 88, October, 15, 1991; v. 88, December 1, 1991; v. 89, June 15, 1993; v. 90, July, 1994; v. 91, November 15, 1994; v. 91, December 15, 1994; v. 91, January 1, 1995; v. 91, August, 1995; v. 92, September 1, 1995; v. 92, September 15, 1995; v. 92, October 15, 1995; v. 92, March 15, 1996; v. 93, October 1, 1996; v. 93, November 1, 1996; v. 93, December 1, 1996; v. 93, April 1, 1997; v. 94, September 15, 1997; v. 94, November 15, 1997; v. 94, December 1, 1997; v. 94, June 1, 1998; v. 95, September 1, 1998; v. 95, January 1, 1999; v. 95, February 15, 1999; v. 95, April 15, 1999; v. 95, May 1, 1999; v. 95, June 1, 1999; January 1, 2000. Copyright © 1980, 1988, 1989, 1990, 1991, 1993, 1994, 1995, 1996, 1997, 1998, 1999, 2000 by the American Library Association. All reproduced by permission.—*Books for Keeps,* July, 1993; July, 1996. © School Bookshop Association 1993, 1996. Both reproduced by permission.—*Books for Young People,* v. 2, October, 1988. Reproduced by permission of the author.—*Books for Your Children,* v. 28, Spring, 1993. © Books for Your Children 1993. Reproduced by permission.—*Books in Canada,* v. 17, December, 1988. "Plasticine Queen" by Ann Jansen. Reproduced by permission of the author.—*Books Magazine,* December, 1988; v. 3, July, 1989. Both reproduced by permission.—*British Book News,* March, 1984. Reproduced by permission.—*The Bulletin of the Center for Children's Books,* v. 30, 1977; v. 34, 1980. Copyright © 1977, 1980 by The University of Chicago./ v. 45, 1991; v. 46, May, 1993; v. 48, January, 1995; v. 49, September 1995; v. 49, January, 1996; v. 50, December, 1996; v. 50, May, 1997. Copyright © 1991, 1993, 1995, 1996, 1997 by The Board of Trustees of the University of Illinois. All reproduced by permission.—*Canadian Children's Literature,* 1989, 1990, 1993, 1996. Copyright © 1989, 1990, 1993, 1996 Canadian Children's Press. All reproduced by permission.—*Chicago Tribune Books,* February 9, 1992. Copyright © 1992 Tribune Media Services, Inc. All rights reserved. Reproduced by permission.—*Children's Book News,* v. 14, Fall, 1991. Reproduced by permission of The Canadian Children's Book Centre, Toronto, Canada.—*Children's Book Review Service, Inc.,* v. 5, 1976; v. 25, November, 1996; v. 25, Spring, 1997. Copyright 1976, 1996, 1997 Children's Book Review Service Inc. All reproduced by permission.—*CM: A Reviewing Journal of Canadian Materials for Young People,* v. XVI, January, 1988; v. XVII, January, 1989; v. XIX, September, 1991; v. XX, March, 1992; v. XX, October, 1992. Copyright 1988, 1989, 1991, 1992 The Canadian Library Association. All reproduced by permission of the Manitoba Library Association.—*The Critical Quarterly,* v. 2, Winter, 1960. Reproduced by permission of Blackwell Publishers.—*Curriculum Review,* v. 17, October, 1978. Reproduced by permission.—*English Journal,* v. 79, March, 1990. Copyright © 1990 by the National Council of Teachers of English. Reproduced by permission.—*Essays in Literature,* v. XI, Fall, 1984. Reproduced by permission.—*Extrapolation,* v. 13, May, 1972; v. 20, Summer, 1979; v. 21, Winter, 1980. Copyright © 1972, 1979, 1980 by The Kent State University Press. All reproduced by permission.—*Fantasy Review,* v. 10, January/ February, 1987 for a review of *Equal Rights* by Pauline Morgan. Copyright © 1987 by the author.—*The Five Owls,* v. VII, May/June, 1993. Reproduced by permission.—*The Horn Book Guide,* v. V, January-June, 1994; v. VIII, Spring, 1997; v. VIII, Fall, 1997. Copyright, 1994, 1997, by The Horn Book, Inc., 11 Beacon St., Suite 1000, Boston, MA 02108. All rights reserved. Both reproduced by permission.—*The Horn Book Magazine,* v. LVI, June, 1980; v. LXIV, January, 1988; v. LXVI, March/ April, 1990; v. LXVII, May/ June, 1991; v. LXVII, September/ October, 1991; v. 69, Sept-Oct, 1993; v. 72, Jan-Feb, 1996; v. IX, Spring, 1998. Copyright, 1980, 1988, 1990, 1993, 1996, 1998, by The Horn Book, Inc., 11 Beacon St., Suite 1000, Boston, MA 02108. All rights reserved. All reproduced by permission.—*Journal of Modern Literature,* v. 18, Fall, 1993. Reproduced by permission.—*The Junior Bookshelf,* v. 54, February, 1990; v. 54, October, 1990; v. 54, December, 1990; v. 56, October, 1992; v. 57, February, 1993; v. 57, August, 1993; v. 58, June, 1994; v. 58, August, 1994; v. 58, December, 1994; v. 60, June, 1996. All reproduced by permission.—*Kirkus Reviews,* v. XLVIII, July 15, 1980; v. XLIX, August 1, 1981; v. LI, August 15, 1983; v. LV, May 1, 1987; February 15, 1989; v. LVIII, January 1, 1990; December 1, 1991; v. 61, February 1, 1993; March 15,

Wolfram Hänel

1956-

German author of books for primary graders.

Major works translated into English include *The Old Man and the Bear* (1994), *Lila's Little Dinosaur* (1994), *The Extraordinary Adventures of an Ordinary Hat* (1994), *Mia the Beach Cat* (1994), *Abby* (1996).

INTRODUCTION

A German with an affinity for the Irish and a belief in fairies, author Wolfram Hänel writes stories for primary graders about the magic of life. He especially likes interesting and extraordinary people who carry with them the whiff of fantasy. He told *Something About the Author*, "I love to tell stories that give room to a child's fantasy, stories where—sometimes—any adult might then say: 'Unbelievable!' And I love to tell about strange people, extraordinary characters." His work is filled with affection for these characters—*The Old Man and the Bear, The Other Side of the Bridge* (1996), and *The Gold at the End of the Rainbow* (1997)—as well as for children and their relationships with animals—*Mia the Beach Cat, Lila's Little Dinosaur, Abby, Mary and the Mystery Dog* (1999), and *Rescue at Sea* (1999).

Hänel wants children to draw lessons from his work, lessons about living in community and helping each other, including the animals who live with us and rely on us. He told *SATA*, "I tell children: believe in your dreams and please never go against those who are on the poor side of life—to help somebody who needs your help makes life more worthwhile than anything money could buy."

Biographical Information

Hänel was born and raised in Fulda, West Germany. He attended the Free University of Berlin, graduating in 1981, and received his teaching degree from the University of Hannover in 1983. His varied career includes stints as a photographer, graphic artist, high school teacher, public relations assistant, copywriter, drama producer, playwright, and social worker. In an interview for *SATA*, Hänel said, "One night in the pub somebody asked me, 'What is your profession?' 'A writer,' I said. 'Well,' said he, 'I'm a butcher, and my brother is a mechanic, and isn't life something beautiful?' What more to say?"

Major Works

Learning to balance cooperation and competition is the theme of *The Old Man and the Bear*. Old man Mahony is fishing for salmon, and so is Big Bill the bear. Caught up in their rivalry, first the bear moves into deeper water, catching the fish before they get to Mahony, then Mahony sets up a net to catch the fish before they get to Big Bill. When both fall into the river and are swept downstream, they discover that collaboration provides better for them both. Critics called this an agreeable book with characters children would enjoy. Hänel wrote a sequel, published in 1997, titled *Old Mahony and the Bear Family*.

After a trip to an exhibit at the Museum of Natural History about dinosaurs, Lila finds that a small, rainbow-colored dinosaur has followed her home. *Lila's Little Dinosaur* can only be seen by children, although the adults can smell and hear him. She awakes from happy dreams to find her new friend gone, and convinces herself that he was only imaginary, but on the way to school she sees him sitting in the back seat of the car, happily munching on the plant that disappeared from the bathroom. A critic for *Kirkus Reviews* wrote that this book "has all the qualities necessary for success. ... And it doesn't lose anything in the translation."

Hänel's best known story in English is *The Extraordinary Adventures of an Ordinary Hat*. A black bowler hat in a shop window daydreams of seeing the wide world and finding happiness with a sweet straw hat. When he is finally purchased, his bald owner carries him into a drab existence, traveling only to and from work, leaving him in a cupboard or on top of a filing cabinet. Inspired by a rabbit dispensing practical advice, the bowler takes off in a gust of wind while on a vacation camping trip and soon finds happiness, and his sweet straw hat, with a new owner in South America. Called "whimsical," "delightful," and "playful," this book was enjoyed by reviewers and won several European prizes.

Designated as a book for early readers, *Mia the Beach Cat* is about a stray cat and the little girl she befriends on the beach. Maggie, bored by her parents idea of a vacation lying on the beach, is happy to have a pet to explore with her. When Mia goes missing, Maggie worries; when Mia shows up as a stowaway in a fishing boat, Maggie is happy again. But when Mia excitedly leaps out of the boat to Maggie before reaching shallow water, she is nearly drowned. All ends happily when Maggie "sneaks" her new friend into the picnic basket to bring her home. A *Books for Keeps* reviewer praised this book as an "engaging story with plenty of dialogue and sufficient detail and suspense to keep [early readers] turning the pages."

Set on an island off the coast of Ireland, *Abby* is the story of a dog and the little girl who loves her. Abby is the farm dog who tends the goats, protects the house, and is the best friend of Moira. When Abby eats some poisoned meat that a neighboring farmer set out for a fox, the grown-ups give her up for dead, but Moira sleeps beside her through the night, caressing her and talking to her, and is rewarded by waking up to Abby licking her face, fully recovered. Carolyn Phelan of *Booklist* commented, "Readers will feel like celebrating, too, though they may shed a few tears, so effective is this simple story."

Awards

Hänel has won awards for his work in Germany and France. He won the Playwright's Prize for Theater from the Bund der Theatergemeinden in Bonn, Germany in 1991 for *Ca Ira! Es war einal eine Revolution.... The Extraordinary Adventures of an Ordinary Hat* won Best Book of the Month from the *Bulletin for Children's Literature* in Hamburg in 1994 and L'Octogonal Prix Creation-Creativite from the Centre International d'Etude en Literature de Jeunesse in Paris in 1995.

TITLE COMMENTARY

THE OLD MAN AND THE BEAR **(1994; in German as *Der Kleine Mann und der Baer*, 1993)**

Martha F. Silbert

SOURCE: A review of *The Old Man and the Bear*, in *The Horn Book Guide*, Vol. V, No. 2, January-June, 1994, p. 274.

After a dousing in the river and an encounter with angry bees, Old Mahony and a big, brown bear turn their salmon-fishing competition into a partnership by deciding to cooperate on procuring salmon and honey. Both the text and the artwork [by Jean-Pierre Corderoc'h] are competent and amusing, although they do not offer many surprises.

The Junior Bookshelf

SOURCE: A review of *The Old Man and the Bear*, in *The Junior Bookshelf*, Vol. 58, No. 4, August, 1994, pp. 128-129.

The northern river is full of salmon and an old man named Mahony fishes there. He is joined by Big Bill the bear, and though neither is happy about the presence of the other there are enough fish for both of them.

Enmity makes the situation unsatisfactory. First of all the bear moves into deeper water, and catches the salmon before they reach Mahony; then the old man fixes a net downstream, which traps the fish before they get to the bear. The enemies squabble, fall into the river and are swept on to an island. Here, the two discover that through collaboration they can not only live amicably together but eat better and more varied meals.

This agreeable book is printed on an unusual, semi-glossy paper particularly well suited to the attractive shades used in the appealing illustrations. [by J.-P. Corderoc'h]

Gale W. Sherman

SOURCE: A review of *The Old Man and the Bear*, in *School Library Journal*, Vol. 40, No. 9, September, 1994, p. 186.

Originally published in Switzerland, this story has universal appeal for youngsters learning to balance competition and cooperation. After plotting to get the best of each other, an old fisherman and a fishing bear fall in the river and are swept into a friendship based on mutual need. Corderoc'h's watercolor illustrations are animated with chubby, appealing characters and a gentle sense of humor. Beginning readers will delight in the fun the two characters have.

LILA'S LITTLE DINOSAUR **(1994; in German as *Lila und der regenbogenbunte Dinosaurier*)**

Christina Dorr

SOURCE: A review of *Lila's Little Dinosaur*, in *School Library Journal*, Vol. 40, No. 10, October, 1994, p. 90.

Make room on the beginning-reader shelves for this delightful story imported from Switzerland. After convincing her father to visit an exhibit of life-sized mechanical dinosaurs at the Museum of Natural History, Lila discovers a rainbow-striped baby dino near one of the display models. They bond immediately, and the cute little fellow follows her out the door; she tucks him under her jacket and takes him home. Lila soon learns that only children can see him, though adults can smell and hear him. That night she broaches the subject of a pet—maybe a baby dino—with her parents. After pleasant dreams, she awakens to find that her friend is gone and decides that maybe he was only imaginary after all. But on her way to school, she is delighted to see him sitting in the back of the car, munching on her mother's fern that had disappeared from the bathroom. [Alex] de Wolf's watercolor cartoons clarify the action for young listeners and broaden the humor. Pair this gem with James Mayhew's *Katie and the Dinosaurs* for a guaranteed read-aloud hit.

Kirkus Reviews

SOURCE: A review of *Lila's Little Dinosaur*, in *Kirkus Reviews*, Vol. LXII, No. 22, November 15, 1994, p. 1530.

The little dinosaur follows Lila home from the Museum of Natural History, where Lila had been explaining to her father all about the different dinosaurs. She tells him to wait for her in the museum, but the incorrigible creature sneaks out anyway. Lila rescues him from the street, brings him to her house, feeds him, and puts him to bed. In the morning, however, the dinosaur is gone, and Lila thinks she dreamt the whole thing. She sadly gets ready for school, only somewhat soothed when her parents offer to buy her a dog or a cat. Then her father drops her off at school, and as he pulls away in the car, who should she see in the back seat but her colorful friend? Who needs a pet dog, thinks Lila, when you have a pet dinosaur?

This easy reader has all the qualities necessary for success: a clever little heroine, dinosaur lore, and an adorable rainbow-colored baby dinosaur that only children can see. And it doesn't lose anything in the translation.

Denia Hester

SOURCE: A review of *Lila's Little Dinosaur*, in *Booklist*, Vol. 91, No. 9, January 1, 1995, p. 820.

A seven-and-a-half-year-old who loves dinosaurs more than anything is thrilled when she encounters a little dinosaur hiding out at a special exhibit put on by the National History Museum. It's not your typical dinosaur. Covered from head to toe with rainbow stripes, this compact dino, about the size of a dog, is a sight to behold—but only a sight for children's eyes. Lila takes her dinosaur home, and the usual antics ensue when a guest that parents can't see has to be accommodated. This predictable tale gets a shot in the arm from the spirited color illustrations [by Alex de Wolf] on each page that should keep readers turning eagerly.

THE EXTRAORDINARY ADVENTURES OF AN ORDINARY HAT* (1994; in German as *Waldemar und die Weite Klelt

Carolyn L. Shute

SOURCE: A review of *The Extraordinary Adventures of an Ordinary Hat*, in *The Horn Book Guide*, Vol. V, No. 2, January-June, 1994 p. 274.

In the whimsical fantasy, the dreams of a black bowler hat to see the wide world and find happiness with a sweet straw hat come true when the wind carries him away from his bald-headed owner. The ink and watercolor illustrations [by Christa Unzner-Fischer] nicely suit the tone of the playful German import, but the book has limited appeal for children.

The Junior Bookshelf

SOURCE: A review of *The Extraordinary Adventures of an Ordinary Hat,* in *The Junior Bookshelf,* Vol. 58, No. 3, June, 1994, p. 101.

The hat daydreams of happy hours in the street outside the shop as seen from the window during his newness. When the bank manager buys his twin he becomes discouraged. Then Mr. Bruno buys *him* and he suffers humiliations and a drab existence until, on a camping holiday, a pragmatic rabbit inspires him to take off, which he promptly does in a high wind and soon is writing from South America to Jonathan, the hat-shop owner, of the exciting life that surrounds him *and* his marriage to a sweet straw hat, worn by his owner's wife who writes his letter for him. The text is plain but never childish and the conversations natural and illuminating. The illustrations are both funny and beautiful—especially the hats.

Deborah Abbott

SOURCE: A review of *The Extraordinary Adventures of an Ordinary Hat,* in *Booklist,* Vol. 90, No. 21, July, 1994, p. 1947.

After years of aging (and dreaming of adventure) on the hat shelf in a store, a black bowler perks up after it is purchased by bald Mr. Bruno. While being out in the world with Mr. Bruno is fun, the hat soon finds itself once again stuck on a shelf. Then, during a summer camping trip, the hat goes to the beach, takes off in the wind, and ends up in South America, where it becomes the property of Don Leonardo. It soon finds happiness with a lovely brimmed straw hat owned by Don Leonardo's bride. This smooth English translation of the book's original German text offers just the right sense of detail and emotion. Color and line drawings [by Christa Unzner-Fischer] on every page, including an expressive face on the bowler, enhance this whimsical story with an unusual point of view.

Mary Jo Drungil

SOURCE: A review of *The Extraordinary Adventures of an Ordinary Hat,* in *School Library Journal,* Vol. 40, No. 7, July, 1994, p. 77.

After years of sitting on a shelf in Jonathan's store, a black bowler is purchased by a bald man and is certain that its dreams of adventure and romance will finally come true. But Bruno only wears the hat to and from work, so it spends most of its time in the closet or the filing cabinet. Then he wears it on a summer camping trip, and it deliberately lets itself be carried away by the wind. Weeks later, Jonathan receives a letter from the bowler, now happily settled in South America, where it is owned by Don Leonardo. Best of all, Don Leonardo's new bride wears a sweet straw hat. The full-color, cartoon-style illustrations underscore the gentle humor in the text; the hats have facial features, and their detailed expressions make the tale come alive. The use of colors—ranging from soft grays and beiges to bright reds and blues—adds to the vibrant tone of the text. Not a first choice, but a nice addition with a surprising twist.

MIA THE BEACH CAT (1994; in German as *Mia, die Strandkatze*)

D.A. Young

SOURCE: A review of *Mia the Beach Cat*, in *The Junior Bookshelf*, Vol. 58, No. 6, December, 1994, p. 214.

Mia the Beach Cat was first published in German in Switzerland and the present translation is by J. Alison James.

Maggie, a bright five year old, is spending a holiday at the seaside with her parents. She finds it incredibly boring playing by herself all day while Mum and Dad want nothing more than to relax in the sunshine. That is until the arrival of Mia, a stray cat, who delights in chasing Maggie in and out of the tumbling waves. Then Mia goes missing in search of food on a fishing boat. Maggie and her Dad wait anxiously for the boats to return. Mia, of course, is on the last one and narrowly escapes a watery grave as he tries to jump ashore before the boat docks.

Maggie succeeds in finding a way to smuggle Mia home and all is well.

With its bright, breezy and sympathetic illustrations [by K. Höcker], its short sentences and simple vocabulary it should take some of the tedium out of the early stages of learning to read.

Christine A. Moesch

SOURCE: A review of *Mia the Beach Cat*, in *School Library Journal*, Vol. 40, No. 12, December, 1994, pp. 75-76.

While her parents sunbathe, Maggie explores the beach and makes friends with a stray cat that says "mia" instead of "meow." When the child's stuffed cat is washed out to sea, she decides to adopt Mia. Dad says no at first, but after several days of playing with the animal, Maggie "sneaks" it home in a picnic basket (which Dad knows about all along). The writing is simple, and the book is filled with enough detail and dialogue to hold young readers' attention. The warm, muted watercolors are filled with action. An easy-to-read story for children ready for more than one sentence per page.

Kirkus Reviews

SOURCE: A review of *Mia the Beach Cat*, in *Kirkus Reviews*, Vol. LXIII, No. 24, December 15, 1994, pp. 1563-64.

Maggie is spending her holiday with her parents and her stuffed tiger at the sea, but her parents' idea of a good time is relaxing for hours in the sun, and her tiger is not really made for water sports. Maggie is left to her own devices. For a while she occupies herself making sand castles and collecting shells, but she is lonely. Then one day Maggie finds Mia the cat, who becomes her summer playmate. Every morning, without fail, she is there on the beach when Maggie arrives. But one day Mia is nowhere to be found. Maggie frantically searches for her friend, and it occurs to her that Mia must be near the fishing boats. Sure enough Mia has stowed away on one of the boats and is now returning to the dock on its prow. Mia sees Maggie and excitedly jumps towards her. She lands in the water, but they fish her out. On Maggie's last day of vacation, she smuggles Mia into her parents' car. Maggie's mother asks innocently about the cat as Maggie and her father share a secret wink and Mia purrs her contentment.

An appealing story for young animal lovers from Hänel.

Roger Sutton

SOURCE: A review of *Mia the Beach Cat*, in *The Bulletin of the Center for Children's Books*, Vol. 48, No. 5, January, 1995, p. 166.

Sated by sandcastle building and shell-collecting, Maggie is slightly bored and lonely at the beach, where her parents remain content to snooze and sunbathe. She's delighted, then, to find a stray cat (who says "mia" rather than "meow," thus her name), and the two have a great time chasing the waves and cuddling. Of course Maggie wants to bring the cat home; of course her mother says no; but time, a little drama, and some surreptitious help from Mia's father bring things to their foregone conclusion. Like the same publisher's *Where's Molly?* by Uli Waas, this is a light breeze of an early-reader book, coaching new readers' skills with a story close enough to real life to be comfortable, but spiked with sufficient suspense to be interesting. The format is clean and open, and amiable, unbabyish pencil-and-watercolor illustrations [by Kirsten Höcker] appear on every page, giving plenty of clues to the text.

Jill Bennett

SOURCE: A review of *Mia the Beach Cat*, in *Books for Keeps: The Children's Book Magazine*, No. 99 July, 1996 p. 9.

On their summer holiday Maggie's parents only want to lie in the sun; they're not the slightest bit interested in her collection of stones, feathers, seaweed and shells. But what good is a collection if you have nobody to share it with, wonders Maggie? As she sits musing, she spies a small grey and white cat playing in the water. A tumbling wave rolls in bringing the little cat to her. From then on Maggie's holiday becomes much more exciting. Soon it's time to return home and Mother has already made one thing clear: 'No cats in my car . . . and that's final.' But Maggie has a plan . . .

There's much appeal for developing independent readers here: an engaging story with plenty of dialogue and sufficient detail and suspense to keep them turning the pages, complemented by delightful, gently humorous, muted watercolours.

JASMINE AND REX (1995; in German as Romeo liebt Julia)

Linda Wicher

SOURCE: A review of *Jasmine and Rex,* in *School Library Journal,* Vol. 42, No. 1, January, 1996, p. 84.

This takeoff on *Romeo and Juliet,* in which the star-crossed lovers are a dog and a cat, is clever and quite well executed; however, the choice of format, a beginning chapter book, is a curious one. Rex and Jasmine are about to talk each other into a suicide pact when Lorenzo the donkey brings them to their senses and suggests they run away together to a land where differences between cats and dogs don't matter. Although young readers may be interested in the theme of fair play, they will not easily understand the concepts of honor and romance. Also, the expressive pen-and-ink and watercolor illustrations [by Christa Unzner] would lend themselves to a larger, picture-book format.

THE OTHER SIDE OF THE BRIDGE (1996)

Martha F. Sibert

SOURCE: A review of *The Other Side of the Bridge,* in *The Horn Book Guide,* Vol. VIII, No. 1, Spring, 1997, p. 58.

Andy, a loner who loves to observe nature, goes looking for signs of spring in the woods one day and gets lost in a spring snowstorm. He is rescued by Jasper, who lives by himself and—despite his scary reputation—turns out to be a nice man, perhaps even a kindred spirit. Engaging illustrations [by Alex de Wolf] accompany this pleasant, if somewhat predictable, story.

Elizabeth Hammill

SOURCE: "Graphic Description," in *The Times Educational Supplement,* No. 4216, April 18, 1997, p. 12.

Perspective is . . . important to Wolfram Hänel's *The Other Side of the Bridge.* This tale celebrates the individualism of Andy, who prefers nature study to sport, and Old Jasper, reputed to "eat children", who saves him when he ventures into the woods in search of Spring and encounters a freak snowstorm. There is genuine drama here, heightened by the lore surrounding Jasper, and a subtle, delicate quality that invites reflection.

ABBY (1996)

Kirkus Reviews

SOURCE: A review of *Abby,* in *Kirkus Reviews,* Vol. LXIV, No. 20, October 15, 1996, p. 1540.

Moira lives on an island off the coast of Ireland with her family and her dog, Abby. Hänel spends about half the book setting up Moira's life on this rural, remote island of fishermen and farmers. The second half tells of Abby's near-fatal experience of and recovery from eating poisoned meat left out for a fox. This gentle, delicate story begins slowly and so generally that new readers will have no idea where it's going. The story of Abby's illness is told straightforwardly and without sentimentality or false suspense, a style that suits the island setting and its inhabitants. The watercolor-and-ink illustrations [by Alan Marks] match the mood, introducing humor that's especially welcome during the sorrowful parts.

Carolyn Phelan

SOURCE: A review of *Abby,* in *Booklist,* Vol. 93, No. 7, December 1, 1996, p. 652.

Set on an island off the Irish coast, this fully illustrated story tells of Moira and her dog, Abby, who looks after the goats, keeps the cats out of the house, and is also the girl's best friend. Abby falls ill after eating some poisoned meat set out by a neighboring farmer. As night falls, the grown-ups shake their heads over the motionless dog, but Moira sleeps with her all night and celebrates her recovery when the morning dawns. Readers will feel like celebrating, too, though they may shed a few tears, so effective is this simple story. There are no chapter divisions; however, readers of early chapter books will find this a rewarding choice. The place, the characters, and the emotions ring true in the text and in [Alan] Marks, sensitive illustrations. Combining deft line drawing and fluid watercolors, the artwork captures the spirit of the story with economy and restraint. Good for reading aloud or alone, this is one of the few books written at this level that is likely to touch the hearts of those who discover it.

Elisabeth Palmer

SOURCE: A review of *Abby,* in *School Library Journal,* Vol. 43, No. 1, January, 1997, pp. 77, 83.

Moira and her family live on a small island off the Irish coast. Abby is Moira's dog and her best friend. Together they watch clouds, sit on the cliffs above the beach, and wave when fishing boats pass by. One day when the girl returns from school, Abby is nowhere to be found. When the dog is carried home by a neighbor, Moira discovers that the pup has eaten poisoned meat intended for some foxes. She stays up all night with Abby, telling her stories and stroking her. The child eventually falls asleep, only to be awakened by Abby licking her face. Moira's love for the animal is pure and understandable to anyone who has ever had a pet. Both text and illustrations [by Alan Marks] depict a beautiful island with hardworking and friendly people. The sweeping pen-and-ink paintings with watercolor washes portray Moira's many feelings as she goes from being happy to sad to relieved. Youngsters who are moving on from easy readers, but still want short books with lots of illustrations, will enjoy this gentle offering.

THE GOLD AT THE END OF THE RAINBOW (1997)

Jackie C. Horne

SOURCE: A review of *The Gold at the End of the Rainbow,* in *The Horn Book Guide,* Vol. VIII, No. 2, Fall, 1997, p. 266.

Brendan and Grandpa set out to capture a leprechaun and the pot of gold he guards, even though Grandpa thinks the creature only a fairy tale. Find the leprechaun they do, but Grandpa lets him go and is rewarded for his kindness. The pleasantly told tale is illustrated [by Loek Koopmans] with watercolors that are sometimes strikingly, other times awkwardly, rendered.

Children's Book Review Service, Inc.

SOURCE: A review of *The Gold at the End of the Rainbow,* in *Children's Book Review Service, Inc.,* Vol. 25, No. 12, Spring, 1997, p. 135.

Brendan and his grandfather had little to eat for they had only one cow. Grandfather told Brendan the story of the rainbow, the island, the leprechaun and the pot of gold. The next day there was a rainbow so they rowed across to the island and dug and dug. They didn't find the gold, but they met the leprechaun and did a good deed. As in all fairy tales, the next morning when they awoke there was a happy ending. The beautiful illustrations and the story will appeal to the young.

Julie Corsaro

SOURCE: A review of *The Gold at the End of the Rainbow,* in *Booklist,* Vol. 93, No. 15, April 1, 1997, p. 1337.

During their search for the gold at the end of the rainbow, young Brendan and Grandpa encounter a leprechaun. Although the old man inadvertently lets the pixie escape, the duo agree that it would have been wrong to steal the creature's treasure. For their generosity and honesty, Brendan and his grandfather are rewarded with the food and livestock they really need. [Loek] Koopmans' watercolors, dominated by deep shades of blue, are strongest in their depiction of landscape; the scenes, infused with bright colors, are reminiscent of the work of Stephen Grammel. This tale steeped in Irish folklore isn't a first pick. However, larger libraries looking for picture books to meet the demands of St. Patrick's Day may want to give it a try.

Janice M. Del Negro

SOURCE: A review of *The Gold at the End of the Rainbow,* in *The Bulletin of the Center for Children's Books,* Vol. 50, No. 9, May, 1997, pp. 322-323.

Young Brendan lives with his grandfather on an unnamed coast. Wishing for bacon and eggs one rainy morning as they eat their potatoes, Grandpa laughingly says, "We might as well wish for the gold at the end of the rainbow." In the morning, a rainbow arches from the coast to a small island, and Brendan insists on rowing over to dig for the gold. No gold is found, and the two dejectedly head for the boat, but Grandpa catches and releases a leprechaun, who rewards them not with gold but with a calf, a pig, some chickens, and a bottle of elderberry juice that, no matter how much you drink, is never emptied. Hänel's gentle narrative is engaging but bland, though the young Brendan's innocent belief in gold and leprechauns is easy to accept. While the figures and faces of Brendan and his grandpa are awkwardly drawn, [Loek] Koopmans' watercolors of the windswept cabin, the rolling sea, and the ever-changing sky (reminiscent of a kinder, gentler Stephen Gammell) are satisfyingly idyllic.

OLD MAHONY AND THE BEAR FAMILY (1997)

Dina Sherman

SOURCE: A review of *Old Mahony and the Bear Family* in *School Library Journal,* Vol. 43, No. 7, July, 1997, p. 68.

The translation in this sequel to *The Old Man and the Bear* is stilted and awkward, and the cartoon artwork is dull. The story itself is slow and predictable, and even a bit preachy. Old Mahony and his friend Big Bill (the bear) like to fish together, each in his own way. When Big Bill's family shows up—a mom, dad, some small cubs, and even old Grampa Bear, things get out of hand, and Old Mahoney can no longer fish in peace. To solve his problem, he builds a trap, planning to sell the bears to a zoo or circus (except for Big Bill). As expected, his plan backfires, and he finds that he needs the bears to help him out of his own trap. While the text is age appropriate for beginning readers, there are many better books out there, about bears or otherwise. Pass on this one.

Michael Kirby

SOURCE: A review of *Old Mahoney and the Bear Family,* in *The School Librarian,* Vol. 45, No. 3, August, 1997, p. 145.

In this sequel to *The Old Man and the Bear* Big Bill the bear stretches his fishing friendship with Old Mahoney by introducing a whole family of bears who splash and play in the river and scare away all the fish. Thinking dark thoughts about zoos, Old Mahoney digs a pit to catch the bears. Needless to say, it is the old man himself who falls into the pit, and it takes a magnificently co-ordinated team effort by all the bears to rescue him. Old Mahoney learns a painful lesson, and the story ends happily. Beautifully illustrated in blues, browns and greens by Jean-Pierre Corderoc'h, this is a delightfully cosy read.

Susan DeRonne

SOURCE: A review of *Old Mahoney and the Bear Family,* in *Booklist,* Vol. 94, No. 2, September 15, 1997, p. 235.

Gruff Old Mahony enjoys the company of Big Bill the bear, as they fish for salmon, each in his own way. When Big Bill's entire family shows up, Old Mahony fears there won't be enough salmon to go around. After unsuccessfully attempting to shoo them away, he builds a trap with the intention of selling the entire bear clan to a circus. Young readers will delight in the quirky turn of events that teaches a valuable lesson to Old Mahony. Numerous color illustrations will help the very youngest readers with difficult vocabulary. This is a short, sweet story with comfortable characters and a happy ending that beginning independent readers will like.

Carolyn L. Shute

SOURCE: A review of *Old Mahony and the Bear Family,* in *The Horn Book Guide,* Vol. VIII, No. 2, Fall, 1997, p. 291.

Furious when his ursine friend Big Bill's raucous family scares away all the salmon, avid fisherman Old Mahoney sets a trap to get rid of the noisy bears but learns lessons in cooperation and camaraderie instead. Neither text nor watercolor pictures are outstanding, but the story's pleasant humor makes it a satisfactory choice for transitional readers.

MARY AND THE MYSTERY DOG (1999)

Carloyn Phelan

SOURCE: A review of *Mary and the Mystery Dog,* in *Booklist,* Vol. 95, No. 16, April 15, 1999, p. 1528.

Visiting the beach on a cold, windy day, Mary befriends a dog and assumes that he is "the Mystery Dog who lived all alone at the beach," a character she has read about in stories. When she brings her parents out to see the dog, they also meet his owner, a fisherman who leaves his pet to play on the shore each morning, while he goes out in his boat. Mystery Dog or not, he's a good playmate for Mary. First published in Switzerland, this book tells a simple, satisfying tale with immediacy and humor. Children will enjoy the pleasing animal story, illustrated [by Kirsten Höcker] with watercolor paintings that conjure up the feelings of the characters and the feel of a wet, cold day by the ocean. A rewarding short choice for children just a bit beyond the beginning readers stage.

Mary Ann Carcich

SOURCE: A review of *Mary and the Mystery Dog,* in *School Library Journal,* Vol. 45, No. 5, May, 1999, p. 90.

Mary cavorts with a "mystery dog" during a cold week at the beach; her parents are skeptical about his existence at first, but eventually join in on the fun of playing with him. It turns out that the pup belongs to a fisherman, who leaves him at the beach while he's out on his boat. Mary is disappointed that the animal is no longer "mysterious" but resolves, with her parents, to continue to play with him. The illustrations, rendered in cheerful pastel hues, are charming and playful evocations of beach scenes, but they cannot overcome the blandness of the writing and the lack of a compelling story line.

RESCUE AT SEA! (1999)

Annie Ayres

SOURCE: A review of *Rescue at Sea!,* in *Booklist,* Vol. 95, No. 19, June 1, 1999, p. 1829.

While a fierce storm rages outside, nine-year-old Paul tells his father that he wants a dog, but his father replies that getting a dog isn't like buying a toy; first Paul will have to prove himself worthy. Going with his fisherman father and the other men of the coastal village to rescue a fishing boat caught in the storm, Paul gets his chance to prove himself when he rescues a dog from the wreck. And, of course, as a reward for his saving the dog, the crew from the wrecked boat decide that Paul can keep it. Generously illustrated [by Ulrike Heyne] with watercolors featuring turbulent seascapes, dramatic rescue scenes, and a scrappy black-and-white dog, this briskly paced first chapter book offers a taste of action-adventure at a slightly higher reading level than that of the Henry and Mudge easy-reader crowd.

Mary Ann Carcich

SOURCE: A review of *Rescue at Sea!*, in *School Library Journal*, Vol. 45, No. 7, July, 1999, p. 72.

While a storm rages at sea, young Paul stays inside his coastal home and yearns for a dog of his own. When a fishing boat founders nearby, he assists his father and other villagers in a rescue; lo and behold, a dog named Johnny is onboard, and Paul resolves to save it. You guessed it: Paul succeeds and the crew decides that he deserves to keep Johnny as his own. While the story is a tad trite, the illustrations are lively and highly evocative of storm-whipped sea and spray. Rendered in muted sepia tones, the artfully depicted scenes sweep across double pages and breathe life into a drama that is otherwise curiously wooden.

Additional coverage of Hänel's life and career is contained in the following sources published by The Gale Group: *Contemporary Authors*, Vol. 155 and *Something about the Author*, Vol. 89.

Kyoko Mori

1957 -

Japanese author of fiction and nonfiction for young adults.

Major works include *Shizuko's Daughter* (1993), *The Dream of Water: A Memoir* (1995), *One Bird* (1995), *Polite Lies: On Being a Woman Caught between Cultures* (1998).

INTRODUCTION

In all her work, Kyoko Mori reflects the pain, confusion, and anger of her own life, and reflects upon her methods of coping with these powerful emotions. Although she did not start out to write for a young adult audience, that audience emerged as she began to adjust the original manuscript for her first book, *Shizuko's Daughter*, under the guidance of her editor. She has said that writing for a young adult audience has made her writing clearer and more focused. Her work, as her life, has been most influenced by her mother's suicide, when Mori was just 12 years old, and the severely abusive treatment she subsequently received from her violent father, coupled with the psychological abuse engendered by her step-mother. She has published two books of memoirs detailing her experiences and reactions to them. Her works of fiction are so filled with autobiographical elements that it is difficult to separate fiction from nonfiction.

What makes these remembrances palatable is Mori's writing. She has said that she has always been more comfortable writing in English than in her native Japanese. Since her reading in English was cultivated and nurtured by her highly cultured and educated mother, her own writing reflects the highest standards. Critics have described her work as "quietly moving," "poetic and emotionally charged," "brief yet perceptive," "intensified by exquisite sensory motifs," and subtly transforming "aesthetic observation into readers' experiences." Withal she is considered abundantly gifted. In an interview for *Something About the Author* Mori said, "I like affecting my readers, touching them and making them look at their lives. But I do not want to be the whole influence. I want to be only one part of a constellation of ideas that touches and affects a person.... I hope to evoke rather than prescribe. To create, through feelings and concrete details, a life. To put something out there between past and present that presents images, characters, and events that seem real to the reader."

Biographical Information

Born in Kobe, Japan, Mori was especially close to her mother. She credits her mother and her mother's family

with introducing her to reading, writing, and art as serious endeavors, and her work is filled with many memories of their influence. Her father was absent most of the time, but he was so unpleasant when he was around that the family was more comfortable with him away. When Mori was twelve years old, her mother, who had been suffering from depression for a year, committed suicide. It was the end of Mori's comfortable childhood. Her father became violently abusive and, after marrying his mistress, began to beat her severely at least once a week and forbade her to see her mother's family.

Unable to speak of her suffering to others because of the restraints of Japanese society and the importance of "saving face," Mori's escape was school. She involved herself in a host of after school activities, athletic, academic, and cultural, to avoid coming home. It was during this time that she decided she wanted to be a writer, but a writer of English, not Japanese. During her junior year in high school, she spent a year as an exchange student in Mesa, Arizona. It was the happiest year of her adolescence because she felt free and accepted as part of her American family. On her return to Japan, her home life was even worse, so she determined to win a scholarship to an American university and escape her miserable home life for good. She was thrilled to win a full scholarship that made her financially independent of her father. She knew when she left, she would never live in Japan again, and was happy that she could once again resume communications with her mother's family.

She graduated from Rockford College in 1979 and continued her education at the University of Wisconsin in Milwaukee, earning her M.A. in 1981 and Ph.D. in 1984. She became associate professor of English and writer-in-residence at Saint Norbert College in De Pere, Wisconsin where she teaches creative writing. Her first novel, *Shizuko's Daughter,* began as part of her doctoral thesis for her degree in creative writing. After extensive revisions that turned it from a collection of short stories into a novel, it was published in 1993.

Major Works

 Mori's first novel, *Shizuko's Daughter,* although a work of fiction, contains many autobiographical elements. In it 11-year-old Yuki's mother Shizuko commits suicide, and a year later her father marries his mistress. Resentful of them both, and uncomfortable at home, Yuki begins to run long distances and to paint pictures of happier times when her mother was alive as a means of consolation. The book follows Yuki for the next seven years, until she finally breaks free by going to a distant art school, but every experience of her growth from girlhood to womanhood is colored by her mother's death. A reviewer for *The Bulletin of the Center for Children's Books* called this work, "A first novel that truly bridges the interests of young adults and adults ... written in a spare, intricately balanced style interweaving several viewpoints without losing sharp focus."

On her first trip back to Japan after 13 years in exile, Mori took notes about returning to the places of her childhood and visiting relatives. She turned those notes into *The Dream of Water: A Memoir.* It covers her departure from America, her rediscovery of Kobe, and many memories of her mother's suicide and the severe physical abuse she suffered at the hands of her father. During the course of the trip, she initially honors the Japanese customs of restraint, but after visiting her mother's grave, changes her approach to accommodate her anger and the person she has become. A critic for *Kirkus Reviews* stated, "Mori opts for the most complicated, interesting, and difficult answers.... This beautifully written voyage through a 'legacy of loss' is a trip well worth the taking."

One Bird recounts the story of Megumi, 15, who must live with her father, as is the custom in Japan, after her unhappy mother abandons the family. Her cold and unfeeling father forbids her to see her mother, and Megumi lives a miserable life with her domineering grandmother. She has lost her mother and her faith and lives in anger and frustration. She is helped in large part by the attentions of a kind veterinarian who rehabilitates wounded birds. In the course of the book, Megumi saves many wounded birds, and is herself saved. Critics were enthusiastic in their praise of this book, commenting on "the keenly observed atmosphere," Mori's "writing with her startling combination of delicacy in observing moods and incisiveness in defining individual actions," the discipline "with which every detail of the accomplished work is orchestrated," and the "lively and affecting" story.

Polite Lies: On Being a Woman Caught between Cultures is a collection of essays about lies and their consequences. They detail Mori's perspective on Japanese restraint and the code-of-silence observed in polite households and how this tradition affected her life. She also ruminates on religious rituals, women's place, marriage, death, divorce, and personal sacrifice. A reviewer for *Publishers Weekly* wrote, "This engagingly insightful discussion from one who has intimately experienced the two cultures is full of revelations about both."

Awards

In 1992 Mori won the Editor's Prize from the *Missouri Review* for her poem "Fallout." In 1993 *Shizuko's Daughter* won a host of awards, including American Library Association Best Book for Young Adults, *New York Times* Notable Book, *Publishers Weekly* Editor's Choice, Council of Wisconsin Writers Best Novel, and Elizabeth Burr Award for best children's book of the year from the Wisconsin Library Association. *One Bird* won similar notice in 1996 when it accumulated as awards American Library Association Best Book for Young Adults, Paterson Poetry Center Best Books for Young Adults, Council of Wisconsin Writers Best Novel, and Children's Books of Distinction Award from *Hungry Mind Review.*

TITLE COMMENTARY

SHIZUKO'S DAUGHTER (1993)

Publishers Weekly

SOURCE: A review of *Shizuko's Daughter,* in *Publishers Weekly,* Vol. 240, No. 4, January 25, 1993, p. 87.

In this quietly moving novel—the first of the publisher's multicultural imprint—Mori poetically conveys the sentiments of an Asian girl who has lost her mother to suicide. Only a year after Shizuko's death, Yuki's father marries the woman with whom he has been having a long-term affair. Deeply resentful of both her father and his bride, Yuki feels uncomfortable at home, which has been redecorated to suit her new stepmother's tastes. Running long distances and painting pictures that preserve memories of happier times are the only ways the girl is able to find consolation. Throughout this story, set in Kobe, Japan and spanning seven years, the author shows how Yuki's visions, attitudes and achievements are influenced by her mother's tragedy. Although most of the narrative is written from the protagonist's point of view, the thoughts of other characters (Yuki's father, stepmother and grandparents) are also depicted in brief yet perceptive segments. A cast of three-dimensional characters, keen imagery, and attention to detail produce an emotionally and culturally rich tale tracing the evolution of despair into hope.

Kirkus Reviews

SOURCE: A review of *Shizuko's Daughter,* in *Kirkus Reviews,* Vol. 61, No. 3, February 1, 1993, p. 151.

Mori returns to her native Japan for a lyrical first novel with the intensity of remembered grief. Yuki's gentle mother commits suicide after assuring the anxious 12-year-old that she is "all right." Like her mother Shizuko, to whom she was exceptionally close, Yuki is talented and resilient; but she too is thwarted by a restrictive society and a miserable family situation. For Shizuko, there was no hope—though she loved her daughter, her husband was cold, dictatorial, and usually absent; and though (as Yuki will learn) she was once attracted to a more congenial man, she would have lost Yuki in a divorce. Life becomes nearly as bleak for Yuki: her father marries his mistress, who is obsessively antagonistic to Yuki, and he prevents Yuki from communicating with her mother's loving relatives. Even Yuki's talents are stumbling blocks to friendship: highly intelligent, creative, assertive, she doesn't fit into the traditional Japan of the '70s. Only at 18 does she break free by rejecting the fine local university to go to a distant art school. Still compulsively gauche, in the end she mellows toward her grandparents and makes a strong friendship with the promise of blossoming into love. A beautifully written book about a bitterly painful coming of age, intensified by exquisite sensory motifs—flavors and aromas, light and color, the weight and ornamentation of clothing. Yuki's unsympathetically portrayed father may not be fully realized; but like Suzanne Staples's *Shabanu* (1989), Yuki is unforgettable. A splendid debut.

The Bulletin of the Center for Children's Books

SOURCE: A review of *Shizuko's Daughter,* in *The Bulletin of the Center for Children's Books,* Vol. 46, No. 9, May, 1993, p. 291.

A first novel that truly bridges the interests of young adults and adults, this is written in a spare, intricately balanced style interweaving several viewpoints without losing sharp focus. The book opens with the calm, carefully deliberated suicide of eleven-year-old Yuki's beautiful but unhappy mother, Shizuko, who turns on the gas while her daughter's taking a music lesson at the piano teacher's house. Most of the remaining fifteen scenes, each dated sometime in the next seven years, detail Yuki's grief, survival, and understanding of her mother's death, but this journeys far beyond a "problem novel" in scope. It is a fully realized portrayal of a Japanese family to the depth of three generations and at least six individuals, including the cold father and stepmother whom Yuki defies, as well as the warm grandparents whose richly traditional patterns of living bring aching recollections of Yuki's mother. The tension of the characters themselves serves as driving action. The strong will and sense of artistry that isolate Yuki finally save her, and readers will be moved beyond cultural boundaries by the author's ability to render nuances of childhood with an immediacy devoid of nostalgia. Most impressive, technically, is Mori's flow of a narrative voice that subtly translates aesthetic observations into readers' experiences—the color and texture of flowers, of clothing, of pottery, of human love's pain and release. Such authenticity illuminates the fictional realities and motivations without intrusion or distraction, so that readers will feel themselves enlightened by an encounter with that rare achievement, a powerfully understated story.

Susan Stan

SOURCE: A review of *Shizuko's Daughter,* in *The Five Owls,* Vol. VII, No. 5, May-June, 1993, p. 118-119.

While many multicultural books have appeared in the past few years, the need is far from satisfied, and books written from an insider's perspective—by an author who is part of the culture being written about—are especially welcome. Born and raised in Japan, Kyoko Mori now lives in Wisconsin.

In her debut as a novelist, Mori transports readers to Japan two decades ago. Yuki Okuda is twelve when she loses her mother, Shizuko, to suicide, and after a year spent with her aunt in Tokyo, she returns to Kobe to live with her father and his new bride. She knows their life would be happier without her; without a wife, it was understandable that she not live with her father, but his status in society would be compromised if she did not move back after he remarried. So Yuki endures her father's coldness and her stepmother's hostility throughout her high school years, cherishing and reliving memories of her mother. Bright and talented, Yuki fills her spare time with homework, running laps, and an evening job at the library, but nothing can fill the emotional void left by her mother's death. Yuki accepts her situation silently but not passively, and by the time she graduates, she has arranged a leavetaking that will save face for her father and his wife: she goes to art school in Nagasaki, far away.

Thanks to Yuki's artistic eye, which never fails to notice such details as yellow marigolds, pink azaleas, the lime-green dress of a friend's mother, or the tight weave of a straw hat, the text abounds with color and texture. Paradoxically, the story is at once austere and filled with belongings, all removed from sight by her jealous step-mother—Yuki's childhood clothes, which her mother had lovingly sewn and embroidered for her; the pottery tea set they picked out together after watching the potter at work; Yuki's own childhood drawings, neatly boxed for posterity by her mother; and even her mother's clothes, packed away in the attic after the funeral. Though one by one the items are destroyed, they remain in existence for Yuki, both in her memory and in her sketch-books.

Americans have no exclusive claim on dysfunctional families, and some readers will find aspects of Yuki's unhappy family life all too familiar. The effects of Japan's strong patrilinear society, however, may dis-orient readers. Although Yuki's ties to her maternal aunt and grandparents had been closely forged while her mother was living, these relatives can maintain only minimal contact with her for fear of affronting her father. Yet their early ties support her and help in her eventual healing process.

Nancy Vasilakis

SOURCE: A review of *One Bird,* in *The Horn Book Magazine,* Vol. 72, No. 1, Jan-Feb, 1996, p. 79.

Kyoko Mori's skillfully structured novel begins with Shizuko's preparations for her suicide. Memories of her childhood—the sight of festive pink and white rice cakes, the smell of the tiny yellow flowers she passed on her way to school—compete with recollections of her daugh-ter Yuki growing up, until all are crowded out by an overwhelming sadness at her loveless marriage. Twelve-year-old Yuki comes home to find her mother's lifeless body on the kitchen floor. She struggles through the rest of the narrative to come to terms not only with her mother's death, but with the harsh realities of the life her mother abandoned her to. Her distant, unresponsive fa-ther marries his mistress of several years, a woman with none of Shizuko's sensitive, artistic spirit. But Shizuko knew her daughter well. She had once asked her, "What would you do if something happened to me?'" and Yuki had responded truthfully, "I would still go on. I would be very sad. I would never forget you. Still I would go on.'" The ghosts take years to exorcise, in fact. Much of the novel is told in flashbacks that convey the special nature of Yuki and Shizuko's relationship. Yuki graduates from high school and leaves her father's house, as cold in her own way as he. She lives for a while with her mother's parents as she attends art school, meets a young man, and begins to retie family cords that will eventually sustain her. The final chapter belongs to her grandmother, who, with equal care, watches over a young grandson and the altar that houses the spirits of her dead daughter and husband. Life and death commingle, each bearing its own measure of pain and acceptance. Mori paints beautiful pictures with words, creating visual images that can be as haunting and elliptical as poetry. A stunning first novel. Notes and glossary appended.

Sylvia Mitchell

SOURCE: A review of *Shizuko's Daughter,* in *Voice of Youth Advocates,* October, 1993, p. 217.

During the six years in which she grew from child to woman Yuki lived with a mixed legacy. The tragedy of her mother's suicide was mixed with rich memories of their lives together and Shizuko's wish that her daughter would grow to become a strong and happy adult. Within a year of the funeral Yuki must leave her mother's par-ents and live with a new stepmother under the cruel hard-ship of being unwanted. Such a plot could easily become a melodrama, but the author is never maudlin. While the "evil stepmother" theme will provide universal appeal for most female readers, several other factors put this novel well above the competition.

Adversity is overcome by using her mother's heartfelt wish as a spur. Stoically ignoring her father's lack of interest, Yuki becomes a top student, president of her eighth grade class, and a champion in school track events. Her saintly behavior is offset by a realistic mask of adolescent indifference toward the people who love her the most. It takes a grandparent's heart attack to jolt her into more mature behavior. At the conclusion she is working and paying her way through college and has found a potential life companion.

This novel adds to cultural and emotional understanding. The Japan of 1970 is a place where a special girl can grow up to graduate from Harvard and yet have a tra-ditional Japanese wedding complete with ancient rites and unbending custom. Many of the chapters have been published previously in various U.S. literary magazines. This explains the patchwork effect in which each chap-ter has enough detail to stand alone. It is only when the parts are put together that the essence of this brave life can be appreciated.

THE DREAM OF WATER: A MEMOIR (1995)

Kirkus Reviews

SOURCE: A review of *The Dream of Water: A Mem-oir,* in *Kirkus Reviews,* Vol. 62, No. 20, October 15, 1994, p. 1390.

In a poetic and emotionally charged account of a journey back to her native Japan, Mori creates beautiful scenes even as she uncovers painful truths about her family and her past.

Not knowing what else to do for a sabbatical, novelist Mori applied for a grant to travel to Japan, which she had left 13 years earlier, when she was a junior in college. This chronicle covers her departure from her adopted America; her rediscovery of her hometown of Kobe; her reacquaintance with the land and people she had so eagerly fled; and her remembrances of a childhood that included her mother's suicide when Mori was 12 and her father's subsequent beatings and cruelties (he forbade Mori to see her mother's relatives and, whenever his new wife threatened to leave because of Mori, would menace his daughter with a meat knife). Her book, which begins like entries in a conscientious traveler's journal, soon becomes a memoir wrought with suspense and wisdom. Will she contact her father? Will she understand her parents' early love for each other and their subsequent loss? In her initial encounters, Mori has difficulty communicating: Not only is her Japanese rusty, but she also respects the customs of Japanese restraint. So she says little and later dwells on what she should have said. But after visiting her mother's grave and relatives, she arrives at an emotional watershed. The book becomes richly rewarding as Mori opts for the most complicated, interesting, and difficult answers. She has an acute eye for metaphors. Some are delicate—like a stone slab at the bottom of a temple gate over which people step because it is a bad omen to touch it. Others, like the atomic bomb dropped on Hiroshima (whose victims include her relatives), are explosive.

This beautifully written voyage through a "legacy of loss" is a trip well worth taking.

Los Angeles Times Book Review

SOURCE: A review of *The Dream of Water: The Memoir,* in *Los Angeles Times Book Review,* April 9, 1995, p. 6.

What exactly is meant by the word *homeland*? How should one deal with a horrible father? These seem to be the two questions at the forefront of Kyoko Mori's autobiography, *"The Dream of Water."*

In 1990, Mori returned to her native Japan for the first time in 13 years. After traveling around the country for a few weeks, she visits the relatives of her mother, who committed suicide when Mori was 12. She also spends time with her father, Hiroshi, and his wife. Hiroshi is to fatherhood what Attila the Hun was to Europe. With an almost sociopathic lack of caring, he has abused, manipulated and belittled Mori and her younger brother ever since she can remember. One of the underlying reasons for Mori's visit is to see if she can live peacefully in the same part of the world as her father. By the end of her trip, she has an answer: "Kobe will always be a lost land to me, a place to think of with nostalgia, from far away. . . . That is the price of my anger. . . . I am losing the city I love, the place of my childhood, because I won't forgive my father."

In spite of some accomplished writing, *"The Dream of Water"* is a frustrating book. Mori goes to Japan angry

and returns angry, and while her feelings are certainly justified, it is not exactly clear, on a selfish level, what is to be gained by reading her rage. Mori is at her best in the sections dealing with Japanese culture and questions of identity; however, as soon as Hiroshi enters the picture, *"The Dream of Water"* begins to feel like a very expensive therapy session.

Michele L. Simms-Burton

SOURCE: A review of *The Dream of Water,* in *School Library Journal,* June, 1995, p. 145.

A poignant and honest memoir by a Japanese American woman who returns to her homeland after many years' absence. Mori explores the emotional and spiritual complexities of having severed ties with loved ones, and how a change in time and place recasts, taints, and illuminates one's perception. Central to her personal observations is the author's inability to forgive her father for his emotional and physical abuse after her mother's suicide. This narrative is in part about the young woman's journey but it is also about forgiving and forgetting even though Mori, herself, is unable to do either. Although she is unable to come to terms with her relationship with her father, she arrives at a better understanding of her mother's motivations and decisions that positively affected her daughter's life. Reminscent of David Mura's *Turning Japanese* this title by the author of *Shizuko's Daughter* will be good reading for YAs interested in Japanese culture, women's studies, and autobiographical writing.

ONE BIRD (1995)

Kirkus Reviews

SOURCE: A review of *One Bird,* in *Kirkus Reviews,* Vol. 62, No. 18, September 15, 1995, p. 1355.

Megumi, 15, in the course of the crisis precipitated by her parents' divorce, tells readers of her relationships with her mother, father, and friends; examines role models; falls in love; and heals many birds. Every character is three-dimensional and memorable, people that readers will recognize from their own lives, although the Japanese setting leaves an unmistakable imprint: Custom demands that Megumi live with her father, who forbids her to visit her mother until she comes of age; she is a Christian who has ceased to believe in God. The unhurried coolness of the text is luminously punctuated by Mori with the names of flowers, descriptions of birds, and poetic chapter titles. Although the themes flow out of one another by free association in a way that is typical of a first-person narration, each paragraph obeys a rigorous inner logic so that every word is enunciated and no detail is slurred. The trajectory of the plot is straightforward, starting at an emotional low point and building without big twists or turns; as a result, readers become especially sensitive to the small occurrences, each one telling. The text gains an intensity from the discipline with which every detail of this accomplished work is orchestrated, from the first page to the last.

Hazel Rochman

SOURCE: A review of *One Bird*, in *Booklist*, Vol. 92, No. 4, October 15, 1995, p. 396.

A teenager is desolate when her mother leaves home. This is a common theme in YA fiction now, from Creech's 1995 Newbery winner, *Walk Two Moons*, to Woodson's spare, beautiful *I Hadn't Meant to Tell you This*. Mori sets her story in Japan in 1975: 15-year-old Megumi's mother says as she packs her bags: If I don't leave your father now, I can't bear to live long enough to see you grow up." Megumi's father forbids her to have contact with her mother; in their male chauvinistic society, divorce is a disgrace; he has the money, the power, and the freedom to have a mistress, and his domineering mother runs his home. As in her highly acclaimed first novel, *Shizuko's Daughter*, Mori writes with subtlety and drama, but this story is far too ruminative. The first-person, present-tense narrative often reads like an essay as Megumi articulates how she feels and what it means and repeats herself many times. She finds metaphors everywhere and explains them, whether it's the fairy tales her mother read to her as a child or the wounded birds Mori helps fly free. Of course, some serious readers will love all the detail of Megumi's coming-of-age as she loses—and finds—family, faith, friends, and mentor.

Francine Prose

SOURCE: A review of *One Bird*, in *The New York Times*, November 12, 1995, p. 242.

Kyoko Mori's second novel for young adults, *One Bird*, is so lively and affecting that one imagines its readers will be too engaged by its heroine's situation to notice how much—and how painlessly—they are learning about another culture. This gracefully written book involves us so immediately in the emotional and spiritual life of a 15-year-old Japanese girl that only rarely do we pause to register which aspects of Megumi Shimizu's story are specific to her country, and how much her experience has in common with the larger world of adolescence.

Megumi's fractured family may seem all too familiar to a dismayingly large percentage of the novel's audience. Her mother has left her chilly, philandering husband to live with her own father in a village north of Kyoto. Megumi remains in Kobe with her harsh, critical paternal grandmother and, in theory, with her father—who in fact has also left, to live most of the time with his mistress in Hiroshima.

Watching one's homelife disintegrate is not exactly a rare experience among contemporary teen-agers. But this is Japan, 1975, and the pain of abandonment and loss is sharpened by a traditional society that sees Megumi's plight as a freakish departure from any acceptable norm. She believes that "my family is nothing like anyone else's, and that makes me different from all the other girls at my high school." In three years, she broods, "I will be at my graduation, the only girl without a mother."

Not coincidentally, Megumi is undergoing a spiritual crisis. Her grandfather is a Buddhist, her mother a devout Christian; Megumi was raised in the church. But the death of a family friend and her mother's departure have raised doubts about a religion that claims that suffering has a divine and unknowable purpose. She has stopped going to church—a decision that inspires the pity and concern of her well-meaning neighbors and her Bible studies teacher at the Christian Girls' Academy. She is also struggling to gauge the unbearable pressures that drove her mother away:

"Grandmother Shimizu has brought her bonsai trees from Tokyo: three pines with roots knotted and swollen out of the shallow soil like hardened hearts. . . . The bonsai remind me of the kind of person my mother did not want to become—shrunk and old, living with my father in bitterness. I have to admit, if I thought I were turning into such a person, I would have left, too. I would have done what my mother has done."

One Bird is full of small radiant scenes and glints of observation. It begins with one such moment: Megumi's mother has planted flats of spring seedlings, "their heads bent down with the cracked seeds stuck on top like tiny helmets." And suddenly Megumi realizes that her mother has grown the plants only to fool her into thinking she wasn't going away.

Younger readers and adult admirers of Kyoko Mori's work will be reminded of themes from her previous books. Her remarkable memoir, *The Dream of Water*, describes her 1990 return to Japan from the United States, where she lives and teaches, in an effort to understand the country she left and to seek clues to the enduring mystery of her mother, who killed herself when Ms. Mori was 12. Her first novel for young adults, *Shizuko's Daughter*, also concerns a Japanese girl who must learn to live with the memory of a mother who chose to die. In *One Bird*, of course, the mother's desertion takes a far less drastic form; and yet when Megumi and her mother are briefly reunited, the scene has the intensity of those dreams in which the beloved dead are revealed to have been alive all along.

If I wanted to give a Kyoko Mori book to an adolescent reader, I would pass along *The Dream of Water* with advice to tough it out through the hard parts. The memoir is as complex as adult life and feels as accidental, without the simplifications, the slightly programmatic and convenient structures so often employed in novels for juniors, even good ones like *One Bird*. Here, for example, the hurt protagonist is greatly helped by a veterinarian who rehabilitates wounded birds.

Yet *One Bird* is fine, better than fine, for readers more comfortable with novels written for their age group. Without piety, obviousness or self-consciousness, the novel integrates elements of Japanese culture—the cultivation of bonsai, the concern with reputation—and shows us how they modify experiences and emotional states we all recognize, or remember. Which is something one would like young-adult readers to know: that someone else's teen-age years may be much like their own, though that person may seem different and live on the other side of the planet.

Publishers Weekly

SOURCE: A review of *One Bird,* in *Publishers Weekly,* Vol. 242, No. 46, November 13, 1995, p. 62.

Writing with her starting combination of delicacy in observing moods and incisiveness in defining individual actions, Mori revisits the premise of her first novel, *Shizuko's Daughter.* Once again an adolescent heroine must cope with a mother's desertion and the disgrace it causes in 1970s Japan—this time, however, the mother has not committed suicide, but sought a separation from her husband. Custom dictates that she forfeit her right to see her child, 15-year-old Megumi, even though she is a devoted parent and even though Megumi's openly unfaithful father is frequently absent. Megumi navigates through her anger and frustration and, with the help of strong friends, quietly supplants prevailing conventions with her own sense of what is right and just. While initial passages and conflicts threaten to overwhelm the narrative with metaphors (e.g., Megumi nurses an injured bird back to health, then sets it free), the novel builds in momentum, gaining in complexity, as it progresses. Even so, the finest element here is neither the plot nor the characters, but the keenly observed atmosphere. It is the portrait of Japan, thoughtfully probed for its ironies, that will linger with the reader.

The Bulletin of the Center for Children's Books

SOURCE: A review of *One Bird,* in *The Bulletin of the Center for Children's Books,* Vol. 49, No. 5, January, 1996, p. 166.

Megumi is devastated when her mother leaves home to escape from her unhappy marriage; Japanese custom and family pressures require the fifteen-year-old girl to stay with her disliked father and cut off contact with her mother until Megumi finishes college. Lost and desolate, Megumi finds some solace in the company of an independent local woman, a veterinarian who teaches Megumi how to nurse wild birds back to health, but she finds herself increasingly questioning the strictures and rules of faith, of culture, and of gender roles with which she has been raised. As she did in *Shizuko's Daughter,* Mori paints a compelling portrait of a girl creating herself in her mother's absence; this book, however, doesn't have the delicate intensity that sustained the previous title, and the avian motif is suggestive but never quite takes flight. The introspective prose isn't fast-paced, but it's sharpened by underlying social criticism that offers a broader counterpoint to Megumi's very personal story.

Nancy Vasilakis

SOURCE: A review of *Shizuko's Daughter,* in *The Horn Book Magazine,* Vol. 69, No. 5, Sept-Oct, 1993, p. 603.

The focus of this book, as it was in the author's highly acclaimed first novel, *Shizuko's Daughter,* is on a teen-age girl's struggles to maintain psychic equilibrium after a wrenching separation from her mother. In despair over her unhappy marriage, Megumi's mother has decided to leave her husband and return to her native village—an especially devastating move in contemporary Japan, where divorce is almost unknown. Forbidden by her father and paternal grandmother to contact her mother, fifteen-year-old Megumi chafes at her grandmother's harsh and restrictive rules and feels virtually abandoned, not only by her mother but by her cold, silent father who spends most of his time with his mistress. As Megumi tries to escape from this sense of utter isolation, old friendships give way to new ones, the resulting upheavals reflecting what is happening in her family. She begins to question her belief in God and attends church less and less frequently, gradually slipping away from the embracing warmth of Pastor Kato and his family, her mother's closest friends. When she finds a wounded bird, she takes it to Dr. Mizutani, a divorced and independent young veterinarian, who offers Megumi a job as her assistant. As Megumi aids in the nursing of wounded birds so that they can be released back into the wild, she begins to see a new life for herself taking form. One of her first steps is to visit her mother. While this novel lacks the poetic touch of Mori's earlier, more tautly structured work, it offers some telling insights into the position of women in middle-class Japanese society.

POLITE LIES: ON BEING A WOMAN CAUGHT BETWEEN CULTURES (1998)

Kirkus Reviews

SOURCE: A review of *Polite Lies: On Being a Woman Caught Between Cultures,* in *Kirkus Reviews,* Vol. 65, No. 21, November 1, 1997, p. 1628.

In spare essays dealing with topics such as "Secrets," "A Woman's Place," "Tears," and "Home," novelist and memoirist Mori examines the ways truth is circumvented in America and in her native Japan.

Now making her home in Wisconsin, the author sees herself as more American than Japanese, and from her newfound perspective she exposes such "polite lies," or socially condoned and expected dissimulations, as the Japanese code of silence regarding matters of health (her father was not informed that he had malignant cancer), finance (the reticence of her father's bank cost Mori her inheritance), and family (the need for family secrecy kept her from seeking a lawyer). Of course, she argues, there are polite lies—religious rituals, for example, or the platitudes we utter in the face of adversity—that we need, that offer us comfort and may actually be preferable to harsh truths. Mori—who was 12 when she lost her mother to suicide—sees that death as a rejection of the polite lie of marital harmony and stability. For herself, unable to decide on a way of life that didn't involve compromise, the author chose divorce: "If marriage meant sacrifice, mutual or one-sided, I wanted to be alone." This terse explanation, however, seems an oddly incomplete accounting for the end of her marriage. While she bravely sees through what she calls the polite fictions of her Japanese family and friends, Mori is rarely condemnatory. Her quiet prose seems to reflect the discipline of her personal belief system; it's as if the stoicism she was raised to practice in her behavior and thoughts is embedded even in her writing style. She is frank—but never deeply angry.

Though there is a sameness to some of these essays, Mori's observations about lies and their consequences build to powerful effect.

Publishers Weekly

SOURCE: A review of *Polite Lies: On Being a Woman Caught Between Two Cultures,* in *Publishers Weekly,* Vol. 244, No. 45, November 3, 1997, p. 71.

For the first 20 years of her life, Mori felt straitjacketed by the Japanese culture in which she was raised; for the last 20, she has found liberation in Green Bay, Wis., of all places, where she teaches creative writing. In 12 plangent, autobiographical sketches, she recalls her experiences in both cultures and reflects on a series of defining issues, among them women, marriage, family, death, emotion, bodies and significant language characteristics. She claims she doesn't like to speak Japanese because to do so, "you have to agree on . . . which one of you is superior, how close you expect to be . . . and who defers." Although she excoriates the Japanese for elevating politeness above honesty, she values the comfort that traditions and rituals can offer, for example, at such times as death. This engagingly

insightful discussion from one who has intimately experienced the two cultures is full of revelations about both.

Kay Meredith Dushek

SOURCE: A review of *Polite Lies: On Being a Woman Caught Between Cultures,* in *Library Journal,* Vol. 122, No. 17, October 15, 1997, p. 79.

Creative writing professor Mori offers a poignant portrait of her dichotomous life: a childhood in Japan and an adulthood in the American Midwest. These 12 personal essays show the insight evident in Mori's previous works. "Polite lies" refers to the imbalance present in the two cultures and the resulting balance Mori establishes for herself and her readers with wit and warmth. Topics include family, secrets, the body, and tears. The distinction between the public and the private colors the double world that Mori speaks of so eloquently. Sacrificial deaths, tragic suicides—all these may be exalted in Japanese art and literature, yet the personal tragedy of Mori's mother's suicide was "shameful instead of glorious"—she was never to mention the event. This strong collection binds one woman's old country with her new one, repeating her impassioned desire not to be swept up in a lifetime of polite acquiescence as were the women of her youth.

Nancy Pearl

SOURCE: A review of *Polite Lies: On Being a Woman Caught Between Cultures,* in *Booklist,* Vol. 94, No. 7, December 1, 1997, p. 590.

Mori, who explored her past in her three previous books, sensitively examines differences in manners and mores in Japan and the U.S. Using parts of her own life as examples, Mori, who spent her first 20 years in Japan and the next 20 in the American Midwest, delineates the ways in which people's lives, especially the lives of women, differ in the two countries. Mori finds Japan to be a country where life is a complicated system of symbols, in which every behavior stands for something else and conversation is an exercise in decoding the polite lies that obfuscate the truth of a situation. She compares Japanese behavior with the American method of handling the same situation through a series of essays focusing on topics such as lies, rituals, and a woman's place. Mori's exquisite language—she teaches creative writing at a small Wisconsin college—leads readers to an understanding of a civilization as highly developed as ours but one that has developed much differently in the area of human relations.

Additional coverage of Mori's life and career is contained in the following sources published by The Gale Group: *Authors and Artists for Young Adults,* Vol. 25; *Contemporary Authors,* Vol. 153; and *Something about the Author Autobiography Series,* Vol. 26.

Terry Pratchett

1948-

English author of fiction and short stories.

Major works include *The Colour of Magic* (1983), *Mort* (1987), *Wyrd Sisters* (1988), *Truckers* (1989), *Reaper Man* (1991), *Johnny and the Dead* (1993).

Major works about the author include *The Streets of Ankh-Morpork* (by Terry Pratchett and Stephen Briggs, 1993), *The Discworld Companion* (compiled by Terry Pratchett and Stephen Briggs, 1994), *A Tourist's Guide to Lancre* (by Terry Pratchett, Stephen Briggs, and Paul Kidby, 1998), *The Science of Discworld* (by Ian Stewart and Jack Cohen, 1999).

INTRODUCTION

A prolific and popular author of fantasy and science fiction, Pratchett is considered an unorthodox, strikingly original writer who irreverently satirizes contemporary culture, morality, and behavior in hilarious, well-written books. Compared to such authors as Jonathan Swift, Charles Dickens, J. R. R. Tolkien, P. G. Wodehouse, Kurt Vonnegut, and Douglas Adams as well as to the British/American comedy troupe Monty Python, he is regarded as a comic genius whose works have enriched and expanded the genres of both high comedy and fantasy literature. Pratchett, a best-selling writer who directs his works to middle graders and young adults as well as to adults, is best known as the creator of Discworld, a complete universe with strong parallels to our own that is the setting for approximately thirty of his books. Discworld is a flat, circular planet that is carried through space on the back of a giant cosmic turtle and is supported by four huge elephants. Overseen by gods and run by wizards, it includes a multicultural cast comprising both real and supernatural beings—sorcerers, witches, vampires, werewolves, dwarfs, trolls, elves, dragons, monsters, soldiers, constables, and barbarians, among others, as well as a librarian (a former human) who is an orangutan. Although there is no central character in the series, one figure appears in all of the Discworld books: Death, a Bergmanesque specter who is both fascinated with and bemused by the human race. Other popular characters include Rincewind, an incompetent wizard; Twoflower, a naïve, enthusiastic tourist; the Luggage, Twoflower's unpredictable, carnivorous suitcase, which follows its owner on thousands of little legs; Constable Carrot, an adopted dwarf who is over six feet tall; and the witches Esmeralda Weatherwax, called Granny; Gytha Ogg, called Nanny; Magrat Garlick; and Agnes Nitt. All of these characters are key players in several volumes of the Discworld series.

As a writer for the young, Pratchett is well respected as the creator of *The Carpet People,* a fantasy about Borrower-like creatures that he wrote at seventeen and revised at forty-three, and two series, the *Trucker* books (called the *Bromeliad* in the United States), a trilogy about another group of small beings who crashed to Earth from outer space thousands of years ago, and the *Johnny Maxwell* books, a series that features a teenage computer nerd who becomes involved with the paranormal.

Thematically, Pratchett spoofs modern society with sharp social commentary while underscoring his books with optimism and an affection for humanity. The author takes digs at such subjects as New Age philosophy and Hollywood movies while exploring topics such as death, politics, religion, and the educational system. Writing in *West Australian* magazine, Todd Owen noted that Pratchett's books "parody many aspects of our own lives and history, covering topics from religion to gender equality, death, folklore, rock and roll, death and Shakespeare (which has plenty of death)," while Edward James of the *Times Literary Supplement* added that in Discworld, "our institutions, our follies, even our laws of nature all appear—but twisted, distorted, magnified, and ridiculed." Throughout his works, Pratchett stresses the importance of strong individuality—his protagonists are often called anti-heroes and his female characters are independent and accomplished—while expressing an intense dislike of coercion by the status quo. Pratchett receives much acclaim for his abilities as a humorist. His works, which range from gently humorous to outrageously bizarre, are noted for reflecting their author's keen sense of the absurd as well as his self-deprecating humor. As a literary stylist, Pratchett favors creative wordplay, puns, allusions, asides, and in-jokes (which the author calls "resonances"). In addition, Pratchett fills his plots with complicated twists and uses the footnotes in his texts to deliver comic punch lines.

Biographical Information

Born in Forty Green (now Beaconsfield), Buckinghamshire, England, Pratchett is the son of an engineer and a secretary. In an interview published in *The Discworld Companion,* Pratchett credits his parents with "pointing me in the right direction and just letting me get on with it. They took the view that if I was reading, that was all right." Pratchett has noted that his major source of education was the Beaconsfield Public Library. He told *Midweek* radio interviewer Christine Hardimant, "Fantasy and science fiction got me reading, because they blew my socks off and made my brain fizz ... and the books that I was being given to read at school didn't have the same effect." In addition to fantasy, Pratchett immersed himself in mythology and ancient history—he told Hardimant, "We're still talking guys in helmets bashing one another with swords"--as well as in books on astronomy. While still at school, Pratchett became a serious writer. "The Hades Business," a short story published in his school magazine when its author was thirteen, was denounced for its moral tone by the headmaster in front of an assembly; consequently, the magazine containing the story sold out. Pratchett sent "The Hades Business" to the commercial magazine *Science Fantasy,* where it appeared in 1963. He used the proceeds from the sale to buy a typewriter, and left school in 1965 to become a journalist with the *Bucks Free Press.*

Pratchett completed his first book, the children's story *The Carpet People,* at seventeen. The tale, which describes a whole civilization of tiny individuals known as Munrungs, was published in 1971. In 1968, Pratchett married his wife, Lyn; the couple have a daughter, Rhianna. While working as a provincial journalist, Pratchett continued to write fiction. His second novel, *The Dark Side of the Sun,* a parody of space-opera conventions for adults, was published in 1976. In 1980, Pratchett was appointed publicity officer for the Central Electricity Generating Board; his responsibilities included handling three nuclear power stations. *Strata,* an adult novel published in 1982, premiered Pratchett's first conception of Discworld. Influenced by such sources as creation myths

and the role-playing game *Dungeons and Dragons,* the initial version of the planet was controlled by robots and peopled with knights, Vikings, demons, and genies.

The Colour of Magic, a novel published in 1983, marks the first appearance of the now-familiar Discworld and introduces Rincewind, Twoflower, and the Luggage. In this volume, the characters tour Discworld, encountering a variety of exotic inhabitants and dangerous situations. Pratchett's first books were published by a small press and distributed through specialty shops. However, they became immediately popular, and Pratchett soon moved into mainstream publishing. He became a full-time writer in 1987. In the same year, the Discworld novel *Mort,* the story of how Death takes on a young apprentice, became the first of Pratchett's best-sellers. Since then, every Discworld book has been a best-seller in the United Kingdom in either hardcover or paperback; most often, both editions have reached best-seller status, and Pratchett has often held the top positions on both lists simultaneously. In 1989, *Truckers* became the first children's book to appear on the British best-seller lists for paperback fiction. Pratchett became recognized as the most popular author in Britain in the late 1990s and is now considered the country's best-selling living fiction author of the decade. At the close of the century, it was reported that one percent of all books sold in the United Kingdom were written by Pratchett. The Discworld series has also become a burgeoning industry. In addition to the books themselves, companion volumes such as an encyclopedia and a quiz book have been published as well as stage adaptations and graphic novels. Many spin-off products have appeared, including concept albums, audio and video tapes, computer games, T-shirts, figurines, doll houses, cross-stitch kits, plates, plaques, and even a Toby jug of Pratchett's head. In addition, the Discworld series has acquired an avid fan base and has prompted hundreds of electronic resources, such as web sites and chat rooms. Although his books appeal to both children and adults, Pratchett told Grant Stone of *Magpies,* "Generally, my books are for adolescents. I just write books. I might change the language slightly to make it more accessible to younger people but I think a good book is a good book and can be read by anyone."

Critical Reception

Initially, Pratchett's Discworld books were considered purely comic. However, as the series progressed, the author was credited with investing his volumes with increased depth and complexity. The Discworld series is now acknowledged for balancing comedy, philosophy, satire, fantasy, and action in an especially creative manner. In addition, Pratchett is acclaimed for his shrewd observations of humanity and his fertile, offbeat imagination, as well as for creating a completely realized world. Lauded for breaking the conventions of the novel while lampooning genre fiction, he is considered a master humorist and superb storyteller as well as a writer who understands his audience, both children and adults, and knows how to please them. Pratchett is often considered an acquired taste: his books are sometimes regarded as manic, demanding, and overlong, and his humor is occasionally thought to be sophomoric and self-referential. He has not received the level of success in the United States that he has throughout Europe. In addition, some of his works are thought to be above the heads of young people, especially due to their themes, references, and allusions. However, most observers regard Pratchett as a gifted, adroit writer of works that are both astute and entertaining. P. Smith, writing online on the *Terry Pratchett Page*, proclaimed Pratchett "the best thing that has happened to the written word for a very long time." Writing in the *Times Literary Supplement*, Edward James said, "Pratchett's humour takes logic past the point of absurdity and round again, but it is his unexpected insights into human morality that make the Discworld series stand out from other fantasies. Pratchett is pro-feminist, pro-pacifist, pro-anarchist, and pro- just being a thoughtful human being without any of that silly heroism which gets people killed, but is without any patronizing pedantry." Faren Miller of *LOCUS* added, "Pratchett demonstrates just how great the distance is between one- or two-joke writers and the comic masters whose works will still be read well into the next century.... He reached the top of his form some time ago, and should remain there for years, to everyone's benefit." Writing in *New Statesman*, David V. Barrett concluded of the Discworld novels, "You could whistle them in the street if you could.... The function of humour is to help us cope with the dark side of life. Terry Pratchett is worth a dozen psychotherapists."

Awards

In 1987, *Mort* was named the Best Gothic Novel of the Year by the Dracula Society. Pratchett won two British Science Fiction Awards, for the Discworld series in 1989 and for *Good Omens: The Nice and Accurate Predictions of Agnes Nutter, Witch,* in 1990. He received the Best Children's Book Award from the Writers' Guild of Great Britain in 1993 for *Johnny and the Dead* and was named the Fantasy and Science Fiction Author of the Year in the same year. Pratchett is also a past chairman of the Society of Authors and was chairman of the panel of judges for the Rhone-Poulenc Prinze in 1997. In 1998, he was appointed an Officer of the Order of the British Empire for his services to literature. In 1999, Pratchett received an honorary doctorate of literature (D.Litt.) from the University of Warwick.

AUTHOR COMMENTARY

Grant Stone

SOURCE: An interview with Terry Pratchett, in *Magpies,* Vol. 8, No. 1, March, 1993, pp. 15-19.

When were you first called a children's writer?

I wrote my first book when I was seventeen. That was a "children's book" and I suppose that was the first time I was described as a "children's author". I don't really like the term; I just like the term author. I think that there are no such things as "children's books" or "adult books", I think there are just books.

My reading of your books, particularly the Discworld titles, is that they are just books. Was it the publishers who made some children's titles or was it a contract to write some specifically?

My Discworld books were always published as "adult books". Then there was the **Truckers** trilogy; they were published as "children's books" and for a very specific reason: the main characters were all four inches high. You can't write a book for adults in which the main characters are four inches high. The whole subject matter was considered to be for children. (Jonathan Swift would definitely be sent home with a flea in his ear.)

Is this a publisher's notion of "sizeism"; if the protagonists aren't large enough it can't be a children's book?

No. My publishers in both cases were Transworld and they have been very kind to me. It's the market's notion of what is for adults and what is for children.

But from your author's viewpoint there isn't a difference in addressing a particular audience?

There are presumably some books that are children's books: books where the pages are a quarter of an inch thick and you can cut your teeth on the edges of them. I don't know if the code is the same in Australia as it is over here, but if you see a sign outside a grubby little shop saying "adult books" you know exactly what you are going to find inside.

Generally my books are for adolescents. I just write books. I might change the language slightly to make it more accessible to younger people but I think a good book is a good book and can be read by anyone.

Indeed. Talking of signs over the door, it's a sadness for me that the sign "children's books" might limit the readership of your Truckers trilogy: **Diggers, Truckers,** *and* **Wings** *and readers might also miss a great delight in* **The Carpet People** *where the protagonists are even smaller.*

Oh, yes, they're microscopic.

That is one of the advantages of the way British bookshops are arranged. There are very few specific children's bookshops so there is a certain amount of cross-over. In America it's very, very hard because there is strong division between books that are seen as being for children and books that are seen as for adults. What tends to happen over here is that all my books are put in one place; it might be the children's section, it might be the adult's or it might be somewhere in between.

Do you feel doubly subdivided in that you're divided off from the fiction into the science fiction/fantasy area and now you have a bit divided off into the children's books on some occasions?

Ah, yes. This is where it gets kind of tricky. Fifteen of my books have been on the best-seller lists here, including my children's books which ended up on the best-seller lists because they were selling so well to adults.

Every country has a literary establishment (and I don't mean this in the specific nasty way). They're basically a few hundred people who define what it is that's going on. Science fiction and fantasy aren't considered respectable genres. There is still something a bit 1950s, a bit Star Trek about it. So they were sort of saying here's this guy, he's selling lots of books but he's a kind of fantasy writer. (You could hear them spitting out of the corner of their mouths). But then they thought, but he writes books for children as well so therefore he's a children's writer and it's perfectly respectable to write fantasy for children. So in a sense I've been pigeonholed as a fantasy writer for children because that way they can invite me to their Arts Festivals without thinking I'm going to play the banjo and drink lager all the time.

That's interesting because on contemplation I would think a Children's Fantasy Author label has much more going for it than just Fantasy Author.

Oh, yes. I'm quite happy with this. It really is the case that fantasy, to be frank, is considered to be no more than Conan the Barbarian and fairytales for adults—and is looked down upon. However, fantasy for children is fine and I get invited to all the best literary events.

Terry, what is it about smallness of size for protagonists that is so appealing for you as you have used it now on a number of occasions?

I suppose you would have to ask a psychologist . . . I mean a psychiatrist (no that would be a bit tricky) . . . a psychologist. There are some obvious things. If you are small then you are under threat. If you are under threat then there is a story there already. With *The Carpet People* they are literally microscopic, invisible to the human eye.

And constantly under threat.

Yes—and the same with the nomes. They were four inches high and lived under floor boards. In circumstances like that the world is a different kind of place and it's a threatening one and, therefore, from an author's point of view it's a particularly interesting one.

I was recently reminded by an old friend of mine, who now lives in Australia, of how the *Truckers* trilogy got to be written. The nomes actually live under the floor in a giant department store. When I was six years old I was taken up to London for the first time from the tiny little village where I lived. Imagine: you are taken up to London, at Christmas; you are taken to a big department store. It's got moving staircases, it's got bright lights, it's got more toys than you ever thought could ever be made, and you're six years old. I think my brain went into a media overload for the whole day. I just stood there with my mouth open and rode up and down on the moving staircases for a half hour. Thinking of that, I thought that is how *Truckers* got started. That was what I remembered, that moment of just sheer amazement that there was such a thing like this in the world.

Yes, indeed. In the Discworld universe how did the picture book **Eric** *come about? Was it a contractual obligation? Was it a friendship to Josh Kirby who has drawn the covers for all your books?*

It's not exactly a picture book; there are about twelve full-page illustrations. It was simply the case that one day the editor said it would be nice to do something that had a number of Josh Kirby illustrations in it if you can think of a plot that would be interesting for him to illustrate. So I wrote a very short novel and sent it to Josh and that was that. It was just something that I did. There was no significant reason behind it. It was just something people thought would be interesting.

I look upon it as being a cornucopia of Discworld, a place where you can be introduced to the characters in short sketches. Was there something of that in your mind when you wrote it?

Well . . . I wrote a letter to Josh Kirby saying "Hey, Josh what do you like to illustrate?" He sent me back a four page letter that was just a list—I like to do castles, hills, clouds, kings, fairies, shoes . . . it went on, so I said: "OK. How about Aztecs?" He replied, "I don't like Aztecs." So I had to talk him into that.

It sold a great deal over here. Strangely, last year the publishers republished it without the illustrations, which made it significantly cheaper, and it sold out all over again. I don't know if I'll ever do anything like it again but it was fun to do, and it's been done.

Indeed.

One of your recent books **The Carpet People** *is also your earliest—the publisher's line "This book had two authors one seventeen and one forty-three. They were both Terry Pratchett". How different did you find that earlier voice?*

I had a contract with Transworld for some years to do *Carpet People* in hardback and they phoned up one day and said we would like to do this next August, or whenever. I said "Yeah, fine", and then thought I had just better have a read of this. I read through it with mounting horror. It was written when I was seventeen and I had been hit over the head with *Lord of the Rings*. It was obvious. But there was also a point of view that was no longer my point of view. I actually believed then in the natural wisdom of wizards and the kingliness of kings and I don't believe in either of those things now. (I may be a bit more cynical about things now). I thought I can't let it go like this. Besides which, parts of it were just very badly written. I don't mean the background was badly realised; it just wasn't written very well. So I phoned up the publisher and said, "I can't let this happen. You must let me rewrite it."

We put a copy of the book through an optical character recognition thing at a university so I could get it back onto computer disc. I spent a month hacking my way through it. Every time I read a bit that made me wince I went in and altered it. Every single bit of it got re-written in some sort of way and that is why I now say the book had two authors.

Did the earlier Terry Pratchett have the same sense of timing, in terms of smiles per minute?

If I hadn't learnt anything in the intervening years that would have been a bit of a shame. I could almost see little holes where the timing wasn't working properly and where one word would make the sentence read better. It was an interesting project to do. I haven't done it for any other book (**Strata** and **Darkside of the Sun** were not published long after that) because I think in most cases an author has to say: "I wrote it a long time ago, I wouldn't write it like that now. If you don't like it that's not how I write now." But *The Carpet People* was a bit different. Apart from anything else people were really waiting for it. It had been in the shops for years and years and copies were changing hands in antiquarian bookshops for £250. It was going to be a big production when it turned up so I thought it had to appear looking reasonably good. I thought I can't really show people the first book I ever wrote with all the faults in it because it will simply not be sold and bought on that basis. People wouldn't be buying it to see what Terry Pratchett wrote when he was seventeen, they would be buying it because it was the new Terry Pratchett book; I didn't want them disappointed.

And it isn't a disappointment. It was fantastic. You re-covered a universe that I for one would be happy to see more of. You have a great world in the carpet and a great set of characters.

Oh. Don't. Don't. There are other things I want to do.

You mean I'm never going to hear more about "achairleg" or experience the "flatland"?

When the book says "and they all lived happily ever after", it's not a good idea to find out what really happened.

I get this all the time because in the Discworld books I often pick different characters, different areas and different plots. A character will take part in a book and at the end will "ride off into the sunset." I do get fans who write and ask: "Can we have a book to find out what happens next." My reaction is, "Well, no." You're not supposed to find out what happens next day; that's not how stories go. Sometimes characters ride off into the sunset.

I think the carpet people have come to an end, but ask me again in five years time and you might get a different answer.

My thinking was more that in **Discworld** *you have the Disc and in* **Carpet People** *the carpet. Surely there is scope in both for the unravelling of tales?*

But the discworld is far more flexible. The discworld is there for humorous purposes. I can put things in the discworld. I can put words in the characters' mouths. That's on a different scale to the carpet. The carpet has to be taken seriously; in a way, the discworld only takes itself seriously. We don't have to do the same thing.

No we don't.

Terry, lastly, your most recently available work here **Only You Can Save Mankind** *is a different sort of tale for you. This is the first work where I get the feel that this is a work of 'teen fiction' given everything we discussed above. This work goes most to the heart of matters of being a contemporary teenager, particularly a male one, no matter where you are in the universe where there is technology. Was that a construction?*

Yes, although I think you have to be slightly careful about this. I found for example, that in the United States my third discworld book, which was *Equal Rites,* got put on the children's shelves because one of the characters (the heroine) was seven years old. That's very much part of the American publishing scene; the age of the character defines the age group the book's for. Therefore, you cannot write a book for children with an adult hero and you cannot write a book for adults with a hero who is a child. This a bit of an over simplification on their part. I say there is no such thing as a children's book and no such thing as an adult's book, but when you are 13 or 14 you're in a very strange kind of world that isn't exactly of the world that belongs to either children or adults. I remembered something about being alive then and I thought I'd like to do this. While I think the book has had a readership from either side of the 13/14 age band I thought there is stuff there that would mean more to people at 13/14 than at 10 or 18.

I enjoyed it a lot and in fact this year there will be another book set in the same world with the same hero. It is dealing with entirely different things; there is very little technology involved this time. Perhaps the reason for writing it is I found another voice and I really enjoyed doing it.

The group of boys you have here, apart from hero Johnny, Wobbler, Bigmac and Yo-less struck me as being the quintessential group of nerdish males from diverse ethnic backgrounds you might find in any High School playground anywhere.

Yeah. The thing is that there is only one girl in the book and she's got more intelligence than all of the boys added up. Although they are all males they are only just. They have about as much charisma as a duck egg. They are all only one step above being totally useless but, frankly, when you are male and about thirteen you are more or less totally useless. Your joints all feel they are held together with elastic bands, you worry about all kinds of things and the world's a very strange place.

I've certainly found over here that the fact that most of the characters in it are male hasn't put off the female readers. I think they rather like the fact that the girl is so much brighter.

Your alien commander is certainly something, as well.

Giving away a bit of the plot: My hero finds that he can communicate with the aliens in the computer game he is playing. Like a lot of kids his age, quite unthinkingly, he's a kind of male chauvinist piglet—girls just can't do things as well as boys. It turns out that all the aliens are female (Their warriors are the females) and they have exactly the same view about males. As a result there is a kind of culture clash because both of them can understand how the other one thinks but they are thinking 180 degrees away from each other. It was fun to do because of the kids in there. I think they are very human. I've decided to keep them on, and there is going to be at least one more book.

Terry, I was surprised at how often in **Only You Can Save Mankind** *I found myself smiling at the humour in the description. I became aware that that is one of the greatest arrows in your armoury of humour—its often the way you describe things that makes them humorous rather than the things you are describing.*

Ah. yes. Recently I've been working on a graphic novel. (I hate that term. I don't think there is such a thing. It takes more than quality paper, moody illustration and an absence of "socko" bubbles to turn a comic into a graphic novel.) But anyway . . . I'm working here on a "big comic" of *Mort,* the fourth Discworld book, the one most people would like to see, and I've had to discuss this with the artist. The discworld is funny because we are looking at it but there isn't any internal humour. Everyone takes themselves seriously. The humour comes from us looking in, seeing these strange people in strange circumstances and realising that to them it is normal life.

There aren't any jokes in *Only You Can Save Mankind.* The things that the kids are doing and the things that actually happen are very, very serious things. The hero's parents are splitting up, he doesn't feed himself properly,

he's a kid on the edge of having bad things happen in his life, but he's got something in his make-up that makes him keep going on. Those who feel like having a good cry after having read the book should know that in the next one, *Johnny and the Dead* he comes through most triumphantly.

The poor kid is such a nerd you can't help feeling sorry for him.

GENERAL COMMENTARY

Gregory Feeley

SOURCE: A review of *Small Gods and Others,* in *Book World—The Washington Post,* No. March 27, 1994, p. 11.

Terry Pratchett's **Small Gods** tells of torture, religious repression, death, and the persistence of folly in human affairs. It is an unusual set of themes to come from a writer famous for his delirious comedy, but Pratchett—whatever his reputation as a hip writer of frequently side-splitting humor—has always been a humorist of the most mordant, darkest shade.

His earlier novels, nearly all of which feature death and mayhem in various comic ways, include **Reaper Man** and **Mort,** while a third begins by promising to answer the question of what our ancestors would be thinking if they were alive today. (The answer proves to be: "Why is it so dark in here?") Like Tom Sharpe's novels and the diaries of Adrian Mole, Pratchett's books about the Discworld (which rests upon four elephants standing atop a great turtle; folks get burned for suggesting the world is round) do not enjoy the fanatical popularity here that they do in Britain, which prompts one to wonder whether the failing is ours. Adrian Mole, like Brian Aldiss's novels of the Hand-Reared Boy, may be too English to find a large audience across the Atlantic; but certainly Pratchett should travel as readily as Monty Python.

Small Gods is the story of Om, formerly one of the billions of minuscule deities that swarm invisibly through the Discworld, hoping to be noticed: "Most of them are too small to see and never get worshipped, at least by anything bigger than bacteria, who never say their prayers and don't demand much in the way of miracles." A great god in his time, commanding the belief of millions, Om has lately fallen into decline: Although he is worshipped by an enormous theocracy, his ranks of actual believers have dwindled to one, a novice monk named Brutha. As a result of this dwindling of assets, Om has found himself incarnated as a tortoise.

The attempts of Brutha (who alone can hear Om's entreaties) and Om to restore the god's fortunes set a great creaking plot into motion, one that is notably funnier for its asides—"This suggested that the Universe had probably been put together in a bit of a rush while the Supreme Being wasn't looking, in the same way that Boy Scouts' Association minutes are done on office photocopies all over the country"—than for its design. There is a city full of Greek-sounding philosophers, and an Alexandrian-like library, and an Omnian army intent on destroying both, and quite a few things happen. Various important issues (the evils of religious intolerance, the unanticipated applications of pure research) are discussed, rather more earnestly than Pratchett has hitherto done.

The problem with *Small Gods* is that its plot is complicated without being especially deft, and many tiny scenes exist solely to move stage scenery. Since a fair number of Pratchett's jokes recur from one book to the next, and many of the jokes in this novel are of the running or repeating variety (virtually every character, seeing Om as a tortoise, remarks, "There's good eating on one of those things"), the reader can end up looking for the good lines, like a partygoer digging through a dish of peanuts for the odd cashew.

Pratchett's previous novel (in America, at least) *Witches Abroad,* reunites Granny Weatherwax, Nanny Ogg, and Magrat Garlick from *Wyrd Sisters* and sends them on a mission to a distant city after Magrat becomes fairy godmother following the death of the previous incumbent, a witch splendidly named Desiderata. In addition to revealing what witches actually say at a sabbat ("Did everyone bring potato salad?"), the story offers a travelogue across the face of Discworld, where the distinctly unrefined trio must deal not only with the rigors of travel—"More than a couple of hours on a stick and I've gone rigid in the dairy air . . . That's foreign for bum"—but also with an evil fairy godmother who wishes to use the power of storytelling to impose happy endings upon everyone.

Perhaps because the novel's picaresque structure seems commodious rather than contrived, one reads with less of an obtrusive sense of stage machinery being wheeled into place. Still, Pratchett's taste for complicated climactic scenes remains, so that his novels, rather than coming to a point as much comedy does, tend to blow apart like a firecracker.

If *Small Gods* and *Witches Abroad* often seem labored, part of the reason may be their outsized dimensions. The first batch of Pratchett's novels to be published in this country—*The Color of Magic, The Light Fantastic,* etc.—ran between 170 and 200 pages in length, traditionally the perfect length for a comic novel (one thinks immediately of those by P. G. Wodehouse). Like everything else in the '80s (the trade deficit, Rush Limbaugh), comic fantasy novels grew bigger without becoming any funnier. The extra hundred pages that Pratchett's recent novels have been carrying weigh heavily upon them; one need only to look to his infrequent short stories (such as **"Troll Bridge"** in the anthology *After the King*) or his shorter novels—the trilogy *Truckers, Diggers,* and *Wings,* ostensibly for younger readers, is an excellent example—to see how much defter and funnier Pratchett is when he keeps his timing taut.

Edward James

SOURCE: "Unseen University," in *Times Literary Supplement,* No. 4786, December 23, 1994, p. 21.

When a new Discworld (or Discworld®) novel is published, it goes straight into the bestseller lists. Pratchett's loyal band of followers has, since the mid-1980s, grown into a dedicated army, and, in the past twelve months alone, it has been rewarded with two new Discworld novels, a series of audio tapes, *The Discworld Companion* and a detailed street-map of Ankh-Morpork, Discworld's greatest city (motto: QVANTI CANICVLA ILLA IN FENESTRA). Students applying to my department at York University often claim on their entrance forms that their favourite authors are Thomas Hardy and Terry Pratchett. One is a set author; the other is someone they really enjoy reading. Pratchett may well last as long as Hardy, or, more appositely, as P. G. Wodehouse. For the army is not made up just of teenagers (male and female in roughly equal numbers), but of their parents too. Some of the jokes, one suspects, are only understood by the well read; others, perhaps, are missed by all but the young.

A newcomer wanting to understand the Discworld phenomenon would be advised to begin, not with *The Colour of Magic* (1983) the first of the series, nor with *Interesting Times,* the seventeenth, but probably with *Small Gods* (1992) or *Wyrd Sisters* (1988). It is an odd thing about the Discworld books that they contravene the general law of series, and get better as they go on. The early books had some good jokes and memorable characters, as well as the benefit of novelty, but they did not have strong plots; since then the plots have matured, along with the characters. Pratchett's satire is no longer aimed at the worlds of other fantasy writers (Anne McCaffry's Pern, Fritz Leiber's Lankhmar, Larry Niven's Ringworld), but at twentieth-century Earth. In Discworld, our institutions, our follies, even our laws of nature all appear—but twisted, distorted, magnified, ridiculed. There is a slight scholarly cast to the humour; as in Gibbon, many of the jokes are in the footnotes and Discworld itself is explained rationally, within a science that operates at least one dimension away from our own. For example, academics have begun to explore fuzzy logic; in Pratchett, the Unseen University has a chair of woolly thinking—which is like fuzzy logic, only more so. Living is not easy on Discworld: "life is like a bird which flies out of the darkness and across a crowded hall and then through another window into the endless night again. In Rincewind's case it had managed to do something incontinent in his dinner."

Pratchett's humour takes logic past the point of absurdity and round again, but it is his unexpected insights into human morality that make the Discworld series stand out from other fantasies. Pratchett is pro-feminist, pro-paci-fist, pro-anarchist, and pro- just being a thoughtful human being without any of that silly heroism which gets people killed, but he is without any patronizing pedantry.

TITLE COMMENTARY

THE CARPET PEOPLE (1971; Revised, 1992)

Times Literary Supplement

SOURCE: "Fantastic Invention," in *Times Literary Supplement*, No. 3661, April 28, 1972, pp. 474-5.

More than any other form of invention, fantasy needs to convey an absolute conviction; where the author flags or fails, the reader also dies. Are there thin places in Grimm, or in Tolkien? This applies to magic themes in younger books no less than the older and more sophisti-cated . . . Conviction certainly keeps **The Carpet People** in motion. It's a strange and tangled book, not for everyone's digestion: the obvious reader seems to be one who has raced through Norton (*The Borrowers*), Sutcliff, Kipling perhaps (the Roman-British items), and Tolkien, and looks around for more. (The Tolkienian echoes may draw in some older readers, even.) Derivative, yes—but the idea also generates a disturbing energy of its own. Quotation best suggests the flavour:

> "In the beginning," said Pismire, "there was nothing but the endless Flatness. Then came the Carpet, Mother of us all. . . . Then came the dust, which fell upon the Carpet, drifting among the hairs, taking roots in the deep shadows. First came the little crawling creatures that make their dwellings in burrows and high in the hairs. Then came the soraths, and the weft borers, tromps, goats, gromepipers and the snargs. But there was a thread missing from the weave on the loom of life. . . ."

And so, from the dust, the Mother Carpet wove the Carpet people. They are minuscule. Each carpet hair is a mighty trunk, each colour of the pattern a vast region. Beyond the uttermost fringes is the Woodwall: beneath is the mysterious Underlay, with its "deep crevasses and windy caves." The people include the deftmenes (good), the mouls (appalling), and wights, the first created of all. ("They are now of another Age, those wights, who polish wood and carve trinkets for anyone who will buy. Now their time has gone.") But the wights once built the beautiful city of Jeopard, glittering with jet from the Hearthlands, and crystals of sugar and salt, and now in deadly danger. The story tells how Snibril the Munrung, a sort of Frodo, goes forth with his brother Glurk into unknown Carpet lands, and becomes involved in countering the advancing power

of Fray. Travel along with Snibril if it's your kind of road; you will drink groad beer, eat fried tromp, baked gromer, behold strange beasts, see tumblers leap to the sound of the flutleharp, and battle with bone-tipped spears. One need not worry too much about the allegory; which is about human rifts in the larger world; it rises up from time to time, but only when the action clears sufficiently.

W. Magee

SOURCE: A review of *The Carpet People*, in *The Junior Bookshelf*, Vol. 56, No. 5, October, 1992, p. 210.

The name Terry Pratchett sounds rather like an old pro playing left half for Millwall. Far from being a clogger, Pratchett is the multi-mega-cosmic best-seller of such sci-fi books as **The Truckers** trilogy and **The Discworld** series. Now we have **The Carpet People** being a novel T.P. wrote while a teenager. Some 26 years later the author has revised and rewritten the story. The notion of a carpet hiding a universe of characters and actions is similar to that seen in the Clive Barker's blockbusting *Weaveworld*. In **The Carpet People** we find the Munrungs (True Human Beings), and then soraths, weft borers, tromps, goats, grome-pipers, snargs. This typifies the novel's mouth-watering attention to names and place names . . . Tregon Marus, Snibril, Glurk, Woodwall, Fray, Dumii, and Damion Oddfoot adding greatly to the story's enjoyment factor. And the story itself—part saga, legend, and adventure—swings along at a fair old clatter. Terry Pratchett's writing is vivid and immediate. He wastes no time. There is little padding. The swiftness of the storyline is everything . . .

> 'When it began to seem to Snibril that the dark Carpet had no ending they reached the road again and, ahead of them, torches burning along its walls, was the city of Jeopard.'

For young readers unaware of Pratchett's oeuvre (can there be any left?) **The Carpet People** is a fine introduction. One can see it generating a new surge of sales for the **Truckers** and the **Discworld** series. Success breeding success. . . .

Jessica Yates

SOURCE: A review of *The Carpet People*, in *The School Librarian*, Vol. 40, No. 4, November, 1992, p. 159.

Terry Pratchett has become a young person's writer by an unconventional route: leaving school at sixteen for local journalism; writing his first Sci-Fi/fantasy for adults while press officer for the CEGB; full-time writer of humorous fantasy becoming a 'cult' writer for teenagers; accomplished children's writer with his first trilogy a permanent best-seller!

However, his very first book, written at seventeen and published when he was twenty-two, was a children's fantasy, and there has been so much demand from his fans for a reprint that he decided to revise it for republication. **The Carpet People** therefore retains its setting, characters and quest structure with Pratchett's more mature observations about the folly of human nature blended into the text, and now appears a fitting companion piece to **Truckers,** which is also about small autonomous adults instead of immature children, the usual subjects of children's literature (not the only feature **The Carpet People** has in common with *The Hobbit*).

These carpet people are miniscule and really do inhabit a carpet. Their capital city is the size of a full stop. They are men, women and children, possess language and several cultures, herd animals, make war and negotiate peace. They venerate huge tokens which once appeared from the sky, such as a matchstick or a penny, without knowing about us big people, and they live in fear of Fray, which causes earthquake-like disasters. The story describes the quest of a village tribe for a new home after Fray destroys their settlements, and centres on five well-defined male characters: the chief, his intelligent younger brother, the tribe's shaman (a Gandalf-type), a wandering warrior, and a deposed king. They discover a plan by the 'mouls', misshapen creatures rather like goblins, to conquer the empire of the carpet people, and they gather allies on their journey to devise a strategy for defeating the mouls.

The concept is fascinating and is told with Pratchett's customary wit plus touches of cynicism. The carpet people's culture appears to be modelled on Roman Britain versus the barbarians—some influence of Asterix as well as *The Hobbit,* perhaps? It's a winner.

David Bennett

SOURCE: A review of *The Carpet People,* in *Books for Keeps,* No. 81, July, 1993, p. 15.

This is 17-year-old Pratchett's first published novel, co-written with his 43-year-old self for the hardback version. After reading it you'll never look at a carpet again without seeing the host of grain-sized people that Pratchett vividly describes as its inhabitants, living in a world that is in danger of destruction from the Mouls, who crave total power. Fortunately there are heroes, albeit reluctant ones, willing to restore the balance by fighting a battle to end all battles.

The pace is fast, the humour wry and the wisdom profound. I already have a waiting list for my review copy.

THE DARK SIDE OF THE SUN (1976)

Sister Avila

SOURCE: A review of *The Dark Side of the Sun,* in *Library Journal,* Vol. 101, No. 14, August, 1976, p. 1661.

There is a current of laughter barely beneath the surface of this delightful story by a young Englishman. The hero, Dom Sabalos, from the planet Widdershins, moves through his galaxy via gravity sandals, sun dogs (sapient and vehicular), and plain space ships, in search of the Jokers, "a race that had died before human times began." He is accompanied by his Phnobic tutor, Hrsh-Hgn; his pet, Ig; and a class-5 robot, Isaac, the most interesting character in the book. After amazing and amusing adventures they reach the surprise ending. A preposterous story written with uninhibited imagination and love for words. Good entertainment.

STRATA (1981)

Kirkus Reviews

SOURCE: A review of *Strata,* in *Kirkus Reviews,* Vol. XLIX, No. 15, August 1, 1981, p. 971.

A well-handled, inventive, gleefully madcap flat-Earth jaunt where things are never quite what they seem. Two-centuries-old Kin Arad, planet-builder from the *real* Earth (where Remus, founded "Reme" and Europe was defeated by a Norse-American Indian coalition) is contacted by mad starship pilot Jago Jalo, who has discovered an astonishing object: a disk-shaped Earth replete with valuable artifacts of the Great Spindle Kings (a vanished alien race of superior accomplishments who, among other things, built the Earth). With alien companions Marco (a paranoid, four-armed warrior Kung), Silver (a cannibalistic Shand), and a stowaway raven who turns out to be a spy (Jalo himself soon succumbs to a heart attack), Kin travels to the disk Earth, which features a protective barrier, recycling oceans, and artificial planets describing epicycles in the sky. On arrival, their ship accidentally rams a "planet" and they crashland on the disk—just in time to save Leif Eriksson's longship, vainly searching for Vinland, from falling off the edge. And a wacky journey ensues, deftly parodying *Ringworld*. With everything from dragons to robots: bright, bubbly fun.

Publishers Weekly

SOURCE: A review of *Strata,* in *Publishers Weekly,* Vol. 220, No. 9, August 28, 1981, p. 391.

Pratchett is a British author who deserves to be better known to American SF readers. His new novel is a fine, light entertainment, full of wit and surprises. Comparable in broad outline to Clarke's *Rendezvous with Rama,* Varley's *Titan* and Niven's *Ringworld,* it is especially influenced by the latter in the area of casting; but despite generic similarities to the aforementioned trio, **Strata** is very much its own book. How could it be otherwise when the place being explored is a disklike flat version of Earth with the oceans falling over the edges, a world inhabited by knights and vikings, demons and djinns and run by robots? Our heroes come from a culture that shapes planets to order, but they leave the disk with the help of a giant roc, having discovered that neither the diskworld nor the universe is quite what it seemed. Let's see more of Pratchett.

Rosemary Herbert

SOURCE: A review of *Strata,* in *Library Journal,* Vol. 106, No. 18, October 15, 1981, p. 2052.

In his latest novel, Pratchett proves himself once again to be particularly adept at building an intriguing imaginary world. The author of **The Carpet People** (concerning a world located in and beneath a carpet) here describes the adventures of Kin Arad, a 210-year-old planet surfacer who has seen much in her long life but remains capable of amazement when she learns of a flat earth with an uncanny physical resemblance to the medieval view of Earth's geography. In the company of two unlikely companions, both inhuman, Kin makes a voyage of discovery to a new but faltering world where "on some nights the stars flicker out." A satisfying blend of wonderment and adventure.

THE COLOUR OF MAGIC (1983)

Kirkus Reviews

SOURCE: A review of *The Colour of Magic,* in *Kirkus Reviews,* Vol. LI, No. 16, August 15, 1983, p. 913.

Pratchett borrows from Babylonian cosmology for his second, wacky flat-Earth yarn—set on an Earth-disk that rests on the backs of four elephants, who themselves stand on the shell of an enormous turtle. (And only Pratchett's characters would think of lowering themselves over the edge of the disk—in order to determine the sex of the turtle!) This time failed wizard Rincewind runs into problems when he encounters rich, bumbling circum-disk tourist Twoflower—whose luggage consists of a sapient pearwood box that trots around after him on hundreds of tiny legs . . . and snaps its lid at anyone it doesn't like. The innocent Twoflower sells some fire insurance to a shifty innkeeper, who proceeds to burn down his inn and the entire city of Ankh-Morpork. And what follows is madcap travelogue, involving: the disk's zany, often magical inhabitants; the Gods (atheists are liable to get their windows broken); a watery being who splashed down in the ocean, having fallen off a different Earth-disk; and Death with his scythe (whose timing is so poor that Rincewind keeps evading him). Not quite the gleefully insane parody **Strata** was, but frothy, inventive, and fun.

Publishers Weekly

SOURCE: A review of The Colour of Magic, in *Publishers Weekly,* Vol. 224, No. 8, August 19, 1983, p. 373.

Pratchett's U.S. debut, **Strata,** was a delightful spoof of certain well-known science fiction novels that could also be enjoyed on its own as an inventive comic adventure. Now Pratchett does for sword and sorcery, with equal success, what he did for SF. In much the same vein as de Camp and Pratt's perennially popular *Incompleate Enchanter* series, he gives us an inept wizard named Rincewind shepherding a naive actuary, Twoflower, his world's first tourist, through a series of increasingly hazardous and outrageous adventures. Assisting Rincewind's rather inconsistent powers in protecting Twoflower is the Luggage, a sentient trunk that doggedly follows him through all manner of adversity on its hundreds of little legs. Heroic barbarians, chthonic monsters, beautiful princesses and fiery dragons; they're all here, but none of them is doing business as usual. Nor would you expect them to, in a book that ends with the heroes falling over the edge of the world. It's all lots of fun.

Richard Geis

SOURCE: A review of *The Colour of Magic,* in *Science Fiction Review,* No. 49, November, 1983, p. 59.

This world is 'supported on the back of a giant turtle—of unknown and disputed sex—and by four huge elephants upon whose shoulders it rests.

'If you get too close to the edge of this disc-world you fall off!

'**The Colour of Magic** is the story of the trials and tribulations of two very unlikely adventures: Rinceworld, the inept, drop-out wizard whose spells work only some of the time and the blissfully naive interplanetary tourist—an actuary from the Agatean Empire—called Twoflower. With Rinceworld as the chaperon, and with Twoflower's luggage, supported and propelled by hundreds of little legs, scurrying close behind, they encounter a wonderful array of characters: princesses, dragons, heroic barbarians, and thieves on this decidedly off-center world.

'A Main Selection of the Science Fiction Book Club.'

Mockery of all we hold dear and sacred had better be damned good! Alas, from a quick dip and a chortle, this is. More later.

Louis James

SOURCE: A review of *The Colour of Magic,* in *British Book News,* No. March, 1984, p. 176.

What is shaped like a trunk, has hundreds of legs, can see without eyes and gulp down a thief or provide clean socks or unlimited gold coins, according to whose side you are on? The answer is Luggage, the invincible valet of Twoflower. Twoflower is a pioneer galactic tourist visiting the discworld of Ankh-Morpork with his imp-operated picture box. By a turn of bad luck inevitable in this topsy-turvy world he is allotted, as guide, a chronically incompetent failed magician called Rincewind. Threatened by everything from space bandits to dragons, their adventures contrive to be at once hilarious and absorbing, ending in a sequence at the edge of the discworld where the waters fall away into infinite space.

Terry Pratchett has been writing science fiction stories since he was thirteen. In **Strata** he turned to parody; in **The Colour of Magic** he turns a satirical eye on the related genre of sword-and-sorcery fantasy. Everyone—from Tolkien to Robert E. Howard, Camp and Pratt, Anne McCaffrey and many others—seems to be remarked upon at some point. The parody is dangerously easy, but Pratchett is saved from archness by his obvious enthusiasm for the writing he so joyously takes over the top. Verbally witty, imaginatively resourceful and with a nice line in comic-book action, the novel will be enjoyed by those who enjoy high-spirited fantasy, whether or not they recognize all the models being so affectionately caricatured. The 'colour of magic' turns out to be the dimension of imagination itself. And imagination, Terry Pratchett hints, ultimately is a magic that everyone (including his readers) can practise.

THE LIGHT FANTASTIC (1986)

Publishers Weekly

SOURCE: A review of *The Light Fantastic,* in *Publishers Weekly,* Vol. 231, No. 16, April 24, 1987, p. 64.

Pratchett's comic novel **The Colour of Magic** introduced the magical world of the Disc, which is in imminent danger of destruction as this sequel opens. The only hope lies in finding the inept wizard Rincewind, who has inadvertently gotten an essential spell lodged in his brain. Rincewind, however, has his own problems. While his steps are dogged by the traveling trunk, a sentient piece of luggage with 100 feet, Rincewind and his companion Two-flower wander, lost, through the forest of Skund. Their encounters include a misplaced computer salesman who discusses his trade with a Druid ferrying rocks to Stonehenge and the legendary Cohen the Barbarian, now aging and toothless. This sort of whimsical, prep-school playfulness with words and concepts isn't for everyone, but fans of the similar *Hitchhiker's Guide to the Galaxy* should enjoy it.

Kirkus Reviews

SOURCE: A review of *The Light Fantastic,* in *Kirkus Reviews,* Vol. LV, No. 8, May 1, 1987, p. 679.

That rare event, a comedy sequel that is twistier, plottier, and *funnier* than its predecessor.

"The sun rose slowly, as if it wasn't sure it was worth all the effort." So begins Pratchett's latest yarn about Disc Earth, which rests on the backs of four huge elephants, who stand upon the shell of A'Tuin the Great Turtle; the latter is heading through space towards a huge, malevolent red star, but nobody knows why. Rincewind the failed wizard, his companion Twoflower the naive tourist, and Twoflower's aggressive luggage (a sapient pearwood box that trots around on hundreds of tiny legs), having fallen off the Disc at the end of **Magic,** now find themselves safe back on the Disc—thanks to the Octavo, the highly magical repository of the Eight Great Spells. One of the spells has taken up residence in Rincewind's head ("The spell wasn't a demanding lodger. It just sat there like an old toad at the bottom of a pond"), and so most of the Disc's wizards are chasing after Rincewind to try and get the spell back. The rest is riotously impossible to summarize but includes warrior princesses, Cohen the Barbarian, trolls, demons, Death, Druids, false teeth, argumentative spells, flying rocks, and talking trees.

You won't stop grinning except to chuckle or sometimes roar with laughter. The most hilarious fantasy since—come to think of it, since Pratchett's previous outing.

Jackie Cassada

SOURCE: A review of *The Light Fantastic,* in *Library Journal,* Vol. 112, No. 9, May 15, 1987, p. 100.

As Great A'Tuin, the cosmic turtle, carries Discworld through space toward almost certain doom, the mages of Unseen University search frantically and murderously for the possessor of one of the Eight Great Spells—the failed Wizard Rincewind. This sequel to **The Colour of Magic** chronicles the further adventures of its "un-hero" and his companions Cohen the Barbarian, Twoflower the Tourist, and The Luggage in grand, uproarious style. Pratchett excels in both slapstick comedy and tongue-in-cheek wit. Recommended.

EQUAL RIGHTS (1987)

Pauline Morgan

SOURCE: A review of *Equal Rights,* in *Fantasy Review,* Vol. 10, No. No. 1, January/February, 1987, p. 45.

This book, according to the author, is not wacky or zany, but it is undeniably fun to read. It is a sequel to **The Colour of Magic** and **The Light Fantastic,** but only in that it is set later on the same fantastic world. (This is a disc-shaped world, carried on the back of four gigantic elephants standing on the shell of a great turtle.)

When an old wizard dies, he passes his staff to the eighth "son" of an eighth son in an obscure mountain village. The problem is that this child is a girl, and women can't be wizards. As soon as she is old enough to recognize her powers (nearly nine), Eskarina is determined to strike a blow for women's liberation (although she wouldn't explain it that way) and go to the Unseen University. With her goes the witch Granny Weatherwax.

It all reads very much like the kind of children's book that can equally charm and captivate adults, and indeed Eskarina is the kind of child any little girl would love to be—independent, adventurous, and able to turn her irksome brother into a pig. For most of the book the tone is just right, but towards the end something is lost and the climax becomes confusing. Nevertheless, the novel will be enjoyed by children between eight and eighty-eight—and on the disc-world, eight is a magic number.

Roland Green

SOURCE: A review of *Equal Rights,* in *Booklist,* Vol. 85, No. 1, September 1, 1988, pp. 42-3.

Pratchett's approach to fantasy strongly recalls Douglas Adams's approach to sf—create a zany premise and introduce a series of still zanier events and characters. Here we have Discworld, a flat world riding on the backs of four elephants standing on an even bigger turtle. The characters and incidents are too numerous to mention; in fact, it would be stretching a point to say that this book has a plot. It does, however, have a great deal of what a growing number of readers regard as entertainment value. This volume will probably entice readers wherever Adams's books have a following.

English Journal

SOURCE: A review of *Equal Rights,* in *English Journal,* Vol. 79, No. 3, March, 1990, p. 82.

An aged wizard passes his powers to a newborn eighth son of an eighth son, who turns out to be a *daughter.* Against all tradition, Eskarina struggles to obtain a wizard's education, assisted by a witch, the wizard's staff, and a young apprentice wizard who unknowingly has powers greater than those of any of the Discworld's accomplished wizards. This book is a great starting place for readers who have been avoiding the fantasy genre because they do not know the rules, for it is humorous and unpredictable, a thoroughly well-written book about wizardry that refuses to take even itself seriously.

MORT (1987, U.S. edition, 1989)

Colin Greenland

SOURCE: A review of *Mort,* in *New Statesman & Society,* Vol. 115, No. 2966, January 29, 1988, pp. 30-1.

Mort is the fourth book of Terry Pratchett's *Discworld* series, which began as wry spoof sword-and-sorcery but is growing in to some moral pretensions of its own. This one, in which an awkward adolescent finds himself apprenticed to a tall bony man who carries a scythe and consults hourglasses a lot, is only partly good. The material requires a black humour Pratchett is constitutionally too merry to manage; and he keeps repeating jokes, sometimes within a few pages. Pratchett has two publishers but apparently no editor. Wrap 'em up and sell 'em, that's the way.

The fantastic conventions Pratchett is ridiculing, all the fatalistic feudal furniture, are so established these days that merely choosing a different epoch to play with guarantees a breath of fresh air.

Publishers Weekly

SOURCE: A review of *Mort,* in *Publishers Weekly,* Vol. 235, No. 8, February 24, 1989, p. 226.

The slightly askew fantasy realm of Discworld is the setting of several Pratchett novels which, however uneven, have an engagingly droll sense of the absurd. In the latest, a Death grown weary of his duties takes as apprentice an absent-minded scarecrow of a boy named Mort. While Death is out finding himself by way of such ordinary human pleasures as drinking and dancing, he leaves to Mort the serious business of gathering in the dead. The immediate result is a botched job in which Mort's beloved Princess Keli is saved from an assassin. In the long run, though, the bumbling creates a pocket of reality at odds with major historical forces. Although Pratchett tends to go on a bit longer than his material warrants and the cleverness occasionally waxes as self-satisfied as it is self-referential, his playfulness with words, clichés, concepts and conventions is, at its best, laugh-out-loud funny.

Don D'Ammassa

SOURCE: A review of *Mort,* in *Science Fiction Chronicle,* June, 1989, p. 42.

Terry Pratchett is the only humorist working in the field who rivals and sometimes even surpasses Douglas Adams. This latest tale of the Discworld features a young man, Mort, who is desperate to find a profession. As a consequence, he finds himself apprenticed to Death himself, and part of his duties include going out into the world and claiming the souls of those who are scheduled to die. But Mort has a soft heart, and sometimes he decides not to do his duty. Unfortunately for those he spares, the rest of the universe remains convinced that they are dead, and the consequences are frequently hilarious. Pratchett is one of those rare writers whom you can read snatches of at a time, out of order, out of context, and still find amusing.

WYRD SISTERS (1988; U.S. edition, 1990)

Mary Cadogan

SOURCE: A review of *Wyrd Sisters,* in *Books Magazine,* No. 21, December, 1988, p. 22.

The trouble with books as funny as the Terry Pratchett *Discworld* series is that the best way to review them may be not to write a review but to stick a finger into the text at random, and transcribe what first comes to hand, in the confident expectation that it will reduce all readers to paroxysms of giggles. (It is unclear how proofreaders and typesetters manage ever to get books like this into print in the first place, except by working through the text backwards.)

By one of the ironies in which life and genre fiction specialise, what started as a parody of the excesses of popular sword-and-sorcery fantasy has become, without any significant change of direction, one of the most successful examples of that genre ever to hit the stands. Pratchett has taken the extravagances and warrior heroes of Tolkien and Howard and subjected them to the relentless undercutting of the mundane, and of the logical mind of the average person. No magician is allowed to wander onto Pratchett's stage set without sarcastic remarks about the tatty stars on his hat; no warrior without problems with thermal underwear. Even Death keeps looking for other careers, most notably as the sort of short order cook that always turns up in author's resumes.

Wyrd Sisters brings back Granny Weatherwax, the stroppy ancient crone of *Equal Rites,* and involves her in a small coven ('When shall we three meet again?' - 'Well, I can do next Tuesday.') with Nanny Ogg, matriarch of a large tribe of Jasons and Sharleens, and Magrat, a young witch heavily into wholefood, clanky silver jewellery and doing magic the proper way, with lots of incense and chanting. The plot in which these three find themselves embroiled involves a usurper, a lost heir, a ghost seeking vengeance, a fool loyal to a bad master and the staging of a play for political reasons; a cauldron of a plot into which the tragedies of Shakespeare have been comprehensively chopped. The only things funnier than Pratchett's one-line gags are the extended sequences of dialogue in which his characters fail entirely to communicate with each other, and the long sequences of farcical climax in which he juggles running jokes, sudden entries and surprise twists until your eyes hurt from following all the things he has in the air.

It is the one-liners that have brought about the regular comparisons with Douglas Adams; Pratchett is quite as inventive as Adams while having altogether greater skills as a manipulator of character and situation. When Adams tries to humanise and develop his characters, the result is often mawkishly sentimental: Pratchett can humanise and deepen his characters while making them act in achingly funny ways.

You do not have to like heroic fantasy to enjoy Pratchett's spoof version of it, but, if you do, you will.

Faren Miller

SOURCE: A review of *Wyrd Sisters,* in *Locus,* Vol. 22, No. 1, January, 1989, pp. 15, 17.

Terry Pratchett continues to defy the odds. An open-ended series that just keeps getting better? Humorous fantasy with resources beyond puns, buffoonery, and generations of cardboard characters? Unheard of—until Pratchett. In *Wyrd Sisters,* sixth of the *Discworld* series, he brings back Granny Weatherwax, provides her with two ill-assorted coven sisters, and plunges them into realms of Shakespearean horror . . . though the witches don't see it quite that way.

King Verence has been murdered by a usurper, and his infant son stolen, along with the crown of Lancre. While Verence begins to learn the ropes of haunting one's own castle, the kidnappers encounter the coven on a dark and stormy night. Before you can say "Hogswatchnight," young Tomjon the king's son has been bundled off to a troupe of traveling players, and the witches are keeping a close eye on the murderous Lord Felmet and his ambitious wife.

The interplay between the witches is a continuous delight, as the strong-minded, rather prim Granny Weatherwax tries to cope with old Nanny Ogg's peasant earthiness and young Magrat Garlick's New Age fripperies. Add in a serious-minded Fool, a playwriting dwarf with a talent so large it bursts the bonds of time (to universal puzzlement), assorted sentient rocks, trees, and storms, and a stubbornly reluctant hero, and the result is a wise nonsense which should set Shakespeare to chuckling in his grave. Once again, bravo Pratchett!

SOURCERY (1988; U.S. edition, 1989)

Publishers Weekly

SOURCE: A review of *Sourcery,* in *Publishers Weekly,* Vol. 236, No. 19, November 10, 1989, p. 57.

This fifth Discworld tale, about a barely averted apocalypse there, reasserts Pratchett's adroitness as a storyteller. Inventive, satirical of the contemporary scene, Pratchett does not merely play with words, he juggles shrewd observations with aplomb. His creations are gently allegorical: for instance, the Unseen University Library is the repository of magic, its librarian an orangutan and its arch-chancellorship reserved for the most powerful magician, a "sourcerer" named Coin. But the author never takes himself or his message too seriously, and maintains a feather-light touch throughout. Even Death, an important minor character here, receives a distinctive voice.

Jodi L. Israel

SOURCE: A review of *Sourcery,* in *KLIATT,* Vol. 24, No. 3, April, 1990, p. 27.

Pratchett's innovative, humorous novel, **Sourcery,** reads like Douglas Adams in outer space. This is one of several Pratchett novels set on Discworld, which is run by wizards, overseen, in a vague sort of way, by the gods. It should be noted, for the uninformed, that wizardry and sorcery are barely related. Wizards, by and large, are not particularly powerful. A sorcerer, on the other hand, does whatever he wants to. This is not a good thing. It should also be noted that the eighth son of an eighth son is always a sorcerer. Ten-year-old Coin fits this description.

No story would be complete without the good guys. (Figure that sorcerers are the bad guys.) In this case we have three-ish. Rincewind, the "wizzard," it says so on his hat, although that is about the extent of his abilities; Conina, daughter of Cohen the Barbarian, who really wants to be a hairdresser but can't help killing people, a trick of "herrydeterry"; and Nijel, a barbarian wannabe, who carries with him his trusty barbarian rule book.

The "ish" would be the Librarian, former human-turned-orangutan, by all the magic floating around in the library, and the Luggage, best described as a sapient pearwood chest with a nasty disposition and legs. This motley crew is given the task of saving Discworld from the Sorcerer.

Pratchett's sense of the bizarre shines in this novel and his footnotes are almost funnier than the story. Highly recommended.

PYRAMIDS (1989)

Roz Kaveney

SOURCE: A review of *Pyramids,* in *Books Magazine,* Vol. 3, No. 4, July, 1989, p. 12.

Pyramids is yet another Terry Pratchett Discworld novel, and stretches hardly at all our sense of the sort of writer Pratchett is. Yet, when comedy is as accomplished and hard-working as this, who needs the shock of the new? This time around, Pratchett deals expeditiously with a lot of clichés about Ancient Egypt, about the power of Pyramids and the Curses of Mummies; in passing, he disposes expeditiously of Assassins' Guilds in a section that impartially puts the boot into Hughes's *Tom Brown's Schooldays* and Gene Wolfe's *Shadow of the Torturer.* Pratchett has reached a level of accomplishment such that he can parody a writer as good as Wolfe and not look presumptuous.

Faren Miller

SOURCE: A review of *Pyramids,* in *Locus,* Vol. 23, No. 2, August, 1989, pp. 11, 13.

If you feel less guilty laughing where the author intended you to, you'll prefer the Egyptological mayhem of Terry Pratchett's **Pyramids.** Here too you'll find temples, tombs, and centuries-undead pharoahs, along with mummies in hordes (and hoards), but this latest *Discworld* saga makes no effort to reach for the sublime.

Pyramids is Pratchett in one of his less novelistic moods, not letting the characters get in the way of the jokes. He romps through his new playground of Djelibeybi the river kingdom, having a better time than his earnest young hero, a newly crowned pharoah known as Teppic. The plot—such as it is—involves an alarmingly outside Grand Pyramid and its drastic spaciotemporal consequences, which set Teppic on a quest, while the Discworld equivalent of Greeks and Trojans muster for another war.

After the fusty melodrama of Ramses and company, it's a relief to encounter Pratchett's crew of new-fangled monument builders, talented camel, and (in passing) a hilariously inept Homeric bard. Of course it's silly. It's supposed to be.

GUARDS! GUARDS! (1989; U.S. edition, 1991)

Faren Miller

SOURCE: A review of *Guards! Guards!,* in *Locus,* Vol. 24, No. 1, January, 1990, pp. 15, 54.

Enter another large young man just out of the sticks and "heading for the city with all the openness, sincerity and innocence of purpose of an iceberg drifting into a major shipping lane." This time it's Carrot, the massive-but-tapering hero of *Terry Pratchett's* new Discworld novel, **Guards! Guards!.**

Carrot isn't particularly clever, and his sword is remarkably free of runes, gems, or other marks of destiny. Just as well, for the newest member of Ankh-Morpork's woefully inadequate Night Watch. It wouldn't do to attract too much attention in a place where the members of the Thieves' and Assassins' guilds are pillars of the community, where the Patrician rules amid sinister austerity, a demonic cult plots havoc, and a dragon is on the loose.

Of course Carrot fails to keep a low profile. (Did the iceberg miss the *Titanic?*) But he shares center stage with his fellow misfits in the Watch, most notably Captain Vimes, whom we first encounter drunk in a gutter, having trouble with his vocabulary. As the gutter becomes metaphoric and Vimes clambers out of it, the Night Watch loses some of its pathetic ineptitude. On their road to something almost resembling greatness, the guards will encounter Lady Ramkin (tweedy breeder of miniature dragons), a young man with a *very* flashy sword, the Supreme Grand Master of a cult which thrives on petty bickering, the orangutan Librarian (now revealed as an initiate into the awesome secrets of "L-Space"), and assorted fire-breathing beasts who resolutely defy the laws of aerodynamics.

Need I say it's hilarious, with moments of genuine poignance and grandeur? Pratchett demonstrates just how great the distance is between one- or two-joke writers and the comic masters whose work will still be read well into the next century. So, no more talk about his "getting better with each book." He reached the top of his form some time ago, and should remain there for years, to everyone's benefit.

Roland Green

SOURCE: A review of *Guards! Guards!*, in *Booklist*, Vol. 87, No. 19, June 1, 1991, p. 1861.

This eighth novel in Pratchett's Discworld saga takes us to the city of Ankh-Morpork, with its unionized criminals. This arrangement is fine with the captain of the night watch, but then an oversize dwarf arrives, and he is determined to clean up the city in the best Wyatt Earp tradition, even if he has to fight a dragon to do it. The zaniness sometimes gets out of hand, but the novel is good, rowdy fun and can be enjoyed independently of the rest of the series, which is emerging as the most ambitious humorous science fiction project since Douglas Adams launched his *Hitchhiker's Guide to the Galaxy*.

TRUCKERS (1989; U.S. edition, 1990)

Kirkus Reviews

SOURCE: A review of *Truckers*, in *Kirkus Reviews*, Vol. LVIII, No. 1, January 1, 1990, pp. 49-50.

A four-inch Moses leads his people in the general direction of the Promised Land in this funny satire from the author of ***The Colour of Magic*** (published for adults but also enjoyed by young people).

Thousands of years after being shipwrecked on Earth, the Borrower-like Nomes have forgotten their origins and are living happily under the floors of a department store full of goods and huge, stupid humans, all created for them by their god, Arnold Bros (est. 1905). Thanks to the labors of the Stationeri tribe, the demesnes of Haberdasheri, Ironmongeri and the rest are uneasily at peace; but there are Signs—"Final Reductions," for instance, and "Everything Must Go"—that all is not well in the "world." Then a group of strangers, led by an often-bewildered and always self-pitying antihero named Masklin, appears from the mythical Outside bearing the Thing, a

small black box that suddenly lights up and announces that the store will be destroyed in less than a month. How to move several thousand Nomes and all their possessions in a hurry? Desperate, Masklin decides to steal a human truck. How to drive it? No problem: he asks the ingenious inventor Dorcas del Icatessen to form a steering committee! Nomes and readers are both in for a wild ride, as time is even shorter than Masklin thinks.

Again, Pratchett gives his cast plenty of personality and fuels the plot with non-stop comedy; he also wields a satirist's blade against human politics, mores, and preconceptions. Though Masklin settles the Nomes in an old quarry, sequels are obviously planned.

Marcus Crouch

SOURCE: A review of *Truckers*, in *The Junior Bookshelf*, Vol. 54, No. 1, February, 1990, p. 52.

Don't be put off by a garish jacket and an uninviting typographical layout. This is a lively and amusing story in the 'Borrowers' tradition.

Truckers is a view of modern life from the level of nomes. Nomes (the initial G is reserved for 'tall, chubby-faced gnomes' and 'pink-cheeked painted gnomes . . . every single one of them grinning' in the Gardening Department) are a race apart, living alongside humans. Masklin and his family live perilously on the Outside, within sight of the motorway, victims of cold and hunger, rats and foxes. They hitch a ride on a lorry and are taken to Arnold Bros (est. 1905) 'All Things Under One Roof,' a massive department store clearly designed with nomes in mind. Between the floor boards of this vast building live nomes by the thousand, in strictly departmentalized tribes. But 'Everything Must Go.' The store is scheduled for demolition, and Masklin finds himself reluctantly in the role of Leader in a Noah's Ark operation of enormous proportions. The nomes evacuate the Store—a hilarious episode—and we leave them adapting to a new life Outside. A sequel is inevitable.

In books of this kind a sense of scale is essential. This Terry Pratchett has. All the details of a man-sized world are seen here from nome-height. Through nome eyes we examine all the complex operations of a man-made society, and interpret them according to nome rules. The management of the story is most skilfully done. The book turns out to be an essay in social criticism. By nome standards we are a queer lot! Mr. Pratchett manipulates his large cast confidently. Some of them are stereotypes, like Granny Morkie and old Torrit who are straight out of the Archers, but Masklin himself, and Dorcas, the technical expert, Gurder, the reluctant Abbot, and Grimma, who, although a girl, learns to read without her brain exploding, are complex individuals whose potential can not be fully realized in a single book.

Some of the satire may escape the young readers who are attracted by this picture of a miniature world, but the story is surely destined for success. A sequel will be eagerly awaited.

Denise Wilms

SOURCE: A review of *Truckers,* in *Booklist,* Vol. 86, No. 14, March 15, 1990, p. 1457.

This is a wry, somewhat tongue-in-cheek fantasy about "nomes," creatures something like gnomes. They're little but, if the picture on the dust jacket is to be believed, quite human looking; in fact, the hero, Masklin, looks much like any modern young man. His job is to save his foundering little community from extinction. He accomplishes this by stowing everyone away in a truck that takes them to Arnold Bros. Department Store. Under the floorboards of the great, lumbering emporium is an entire world inhabited by nomes, who in the sheltered comfort of the store, have developed a complicated society. Arnold Bros., however, is set to be demolished, and Masklin must convince his new friends that the end is near and show them a way to save themselves. This tall order, which Masklin undertakes with some reluctance, is the core of Pratchett's enterprising tale. A sense of humor permeates the story, which unhesitatingly lampoons the ingrained habits and complacent attitudes found in any society. Pratchett's tale winds down to a satisfactory conclusion, but there's a strong sense of more to come—a fact confirmed by the flap copy. Lively fantasy adventure.

Ann A. Flowers

SOURCE: A review of *Truckers,* in *The Horn Book Magazine,* Vol. LXVI, No. 2, March/ April, 1990, p. 202.

Masklin is the rather surprised and reluctant leader of a small group of nomes, beings in the form of miniature but burly humans. They have lived alone in the hazardous Outside for some time, treasuring their Thing, a black box that they have handed down through the generations from leader to leader. But times are tough, and they seek shelter in a department store called "Arnold Bros., (est. 1905)." There they find many more nomes—to their immense surprise, for they had always thought they were the only ones left. Masklin makes many discoveries in the Store, as it is reverently called, and receives messages from the hitherto silent Thing, which informs them that nomes originally came from another planet in a spaceship. The Store's inhabitants, the Stationeri, the Ironmongri, the del Icatessens, do not believe in Outside—they have always lived in the Store. But when the Thing tells them that the Store is about to be torn down, Masklin gathers a group of trusty friends who first learn how to read and then learn how a truck is driven. A fancy rig, made of levers and wires, enables a cooperative company of nomes to drive the truck, laden with supplies and the entire nome population of the Store, right out of the building just before it is completely destroyed. A wild and hilarious chase sequence follows, with the baffled police doubting their sanity. Clearly a sequel is called for, as, when last seen, the nomes are living in a quarry and thinking of learning to fly an airplane. The strong overtones of Moses leading the Israelites out of Egypt are accentuated by quasi-biblical entries at the beginning of each chapter. Fascinating and funny.

GOOD OMENS: THE NICE AND ACCURATE PROPHECIES OF AGNES NUTTER, WITCH (with Neil Gaiman, 1990; U.S. edition, 1991)

Publishers Weekly

SOURCE: A review of *Good Omens: The Nice and Accurate Prophecies of Agnes Nutter, Witch,* in *Publishers Weekly,* Vol. 237, No. 29, July 20, 1990, p. 50.

When a scatterbrained Satanist nun goofs up a baby-switching scheme and delivers the infant Antichrist to the wrong couple, it's just the beginning of the comic errors in the divine plan for Armageddon which this fast-paced novel by two British writers zanily details. Aziraphale, an angel who doubles as a rare-book dealer, and Crowley, a demon friend who's assigned to the same territory, like life on Earth too much to allow the long-planned war between Heaven and Hell to happen. They set out to find the Antichrist and avert Armageddon, on the way encountering the last living descendant of Agnes Nutter, Anathema, who's been deciphering accurate prophecies of the world's doom but is unaware she's living in the same town as the Antichrist, now a thoroughly human and normal 11-year-old named Adam. As the appointed day and hour approach, Aziraphale and Crowley blunder through seas of fire and rains of fish, and come across a misguided witchhunter, a middle-aged fortune teller and the Four Horsepersons of the Apocalypse. It's up to Adam in the neatly tied end, as his humanity prevails over the Divine Plan and earthly bungling. Some humor is strictly British, but most will appeal even to Americans "and other aliens."

Joe Queenan

SOURCE: A review of *Good Omens: The Nice and Accurate Prophecies of Agnes Nutter, Witch,* in *New York Times Book Review,* No. October 7, 1990, p. 27.

Good Omens is an ostensibly funny novel that deals with the efforts of a London-based angel named Aziraphale and a demon named Crowley to prevent Armageddon from taking place on the following weekend, as predicted in a book written by a 17th-century witch. In order to insure their continued survival in a world they have grown quite fond of over the centuries, the two old friends must intercept the Four Bikers of the Apocalypse before they have a chance to join forces with the "Destroyer of Kings, Angel of the Bottomless Pit . . . Father of Lies, Spawn of Satan, and Lord of Darkness"—or, as he is more commonly known, the Antichrist, currently residing in the village of Lower Tadfield.

Good Omens is a direct descendant of *The Hitchhiker's Guide to the Galaxy,* a vastly overpraised book or radio program or industry or something that became quite popular in Britain a decade ago when it became apparent that Margaret Thatcher would be in office for some time and that laughs were going to be hard to come by.

Just as Douglas Adams worked his joke to death by juxtaposing the tedious lives of ordinary people with events of cosmic significance, so Neil Gaiman and Terry Pratchett, two former journalists, go on and on for 354 pages with their schoolboy wisecracks about Good, Evil, the Meaning of Life and people who drink Perrier. Here's a typical example:

> "Over the years a huge number of theological man-hours have been spent debating the famous question:
>
> *"How Many Angels Can Dance on the Head of a Pin?*
>
> "In order to arrive at an answer, the following facts must be taken into consideration:
>
> "Firstly: angels simply don't dance. It's one of the distinguishing characteristics that marks an angel. They may listen appreciatively to the Music of the Spheres, but they don't feel the urge to get down and boogie to it. So, *none.*"

Chuckle when ready.

Mr. Gaiman and Mr. Pratchett are the sorts of writers who feel that anything having to do with nuns is uproariously funny—and, in point of fact, virtually anything having to do with nuns, the planet's original terrorists, *is* uproariously funny. But when the reader is introduced to Sister Mary Loquacious of the Chattering Order of St. Beryl on page 16, he may well have the feeling that he has been down this road many times before, if not with Peter Cook and Dudley Moore, then with Father Guido Sarducci.

In fact, the whole Supernatural in Your Own Backyard shtick was pretty well milked dry years ago by everyone from Woody Allen (*Mr. Big*) to Monty Python (*Life of Brian*) to John Denver and George Burns (*Oh, God!*). There is no more damning statement one can make about a satirical novel than to note that a film starring John Denver was funnier.

Obviously, it would be difficult to write a 354-page satirical novel without getting off a few good lines. I counted four. There is also a nice passage about an ancient prophesy warning denizens of the Future to avoid buying Betamax, a snippy remark about Welsh-language television and one truly funny bit about the decision made by the Four Bikers of the Apocalypse to change their names from the likes of War and Famine to All Foreigners Especially the French and Things Not Working Properly Even After You've Given Them a Good Thumping.

Other bits that will pass muster include a sequence dealing with an apocryphal scriptural text called the Buggre Alle This Bible, a proposed recipe for leftover toad and the intervention of extraterrestrial forces in the workings of the London cellular phone system.

But to get to this material, the reader must wade through reams and reams of undergraduate dreck: recycled science-fiction clichés about using the gift of prophesy to make a killing in the stock market; shopworn jokes about American television programs (would you believe the book includes a joke about "Have Gun, Will Travel"); and an infuriating running gag about Queen, a vaudevillian rock group whose hits are buried far in the past and should have been buried sooner.

Add to this names that are not funny (Citron Deux-Chevaux), jokes that fall flat ("a plaque on both your houses") and pointless wisecracks about people and institutions that are impregnable to satire because they are self-parodying entities—televangelists, the British monetary system, any publication involving Rupert Murdoch—and you have a book that reads like Benny Hill's version of "The Tibetan Book of the Dead." Or John Denver's.

Gene LaFaille

SOURCE: A review of *Good Omens: The Nice and Accurate Prophecies of Agnes Nutter, Witch,* in *Wilson Library Journal,* December, 1990, p. 128.

Neil Gaiman and Terry Pratchett's *Good Omens: The Nice and Accurate Prophecies of Agnes Nutter, Witch* is truly a work of understated British comic genius. According to the centuries-old prophecies of Agnes Nutter, the Apocalypse will end life as we know it on a Saturday, just before dinner, eleven years after the birth of the Antichrist. The only minor problem with this plan is that the forces of heaven and hell that have been sent to Earth over the years to prepare for this eventuality have become institutionalized in our society and like it just fine as is, thank you very much. In fact, the prophecies are further thwarted from happening by the switching at birth of the Antichrist, who turns into quite a sweet child; the transformation of the Hound of Hell into an equally gentle dog; and the interjection into the plot of the most loony group of people since the assemblage of the tragicomic Watergate cast of characters and criminals. *Good Omens* is not an easy novel to describe, as its strength is its scatterbrained approach to the art of writing—a style that results in more chuckles per page than Donald Trump has deals. Who else but Gaiman and Pratchett could philosophize upon the British monetary system and central heating and make them such fascinating subjects? The playful and witty use of words, combined with nutty but plausible footnotes, add up to a fine reading experience. Gaiman and Pratchett very quietly build a mood by providing oodles of sly humor and, along the way, leave very little unsatirized. I only hope that **Good Omens** finds a wide audience, including mainstream readers who appreciate the intelligent use of language, as well as science fiction and fantasy fans, especially Douglas Adams devotees. Very highly recommended for high school to adult collections in school, public, and academic libraries.

Diana C. Hirsch

SOURCE: A review of *Good Omens: The Nice and Accurate Prophecies of Agnes Nutter, Witch,* in *School Library Journal,* Vol. 37, No. 2, February, 1991, p. 104.

The end of the world is nigh! At least according to the prophecies of Agnes Nutter, a witch whose predictions are usually accurate but seldom heeded. Eleven years before the deadly Last Saturday Night, the ancient rivals of good and evil personified by the angelic Aziraphale (otherwise living as a London book dealer) and the demonic devil and former serpent Crowley clash in substituting the Antichrist during the birth of a baby. But the babies are switched as an unexpected third child enters the picture. The confusion picks up pace as witch hunters Sgt. Shadwell and Newton Pulsifer pursue modern Nutter follower Anathema Device. Along the way, countless puns, humorous footnotes, and satirical illusions enliven the story. A book that's sure to appeal to devoted fans of Douglas Adams.

DIGGERS (1990, U.S. edition, 1991)

Marcus Crouch

SOURCE: A review of *Diggers,* in *The Junior Bookshelf,* Vol. 54, No. 5, October, 1990, p. 249.

The first volume of the story of the Nomes appeared last year. It was a book that I approached with some reluctance, put off as much by the publisher's extravagant claims as by a horrid jacket. In the event it proved to be a lively, humorous and at times provocative tale. The second instalment has an equally discouraging jacket, and it is nearly as enjoyable. (Some of the pleasure of the first came from the reader's adjustment to the concept of small 'Borrower'-like creatures co-existing with humans; there are no such surprise discoveries in this book.) The Nomes have escaped from the Store where they had their haven and have set up their community in a disused quarry. Disused, but not for long. The arrival of men preparing to reopen it precipitates a crisis. Masklin and Abbot Gurder and the 'Thing' are away from base, exploring the possibility of making contact with the Nome

homeland in space, and authority is divided. Dorcas is an engineer and no politician, Nisodemus is certainly a politician but one made mad by his own obsessions. Thank goodness for Grimma who, although only a girl, has more sense than all the rest; thank goodness even for Granny Morkie whose memory of the old days is still keen; thank goodness above all for Jekub. Jekub is a JCB, long neglected but still capable of action with Dorcas' coaxing. Jekub provides the grand climax to the story, after which we are, in true serial tradition, left with a cliffhanger. The third volume must surely be the last. It would be difficult to squeeze much more excitement and fun out of the situation.

Diggers has many of the virtues of *Truckers,* especially its firm sense of scale, but it is kept going mainly by the momentum of the original book. It is likely to have the same popular success as that book, but I am beginning to doubt the staying power of the sequence. Apart from Nisodemus' demagogy there is nothing very new here. The jokes are a little tired, the thrills fairly low-key. I hope Mr. Pratchett will wind it all up neatly in a concluding volume, and then turn his formidable inventive talents to a different theme.

Bruce Anne Shook

SOURCE: A review of *Diggers,* in *School Library Journal,* Vol. 37, No. 2, February, 1991, pp. 82-3.

This newest addition to what will become the **Bromeliad** trilogy continues the adventures of a race of miniature creatures called nomes, whose story began in **Truckers.** The nomes, a Borrower-like folk, have fled from their comfortable homes beneath the floorboards of a large department store after learning that it is about to be demolished. They now live in an old rock quarry where they are at the mercy of humans, wild animals, weather, and changing seasons. The nomes' salvation seems to rest in their ability to take over and drive the Cat, a huge yellow piece of earth-moving equipment, which will take them to the Barn, a place of relative safety. Their efforts to drive the monster fail just as a mysterious "airplane without wings" floats over them. Dorcas, one of the older, wiser nomes, is convinced that this signals the return of their leader Masklin, who has been off exploring. As the story ends, Dorcas is wondering just what Masklin has been up to, and that, obviously, is what readers will find out in the yet-to-be-published part three of the trilogy. While this tale may work well as a sequel, it will not have wide appeal to readers who missed the first installment. Background information is needed to follow the plot, and character development is dependent on prior knowledge of the major players. The tongue-in-cheek humor that pokes fun at the nomes' many foibles and the satirical slant of the fantasy will be lost on many youngsters. Still, for those who read and enjoyed **Truckers,** this will be a welcome continuation of those adventures.

Ann A. Flowers

SOURCE: A review of *Diggers,* in *The Horn Book Magazine,* Vol. LXVII, No. 3, May/June, 1991, p. 332.

A sequel to **Truckers** and the second book in the **Bromeliad** trilogy, this very funny fantasy follows the further adventures of the nomes in their search for a safe haven. Nomes are four-inch-tall creatures much like humans, showing all the faults and foibles of their counterparts. The nomes now live in a deserted quarry after their escape from their immemorial home, the department store "Arnold Bros. (est. 1905)." Their leader, Masklin, leaves on a perilous trip to find them a permanent home, and the guidance of the group unexpectedly falls on his friend Grimma, a strong-minded female nome, and Dorcas, an elderly nome with an aptitude for machinery. They are forced to deal with humans who intend to reopen the quarry; their desperate attempts to preserve themselves unseen lead to an episode similar to Gulliver's capture in Lilliput and a number of hilarious car chases and hair-breadth escapes. Satire and allegory abound, but so fascinating are the nomes as a microcosm of human society that their trials and emotions are both moving and amusing.

Leone McDermott

SOURCE: A review of *Diggers,* in *Booklist,* Vol. 88, No. 1, September 1, 1991, p. 52.

This second volume of the **Bromeliad Trilogy** is as spirited and wryly funny as the first. In **Truckers,** Pratchett introduced the "nomes," a race of tiny people reminiscent of the Borrowers, who had, for generations, inhabited the Arnold Bros. Department Store. Narrowly escaping the store's demolition, the nomes moved to a rural quarry, where **Diggers** follows them through another set of troubles. To begin with, the nomes are ill-equipped for country life: they mistake the wind for air conditioning and the rain for a sprinkler system. Furthermore, the move has shaken up the nomes' social hierarchy and their department-store-based religion. But the gravest blow comes with the unexpected return to the quarry of human beings. As in **Truckers,** Pratchett gets a lot of laughs from depicting the rigid and ingrained attitudes common in any culture. This deftly written fantasy will leave **Bromeliad** fans eager for the final installment.

ERIC (1990; U.S. edition, 1995)

Faren Miller

SOURCE: A review of *Eric,* in *Locus,* Vol. 25, No. 4, October, 1990, pp. 15, 17.

Ah, for the relief of comedy! Particularly the elegant comedy of Terry Pratchett, where a budding wizard may conjure up another wizard (of sorts) in his magic circle, where the worst demons are upstart bureaucrats, and the worst situations can be saved by the tumultuous advent of the Luggage. Thus **Eric,** the new **Discworld** novella, riotously illustrated by Josh Kirby. To give the name as it appears on the cover, it's **"Eric".** Right, *that* story, with the three wishes, the dark conjurings, the final trip to Hell—but no Marguerite. After all, Eric is only 14. He's a demonology hacker, your basic precocious/obnoxious nerd, enough of the neophyte to mistake the hapless Rincewind for a wish-granting demon, when Rincewind lands in the magic circle. Oddly enough, the elder wizard finds that he can snap his fingers, and lo, things actually happen. They're never what Eric expects, though.

"The most beautiful woman who has ever lived, mastery of all the kingdoms of the world, and to live for ever" . . . well, we all know how ambitious wishes can go awry. Lucky for Eric that Rincewind is such an expert at running away, with the Luggage never far behind. Meanwhile, the wizards encounter heroes, demons, a somewhat absent-minded Creator, and *the* Elenor of Tsort. Eric grows up a little. And an egg and cress sandwich plays a vital part in world history.

Irreverent, charming, absurd, and unobtrusively wise, **Eric** is nothing at all like its eponymous hero. Artist Kirby outdoes himself (in full color), and Pratchett continues to turn everything he touches to comedic gold.

Roland Green

SOURCE: A review of *Eric,* in *Booklist,* Vol. 92, No. 1, September 1, 1995, p. 48.

The latest in Pratchett's **Discworld** series plays a variation on the Faust theme. Eric is a singularly inept sorcerer who conjures up an even more inept wizard, Rincewind, and a sentient (also treacherous, vindictive, and unruly) footlocker named, of course, the Luggage. Not having got anything like what he bargained for, Eric is fated to go through the usual zany ordeals of a Pratchett protagonist, until he wishes he'd never been born. Nor do things really all work out in the end, even if Eric is better off than he expected to be through most of the book. The Discworld books are building a following that is beginning to resemble that of Piers Anthony's *Xanth* stories, although it can be said that Pratchett is rather more sophisticated than Anthony. In any case, there should be a lot of readers for this one. Fantasy collections, provide accordingly.

Karen S. Ellis

SOURCE: A review of *Eric,* in *KLIATT,* Vol. 30, No. 1, January, 1996, p. 17.

A demonologist summons a demon from Hell, binding it to his will, and demands three wishes—to rule the world, to meet the most beautiful woman who has ever lived, and to live forever. Hmmm . . . Does the plot sound strangely familiar? However, this is Discworld. The summoned demon is really a second-rate wizard and the demonologist is really a 14-year-old boy, Eric. Though Rincewind the wizard appeared by mistake, he does seem to have the power to grant Eric's wishes—sort of. Pratchett happily parades his characters through the confusing and mixed-up realm of Discworld, setting for many previous fantasy stories. His pun-filled, sometimes black humor is comparable to Piers Anthony's *Xanth* series, though a little darker. The plot is simply a vehicle for the outrageous situations and parodies. This is a riot to read, though some familiarity with previous Discworld novels might help. Buy where Pratchett or humorous fantasy is popular.

MOVING PICTURES (1990; U.S. edition, 1992)

Faren Miller

SOURCE: A review of *Moving Pictures,* in *Locus,* Vol. 25, No. 4, October, 1990, pp. 15, 17.

In this year alone, Terry Pratchett will have two young adult books of the "nomes," the collaboration *Good Omens,* a *Discworld* novella, and the forthcoming "Discworld" novel *Moving Pictures.* (How does he do it? A snap of the fingers and some feverish negotiations with dark powers, perhaps?) If *Eric* is something of a bonbon, *Moving Pictures* is a banquet, featuring mostly new characters and an entirely different spin on that adaptable Disc: an outbreak of movie madness.

It starts when the last practitioner of an obscure rite dies on a lonely shore known as Holy Wood, and the watchfire no longer burns. Something insidious creeps back into the world . . . and when the Alchemists Guild (known for an ability "to turn gold into less gold") discovers both octo-cellulose film and "banged grains" with butter, it's not long before gaggles of imps are shoved into boxes to paint series of pictures *very* fast, and all of Discworld seems to be converging on that once-deserted shore.

The most appealing thing about Pratchett's humor is its humane intelligence, capable of finding more than two dimensions in characters and concepts alike. The movies (or "clicks") are a dangerous, snowballing form of insanity inspired by creatures from the Dungeon Dimensions—but they offer a means of freedom and fulfilment to ex-milkmaid Ginger (*née* Theda) and perennial-undergraduate-wizard Victor (a master at scoring 84% when the passing grade is 87). Once they're taken in hand—or paw—by scruffy but articulate Gaspode the Wonder Dog, it's clear they're bound for filmic glory. If only they could remember what happens when some outside power takes over and acts *through* them, and the golden stars glitter in their eyes. . . .

From primitive slapstick to the reenacted Burning of Ankh-Morpork in the Civil War epic *Blown Away,* the filmmakers of Holy Wood manage to recapitulate decades of cinematic history, cliché, and legend in a few short months. It's mad, it's glorious, it's (need I say?) hilarious, and it's putting a terrible strain on Discworld's already fragile fabric of reality.

The little world that stands on the backs of those four giant elephants, in their turn supported by star-turtle Great A'Tuin, has always seethed with myths and the stuff of fantasy. But now the citizens of Discworld encounter a force greater than any of them, a power capable of reconciling dwarf with troll, making senior wizards play hookey, and setting ten thousand elephants on the march. It's a very modern magic, and we've all felt its touch. Did you think the age of miracles was long gone?

David W. Barrett

SOURCE: A review of *Moving Pictures,* in *New Statesman & Society,* Vol. 121, No. 4065, January 3, 1992, p. 33.

Speaking of Marilyn Monroe, the latest paperback sees the sudden arrival of Holy Wood in the Discworld, as alchemists find a way to make dozens of little demons in a box paint lots and lots of individual pictures very quickly. *Moving Pictures* relentlessly shows the squalor and emptiness inside the glamour, the dreadful living power that Holy Wood exerts over everyone caught up in it: "I'm going to be the most famous person in the world, everyone will fall in love with me, and I shall live forever." Yet even in the darkest moments of the book, Pratchett's humour bubbles as he upturns every film cliché—including, of course, a wonderful reversal of the famous scene of King Kong and the Empire State Building.

WINGS (1990; U.S. edition, 1991)

Marcus Crouch

SOURCE: A review of *Wings,* in *The Junior Bookshelf,* Vol. 54, No. 6, December, 1990, p. 300.

This concludes the sequence of *Truckers* and *Diggers.* Contrary to expectation and experience of such trilogies this last instalment is perhaps the best. It brings Terry Pratchett's invention to a satisfying and consistent climax.

The focus, which in *Diggers* had been on Grimma and the engineering genius Dorcas, now returns to Masklin who, with Abbot Gurner and Angalo, had gone to look for Grandson Richard and through him find a way to return to the nomes' original home in space. Grandson Richard is booked on Concorde, so the nomes hitch a ride on it to Florida where a new satellite is to be launched. The Thing has ideas of its own, and the launch does not proceed according to schedule. There are some very funny moments, including the discovery of a tribe of Floridian nomes who use geese as transport, before the nome spaceship picks up its passengers, including Grimma, and departs for home. But Gurder stays behind to deal with some unfinished business.

Now that the trilogy is complete it is possible to see its proportions justly. It is indeed more than the sum of its parts. The fun is still there, much of it of a farcical knockabout kind, but the story has several layers of meaning. The irony is more penetrating, the social comment sharper. Perhaps the effect might have been greater if the author had exercised his powers of self-censorship. The force of some of its message is dissipated over three volumes. But let me not attempt to belittle Mr. Pratchett's achievement. Here is a real effort of creativity, and a criticism of society no less forceful for being clothed in the garb of comedy. Children, thank goodness, will read it for the fun and the gallery of memorable eccentrics. They will not on that account escape the satire and the philosophy. Great stuff!

Virginia Lowe

SOURCE: A review of *Wings,* in *Magpies,* Vol. 6, No. 4, September, 1991, p. 31.

Wings: the Third Book of the Nomes is, like the others in the trilogy, a highly entertaining look at our world through other eyes. Nomes are tiny creatures who have "settled down under the floorboards of mankind". They live in and around human habitation, largely unnoticed, rather like Mary Norton's Borribles of an earlier generation. In keeping with our technological modern world, Nomes are as interested in methods of transport as they are in homes, and once this particular group realise that they once came from outer space, they are anxious to try space flight as well. This is the story of their desperate attempt to get to NASA's launching site in time to load the Thing (to us, obviously a very sophisticated computer) onto it, to contact their mother ship, which has been waiting for hundreds of years. There are obvious difficulties, if you are four inches high, in coping with any type of human transportation. The two earlier volumes are entitled ***Truckers*** and ***Diggers,*** as these intrepid and ingenious creatures learn to obtain, control and drive these human devices. Now it is first Concorde then a NASA rocket that they are tackling.

"AIRPORTS: A place where people hurry up and wait. From *A Scientific Encyclopedia for the Enquiring Young Nome* by Angalo de Haberdasheri". This is where it all begins. The plot is exciting—Masklin, Gurder and Angalo trick their way onto Concorde ("I thought jet planes were just trucks with more wings and less wheels," Masklin complains, as he discovers that they are much more complex), and do even get a chance to drive it, without the permission of the humans in control, of course. On this level, with side swipes at the stupidity of the huge slow humans, it will be appreciated by 11- and 12-year-olds.

Sophisticated readers, including those of Pratchett's adult fantasy comedies, will enjoy it for other reasons as well. It plays with philosophy, even theology, in a rumbustious way. Gurder is an ex-Abbot who "believed that Arnold Bros made the Store for nomes. And he still thinks there's some sort of Arnold Bros somewhere, watching over us, because we are important." On the other hand, Angalo "doesn't believe in Arnold Bros but he likes to think Arnold Bros exists just so that he can go on not believing in him". And the ideas of belief and faith are played with throughout.

Ann A. Flowers

SOURCE: A review of *Wings,* in *The Horn Book Magazine,* Vol. LXVII, No. 5, September/ October, 1991, p. 598.

Nomes, four-inch-high replicas of humans, have lived hidden from human sight for many years. In the concluding volume of the ***Bromeliad*** trilogy, Masklin, leader of the nomes, sets out to find the spaceship that is waiting to receive the nomes who live on earth. Masklin's goal—to place Thing, their small black box of artificial intelligence, on the Florida space shuttle—is obviously an impossible undertaking. But Masklin starts out anyway, accompanied by two nome companions: Angalo, who yearns to drive high-tech vehicles; and Gurder, a religious leader rapidly becoming disillusioned. Masklin manages to get them onto the Concorde to Miami and then to the launch of the space shuttle. Their wildly funny adventures include attempts to get food while on the Concorde by having Gurder dangle from the ceiling and give the raspberry to a flight attendant, causing predictable chaos. Even when, to their surprise, they find other nomes in the Florida swamps and their spaceship does, improbably, arrive and rescue the beleaguered group of nomes back home, Masklin feels restlessly that there is always more to be learned and done. The adventures of the nomes are clearly our world in microcosm as they fall prey to human insecurities and fears; and a nome's-eye view of humanity, though humorous, is far from reassuring. Both thoughtful and hilarious; unusual science fiction for young readers.

Katherine L. Kan

SOURCE: A review of *Wings,* in *Voice of Youth Advocates,* Vol. 14, No. 4, October, 1991, p. 248.

Concluding volume of ***The Bromeliad,*** which began with ***Truckers*** and continued with ***Diggers.*** Nomes are four-inch high people, very literal-minded beings who have lived secretly on Earth for thousands of their years (their lives pass by more quickly than those of humans). When their new home in a quarry faces destruction, three of them set out on a quest to communicate with their Ship, which has orbited Earth for all this time. At this volume's opening, Masklin of the Outside nomes; adventurous young Store nome Angalo; and Gurder, former Abbot of the Store nomes, hitch a ride on the Concorde to Florida, where their computer, Thing, tells them a satellite will be launched. Angalo gets them into trouble when he sneaks into the pilot's cabin, determined to "drive" the Concorde, and humans see him. Once they escape from the jet at the airport, they must find their way to Cape Canaveral, where they must reach the launching pad so Thing can make the satellite communicate with Ship. Along the way they encounter the grandson of the Arnold Bros. (est. 1905) department store which had been home to the Store nomes for more than eighty human years, strange goose-flying Floridian nomes, and more adventures than they care to have.

Wings is humorous science fantasy for middle school and intermediate school readers, written by the author of the hilarious *Discworld* series. It will make more sense to those who read the first two books, although Pratchett does give some background information in a brief introduction. The interaction between Thing and the nomes is very similar to the banter in the Norby books by the Asimovs, although Pratchett's story has more substance and sophistication and can appeal to adults as well as its intended audience. He tells the story almost entirely from the nomish viewpoint, which allows the reader to look at our present world from a different perspective. The parallel story of the bromeliad frogs sheds light on the nomes' situation while also providing a humorous "sidebar" to the main action, and the nomes' stubborn literal-mindedness leads to ironic humor which appeals greatly to YAs. The book makes great transitional reading for those who are ready to leave children's books but aren't yet able to handle the books of Piers Anthony or Robert Asprin, or for that matter Pratchett's own books for adults. Recommended for all libraries that want to provide intelligent, fun fiction for younger YAs.

Sheilamae O'Hara

SOURCE: A review of *Wings*, in *Booklist*, Vol. 88, No. 7, December 1, 1991, p. 698.

In the third entry in the **Bromeliad** series, following **Truckers** and **Diggers,** the four-inch-tall gnomes, who resemble humans, are trying to get close enough to a communication satellite to summon their ship to take them away from Earth. They hitchhike from England to Florida on the Concorde, encounter still more gnomes, find the launch pad, permit themselves to be seen by humans who refuse to believe their eyes, and finally gain control of their ship. A lighthearted story with serious underlying themes about sharing resources, seeking adventure, and taking care of others, even if they are "others" you haven't met, *Wings* can be enjoyed by itself, but characterizations pale without the background of the other two books. The story offers metaphors and symbols galore, from the tiny frogs who live their whole lives in the bottom of a large flower, never dreaming of the existence of a larger world, to the ship that is as self-contained and secure as the department store once seemed,

but the parallels and analogies never get in the way of the story. The gnomes are perceptive and appealing, their adventures are fast paced and engrossing, and the tale is told with rollicking good humor.

WITCHES ABROAD (1991; U.S. edition, 1993)

Faren Miller

SOURCE: A review of *Witches Abroad,* in *Locus,* Vol. 27, No. 4, October, 1991, pp. 15, 17.

[L]et's spend some time in the domain of high comedy, a paradoxical realm governed by peculiarly logical laws, conceived by an intellect both rigorous and humane, and—for all that—very, very funny. To wit: Terry Pratchett's **Discworld.**

Witches Abroad brings the series to an even dozen. A long-term reviewer may feel a bit guilty about discussing yet *another* one at length, and liking it so much. Aren't we supposed to be stalwart defenders of genres assailed by shoddiness, mediocrity, and the scourge of the endless series? Well, Pratchett is never shoddy, and under the laughter there's a far from mediocre mind at work.

The new book deals with the awesome power of stories, those "great flapping ribbons of shaped space-time" which "have been blowing and uncoiling around the universe since the beginning of time." Try to stop the poor servant girl from marrying the prince? You'll find yourself standing in the path of a hurtling juggernaut with centuries of accumulated momentum. If you're Granny Weatherwax, however, you'll cope.

Granny is one of the title's traveling witches; her cohorts in this anti-Cinderella tale are the cheerfully low-minded Nanny Ogg, and newly anointed fairy godmother Magrat Garlick, a gangling girl afflicted with wimpishness, youth, and a regrettable fondness for the New Age philosophies of such as Grand Master Lobsang Dibbler. When Magrat inherits the magic wand, she is instructed to set off for Genua, a distant city that resembles a cross between New Orleans and Orlando Disneyworld, to put a stop to a reign of godmothering run amok. Aside from the general Weatherwax pushiness, Granny has a more urgent reason for inviting herself along. It involves mirrors. . . .

In between the judicious sprinkling of funny footnotes, and exploration of the boundless potential for humor when the trio of Maiden, Mother, and Crone are idiosyncratic British females coping with a world of foreigners, Pratchett slips in his analyses of power, solipsism (those mirrors), and the tyranny of enforced happy endings. "Cinderella" is only one of many tales to be sideswiped and upended in the course of the book (keep an eye out for the delicious Tolkien parody). . . . *Witches Abroad* enters the realm of traditional stories with patently subversive intent. Is it any less significant if the author makes you weep with laughter rather than with righteous rage?

David W. Barrett

SOURCE: A review of *The Colour of Magic* and *Witches Abroad,* in *New Statesman & Society,* Vol. 121, No. 4065, January 3, 1992, p. 33.

Terry Pratchett's **Discworld** novels snuck into an unsuspecting world fewer than nine years ago with ***The Colour of Magic;*** after a slightly dazed start (with fantasy readers uncrossing their eyes and whispering "What the hell was *that?*"), they have multiplied with almost fearsome fecundity. The newest paperback edition now tends to be two behind the latest hardcover—which in this case is ***Witches Abroad.*** This time last year Pratchett was the only adult novelist with three books in the top hundred best-selling paperbacks; he's probably there again now.

Pratchett is Gilbert and Sullivan to the Wagner of Tolkien's *Ring:* both the acceptable, popular face of the genre, and *fun.* But like G & S, Pratchett's work is much more than simply a parody, pastiche or piss-take of the real thing; there are plenty of those, and they deservedly die the death. The **Discworld** novels, to continue the metaphor, are works of marvellous composition and rattling good stories. You would whistle them in the street if you could.

And like G & S, in among the slapstick and clever wordplay are serious concepts. In ***Witches Abroad,*** it's the idea of the deep power of myth, folk tale or fairy story: that these child-like narratives contain awesome archetypes of power and lust and envy and greed, of love and beauty and sacrifice. There's a terrifying downside: once you get caught up in a myth, you can't escape it—Norma Jean Mortensen, for example, was completely lost inside Marilyn Monroe.

"Granny Weatherwax wouldn't know what a pattern of quantum inevitability was if she found it eating her dinner . . . She just knew that there were certain things that happened continually in human history, like three-dimensional clichés. Stories."

"'And now we're part of it! And I can't stop it,' said Granny."

What if the fairy godmother wants to *control* the lives of her charges in an unremittingly *good* world? What if the scullery maid doesn't actually want to go to the ball where she will meet the handsome prince and eventually marry him?

It's the inevitability of mythic outcomes that Pratchett's gloriously awful witches (two old hags and a wimp of a girl who's into "finding herself") set out to counter, with the author cheerfully ransacking the fairy tales we all grew up with as the witches pursue their goal.

REAPER MAN (1991; U.S. edition, 1992)

David W. Barrett

SOURCE: A review of *Reaper Man,* in *New Statesman & Society,* Vol. 121, No. 4065, January 2, 1992, p. 33.

[In] ***Reaper Man*** . . . Death (who always speaks in small capitals) is pensioned off with a gold hour-glass because he's becoming too personally interested in his work. How does Death cope with knowing that soon his own sands will run out? "How could they live with it? . . . To feel you were a tiny living thing, sandwiched between two cliffs of darkness. How could they stand to be alive? Obviously it was something you had to be born to."

The function of humour is to help us cope with the dark side of life; Terry Pratchett is worth a dozen psychotherapists.

Don D'Ammassa

SOURCE: A review of *Reaper Man,* in *Science Fiction Chronicle,* Vol. 13, No. 9, June, 1992, p. 33.

Each time Terry Pratchett returns to Discworld, I expect the well of humor to have run dry, but on each occasion, he surprises me again. This time, Death has more or less been fired from his job and transformed into a mortal. As a consequence, there are some temporary difficulties during the transition, and those who should be dead find themselves, well, not exactly alive, but perhaps not undead either. The scene where Death gets a job on a farm and harvests crops with a scythe is priceless. The book on the other hand does have a price, but it's worth every penny.

Judith H. Silverman

SOURCE: A review of *Reaper Man,* in *KLIATT,* Vol. 26, Nos. 7 & 8, November, 1992, p. 18.

Pratchett has taken us on another trip to Discworld, that flat planet carried on the backs of four elephants that travel though space on the shell of the world turtle, Great A'Tuin. This time, Death (a being not quite alive) is the problem. He has been relieved of his duties, so that until a suitable replacement is found, nothing on Discworld dies. This lack of death means that when Windle Poons, oldest wizard on the faculty of Unseen University, dies, he's not really dead, and he's buried alive. He manages to tunnel out of his grave and into a faculty meeting, where the other wizards accept him as a zombie. They soon realize that life force is running uncontrolled all over the city of Ankh-Morpork. They also realize that something must be done, as soon as possible, or there will be more zombies than there are live people. With some help from our old friend the Librarian (who, due to an unfortunate experiment, is now an orangutan), they manage to get everything back to normal. Or what passes for normal on Discworld. Pratchett keeps everything going at his usual manic pace, giving us all a great time. Pratchett's many fans will love this, fantasy fans will like it, and readers new to fantasy will enjoy this irreverent and funny introduction.

LORDS AND LADIES (1992; U.S. edition, 1995)

Kirkus Reviews

SOURCE: A review of *Lords and Ladies,* in *Kirkus Reviews,* Vol. LXIII, No. 15, August 1, 1995, p. 1068.

So you think elves are handsome and high-minded, or cute, cuddly, and bring good luck? Nope. Elves are vicious and sadistic, and they stink, according to Pratchett's latest Discworld fantasy romp, and only their magical glamour enables them to bamboozle humans into believing the opposite. So when the horrid elves threaten to invade, only the savvy witches Granny Weatherwax and Noann Ogg, somewhat assisted by the bumbling wizards of Unseen University, can save the Discworld. As always, Pratchett's brand of comedy has an agreeably wry, self-deprecating quality: "The chieftain had been turned into a pumpkin, although, in accordance with the rules of universal humor, he still had his hat on."

A so-so addition to a mostly hilarious series.

Publishers Weekly

SOURCE: A review of *Lords and Ladies,* in *Publishers Weekly,* Vol. 242, No. 37, September 11, 1995, p. 80.

Pratchett has won an ardent following with his tales of Discworld and his particular brand of comedic fantasy. This latest installment, however, is unlikely to widen his readership. It's circle time on the Discworld; portentous round depressions are showing up everywhere, even in bowls of porridge. Worlds are weaving closer to one another, with unpredictable results. Only the three wacky witches, formidable Granny Weatherwax, crusty Nanny Ogg and scatterbrained Magrat Garlick, can ensure that the worst does not happen: the return of the elves. Trouble is, almost everyone else in the kingdom of Lancre is eager to welcome the "lords and ladies" back. They've forgotten that elves are nasty creatures who live only to torture their prey—humans especially. It's a tempting premise, but underdeveloped by Pratchett, who relies too heavily on his trademark humor, veering into the silly and sophomoric, to fuel the early portions of this fantasy. Only in the last third of the novel does he strike a successful balance among action, imagination and comedy. There is much fun to the tale once the smiling, sadistic elves actually appear, befuddling the townfolk with their beauty and illusion. An earlier arrival would have done much to strengthen this uneven novel.

Roland Green

SOURCE: A review of *Lords and Ladies,* in *Booklist,* Vol. 92, No. 2, September 15, 1995, p. 145.

This particularly excellent example of Pratchett's Discworld tales tackles the subject of elves. These elves present the image of being cute only to deceive humans. In fact, they are about as agreeable as Hitler's SS. So when a bunch of them decides to crash an entire human kingdom and all its activities, problems arise. The solution is Granny Weatherwax and the witches she leads, who are not exactly nice people, either, exhibiting, as they do, positive glee in slaughtering elves. When applied to as large a body count as this novel affords, Pratchett's light tone is a little unsettling, but otherwise the book is a superior example of Pratchett's inimitable, seemingly endlessly fertile wit. Discworld's loyal readers are beginning to constitute as doughty a band as Xanth's, and all fantasy collections should provide for them accordingly.

Jackie Cassada

SOURCE: A review of *Lords and Ladies,* in *Library Journal,* Vol. 120, No. 15, September 15, 1995, p. 97.

When an invasion of elves from another world threatens the Kingdom of Lancre, only the intervention of Granny Weatherwax and her sister witches can keep the human populace from succumbing to the enemy's fatal spell. This latest addition to the whimsical *Discworld* series features a tireless flow of tongue-in-cheek humor, lowly puns, and broad, comic vision. Pratchett demonstrates why he may be one of the genre's liveliest and most inventive humorists. A good selection for libraries in possession of previous titles in the series.

ONLY YOU CAN SAVE MANKIND (1992)

A. R. Williams

SOURCE: A review of *Only You Can Save Mankind,* in *The Junior Bookshelf,* Vol. 57, No. 1, February, 1993, pp. 33-4.

One has to assume that Terry Pratchett's technically brilliant fantasy will mean more to readers who are into computer games than to others perhaps only casually acquainted with them. Between Two Worlds' might have suited as title had it not been used in a different context. The latest Game from Gobi Software is interrupted for Johnny in the midst of an 'attack' by the space fleet of the ScreeWee Empire whose commander, unexpectedly, wishes to talk, thus putting Johnny in the role of attacker against a 'friendly' enemy. This is not all, for Johnny, through his dreams and ruminations on the strangeness of the situation (or through the computer) alternates between flying a starship and visiting the mother ship of the female commander whose physiology will not here be revealed. Johnny's game-playing schoolmates offer explanations which do not resolve Johnny's inner dilemma. Complications within the dilemma evolve when Johnny co-opts a very bright if abrasive girl gamester who insists he should *do* something to save the alien fleet. He does, manoeuvering his starship and firing his missiles with skill and certainty. Meanwhile the lady captain has suffered a mutiny and Johnny goes to the rescue. That is not all by a long inter-galactic mile. The dialogue is something else again; but genned-up on computers or not most teenagers should thoroughly enjoy the teasing competence of Mr. Pratchett's high-tech conundrum, by turns comical, whimsical and downright terrifying.

N. Tucker

SOURCE: A review of *Only You Can Save Mankind*, in *Books for Your Children*, Vol. 28, No. 1, Spring, 1993, p. 27.

Terry Pratchett is one of today's very best-selling writers for children, and on the evidence of this novel it is easy to see why. He is witty, concerned, unpredictable and absolutely bang up to date.

Caught up in a computer game that turns dismayingly real, Johnny has to revise all his habits of unthinking aggression in favour of trying to save the alien race on the screen that decides one day to surrender rather than fight back as expected. Details of the latest software may mean little to some parents, but their children will almost certainly lap up this gripping, brilliantly imaginative story without need of any further encouragement.

SMALL GODS (1992; U.S. edition, 1994)

Gene LaFaille

SOURCE: A review of *Small Gods*, in *Wilson Library Journal*, June, 1994, p. 106.

If wacky sophistry such as "It's a wise crow that knows which way the camel points" is your cup of tea, you must read Terry Pratchett's *Small Gods*, the zaniest fantasy novel to come down the pike in some time. *Small Gods* is the thirteenth volume in Pratchett's *Discworld* series, which posits a world balanced on the back of an elephant, which itself rests atop a turtle. It tells the tale of a simple apprentice priest named Brutha who is suddenly privy to the thoughts of the great god Om, who takes the form of a turtle. From then on, Brutha's quiet life of gardening and contemplation is shattered. He participates in a religious mission to a hostile land, where the government is overthrown by a zealous church deacon named Vorbis. Brutha has become the protector and spokesperson for the once mighty Om, who is now reduced by circumstances to repeated attempts at convincing Brutha that he

is indeed a god and to obsessive concerns about his next meal and a certain eagle who keeps circling ominously. After all, there's lots of good eating in a turtle—god or otherwise!

Small Gods is wicked good fun, the type of novel that produces bubbling inner laughter long after it's finished. Pratchett perfectly mixes some of the serious religious-philosophical issues of Walter M. Miller's *A Canticle for Leibowitz* with the looniness of Neil Gaiman and Terry Pratchett's *Good Omens: The Nice and Accurate Prophecies of Agnes Nutter, Witch.* The result is a work that tickles your funny bone as it makes you think about the conventions and restraints of fantasy literature. *Small Gods* is so delicious a parody of various fantasy series that you must force yourself to ration its reading. It is very highly recommended for grade nine to adult collections in school, public, and academic libraries, but it is especially for adult fantasy readers who want a taste of something fresh.

JOHNNY AND THE DEAD (1993)

Marcus Crouch

SOURCE: A review of *Johnny and the Dead*, in *The Junior Bookshelf*, Vol. 57, No. 4, August, 1993, p. 157.

I missed an earlier book about Johnny Maxwell, so the new story surprised with its depth and seriousness. This is not to say that it is dull. Terry Pratchett's philosophy is based on a humorous view of life and humanity, and the fact that most of the characters in *Johnny and the Dead* are indeed dead does not mean that they are the less funny. The comedy and the philosophy are inseparable.

Blackbury Council, inspired no doubt by the real-life example of the City of Westminster, have resolved to sell off the old cemetery to United Amalgamated Consolidated Holdings (what does this great undertaking actually *do*?) who will replace the graves of past notables with an 'exciting development.' A few traditionalists are unhappy. So too is Johnny when he has discussed the matter with Alderman Thomas Bowler (1822-1906) and other residents of the graveyard. The dead—'ghosts' is a description which they firmly reject—need the cemetery. After all it is where they, so to speak, live. Johnny's efforts to mobilize public opinion against United Amalgamated produce some very funny situations, and make him face up to some important decisions and develop profound concepts. Here is Johnny, driven to address a public meeting on the subject of Time. 'It's wrong to think that the past is something that's just gone. It's still there. It's just that *you've* gone past. . . . Time is a road, but it doesn't roll up behind you.' A little later he is meditating about 'dark forces': 'Real dark forces . . . aren't dark. They're sort of grey. . . . They take all the colour out of life. . . . The *dead* seem more more alive than us.' Profound stuff; but Johnny is still just a small boy with a boy's sense of fun. After successfully getting where he shouldn't by inventing a school project, he reflects: 'If Saddam Hussein had said he was doing a school project on Kuwait, he'd have found life a lot easier.'

A lovely, funny, witty, sometimes wise book, exciting and entertaining and always highly readable. I like Johnny.

The Times Educational Supplement

SOURCE: A review of *Johnny and the Dead,* in *The Times Educational Supplement,* No. 4073, July 22, 1994, p. 24.

A group of no-hope lads in a ground-down town take up cudgels on behalf of the residents of the local cemetery when it is sold for fivepence by the council to speculative builders. Then the dead take up their own cudgels, as it were. Not only as funny as everyone says it is, but gently sorrowful, too.

MEN AT ARMS (1993; U.S. edition, 1996)

Kirkus Reviews

SOURCE: A review of *Men at Arms,* in *Kirkus Reviews,* Vol. 64, No. 1, January 1, 1996, p. 32.

In Pratchett's latest Discworld fantasy romp, Captain Vimes of Ankh-Morpork's City Watch is retiring in order to marry the city's richest lady and become a Gentleman. The Watch, you see, thanks to affirmative action, has been forced to hire both dwarfs and trolls—they loathe each other—and even *women* (actually, a she-werewolf). But before he goes, Vimes, with Corporal Carrot—he's probably the lost heir to the throne of Ankh-Morpork—and Gaspode the talking dog must solve a series of horrible murders involving a strange explosive device, meddling Assassins, and the doddering denizens of the Unseen University.

An about average installment in this always entertaining, sometimes hysterically funny series.

Publishers Weekly

SOURCE: A review of *Men at Arms,* in *Publishers Weekly,* Vol. 243, No. 5, January 29, 1996, p. 96.

In his latest effort, Pratchett skewers the hard-boiled detective novel as effectively as he's satired fantasy fiction all these years. Set on Discworld, there are a few more gargoyles and exploding dragons than Sam Spade ever had to deal with. But there's a trail of corpses and a hero named Carrot determined to track down the killer. His partners—the token dwarf, troll and werewolf on the police force—must overcome discrimination as well as

the occasional rampaging orangutan. Although *Men at Arms* isn't as consistently funny as his earlier novels, the dialogue is hilarious, and Pratchett's take on affirmative action is a whole lot of fun. There's not a lot of rational narrative cause-and-effect here, but it doesn't really matter. As usual, Pratchett provides enough bad-tempered clowns, bloodthirsty trolls and dogs with low self-esteem to keep readers entertained.

Roland Green

SOURCE: A review of *Men at Arms,* in *Booklist,* Vol. 92, No. 14, March 15, 1996, p. 1245.

The umpteenth Discworld novel introduces Captain Vines, who is about to leave the City Watch of Ankh-Morpork. The ensuing efforts to replace him are quite as zany, as devoid of conventional plot, as rich in displays of offbeat imagination, and as satirical (particularly of affirmative action and the hard-boiled detective thriller) as we have come to expect from Pratchett. Although not an outstanding Discworld novel and absolutely not the place to start with Pratchett's best-known creation, *Men at Arms* upholds Pratchett's reputation as a master of humorous fantasy and is good, highly recommendable fun for those who have already acquired a taste for Discworld.

Sue Krumbein

SOURCE: A review of *Men at Arms,* in *Voice of Youth Advocates,* Vol. 19, No. 4, October, 1996, p. 220.

On page 204 of *Men at Arms,* the Librarian, who has only a cameo appearance, shares his opinion that books should be left "on the shelves where Nature intended them to be." This is just one in a series of jokes, jabs, puns, and satirical set-ups in the book. I might have barely noticed it if I hadn't been thinking about writing this review, but it reminded me that Pratchett pokes fun at everyone and everything in this sixteenth Discworld novel.

Corporal Carrot, a young dwarf, is suddenly placed in charge of guarding Ankh-Morpork, a large city in Discworld, because his boss, Captain Vimes, is retiring. It is a big job in a city where all kinds of people are organized into guilds, including thieves and assassins. A number of crimes occur during Carrot's tenure. His investigation leads him to believe that the instrument used was the fearsome "gonne." This weapon is understandably much feared by the inhabitants of Discworld who tend to do battle with implements such as cross-bows, truncheons, and axes.

The story itself is interesting, but the major attraction is Pratchett's style of humor and sense of the absurd. His characters who join the Watch include Detritus, a troll, and Angua, a werewolf. Then there's Gaspode, the dog who follows Angua around and talks to her constantly. Carrot is the central character who eventually weaves the story together. He is intent on finding the gonne and solving the mystery. As he does this, he reveals some of his philosophy of life, including that everyone should be treated fairly and that it wouldn't be a good idea to have a king in Ankh-Morpork.

Anyone who has read Pratchett's three book series, *Truckers, Diggers, Wings,* will recognize and appreciate his ability to satirize and to do it with great humor. However, *Men at Arms* is a much more complicated novel which only a few of my middle school readers would find accessible. Of course, Discworld readers will find it a very satisfying new title.

SOUL MUSIC (1994; U.S. edition, 1995)

Jackie Cassada

SOURCE: A review of *Soul Music,* in *Library Journal,* Vol. 119, No. 19, November 15, 1994, p. 90.

When Death takes a holiday—literally—from his job of cutting lifethreads on the planet known as Discworld, it falls to his granddaughter Susan to fill, however reluctantly, his position. Simultaneously, a fortune-seeking bard discovers a magical instrument and proceeds to revolutionize music on a worldwide scale, unmindful that his own life is scheduled for an abrupt ending. Pratchett's continuing comic fantasy saga reaches new heights—or depths—in his latest incarnation. Filled with genuine humor that runs the gamut from slapstick to subtle, this most recent effort by the author of *Good Omens* is a good choice for fantasy collections.

Kirkus Reviews

SOURCE: A review of *Soul Music,* in *Kirkus Reviews,* Vol. LXII, No. 23, December 1, 1994, p. 1577.

Perhaps best considered as parody, with strong infusions of farce and satire, Pratchett's Discworld fantasies consist of elliptical jokes and mad puns delivered in an unobtrusive English accent, and move to their own inimitable logic. This time, Death (you know, skeleton, scythe, and so forth) becomes burdened by his infallible memory—he can even remember things that haven't happened yet—and, in an effort to forget, decides to join the Foreign Legion, whose members forget things, no problem, but only in their own particular fashion (" . . . you know . . . thing . . . clothes, everybody wears them . . . sand-colored"). While Death's away, his granddaughter, Susan, presently attending a posh finishing school, must take over his function. Susan has a helper, a rat-skeleton called the Death of Rats ("Do you just do rats, or mice and hamsters and weasels and stuff like that as well? . . . Death of Gerbils too? Amazing how you can catch up with them on those treadmills"). Meanwhile, talented musician Imp (from a place so wet that "rain was the

county's main export. It had rain mines") has somehow acquired a magic guitar that plays utterly compelling Music With Rocks In It. Susan, scheduled to terminate Imp forthwith, finds herself unable to wield her scythe, thus threatening the magical stability of the entire Discworld.

None of the peerless Pratchett's Discworld yarns are dull, and some are comic masterpieces. This one, unfailingly amusing and sometimes hysterically funny, is recommended for anyone with the slightest trace of a sense of humor.

Carl Hays

SOURCE: A review of *Soul Music,* in *Booklist,* Vol. 91, No. 8, December 15, 1994, p. 740.

Where else except in a Terry Pratchett novel can the consenting reader find not only Death himself but his diminutive rodent counterpart, the Death of Rats? Along with intrepid crime-watchers Constable Detritus and Sergeant Colon, an orangutan head librarian at Unseen University, and a flying horse named Binky, Death distinguishes a motley cast in this latest installment of Pratchett's internationally popular Discworld series. Here, the story concerns Death's granddaughter, Susan, who, unaware of her ghoulish heritage and thoroughly bored in school, is one day made aware of her inborn talents by Death's servant, Albert. Assisted by the Death of Rats and Binky's airborne fleetness, Susan learns the reaper's trade on assorted battlefields and deathbeds and even grows to enjoy it until she hears music emanating from an immortal magic guitar. Pratchett fans will take endless delight in a profusion of puns, wit-laden footnotes, and rambling comic misadventures in this first-rate fusion of humor and fantasy.

Publishers Weekly

SOURCE: A review of *Soul Music,* in *Publishers Weekly,* Vol. 242, No. 3, January 16, 1995, p. 442.

Nepotism is given an unusual spin in Pratchett's 14th Discworld novell, as Death's granddaughter picks up the scythe when the Grim Reaper takes a vacation. Trolls, dwarves, magicians and rock music—music played with rocks—figure in this amusing but overlong romp, which begins with the formation of a band by aspiring musician Imp y Celen (aka Buddy). Arriving in the city of Ankh-Morpork, Buddy finds a magical guitar which enables the group—a rock-playing troll, an ax-wielding dwarf and an Orangutan pianist—to drive crowds wild. But the instrument causes conflict between the motley crew and Susan, Death's granddaughter, who is just adjusting to her new post. Many of the ensuing comic situations involve Death trying to get drunk, though Pratchett's liberal application of jokes scores as many misses as hits. Extraneous plot information slows the pace as the narrative rattles to a colossal, albeit uninspired, conclusion.

INTERESTING TIMES (1994; U.S. edition, 1997)

Boyd Tonkin

SOURCE: "Pratchett's Orient Excess," in *New Statesman & Society,* November 25, 1994, p. 48.

A Martian who scanned the bestseller lists would have no doubt about the identity of Britain's leading novelist. His last novel squats invincibly at the head of the paperback charts; his new one jostles for the hardback top spot. Yes: Terry Pratchett's Pythonesque parodies of sword-and-sorcery fantasy have reached their 17th episode, with *Interesting Times.* Many critics on the quality papers have cheered his wit and wisdom, while sneering at unhip rivals for overlooking such a craze.

It's strange, then, that none of these trend-followers has tackled one large theme of a novel that sets the (undersized) brain of Rincewind the Wizard and the (geriatric) brawn of Cohen the Barbarian against the inscrutable might of the Agatean Empire. Yet this aspect will hit the dullest reader in the face with all the pungency of that Agatean delicacy, the "Dish of Glistening Brown Stuff". For *Interesting Times* translates into Pratchett's own Discworld a familiar cultural clash between the brash, free west and the tyrannous and decadent orient. It works as a kind of Popperian fable, which aims to prove the superiority of an open society of plain-speaking traders and fighters against a rigid hierarchy whose servile peasantry suffer "whips in the soul."

Appalling Agatea is a Discworld version of China. Its emperors still reign with cunning and cruelty, although a polite Red Army demurs with mild slogans: "Regrettable Decease without Undue Suffering to the Forces of Oppression!" Rebels draw inspiration from the tract "What I Did on My Holidays." What its author did was visit the city state of Ankh-Morpork, the Discworld series' usual venue. There he learned all about free speech and free markets.

Pratchett's endless one-liners sharpen the contrast. Aspiring sewage workers in Agatea have to write a 16-line poem "on evening mist over the reed beds"; in Ankh-Morpork, they're simply asked: "Got your own shovel, have you?" We never doubt where the book's heart lies. Genghiz Cohen himself has a tub-thumping speech in praise of his Horde's healthy nordic-style barbarism: "I never knew a barbarian who cut up people slowly in little rooms, or tortured women to make 'em look pretty, or put poison in people's grub." East is East, and West is Best. . . .

Pratchett has a vast fan-club of computer nerds. (And he knows it: one joke refers to the very remote prospect of "intelligent life evolving from arts graduates"). What might happen if most of a hi-tech trade mission to Beijing were to read this book on the plane? Interesting times, indeed.

Edward James

SOURCE: A review of *Interesting Times* from "Unseen University" in *Times Literary Supplement,* No. 4786, December 23, 1994, p. 21.

Interesting Times heralds the return of Rincewind, Unseen University's most incompetent wizard, the aged but still doughty hero Cohen the Barbarian, and Twoflower, the tourist from across the seas whose naivety, enthusiasm and boundless trust brought him into daily mortal danger in the first two books in the series. Twoflower has returned home to the Agatean Empire, a brutal, static autocracy cut off from the surrounding world (Discworld's equivalent of Imperial China), and he has written a book about his time in Ankh-Morpork, "What I Did On My Holidays." By the time Rincewind arrives in the Agatean Empire, this book has become an inspiration to a secret band of less than proletarian revolutionaries. They are not promising material: obedience is so deeply ingrained into all Agateans that their revolutionary songs have titles like "Steady Progress and Limited Disobedience While Retaining Well-Formulated Good Manners." Luckily for the success of the revolution, they have a number of unexpected allies: the Silver Horde (seven very famous but absurdly geriatric barbarian heroes); a battalion of terra-cotta soldiers; and a quantum Weather Butterfly. The revolution succeeds; the revolutionaries are frustrated; we are left waiting eagerly for the next volume.

Kirkus Reviews

SOURCE: A review of *Interesting Times,* in *Kirkus Reviews,* Vol. LXV, No. 5, March 1, 1997, p. 342.

More comic fantasy from Pratchett's Discworld featuring another aspect of the unending strife between humans, fates, and the god that "generally looked after thunder and lightning, so from his point of view the only purpose of humanity was to get wet or, in occasional cases, charred." This time, the incompetent "wizard" Rincewind, hero of several of the earliest Discworld wingdings, makes a reappearance, along with other favorite characters such as the demented tourist, Twoflower, the unpredictable, multilegged Luggage—apparently it's found a mate—and Cohen the Barbarian.

Fun, especially for those susceptible to Pratchett-inspired nostalgia.

Publishers Weekly

SOURCE: A review of *Interesting Times,* in *Publishers Weekly,* Vol. 244, No. 13, March 31, 1997, p. 67.

Discworld continues to spin merrily along in this new addition to Pratchett's successful series about a magical world carried through space on the back of a giant turtle. Here, Rincewind the wizard is drafted to visit the Agatean Empire, which in Pratchett's hands is either a satire of Imperial China or a satire on how that China is handled by other fantasy writers, or possibly both (in Discworld there are few certainties). Arriving complete with the Luggage, Rincewind is dropped into the middle of a succession crisis that's complicated by the presence of Cohen the Barbarian, with his Silver Horde of super-annuated barbarians, and a band of youthful revolutionaries, the Red Army. The plot that slowly emerges sees Cohen become Emperor and will hold Discworld fans' attention despite some of the satirical effects arising from a working knowledge of British popular culture. Pratchett is an acquired taste, but the acquisition seems easy, judging from the robust popularity of Discworld. Certainly there is more verbal elegance in this novel than in most humorous fantasy. Pratchett does try to satirize so many subjects at once here that he resembles the man who jumped on his horse and rode off in all directions, and so the book benefits from being read in small, bracing doses.

MASKERADE (1995)

Meg Wilson

SOURCE: A review of *Maskerade*, in *Voice of Youth Advocates*, Vol. 21, No. 1, April, 1998, p. 60.

Clever puns, plot twists, and witty sarcasm make reading *Maskerade* an enjoyable jaunt into the fantasy world. Pratchett has created a likeable cast of characters and a believable setting, which help move the story along at a rapid pace. His style is funny and intelligent, and will appeal to many adult and young adult fantasy readers.

In "yet another novel of Discworld" (from the cover), young Agnes Nitt has decided to make her mark in the world of Opera in the big city. Although she is enormously overweight, she has been blessed, or cursed, with a wonderful personality, great hair, and an astounding singing voice. Her good sense also makes her a definite anomaly in the looney world of the Ankh Morpork Opera house, where the resident Ghost demands full observance of all superstitions, makes demands regarding the casting of Operas, and occasionally leaves behind the corpses of those who dare cross him. To further complicate her life, Agnes believes, two witches from her home town turn up and do their best to end her career in the opera by recruiting Agnes into their coven. In the end, the good witches prevail and the mystery of the Opera House Ghost is solved.

Nothing about *Maskerade* makes it an intrinsically YA novel, though many YAs would enjoy it thoroughly. It should be included in any collection where fantasy readers appreciate a well-written story and a good laugh.

JOHNNY AND THE BOMB (1996)

Renata Rubnikowicz

SOURCE: "Bombs Away with the Travellers in Time," in *The Times Educational Supplement,* No. 4166, May 3, 1996, p. 8.

With his latest foray into a parallel universe, Terry Pratchett leaps into the Trousers of Time with Johnny Maxwell and the gang who first explored computer-game space in *Only You Can Save Mankind.*

In book three of the series, Johnny's home life is still bogged down in "Trying Times", and he and his mother are still living at his grandad's. Too much is uncertain, too much is changing, he feels unsafe in the present. But instead of swooping into a sci-fi future or dreaming himself into the kind of fantasy world that readers of Pratchett's Discworld series enjoy, Johnny is sent back to the past.

Blackbury's Paradise Street in wartime is a place where jolly evacuees play in the street, old men go off to work their allotments in "special old man's allotment trousers" and the woman in the tobacconist's calls Johnny's friend Yo-less (the only black boy in fiction who's so uncool he wears school uniform) "Sambo." Mrs. Tachyon, the local bag lady, is the mysterious link between past and present. Her Tesco trolley—the one with the creaking wheel—is the time machine that transports Johnny and the gang to May 21, 1941.

Mrs. Tachyon bears a strong resemblance to the Discworld witches. Even Mrs. Tachyon's cat, Guilty, has come from the same spawn-of-the devil litter as Nanny Ogg's Greebo. But here the witchy figure is only a catalyst for the action. It is Johnny and his friends who blunder to the rescue when a German plane bombs Blackbury.

The plot takes off with the trolley on an exhilarating switchback swirl through different but interconnecting versions of the same two days, one in the Nineties and one in 1941, making a story complicated enough to hold the attention of even older teenage boys for whom at first sight a book with a 12-year-old hero might seem too young.

D. A. Young

SOURCE: A review of *Johnny and the Bomb,* in *The Junior Bookshelf,* Vol. 60, No. 3, June, 1996, p. 124.

Terry Pratchett is the creator of the Discworld series chronicled in some fourteen volumes which occupy several feet of bookshelf in the Sci/Fantasia section of the larger bookshops. *Johnny and the Bomb* is the third story involving Johnny Maxwell and his friends aimed at the 11 plus age range. *Johnny and the Dead* won a 1993 Writers' Guild award and has been adapted recently for TV.

Mrs. Tachyon is a well-known 'bag lady' in Blackbury. She wears most of her clothes at the same time and the rest she piles into a Tesco trolley which is shared by a wild eyed untidy cat with very sharp teeth. It may be helpful to learn from a dictionary that a tachyon is a hypothetical elementary particle capable of travelling faster than the velocity of light. The trolley is a time machine. Johnny and his friends find themselves commuting between 1941 and 1996 and trying to cope with the paradox involved. 1941 was the year when the Germans bombed Blackbury and Paradise Street was obliterated and its inhabitants killed. What if some of the grandparents lost their lives before they had the chance to become grandparents? Can Johnny and his friends change what happened in 1941? Or have they already done so?

No summary can give a fair picture of the intriguing events and lively crosstalk that make up this fascinating story for computer literate youngsters with a yen for philosophical problem solving. It does require to be read closely if its purport is to be grasped fully.

Michael Gregg

SOURCE: A review of *Johnny and the Bomb*, in *Magpies*, Vol. 11, No. 4, September, 1996, p.

Oh what fun! Vast numbers of readers will greet the new Johnny Maxwell book with delight. Like its predecessors *Only You Can Save Mankind* and *Johnny and the Dead*, this is a vehicle for Pratchett to play with all manner of challenging concepts in a form accessible and entertaining for all. He's dealt with aliens and the after-life respectively before; this time it is the concept of, and particularly the implications of, time-travel.

Johnny and his friends discover the local bag lady lying injured in an alleyway and, feeling like he should look after it while she's in hospital, Johnny puts her shopping trolley in his garage. Unfortunately, those big bulging black plastic garbage bags seem to be full of time . . .

And so Johnny and his friends find themselves back in 1941 just before the one and only air raid that hit their town during the war. They've studied it in class, they know what's going to happen but what can they, or more importantly, should they do?

It's impossible to summarise a Pratchett plot, so full of twists and turns and witty asides. Mrs. Tachyon, the bag lady for whom time is translucent and the step between parallel universes but a step, is one of his finest and most intriguing creations. The concepts in this book are far from simple—there's much food for thought in his exposition of chaos theory and various scientific theories, enough to occupy a Year Twelve student or entertain a Year Six. There's a giggle on every page and enough to keep the mind mulling over long after the book is put down. Highly recommended.

FEET OF CLAY (1996)

Publishers Weekly

SOURCE: A review of *Feet of Clay*, in *Publishers Weekly*, Vol. 243, No. 40, September 30, 1996, p. 65.

A flat platter of a planet spinning atop the backs of four giant elephants perched on the shell of an immense turtle: it's no surprise that life on Discworld is far from mundane. Pratchett's 17th Discworld novel picks up where his last, **Men at Arms**, left off, following Ankh-Morpork City Watch Commander Samuel Vimes and his fellow cops as they strive to maintain a semblance of order in a city as infamous for its intrigues as for its ethnic diversity. An elderly priest is killed, then the harmless old curator of the Dwarf Bread Museum is found beaten to death with one of his own exhibits. Investigation reveals a link to the city's golems—silent, tireless workers built of clay and brought to life with magic. There's a rash of golem suicides, and Vimes uncovers a plot that could topple the government. Pratchett's latest is full of sly puns and the lively, outrageous characters his readers expect. Those new to Discworld—which first appeared in Pratchett's **The Colour of Magic**, 1983—will have no trouble keeping up with the action. This is fantasy served with a twist of Monty Python, parody that works by never taking itself too seriously.

Roland Green

SOURCE: A review of *Feet of Clay*, in *Booklist*, Vol. 93, No. 3, October 1, 1996, p. 326.

Pratchett brings Discworld, the city of Ankh-Morpork, and Commander Vimes of the city guard back once more, and it comes as no surprise that Ankh-Morpork's assassins and thieves have guilds and that killing or stealing outside guild limits is severely frowned on. So when a non-union assassin goes to work in the city, Vimes has to resort to various expedients, including hiring a dwarf, one Cheery Littlebottom, to deal with the culprit. Pratchett's humor is as off-the-wall as ever, so the pursuit of the assassin is as witty and nonsensical as ever, and raising the question of a king for the city hints of possible future changes. Pratchett hardly needs to alter his combination of whimsy, satire, and subtly intelligent world building in order to hold on to his many readers and win new ones.

Sue Krumbein

SOURCE: A review of *Feet of Clay*, in *Voice of Youth Advocates*, Vol. 19, No. 6, February, 1997, pp. 339-40.

This seventeenth book in Pratchett's *Discworld* series is aptly titled **Feet of Clay** in that an important character in the story is a golem named Dorfl. Golems are not exactly alive, but malleable individuals made of clay—malleable, that is, until they revolt and become a problem. It is not surprising to find golems in Ankh-Morpork; a city with all kinds of unusual citizens, including dwarfs, some of them mustachioed females, werewolves, and trolls.

This latest book finds Commander Vimes facing a serious problem. Someone is trying to kill Lord Vetinari, the Patrician, and Vimes must get to the bottom of it. In the process, Vimes and his men have a series of adventures and misadventures.

Although fans of this series will enjoy this latest title, the reader does have to concentrate to follow the plot and enjoy the humor in what is really a complicated novel, and one slightly more difficult to get into than the previous title in the series, *Men at Arms.*

HOG FATHER (1996)

Publishers Weekly

SOURCE: A review of *Hogfather,* in *Publishers Weekly,* October 26, 1998, p. 47.

The master of humorous fantasy delivers one of his strongest, most conventional books yet. Discworld's equivalent of Santa Claus, the Hog Father (who flies in a sleigh drawn by four gigantic pigs), has been spirited away by a repulsive assassin, Mr. Teatime, acting on behalf of the Auditors who rule the universe and who would prefer that it exhibited no life. Since faith is essential to life, destroying belief in the Hog Father would be a major blow to humanity. It falls to a marvelously depicted Death and his granddaughter Susan to solve the mystery of the disappeared Hog Father, and meanwhile to fill in for him. On the way to the pair's victory, readers encounter children both naughty and nice; gourmet banquets made of old boots and mud; lesser and greater criminals; an overworked and undertrained tooth fairy named Violet; and Bilious, the god of hangovers, among other imaginative concepts. The tone of much of the book is darker than usual for Pratchett—for whom "humorous" has never been synonymous with "silly"—and his satire, too, is more edged than usual. (One scene deftly skewers the Christmas carol "Good King Wenceslas.") Pratchett has now moved beyond the limits of humorous fantasy, and should be recognized as one of the more significant contemporary English language satirists.

JINGO (1997)

Roland Green

SOURCE: A review of *Jingo,* in *Booklist,* Vol. 94, Nos. 19-20, June 1, 1998, p. 1736.

The latest Discworld novel begins with the island of Lesht rising briefly from the Circular Sea and between Ankh-Morkporkh and its archrival Klatch. Both countries immediately become rivals for it, and war soon breaks out.

The least bizarre thing that then happens is Sir Samuel Vimes, head of the Watch, organizing a six-person regiment of his old stalwarts for the invasion. Thereafter the yarn gets jumbled in a way that will befuddle those who have not come to terms with Pratchett's notions of plotting. It will also befuddle those unfamiliar with World War I, at which Pratchett's satirical heavy artillery is mostly directed in a salvo that culminates in Vimes becoming a duke for arresting both armies and thereby preventing war over Lesht, which sinks back into the sea before either side can claim it. This is one of the more demanding Pratchetts, and neophytes might better start the Discworld megasaga with an earlier book. Still, it conforms to Pratchett's high and humorous standards which will gratify faithful fans.

Susan Salpini

SOURCE: A review of *Jingo,* in *School Library Journal,* Vol. 44, No. 8, August, 1998, p. 197.

Jingo, the twentieth Discworld novel to be published in the United States, is a worthy addition to the series. It's a quiet night. Maybe too quiet. Solid Jackson and his son are fishing the waters between Ankh-Morpork and Al-Khali when their boat runs aground. To their amazement, an iron chicken rises out of the water, followed shortly by the island of Leshp. Solid Jackson immediately claims the island as Ankh-Morpork territory. There's only one problem. Greasy Arif and his son are also fishing for Curious Squid, and Arif swears that the island belongs to Al-Khali. Both cities are determined to annex it. By jingo, this means war. Ankh-Morpork is outgunned and out-manned but the city's nobles don't plan to let that stop them from carrying on the noble traditions of chivalry and showing those Klatchians what's what. This book is just as funny, clever, and unpredictable as the previous titles. Pratchett fans will not be disappointed, and new readers will not be confused. *Jingo* expands upon the lives of characters from titles in the series, but readers don't need to be familiar with them to enjoy this one. It's fast-paced, with lots of twists and turns, unexpected events, and football.

CARPE JUGULUM (1999)

Publishers Weekly

SOURCE: A review of *Carpe Jugulum,* in *Publishers Weekly,* Vol. 246, No. 39, September 27, 1999, p. 77.

Carpe Jugulum—seize the throat—is the motto of the family of "vampyres" who attempt a hospitable takeover of the kingdom of Lancre in Pratchett's 23rd *Discworld* novel. When the good-hearted king invited the Magpyrs to celebrate the birth of his daughter, he couldn't know that these modern bloodsuckers would have no intention of leaving. By controlling everyone's mind, they try to turn Lancre into a sort of farm, and no one can think straight enough to stop them. That is, until the vampyres meet up with the local witches: Granny Weatherwax, Nanny Ogg, Magrat Garlick and Agnes Nitt (who is literally of two minds about everything). The perplexing skirmishes that ensue will leave readers shaking their heads in hearty dismay even as they groan at the puns and explanatory notes that pepper the tale. Death (scythe and all) and Igor (of Frankenstein film fame) provide the best gags. The novel exudes the curious feel of old-fashioned vampire and Frankenstein legends—full of holy water, religious symbols, stakes through the heart, angry mobs, bad pronunciation and garlic. The vampyres, however, have risen above these cliches even if their servant, Igor, still has a taste for dribbly candles and squeaky hinges. Pratchett lampoons everything from Christian superstition to Swiss Army knives here, proving that the fantasy satire of Discworld "still ate'nt dead."

THE FIFTH ELEPHANT (2000)

Roland Green

SOURCE: A review of *The Fifth Elephant*, in *Booklist*, January 1, 2000, p. 834.

It is well known that Pratchett's Discworld is supported by four elephants standing on the back of a giant tortoise. Once there was a fifth elephant, which fell off the tortoise's back and crashed onto Discworld with a mighty impact, leaving behind rich deposits of minerals and fat. Now Uberwald, the country that has most of the deposits, faces a succession crisis among the dwarfs, because the Scone of Stone, their emblem of kingship, has been stolen. With a motley but effective team of aides, Chief Constable Vimes and his wife arrive as ambassadors from Ankh-Morporkh to solve the mystery and prevent civil war among the dwarfs, werewolves, and vampires of Uberwald. Vimes needs all the help he can get, as the werewolves, led by one Wolfgang, who would have been at home in the Waffen SS, are busily trying to take over Uberwald by throwing the other races into chaos. As usual, Pratchett satirizes everything in sight and a few things buried in the subtext, always with a great knowledge of and fondness for his fellow primates, even in their more foolish moments. He never lets a proper tone flag; thus, in the midst of all the satire, Vimes's death struggle with the werewolves is as grim as any thriller's climax, and the growing love between Captain Carrot and Corporal Angua the werewolf is handled straight. Pratchett is now inviting comparison with Kurt Vonnegut, but if he ends up with a reputation equivalent only to that of P. G. Wodehouse, the world will be the better for his having written.

Additional coverage of Pratchett's life and career is contained in the following sources published by The Gale Group: *Authors and Artists for Young Adults,* **Vol. 19;** *Contemporary Authors,* **Vol. 143; and** *Something about the Author,* **Vol. 82.**

Barbara Reid

1957 -

Canadian illustrator and author of picture books for preschoolers and primary graders.

Major works include *The New Baby Calf* (1984, written by Edith Newlin Chase), *Have You Seen Birds* (1987, written by Joanne Oppenheim), *Playing with Plasticine* (1988), the *Zoe* series (1991), *Two by Two* (1992).

INTRODUCTION

Dubbed the "Queen of Plasticine," Barbara Reid has received international acclaim for her unusual and humorous illustrations of books for young children, with imaginative artwork done in the humble medium of plasticine sculpture. Winner of the prestigious Ezra Jack Keats Award for Innovative Illustration, she has written and illustrated her own books as well as providing artwork for other writers. A reviewer for *Horn Book* commented, "Reid creates with plasticine in a way that makes one look anew at this unpretentious medium." The rich, dense colors and texture of the layers, coupled with Reid's loony sense of humor, make for a unique presentation. Carol Anne Wien of *CCL* noted, " [T]he pictures are not stylized but are highly expressive, for Reid manages to keep a fluid line and to incorporate marvelous expressions of feeling."

The popularity of her award-winning illustrations for *Have You Seen Birds?* brought her many queries from children about "how she did it." Her response was to write the how-to book *Playing with Plasticine*. Because plasticine is "silly," Reid believes that, compared to other media, it is not as intimidating a material to children who worry that they "can't draw." She produced the book in black and white to avoid children being distracted by specific colors. She also wanted to keep the book open-ended to encourage creativity, to present ideas rather than glossy pictures of a finished product.

Reid's plasticine creations are sensitively photographed by her husband, Ian Crysler, who has a knack for the tricky lighting needed to bring out the depth and color of her artwork. Asked by Susan Gaitskell why she prefers to work in plasticine, Reid replied, "It's flexible. I can change my mind and play with it, keep molding it and working on it. It's really nice for detail.... [It's] a silly medium. People are friendly to it and it makes them laugh."

Biographical Information

Reid has always loved to read and to draw. In both elementary and high school, she was considered a "bright"

student and received high marks for her elaborate dioramas and dazzling science models that obscured the fact that she was taking in very little of the subject matter. She chose to do what she liked, and this led her to attend the Ontario College of Art. Reid once wrote in an essay about herself, "[W]hen I honestly look at my story, it's really a case of doing what I liked and avoiding the rest, with no clear goal in sight. If you keep doing what you like, you get good at it. If you get good enough, you don't have to do the other things anymore."

Reid began her career as a freelance illustrator, working in a variety of media, mostly to illustrate textbooks. A boom in the children's book market in Canada coincided with her evolving use of plasticine, and she was soon both surprised and pleased to find herself making a living doing exactly what she most liked to do, illustrating, and writing, children's books.

Major Works

The first book to showcase Reid's unique illustration techniques was *The New Baby Calf*, a poem by Edith

Newlin Chase about Buttercup the cow and her new calf. The poem follows the baby calf as it grows and becomes stronger and more competent. A critic for *Quill and Quire* commented, "[A]nyone who has ever tried to squeeze a piece of clay into some recognizable shape will marvel at Reid's artwork."

Have You Seen Birds? was received with tremendous enthusiasm by both critics and the public and garnered the five top Canadian awards for children's literature, including the Ezra Jack Keats award. It is a picture book depicting a wide variety of birds in different seasons and different habitats, some of the scenes shown from a bird's eye view. Joan Weller, in her review for *CM*, wrote, "Plasticine ... takes on forms so creative in their depiction of all kinds of birds that one looks again and again at the illustrations and marvels at their conception."

Playing with Plasticine, the first book that Reid both wrote and illustrated, introduces plasticine as an art medium and provides instructions for making basic shapes, then suggests how to use them to create animals, people, miscellaneous objects, board games, pictures, and self-portraits. Called "practical" and "charming"—"if your standing animals topple over, just lean them together"—this book was intended to encourage creativity rather than imitation, and utilizes black and white illustrations because Reid thought they would be less intimidating. In her review, Annette Goldsmith praised the book as "the best kind of craft book, demonstrating easily how to use a particular medium and inspiring original efforts."

The *Zoe* series of wordless board books for preschoolers includes *Zoe's Windy Day, Zoe's Sunny Day, Zoe's Snowy Day,* and *Zoe's Rainy Day,* each one illustrating a different season. One reviewer enthused, "The wordless tales are clear, easy to follow and characterized by Reid's innate ability to realize in plasticine the magical nature of life's simplest events. In Reid's hands snow, rain, wind and sunlight become agents of delight."

Two by Two retells the story of Noah's Ark in the form of a poem that can be either read or sung to the tune of "Who Built the Ark?" Using various perspectives such as long distance, aerial, and close up, Reid's plasticine renderings are accurate and detailed. Reviewer Patricia L. M. Butler of *CM* wrote, "[I]t captures the imagination of both listener and reader with its flow and its wonderful accompanying illustrations," and a critic for *Publishers Weekly* stated, "Readers will ... enjoy counting along as the animals—from the tiniest mice to the biggest elephants—clamber aboard this beguiling ark."

Awards

In 1988 Reid won the UNICEF-Ezra Jack Keats International Award for Illustration, given to a promising young illustrator of international stature. *Have You Seen Birds?* won five major Canadian children's book awards: the Governor General Prize for illustration from the Canada Council in 1986, runner-up for the Amelia Frances

Howard-Gibbon Award in 1987, the IODE in 1986, the Elizabeth Mrazik-Cleaver Canadian Picture Book Award in 1987, and the Ruth Schwartz Award in 1987. The four books in the *Zoe* series each won the Mr. Christie's Award for English illustration in 1991. Reid became the first illustrator to win the Elizabeth Mrazik-Cleaver Canadian Picture Book Award twice when it was awarded to her for *Two by Two* in 1992.

AUTHOR COMMENTARY

Barbara Reid

SOURCE: "Colouring the Road to Oz," in *Canadian Children's Literature,* No. 54, 1989, pp. 46-9.

For me, the subject "My own story: plain and coloured" brings to mind the movie "The Wizard of Oz". Just as Dorothy's home in Kansas appears in black and white with full colour being reserved for the dreamland of Oz, as a child my own life seemed rather plain in comparison to the colourful worlds to be found in books. (It also seemed a very hard task to express my own thoughts with words instead of someone else's with pictures.)

Books have always been important to me. As a small child I was an early riser. House rules kept me in my room until 8.00 a.m. As a result I spent about two hours every morning playing with my books. I knew them all by heart, but their entertainment value could be stretched by making up new stories to match the pictures, or by inventing a story that made sense when I went through the book backwards. I carried on imaginary conversations between the characters. I even chewed on the metallic spines of certain books for the tingling sensation they gave my teeth. It can be said I really *devoured* my first books!

Another wonderful introduction to the book world was being read to. My mother and I would lie on her bed for a quiet time each day and she would read aloud, such books as *The Moffats, The Secret Garden,* Edith Nesbit books, and anything by Gerald Durrell or with animals in it. I could stare into space and visualize the characters and their surroundings. I don't often get the luxury of being read to now, but I still enjoy good radio for the same reasons. The story can flood into my mind, but part of the brain is free to imagine, interpret and "colour" it.

Once I could read for myself there was no stopping me from escaping to other worlds whenever I got the chance. I became very good at reading late into the night under the covers using the illuminated dial of my electric clock to see by. Reading Rumer Godden made me think with an English accent for weeks. I became Elsa the Lion (*Born Free, Living Free* etc., etc.) for a whole summer. My favourite books were C. S. Lewis's *Narnia* series. I was constantly wishing myself into that exciting world to perform noble deeds, instead of sitting trapped in a pastel classroom looking at the clock and reproductions of the "Lone Pine" for what seemed like one hundred years.

A great outlet for this frustration was drawing. I could draw my favourite characters, or myself as I would like to appear in a story. It was possible to prolong a book after it ended by drawing what happened next.

Being very shy, I spent a lot of time observing people and their behaviour, another endless source of drawing material. Drawing is also a super way for a shy person to communicate—a caricature of a teacher or a cartoon of class big shots is a sure ticket to popularity without having to talk much!

It would be nice to think a career in illustration occurred to me back then. When I see some biographical information neatly typed in chronological order it even appears to have been a direct course of action. However, when I honestly look at my story it's really a case of doing what I liked and avoiding the rest, with no clear goal in sight. If you keep doing what you like, you get good at it. If you get good enough you don't have to do the other things any more.

I liked to read and draw. Good reading ability and quiet behaviour in class often convince teachers a student is "bright." I shamelessly exploited this attitude and constantly volunteered for special projects: clearing up the art room, making posters for concerts and fun fairs, producing plays and backdrops improved my artistic skills and neatly sprung me from the monotony of the classroom and some math lessons.

This kind of behaviour worked in high school as well. Dazzling science models and diagrams helped obscure the fact that I wasn't taking much in. High marks in English, history and art helped to establish a studious reputation. On the final math exam I had answered all I could in the first ten minutes. The rest of the paper I filled with an illustrated essay on the John Donne poem that contains the lines "Ask not for whom the bell tolls . . ."— which seemed appropriate. The kind teacher passed me with a 50% on the condition that I never, *ever,* take a math class again. A promise I have kept!

By this time I assumed I would become a writer. I loved what writers did and wanted to be one. It should have occurred to me that as much as I admired writers and their craft, I never wrote myself—except an assignment. (Like this!) Whenever I had ideas to express (which was often) it came out in drawings. While I admired artists and illustrators, my favourites were all dead and it never seemed a realistic career choice.

As usual, it was a case of doing what I like that steered me at the last minute to choose the Ontario College of Art over journalism at Ryerson. On the day each of the colleges and universities displayed their attractions at our high school, I was drawn (no pun intended) into the O.C.A. room for two reasons: there were only three others in the audience and, the two graduate students doing the presentation were extremely handsome, colourful and Bohemian—complete with ponytails. This was a rare thing to see in my very normal North Toronto neighbourhood. After half an hour I was convinced my career was in art.

At least half the first year students at O.C.A. in 1976 naïvely said, "I'd like to illustrate children's books." It was very trendy at the time; reproductions of many classic illustrators' work were appearing on greeting cards, wrapping paper and expensive coffee-table books.

Four years of O.C.A. tore our minds apart and reassembled them. My career plans swung from art direction to typography to storyboard rendering. Illustration won in the end, but like all my fellow grads I knew that *no-one* becomes a children's book illustrator now-a-days and, that all forms of children's illustration were for struggling newcomers only. It was the bottom rung of the illustrator's ladder in terms of respect and especially with regard to money. The word "starvation" was associated with children's illustration.

Starting out as a freelance illustrator (a real job with enforced hours never occurred to me) I had a portfolio with a bit of everything in it. I did lots of jobs in many media, including Plasticine. Just as in school, it was very rewarding to do a good job—to please someone with artwork. Being a beginner, I did much of my work for school textbooks. To my surprise I enjoyed the challenge of making fun, exciting pictures within the strict restrictions imposed by textbooks.

As usual, I put much more energy into assignments I liked and the other jobs began to fall by the wayside. People pictures, humorous work and children's things took over the portfolio and Plasticine work took up the largest share. The children's book scene in Canada was going into a boom time just as I was steering myself into that market—a happy coincidence for me! While textbook, editorial and advertising work continue to pay the bills I am surprised and pleased to find I am primarily a children's book illustrator (and obviously not starving!).

I feel very fortunate, and a little guilty. I don't have to report to an office, I can be alone as much as I like and have found a socially acceptable way of spending most of my time in an imaginary world.

The first read-through of a manuscript opens the doors to the author's world and it's up to me to interpret it visually—a real honour and a thrill. I can surround myself with reference material and props to get in the mood of a book. I can act out the different parts and talk with silly accents in the privacy of my studio. And, most importantly, I can make the story my own in a small way by including very personal images and ideas that the author's words have stirred up.

My happiest moments come when I can solve a problem. For example, how to represent Tweedle-Dum and Tweedle-Dee (*Sing a Song of Mother Goose*) without recalling Tenniel's classic version. After lots of pencil chewing the idea finally came. By turning them into turtles they are already dressed for battle and in combat greens. It's a simple spoof of wars in general and the turtle shells become a perfect device to show their cowardice and retreat from the crow. Bird lore gained from research for **Have You Seen Birds?** made it obvious that the crow should make off with the shiny rattle to round out the story. Most observers won't get all that by looking at the picture, but I always hope that somewhere, someone thinks the same way and enjoys the jokes. At the least, it's personally very satisfying to come up with just the right image.

After all this self-searching, I have to conclude my story is quite a *selfish* one! In my attempts to escape to an Oz or a Narnia I've avoided the plain world as much as possible and done what I enjoy as much as possible—colouring.

Susan Gaitskell

SOURCE: An Interview with Barbara Reid, in *Canadian Children's Literature*, No. 56, 1989, pp. 6-14.

At 2:00 on November 10, 1988, I arrived at the Toronto apartment of Barbara Reid, recipient of the 1988 Ezra Jack Keats Award for Illustration. Tape recorder and question list in hand, I was prepared for this interview. Barbara Reid greeted me and showed me into her living room. We sat down—she on a chair, I on a couch, the tape recorder poised discreetly on a coffee table between us. We began. The tape recorder did not. We began again. The tape recorder showed tentative signs of life. Barbara suggested we move to the floor to accommodate it. The tape recorder was beside itself with joy.

I have enormous admiration for Barbara Reid. She is very spry. Though expecting to give birth in three weeks to her first child, she was a model of cross-legged graciousness. Now and then, in an effort to preserve my dwindling dignity, she would politely inquire after my creaking bones. "Fine," I'd say, "Just fine." Though I remember these exchanges fondly, I have edited them from the transcription that follows.

Gaitskell: When did you first get interested in art?

Reid: I've always been interested in it.

Gaitskell: And in books?

Reid: I was always a big reader. Mom and Dad encouraged it. We didn't have a lot of books at home, but we went to the library all the time.

Gaitskell: Any special favourites?

Reid: The Narnia books. I still read them. I also went through a phase where I read every animal book on the shelf—*The Call of the Wild, Meph the Pet Skunk, Rascal,* and Gerald Durrell's stuff.

Gaitskell: Did you ever draw the characters in the books you read?

Reid: Yes. When I finished stories I'd often draw the characters the way I thought they should look, or sometimes I'd copy illustrations.

Gaitskell: Did you have any favourite pictures when you were a kid?

Reid: I liked realistic pictures. A lot of textbooks at the time were illustrated in a deliberately childish style. I thought, I can do that. I was more impressed by things that I couldn't do.

Gaitskell: Was there a time when you became interested in illustration as opposed to fine art?

Reid: Yes. I started to realize there *was* such a thing in high school. Around that time there was a revival of interest in the classic children's book illustrators. Books by people like Arthur Rackham were showing up everywhere.

Gaitskell: Was Rackham a particular favourite?

Reid: Yes. I went through a real Rackham phase. I also liked Dulac, Tenniel, N. C. Wyeth, and Maxfield Parrish too for a while, but that was in art college.

Gaitskell: You went to the Ontario College of Art?

Reid: Yes. It was really a last minute decision. I wanted to be a writer. I thought that would be a job and I didn't think art had any jobs. At the last minute I decided to go to OCA because I started hearing that there was commercial stuff.

Gaitskell: Was it tough to get in?

Reid: Well, you had to show a portfolio and it was really scary. Three people interviewed you. I'd done a bunch of sketches of my pet rat, and my interviewers thought I'd copied them from a book. I said, "No, this is my pet." "Oh, well, if you're sketching from life," they said, "that's different."

Gaitskell: Did you enjoy OCA?

Reid: Yes, it was great. There was a real wave of people who wanted to be children's book illustrators. Everyone just laughed at us and said, "Forget it. You can do it for fun if you marry someone rich." I said, "Fine. I still want to be an illustrator." I learned a lot at OCA.

Gaitskell: Did you marry someone rich?

Reid: Rich enough. My husband, Ian, is a freelance photographer.

Gaitskell: Do you only illustrate for children, or do you illustrate for adults as well?

Reid: I do everything.

Gaitskell: Which do you prefer?

Reid: I like it all. Kid's stuff has taken over, but I'd like to do some more adult stuff now. It makes you use your brain, dealing with a different audience. You start getting boring when you do the same thing all the time.

Gaitskell: Could you describe the process that you go through once you get a manuscript to illustrate?

Reid: I read it—a bunch—and then I start doing roughs. Usually with a book I know how long it is and whether it's in colour or black and white. Then I do a dummy— a grid pattern that lays out all the pages—to give it a pace. I like to think of the book as a whole before I work through it from beginning to end.

Gaitskell: Why?

Reid: It lets me plan where there are going to be big pictures and keeps me from getting repetitive. I make little notes, then go back and do the roughs in order, tighten them up, use reference if it's necessary. The roughs get shown to the art director. If there are any changes, they happen then. After that I do the finished art.

Gaitskell: Do the roughs take a lot of time?

Reid: With some pages I know from the beginning exactly what I want to do. With other pages I can walk around for days accomplishing nothing. It's really frustrating. I clean the house, I shop, I reorganize cupboards. I do all kinds of stuff just to avoid dealing with it. Then an idea comes somehow.

Gaitskell: Where does it come from?

Reid: It's surprising how much comes from your own experience. The plants or buildings or people I represent often turn out to be the ones I'm familiar with. I've noticed when I make buildings they're brick buildings, and Toronto's brick. I've noticed the same thing with other illustrators; for example, Rackham's trees all look the same. Then you go to England and, wow, the trees all look like that!

Gaitskell: What about the ideas that are outside your direct experience? How do they evolve?

Reid: When I have a project to do, I surround myself with stimuli. I look at different history books to get time periods and colours. I get all kinds of remaindered art books and flip through them to get a mood or a feeling

or a colour. I look through alphabet books, costume books. I go to the picture library. I set up the studio and I sit there waiting. It's important to set up all these little tokens so that, when the idea god comes by, I'll look ready.

Gaitskell: Who discovered Plasticine, you or the idea god?

Reid: Me. I played with it all the time when I was little.

Gaitskell: You liked it better than Play-Doh?

Reid: I hated Play-Doh. I didn't like the smell. It got hard and it tasted bad. But Plasticine was great stuff. Some Saturdays, I'd be in the mood to make something, so I'd spend all day modelling a whole village out of Plasticine. If I was home sick from school, I used to spend hours in front of the TV doing Plasticine. Life hasn't really changed for me.

Gaitskell: When did you decide that Plasticine was something you could use in your art?

Reid: I did it as a project at OCA. We were encouraged to do things with unusual media. It was a lot of fun and it seemed to get a really good reaction.

Gaitskell: Was it a problem convincing art directors to use Plasticine for picture book illustration?

Reid: I originally didn't think of it for kid's stuff. I thought of it for caricature, because that's what I liked to do. It did take a while for art directors to be open to the idea that it had to be photographed. But when I started doing textbook illustration a lot of 3-dimensional work was coming out. Paper sculpture and collage were really popular so the textbook people were open to it. Then I had some samples to show the other people.

Gaitskell: Your husband takes the photographs?

Reid: Yes, and it's great to have someone who knows how to shoot the stuff. It's not just like copying flat work. The lighting is very tricky.

Gaitskell: What do you like about Plasticine?

Reid: It's flexible. I can change my mind and play with it, keep moulding it and working on it. It's really nice for detail. With watercolour, you've got to be right the first time or you've got to redo it; if you're putting in a lot of detail, it gets really boring because you've got to work it up from the beginning. With Plasticine, it starts out very plain: you do the base layers and build on them. Then it gets more and more exciting as you add the little details.

Gaitskell: You add a lot of detail, don't you?

Reid: Yes. I think, especially for kid's stuff, that's the exciting part. By the time I did ***Mother Goose*** I'd started using paint to get shine and tiny pearls and beads. You

"Just the smell of rain
from a shady lane,
and a ride on a garden swing."

Illustration by Barbara Reid for Gifts, *by Jo Ellen Bogart.*

can go farther and farther and start putting in real cloth and building real things, but I don't want to go too far. I think it's part of the fun that the things are made with Plasticine. It's a silly medium. People are friendly to it and it makes them laugh. But I get tired of it. I'd like to do other stuff.

Gaitskell: Have you any other wildly experimental plans, using ostrich feathers or something for your medium?

Reid: I don't think so. I do things I know how to do and come up with ideas as I need them. Plasticine was easy because I knew how to play with it. I'd like to do some traditional stuff—watercolour and line illustration—maybe to prove that I *can* do it, that I'm not just getting by on this weird medium.

Gaitskell: Are there any particular books you would like to illustrate?

Reid: No. I like to do new stuff, contemporary stuff by people who are writing today. Frankly, I'd like someone to tell me what to do. I miss that. I'm finding it hard these days because I'm in a really lucky position. I can pick and choose projects, but it's a big responsibility. I feel I don't just want to do any old book. I want to do something really good and I don't know how to find it. I get manuscripts, but I'm not confident enough of my judgment: is it a really good story or not, I don't know.

Gaitskell: Have you ever thought of writing a story of your own?

Reid: I'd like to, but I'm not ready yet. I don't have anything to say. People always tell me, "Oh, write your own." That's like telling a writer, "Oh, illustrate your own." Writing the Plasticine book was easy because that was explaining what I do, but coming up with a story? All the great stories have already been written. And to stop working and just think up something out of the blue? No, I need the discipline of a manuscript, the size of a page, then I can fight it, work with it.

Gaitskell: Did you like doing the **Playing with Plasticine** *book?*

Reid: Yes, it was fun.

Gaitskell: Whose idea was it?

Reid: Well, Kids Can Press started bugging me right after **The New Baby Calf** to do a How-To. I kept saying no. Anyone can pick up Plasticine and figure it out. But there are some things that take a lot of practice and learning, and I didn't want to tell people the shortcuts. I felt uncomfortable, I couldn't picture the format. I didn't see how it could work without being really crippling for kids. I didn't want to tell them how to do something exactly. I never liked that as a kid. Then Kids Can started saying,

"If you don't, someone else is going to." They got me that way. At the same time, I'd been working on *How to Make Pop-Ups* by Joan Irvine. Four of us—Joan, the designer, the editor, and I—really hammered it out and I started to understand how that kind of instruction can work. It seemed the team was already in place, and I really liked the format. Finally everything was right.

Gaitskell: Was the book a challenge for you in any way?

Reid: Yes. The hardest part was trying to leave it open-ended so that it's a creative book. That's why I wanted black and white, partly so that people could afford it but also, if you make ducks orange and kids only have purple, some don't care and will work with purple, but other kids are real rule followers and I was trying to leave it open for them. If you show glossy photographs of wonderful finished stuff, it's depressing for kids to not be able to do it. It's nice just to give them some ideas.

Gaitskell: How do kids respond to Plasticine?

Reid: It loosens them up. When they see illustrations, they think, oh I can't draw and everyone (except for the three talented kids in the class) gets discouraged. But with Plasticine, everyone tucks in because it's silly and they don't have to worry about it being good—for them, that means photographically real. Modelling's easier than drawing too. The kids don't have to transform anything into two dimensions. They can just stick on an arm instead of having to figure out what angle to draw it from.

Gaitskell: How important is research in your work?

Reid: It varies. *Have You Seen Birds?* needed really tight research. It took a lot of readings, but it finally became clear what kinds of birds the author was talking about on each page. Sometimes she'd cover seven or eight different birds and often I had to pick one to illustrate. The bird had to be fairly generic so that a kid—maybe a European kid—would have a chance of seeing it. I made lists, narrowed things down, crossed things off. I used a bunch of bird guides and library books.

Gaitskell: Why did you chose Plasticine as the medium for that book?

Reid: Initially Scholastic didn't want *Birds* in Plasticine. They felt that Plasticine was fine for things like cows and earth but for birds it was too heavy, and I agreed. I worked for a couple of weeks with different kinds of water-colour and it was getting to look like Audubon—too real—and I was getting very tight and it wasn't any fun. Then I made a couple of Plasticine birds. I realized that because Plasticine's more crude and cartoony and humorous, it takes away that textbook, bird book feeling that I couldn't stop getting in watercolour without making it really cartoony. Now they're quite accurate, but they're not Batemans.

Gaitskell: What kind of research went into **Sing a Song of Mother Goose?**

Reid: I looked at a lot of Mother Goose books and I tried to get a feel for the Edwardian period, with those hats. I've never had a chance to illustrate costumes before. Birds and calves are dressed as they're dressed and you can't play around with it. With Mother Goose, I worked in all kinds of colours. It's so much more exciting to do faces than beaks.

Gaitskell: The farmer's face in **The New Baby Calf** *is fascinating. Is he a particular person?*

Reid: No. I got about 20 pictures of grisly old guys and hung them up around me to get in the mood and see how their faces work.

Gaitskell: I thought it might have been your grandpa.

Reid: No. Mother Goose started out being my grandmother, but it's not really her. It's sort of one of my aunts. There's an imperial old-lady style that's my other grandmother. She was English and very proper and very ladylike. She was in my head when I was doing those characters, but they don't necessarily look like her.

Gaitskell: When a text doesn't mention something, do you feel free to add your own ideas? For example, in **Birds** *the text never mentions a cat, yet the book opens and closes with one.*

Reid: Yeah, I think it's your duty to push the words, to add to the words, as long as you're not changing them. With *Birds* we decided that there shouldn't be people in the book; that would be too distracting. But it would be nice to have a beginning and end because there's really no story. So I thought, okay if we're going to have a bird watcher and there's no people, a cat seems to work. The idea's so obvious once it comes.

Gaitskell: Whose idea was it to make the birds jump out of their frames on the page?

Reid: Mine. I designed the grid of the whole book and arranged the pages. I do very basic design. I tend to centre things, divide them up neatly, but what a real designer can do with type is incredible and that's something else I'd like to do—get hooked up with some really hot designers, people who could take my work and make it look even better.

Gaitskell: Do you have particular designers in mind?

Reid: Well, there's a few. I like working with Michael Solomon at Kids Can Press.

Gaitskell: You use a lot of aerial views. Why?

Reid: I did it in **The New Baby Calf** because there's no story. Nothing happens page after page. It's just this farm and this calf, so I tried to make it interesting by using different points of view. You want the kids to respond, ask questions, say "what's that and look at that." That's what picture books are about. I always try to work with angles, to imagine what if I were this character or that. It's like acting.

*Gaitskell: The tiny subplots you put into your work—the duck family and the pig family in **The New Baby Calf,** for example—do you see this as a form of storytelling?*

Reid: They're little jokes. That's how I've always drawn. There's the main subject of the picture, but then there's always someone doing something in the background. It's like making fun in the back of the classroom. I always did that too.

*Gaitskell: In **Sing a Song of Mother Goose,** how did you decide whether characters were going to be male or female, human or animal?*

Reid: Those are some of the hardest decisions and nobody understands. You go out for a beer after work and someone says, "I had a really rough day," and you say," I did too, I couldn't figure out what to do with Tweedle-dum and Tweedle-dee," and they say, "Oh really, give me a break."

Gaitskell: Why are Tweedle-dum and Tweedle-dee turtles?

Reid: I had a problem. I really liked John Tenniel's *Alice in Wonderland* illustrations—the two little round guys with the striped shirts—but I didn't want to copy them. I wanted to take that verse away from Alice and I couldn't figure out how. I kept coming up with characters and they all looked like Tenniel's. Then I tried to think of animals and it suddenly clicked. Turtles would be good because Tweedle-dum and Tweedle-dee are battling. Turtles are armoured, and when they're afraid you can show it by putting them inside their shells. I was really happy with that one.

Gaitskell: And why is the mouse running down the Hickory, Dickory, Dock clock a girl in a pink frilly dress?

Reid: That's my textbook training. Textbook people are really uptight about sexual stereotyping. I've been drilled: make sure there's an even split of girls and boys, make sure the girls aren't doing anything too feminine, the boys aren't doing anything too masculine, try, whenever possible, to flip the illustration to make it non-sexist. I've learned through textbooks when in doubt, draw an animal, because animals can do sexist things. If a little girl were dressed like that, I'd expect to get flack, but with a mouse I can get away with it for another year, maybe.

Gaitskell: The dish that ran away with the spoon is a bit of a vamp, no?

Reid: Yeah, I switched that one. In most nursery rhyme books the dish is the male, but I thought dishes look more female, and I thought I'd make her kind of tarty. She should be taking charge, taking the guy by surprise and running away with him.

Gaitskell: There's a lot of formal dress in this illustration.

Reid: I thought it must be a party, a fancy-dress ball or maybe it's a pantomime with the cow on stage, but they're just dressed up and carrying on. That seemed to be the mood for that piece.

Gaitskell: Why did you make the speaker in "Where are You Going, My Pretty Maid?" an artist?

Reid: Because that's a fairly sexist poem. I thought if there's an artist ogling this chick going by, maybe it's just for beauty's sake. I thought I'd make him one of those painters out there trying to be an Impressionist. I wanted to make him less leering, more innocent—he's a soldier in most Mother Goose books. I enjoy some of the old stereotyping stuff, but I don't like to show it, and maybe for kids it's a little much.

Gaitskell: The maid's postures are very strong.

Reid: Yes, she's aggressive. I didn't want to make her a shrinking-violet type or have her look crushed that the painter doesn't want to marry her.

Gaitskell: He's the one who looks crushed.

Reid: Yes, his paintbrush shows it. You should be able to cover up the words and know what's happening in that scene from the way the characters are acting. I think that's important in illustration, telling the story without words.

Gaitskell: Did you have problems depicting death and illness in "Solomon Grundy"?

Reid: It's such a morbid little poem. I was thinking of how to do it nicely when I decided, no: he's sick, he's dead, there's no way around it. Actually, as a little kid, nothing ever really shocked me in a book. I think we get more sensitive as we get older, but I know little kids read about horrible dismemberment in fairy tales, and I always liked that part.

Gaitskell: Is there anything you notice about children's senses of humour that you cater to in your work, or is it your own sense of humour that guides you?

Reid: I think it's my own, it's childish probably. Some kids like it and some kids don't. My type of humour is generally making fun of any type of pompous behaviour. I really like to poke fun at people who take themselves too seriously or to make fun of anything bad. That's my way of dealing with things, so that's the kind of humour that comes out.

Gaitskell: What do you like best about your job?

Reid: It's really rewarding—like cooking. You get this story and you turn it into your own; then you take it and show it to someone and they like it. It's the need to please instantly satisfied, like when you were a little kid and you made a picture and showed it off to someone. I've never really gotten over that.

TITLE COMMENTARY

THE NEW BABY CALF (1984)

Bernie Goedhart

SOURCE: A review of *The New Baby Calf,* in *Quill & Quire,* February, 1985, pp. 14-15.

The New Baby Calf has, as text, a little poem by Edith Newlin Chase about Buttercup the cow and her new calf. Taken from an out-of-print anthology, the poem is given new life through the ingenious, brightly coloured Plasticine farmyard images created by Barbara Reid. The book should have immediate appeal for pre-schoolers, but any-one who has ever tried to squeeze a piece of clay into some recognizable shape will marvel at Reid's artwork. Especially intriguing is a bird's-eye view of the barnyard, complete with plump pink piggies, a sturdy farmer, chickens pecking at seeds, and a calf sprawled spread-eagle on the ground after a first attempt at walking—an ideal illustration for nurturing in small children the awareness of perspective. The texture of the Plasticine three-dimensional images is so realistic that there is a constant temptation to pinch the pictures.

Carol Anne Wien

SOURCE: A review of *The New Baby Calf,* in *Canadian Children's Literature,* No. 42, 1986, pp. 66-8.

In *The New Baby Calf,* Barbara Reid unites a simple rhyming text with vivid, detailed landscapes created out of Plasticine. The story concerns a calf's first experi-ences. This experience of gradually growing stronger and more competent is parallel to the child's so that the con-tent reaffirms the child's sense that she/he too will grow strong. The illustrations are masterfully created with the vivid, clear tones of Plasticine. Interesting textures are constructed using tiny dots or stripes or by making pat-terns of indentations. Yet the pictures are not stylized but are highly expressive, for Reid manages to keep a fluid line and to incorporate marvelous expressions of feeling on the farmer's and animals' faces. This is a masterpiece of illus-tration, using an original technique, and has the additional benefit of stimulating slightly older children (four to six) to see the range of things it is possible to do with Plasticine.

Publishers Weekly

SOURCE: A review of *The New Baby Calf,* in *Publishers Weekly,* Vol. 230, No. 29, September 26, 1986, p. 79.

"Buttercup the cow had a new baby calf, a fine baby calf, a strong baby calf. Not strong like his mother, but strong for a calf, for this baby calf was so new." Plasticine-relief illustrations give this book an unusual three-dimensional look, as the baby calf grows up with lots of love and mother's milk. It's a sweet story, which should encourage those readers who despair of ever growing up them-selves. Reid's observations of country life are on target, from the barnyard full of animals to the pink-cheeked farmer who tends them.

Sarah Ellis

SOURCE: "News from the North," in *The Horn Book Magazine,* Vol. LXIV, No. 1, January, 1988, pp. 102-04.

Reid creates with Plasticene in a way that makes one look anew at this unpretentious medium. In her first book, *The New Baby Calf,* she illustrates a text that at first seems to have little potential. A short verse by Edith Newlin Chase about Buttercup the cow and her new calf is typi-cal of the benign, slightly saccharine juvenile poetry of a bygone era. But Reid uses this brief text as a basso continuo to her own exploration of farm life and the changing seasons. In the foreground are Buttercup and her calf, one bony and stolid, the other bony and lanky. The milking scene provides a rear view of Buttercup in which Reid beautifully captures what painter Emily Carr has called the "squareness" of a cow. In the background we see tilling, sowing, and harvesting—the fields turning from brown to green to golden. As the calf grows, an apple blossom border modulates to a crop of apples hanging from the top of the page.

The colors are rich and dense. They recall the childhood joy of a new box of Plasticene, each color lying pristine and separate in its neatly grooved brick. But it is the texture of the pictures that makes Reid's vision unique. The crops in the field and the straw in the barnyard are created from long thin sausages, that time-honored Plasticene technique. The coarse, sharp-edged farm grass in the foreground is scissor-cut. The distant meadows are scored as with a comb, and the bodies of the cows are pushed into shape with the fingertips. The farmer's cheekbones and knuckles and the blossoms on the trees are tiny balls of color, delicately squished. One can feel how much fun it must have been to create these pictures.

HAVE YOU SEEN BIRDS? (1986)

Luann Toth

SOURCE: A review of *Have You Seen Birds?,* in *School Library Journal,* June-July, 1987, p. 88.

A wonderful picture book depicting the wide variety of birds seen throughout the year and in various types of habitats (i.e., marsh birds, sea birds, flat-footed fishing birds). The birds are described throughout in lyrical running verse. It is, however, the stunning, vibrantly colorful plasticine-relief illustrations that make this book so special. This medium gives depth and texture to the pages, the scenes often shown from a bird's eye view. The birds really do appear to dive, dip, glide, and tip. The clever details and excellent page design maximizing use of white space make for an exciting look at the world of birds for preschoolers and beginning independent readers. Even without a key to identify the depicted birds, this is a winner.

Susan Perren

SOURCE: "Picture-Book Plums for Christmas Gift-Giving," in *Quill & Quire*, December, 1986, p. 16.

Reid . . . brings an uncanny realism, a kind of magic realism, to this book with her pictures in relief of birds in landscape, birds in cages, sky birds and sea birds, colourful, exact, and perfect sculptures all. *Have You Seen Birds?* is a delight for both the eye and the ear.

Joan Weller

SOURCE: A review of *Have You Seen Birds?*, in *CM: A Reviewing Journal of Canadian Materials for Young People*, Vol. XVI, No. 1, January, 1988, pp. 7-8.

And to fly with the birds is a wish come true in Barbara Reid's second picture book, *Have You Seen Birds?*. Plasticine, that medium many of us rolled into snakes or at best rolled into a tiny snowman on rainy days in elementary school, takes on forms so creative in their depiction of all kinds of birds that one looks again and again at the illustrations and marvels at their conception—the colours, texture, perspective, depth, and their special sense of movement and activity. Here is a picture book to stimulate the eye and to bring readers back many times to see more. In all their natural habitats birds of every kind in all our seasons are captured in amazingly original pictures. With gentle humour, too, the artist presents her birds not just to young readers and older readers but also to a little cat on the opening page who mysteriously disappears on the last page leaving his tail behind him. We can only ask ourselves the question that one little child asked on having the book read to her: "Is that cat going outside now to see the birds or to catch them?"

Judy Willson

SOURCE: A review of *Birds, Birds and More Birds!*, in *Canadian Children's Literature*, No. 57/58, 1990, pp. 138-39.

A curiosity about birds does not come naturally to all young children, but an interest in the subject can be sparked through literature. For young children, Joanne Oppenheim's book *Have You Seen Birds?* introduces the physical features, habitats and behaviours of a wide variety of birds without even naming them. This is done through rhyme and imaginative, descriptive vocabulary. Barbara Reid's detailed Plasticine illustrations greatly enhance the text by showing the birds in various settings throughout the seasons.

PLAYING WITH PLASTICINE (1988)

Annette Goldsmith

SOURCE: "Barbara Reid Shares Plasticine Secrets," in *Books for Young People*, Vol. 2, No. 5, October, 1988, p. 14.

Barbara Reid is to Plasticine what Camilla Gryski is to string games. She has single-handedly popularized the medium both through her highly original picture-book illustrations and by touring schools. Her first published Plasticine illustrations, in Edith Newlin Chase's *The New Baby Calf*, caused a sensation, and her reputation continues to grow.

This year Reid won the international Ezra Jack Keats Award, a biennial prize given jointly by the U.S. section of the International Board on Books for Young People (USBBY) and UNICEF to a promising new illustrator of "innovative picture books that achieve a fine sense of balance between art and text." She is the first Canadian to be so honoured. Her work for Joanne Oppenheim's *Have You Seen Birds?* alone garnered her the Ruth Schwartz Children's Book Award, the IODE Book Award (Toronto Chapter), and the Canada Council Children's Literature Prize for Illustration.

Playing with Plasticine is the first book Reid has both written and illustrated. It conveys her love of the medium and her sense of whimsy—qualities one would expect from such an accomplished illustrator, but no mean feat for a fledgling author.

Reid begins with an introduction to Plasticine and provides instructions for making the basic shapes (ribbons, sausages, snakes) used throughout. It's important to read this part before proceeding; otherwise, a perfectly reasonable instruction, such as this one for making a tree, won't make much sense: "Start with a ribbon trunk and blend on some sausage roots and snake branches."

The author then demonstrates, in words and pictures, how to create animals, people, a surprising array of miscellaneous objects (cars, food, furniture, etc.), flat pictures, board games, and even self-portraits (look for Reid's on the back cover). For the more ambitious, she explains the "bird's eye view" approach employed so successfully in her own work. And for those well supplied with Plasticine and free time, there are sophisticated models and theatre sets to tackle.

Reid's hints on handling the material are not only practical but often quite charming: if your standing animals topple over, says Reid, just lean them together. And did you know that a Plasticine snail will stick to your refrigerator door?

The book ends with a double-page spread called Plasticine Then and Now, a fascinating look at Plasticine's beginnings and applications other than the purely artistic.

Ever since the publication of *The New Baby Calf,* Reid has been urged to write a book explaining her technique. She resisted, unsure of how such a book might best be done. Eventually she found her inspiration while working on the line drawings for Joan Irvine's excellent *How to Make Pop-ups.* The format of the pop-ups book, with its easy-to-follow instructions and clear layout, proved the perfect model for *Playing with Plasticine.*

At first it's disappointing to discover that the photos heading each section in *Playing with Plasticine* aren't in colour. Apart from the glorious cover, there are no colour samples of the pieces. However, Reid felt strongly that black-and-white illustrations would be less intimidating, particularly if the reader had only one colour at hand. They also encourage creativity rather than imitation.

No reader could expect the artist to share *all* her secrets, of course; Reid explains how to mix colours, for example, but not in such detail that one could reproduce her palette. And anyone following her directions can create equally detailed Plasticine pictures, but no one will mistake them for Reid originals.

The results are thoroughly satisfying, though—and fast. Even young children (with an older friend to explain the instructions) can make something recognizable. Plasticine is an extraordinarily versatile medium: easy to manipulate, non-toxic, available in a wide range of colours, virtually indestructible, and inexpensive. In a word (one of Reid's favourites), it's "neat." It isn't even messy, unless ground into the carpet. Kids Can Press doesn't intend to package the book with Plasticine as a gift set, so plan to buy the two separately.

Playing with Plasticine is the best kind of craft book, demonstrating easily how to use a particular medium and inspiring original efforts. The book is a plentiful source of ideas, and not just for Plasticine. The board games and flat pictures, for example, could also be executed in more conventional media. Another tip: children looking for a science fair project might consider the history and properties of Plasticine. This book belongs in every school and public library collection, and on many private shelves as well.

Ann Jansen

SOURCE: "Plasticine Queen," in *Books in Canada,* Vol. 17, No. 9, December, 1988, p. 15.

Fans and modelling-clay *aficionados* can busy themselves . . . by getting hold of Reid's new how-to book,

Playing with Plasticine. In this, her first attempt at writing as well as illustrating a book, Reid leads children from the basics of classic snakes and sausages to "painting" with Plasticine. Along with her clear and lighthearted suggestions, she provides a history of Plasticine since its invention by an English art teacher in 1887 (the secret ingredient is not divulged). The book has black-and-white illustrations rather than the elaborate and colourful extravaganzas for which Reid has become famous. She explains that she wanted to get kids started on their own, not turn them into smaller-sized Barbara Reids. "I didn't want to say, 'You do this, this and this, and this is a duck.' I never liked colouring books when I was a kid. I don't like anything restrictive," said Reid. "Besides, kids often have only two colours and they're stuck together anyway."

Fond as she is of modelling clay, Reid is wary of being typed as a one-medium illustrator. Admittedly, the books may have been first noticed because of their novel approach—"When a hundred books come out for Christmas, the one in watermelon seeds gets noticed," says Reid, but adds, "I'm an illustrator first. My design of the page is the same whether I do it in black and white or watercolour or Plasticine. I've seen other people work in Plasticine and it looks like that other person doing Plasticine. Mine looks like the way I draw."

In her work, whether in Plasticine or more traditional media Reid always aims at finding the funny side of things. "I think I'm still really immature. I like reading children's books," she said, looking very youthful sitting on a small stool in her blue overalls with her hair drawn into a pony-tail. "Even when I was a kid, I used to make very complicated pictures of all kinds of stuff happening and just hope people would get all the jokes. I guess it's like being a cartoonist. Basically, I spend most of my time stereotyping people. Friendly stereotyping. Just by looking at the picture you should know right away, this person's very tense or this one's a goof—I especially like making fun of pompous people."

Joanne Robertson

SOURCE: A review of *Playing with Plasticine,* in *CM: A Reviewing Journal of Canadian Materials for Young People,* Vol. XVII, No. 1, January, 1989, p. 28.

Barbara Reid's award-winning Plasticine illustrations have delighted many children. In her latest book, *Playing with Plasticine,* she shows you how to make all sorts of bugs, birds, animals, reptiles, and even fish. She'll show you how to build human bodies and some not quite so human. And she doesn't stop there. What will your Plasticine characters need—food, furniture, plants, toys, transportation, a home to live in? Barbara Reid creates a magical Plasticine world and she shows how you can too.

Would you rather make three-dimensional figures or paint a flat, two-dimensional picture from Plasticine? If you can't make up your mind, you can combine the two techniques and make a special scene. She does not expect that her directions will be slavishly followed, but rather that the ideas and directions will serve as a starting point for the reader's imagination.

Playing with Plasticine begins with directions that show how to construct basic shapes. More complex creations are made by using these simple shapes and by adding details. Each step-by-step direction is illustrated by an uncluttered black-and-white drawing. The directions are written in a simple clear style, with easy-to-read vocabulary. A child should be able to follow them with a minimum of adult help. The book includes a table of contents, which is very helpful; more importantly, the material itself is organized in a systematic manner.

Highly recommended.

Kirkus Reviews

SOURCE: A review of *Playing with Plasticine,* in *Kirkus Review,* February 15, 1989, p. 299.

Step-by-step instruction for turning Plasticine and other modeling clay into colorful, cheerful, and whimsical works of art; by the winner of the Ezra Jack Keats Award—who won the award for her picture-book illustrations in this medium, but who uses drawings as well as black-and-white photos here. Three-dimensional zoo animals, food, space monsters, buildings, pictures, plaques, and games are created—with tips on techniques, tools, and possible further explorations. The text is lively and insightful; for those who can't yet read, the black-and-white drawings are abundant and explicit. An unusual book that should provide both the young artist and the art or craft teacher with useful inspiration for work in a popular, accessible medium.

Cynthia Bishop

SOURCE: A review of *Playing with Plasticine,* in *School Library Journal,* May, 1989 pp. 121-122.

This delightful book gives clear, step-by-step instructions for making dozens of Plasticine sculptures and bas-reliefs. Reid systematically demonstrates how to combine several basic shapes into increasingly complex creations. Unique to this book are directions for what amounts to painting pictures with Plasticine. The technique involves spreading thin layers of well-softened Plasticine over flat and solid shapes, and then adding flattened figures to create two- and three-dimensional scenes. The written instructions are effectively illustrated with attractive drawings and photographs. Useful modeling tips are offered along with information on sources, storage, and color mixing. Other modeling books for children are far less detailed, and describe the use of potter's clay rather than Plasticine. This excellent offering is a craft rather than an art book. Reid gives directions for making things; she does not suggest exercises for exploring the nature of this particular modeling medium. A logical, attractive layout; many specific instructions; and a sense of fun make this an appealing book.

Phillis Wilson

SOURCE: A review of *Playing with Plasticine,* in *Booklist,* Vol. 85, No. 17, May 1, 1989, p. 1553.

Soft, lightweight, easy-to-handle: these attributes mark the modeling material called Plasticine, which was invented about 100 years ago in England. Reid's fascination with and facility for manipulating this amazing stuff into myriad creative forms is obvious. Her step-by-step lively instructions are clear and well paced, giving children the prospect of satisfying results. Sections on bugs, animals, people, food, furniture, and vehicles precede more difficult projects, so that a complex three-dimensional plaque or scene utilizes skills already mastered. While Plasticine comes in rainbow hues, the black-and-white illustrations keep the focus on construction technique. A top-notch resource for home or classroom use.

Bernard Schwartz and JoAnn Sommerfeld

SOURCE: A review of *Playing with Plasticine and The New Baby Calf,* in *Canadian Children's Literature,* No. 60, 1990, p. 32.

Plasticene has traditionally been used to create free-standing sculptures of snakes, snowmen and other simply-shaped items. Barbara Reid takes Plasticene to previously undreamed of dimensions when using it as an illustrative medium. *The New Baby Calf* is illustrated by using Plasticene to create pictures: Plasticene is flattened, textured and pressed into place on masonite or cardboard. Colours which previously were found only in a 64 colour crayon box resurface in Plasticene. Reid shares ideas on how Plasticene can be used in her resource book *Playing with Plasticene.* The beauty of the medium can be realized by studying the illustrations for *The New Baby Calf.*

For the art class, the teacher could combine studies in colour, shape and texture with a study of Reid's techniques. Discussion and analysis of the suitability of the medium for illustrative purposes would challenge the students to think of Plasticene in a non-traditional mode. Children across the spectrum of the elementary grades can analyze how particular textures were achieved. They can experiment to create the effects of wood, straw, fur, or hair; they can be challenged to make a variety of colours by mixing only a few basic ones. After discussing the story and the illustrations for the new calf, children could be directed to create their own Plasticene pictures or sculpture. They could continue by working with other modelling materials.

The above are but a few examples of how the art class and the art curriculum can be enriched by using readily available materials from the school library shelves. If information about the authors and illustrators is available it should be shared with the students to broaden their knowledge and appreciation of art and literature. Children should be encouraged to analyze the artwork in books as well as their own and their classmates' work. By making informed judgments based on observation, discussion, analysis, and interpretation, children not only increase their understanding and appreciation of art but are able to increase their own repertoire of art skills. By the use of books designed for children and available to children, a substantial art program can become a more viable and achievable goal.

EFFIE (1990)

Publishers Weekly

SOURCE: A review of *Effie,* in *Publishers Weekly,* Vol. 238, No. 5, January 25, 1991, p. 56.

Effie "was an ant like hundreds of others—in every way but one. All the others had tiny ant voices. Effie's voice was like thunder." Poor Effie merely wants a friend, but even a sociable "hello" in her booming voice sends the other insects scrambling. And when they come running back, it's not to see Effie: they're trying to get away from an elephant that, oblivious to the tiny beings below, is about to crush them. Effie's gigantic lung power saves the day. She wins the respect of the other creatures, and finally finds a friend in the gentle elephant. Allinson's simple, straightforward text is complemented perfectly by Reid's (*Have You Seen Birds?*) rollicking Plasticine compositions. The layering of the material creates a marvelous textural illusion and—especially in a scene depicting a caterpillar bounding away from Effie's big voice—some hilarious perspectives.

Julie Corsaro

SOURCE: A review of *Effie,* in *Booklist,* Vol. 87, No. 17, May 1, 1991, p. 1720.

Illustration by Barbara Reid for her book, Two by Two.

Once again, Reid boosts a simple, direct text with the innovative Plasticine technique that earned her the Ezra Jack Keats Award. At first Effie looks just like any other ant. The big problem is her booming voice, which scares away the caterpillar, the butterfly, the spider, and many others she tries to befriend. When these same creatures are about to be crushed by an elephant, they beat a hasty retreat past Effie. Not only does the little ant with the big lungs save them all, but she also finds a soulmate in the large, gentle elephant. With appealing variety in perspective and placement, the expressive artwork has humorous details, such as a hungry spider complete with bib, utensils, condiments, and parachute. Young children returning for second and third looks will also be pleased with the grandiose and satisfying finale.

Louise L. Sherman

SOURCE: A review of *Effie*, in *School Library Journal*, Vol. 37, No. 7, July, 1991, p. 52.

Effie's loud voice causes her to be shunned not only by the rest of the ants, but also by other small creatures in her world. When an elephant threatens, however, she speaks up and saves them all. There is nothing new about this familiar plot, but the humor and verve with which it is told and illustrated make it stand out. The first page, in which readers are told that "Effie came from a long long line of ants" and shown—literally—will fascinate children. Reid's Plasticine scenes are filled with bold colors and fanciful touches: toe slippers on a balletic butterfly; a salt shaker in the hand of a spider approaching its prey. The texture seems almost touchable; the perspectives add humor—a look down Effie's huge throat, an extreme close-up of her climbing the elephant's trunk. The story works well as a read-aloud, but the very bold type used for Effie's dialogue will convey her volume to silent readers, too. Simpler than Richard Wilbur's *Loudmouse*, this is a good choice for comparison with that title or others in which the outcast makes good.

Terri MacLaen

SOURCE: A review of *Effie*, in *CM: A Reviewing Journal of Canadian Materials for Young People*, Vol. XIX, No. 4, September, 1991, p. 226.

Effie is a small ant with a big problem. Her voice is so loud that whenever she speaks everyone runs to get away from the noise. Effie is very lonely until one day she spots an elephant's foot descending on the ants who had run away from her that same morning. Effie's booming voice saves them all from being crushed, and she and the elephant become friends. Not a terribly original plot, but one which young children will nonetheless enjoy.

What makes the book totally irresistible is the wonderful artwork of Barbara Reid, of *Playing with Plasticine*

fame. Her skilful use of Plasticine to produce texture, colour and detail brings the characters in the story to life. (The grasshopper is wearing red Convers.) Interest is further added by such design details as printing all Effie's words in large bold-face type and the caterpillar's words wiggling across the page.

The book would make a wonderful introduction to an art lesson for Junior grades and would certainly inspire children of all ages to explore the medium of Plasticine. The book would also fit nicely into a Primary unit on insects.

Highly recommended.

ZOE SERIES (1991)

Children's Book News

SOURCE: A review of *Zoe's Windy Day; Zoe's Sunny Day; Zoe's Snowy Day; Zoe's Rainy Day*, in *Children's Book News*, Vol. 14, No. 2, Fall, 1991, p. 17.

Barbara Reid's Plasticine creations have captivated an international audience for many years. Books such as ***Have You Seen Birds?*, *Playing with Plasticine*** and ***The New Baby Calf*** have won the artist numerous prestigious awards and a passionate following. Her newest surprise, a four volume collection of wordless board books, will only reinforce her reputation as one of Canada's finest children's illustrators

Overflowing with detail, colour and humour, each volume in the Zoe series follows a little girl through the adventure of the changing seasons. The wordless tales are clear, easy to follow and characterized by Reid's innate ability to realize in Plasticine the magical nature of life's simplest events. In Reid's hands snow, rain, wind and sunlight become agents of delight.

Children will spend hours with these books eagerly pointing out familiar events and objects. Parents will be tempted to steal these treasures out of the nursery and spend time enjoying the exquisite detail all by themselves.

Bernie Goedhart

SOURCE: A review of *Zoe's Snowy Day; Zoe's Windy Day; Zoe's Sunny Day; Zoe's Rainy Day*, in *Quill & Quire*, October, 1991, pp. 36, 38.

One glance at this new series of four wordless board books shows why Barbara Reid is—and will always be—the Queen of Plasticine. Since bursting onto the children's book scene in 1984 with the publication of ***The New Baby Calf***, Reid has elevated illustration in the lowly medium of coloured modelling clay to a fine art. Others have followed suit—but none have matched Reid's finesse.

In the *Zoe* stories, Reid uses this art form in books aimed at babies and toddlers. Colourful, action-filled double-page spreads illustrate the four seasons, as Reid gives children plenty of familiar images to which they can relate while providing adults with humorous, appealing material for conversation. Reid has modelled the central character on her own daughter. In two of the books (*Rainy Day* and *Sunny Day*) the child is accompanied on an outing by her mom, while the remaining two books show Zoe heading to the park with dad. A calico cat rounds out the family troupe.

The illustrations are richly detailed. The wetness of *Rainy Day* is palpable; leaves all but blow off the pages of *Windy Day;* and we can virtually taste those drops of snow landing on Zoe's tongue in *Snowy Day.* When she skins her knee in *Sunny Day,* we wince in sympathy. And Zoe's toy monkey, in this same volume, proves an expressive example of Reid's mastery.

Kirkus Review

SOURCE: A Review of *Zoe's Windy Day,* in *Kirkus Review,* December 1, 1991, p. 132.

[*Zoe's Windy Day* is] one of four simultaneously published wordless board books concerning an appealingly sturdy child's outings in different kinds of weather (in the others, Zoe enjoys sunny, snowy, and rainy days). As a new illustrator, Reid received the Ezra Jack Keats award for her vibrant art, fashioned in Plasticine and then photographed. The subtlety of her work here is astonishing—she deftly captures the effect of blowing leaves, clouds, and even dandelion seeds, as well as the nuances of her characters' expressions, molding and marking her material to create the textures of a knit sweater or a three-dimensional shape seen in perspective. The medium ensures crisp, clean images, easily "read" by the youngest; the five-inch-square size is perfect for tiny hands. By meeting the challenge of portraying the wind's effect in this uncompromising material, the windy day may be the most virtuoso performance, but young "readers" will enjoy all four books.

Kay Kerman

SOURCE: A review of *Zoe's Rainy Day; Zoe's Snowy Day; Zoe's Sunny Day; Zoe's Windy Day,* in *CM: A Reviewing Journal of Canadian Materials for Young People,* Vol. XX, No. 2, March, 1992, pp. 84-5.

Well, she's done it again! Barbara Reid has produced a series of excellent and innovative Plasticine books. These four wordless board books follow a young girl and her family through a series of adventures on windy, snowy, rainy and sunny days. As usual, Barbara Reid fills in details that would be familiar to all children. I will describe one book in detail and the others more briefly, as the format is similar across the series.

In her four-colour, Plasticine-illustrated books, Barbara Reid is describing the events that happen on an outing with any child during one of the particular weather days.

In *Zoe's Sunny Day* Zoe goes to the park with her mom and accidentally falls on the sidewalk in her eagerness to get to the play area. The next scene shows Zoe's tears being wiped away while sitting atop her mom's knee on the grass. Throughout the rest of the book we will note the red sore on Zoe's knee. But there is much else going on in this picture. Children are sliding, swinging, drinking at the fountain, kicking a soccer ball, and of course there are other parents around to share in all the fun. In the following scene, we see Zoe eating her sandwich and standing intently over top of an anthill. In the background we see the squirrels rummaging around the garbage pail. Her picnic lunch rests on a blanket behind her and we see a little ant snatching up a crumb from it. Finally we see a very familiar site, that of children in a wading pool. Zoe is splashing about with her big beach ball while her mother lies on the blanket and watches her from the background. Looking on are some other people sitting on the bench and another child who is drying off with a towel. After such a busy outing it is time to go home. Zoe is fast asleep in her carriage, with her toy monkey (who appears in all four books) on her chest. Mom is bringing her home as the sun is setting and the neighbour is watering her lawn.

Each of Reid's books portrays Zoe's outing with her family. In *Zoe's Rainy Day* Zoe gets into her raincoat and boots and goes out walking with her mom to the park, where she plays with the other children. Upon returning home, we see Zoe enjoying a bath, cleaning off the mud from the park. In *Zoe's Snowy Day* Zoe goes tobogganing with her dad at the park. They pass by the ice rink and watch the older children playing hockey and then they return home, where we see Zoe asleep in bed. *Zoe's Windy Day* clearly gives the reader the feeling of fall. People are raking leaves that are blowing all around. Zoe's father stops and buys some food from a vendor in the park and then Zoe plays on the swings. After they walk home, they have a warm cup of hot chocolate! All children will love pointing out the familiar and similar experiences that they have had on days such as these.

Reid's illustrations provide amazing detail in lushly coloured scenes that appear to be three dimensional. Parents and children will enjoy hours of visual delight with Zoe, who just happens to be Barbara Reid's daughter!

Other books that Barbara Reid has illustrated are *Have You Seen Birds, The New Baby Calf, Sing a Song of Mother Goose,* and *Jenny Greenteeth.*

Reid has won numerous awards for her illustrations. I highly recommend these books—especially for preschool children.

Tracey Siddall

SOURCE: A review of *Zoe's Snowy Day; Zoe's Sunny day; Zoe's Windy Day; Zoe's Rainy Day,* in *Canadian Children's Literature,* No. 69, 1993, pp. 90-1.

Barbara Reid can do no wrong with Plasticine. This amazing set of books is intricately and artfully crafted to show a young girl named Zoe on outings with her parents. The books are set up like a family photo album; the pictures are fashioned in Plasticine and then photographed. Urban children are sure to recognize and identify with Zoe's activities. For example, at the end of *Zoe's Sunny Day,* Zoe is fast asleep in her stroller on the way home from the park where she's had a busy day swimming, frolicking at the playground, and picnicking on the grass.

There is no text to accompany the artwork, but none is needed. When my two-year old asked where the words were, I realized the need for books such as these in a child's library. Reading stories is important, but it is equally important to learn to use books as a focus for sharing ideas and conversation. These books allow adults and children the opportunity to make up stories, to talk about familiar sights, sounds and smells, remember similar days in their own lives and, most importantly, to spend shared time together in an interactive way. These wordless books can create a shared space of pleasure between children and their caregivers.

The Zoe books are constructed of sturdy cardboard. They are small in size, just perfect for the hands of children. Reid has won international awards in the past for her books (e.g., *Who Has Seen Birds*), and this collection of books is sure to win her more acclaim.

TWO BY TWO (1992)

Patricia L. M. Butler

SOURCE: A review of *Two by Two,* in *CM: A Reviewing Journal of Canadian Materials for Young People,* Vol. XX, No. 5, October, 1992, p. 265.

Barbara Reid needs no introduction in the world of children's book illustration. *Two by Two* is destined to join, among others, her multi-award-winning book *Have You Seen Birds?* as a mandatory part of any home or library collection. This new work finds Reid providing not only the illustrations but also the text, and she proves herself just as adept in molding the lyrical rhythm of words as she is in creating her wonderful Plasticine art.

Two by Two retells the story of Noah's ark in poetry form, to be read or sung (the traditional tune is supplied). In either mode of delivery, it captures the imagination of both listener and reader with its flow and its wonderful accompanying illustrations. Reid uses, amongst other devices, alliteration and humour to retell the story of Noah, the animals, and God's promise that "after rain, the sun will shine."

With the exception of a few grins, all the animals, fish and insects that troop aboard Noah's big boat are rendered in accurate and detailed form, much to the delight of small readers learning the difference between a leopard and an ocelot. Even a full ark rolling on high seas shows every beak and crocodile tooth as it should be!

The animals are shown from several imaginative perspectives (close up, long distance, aerial) as they clamber aboard, complementing the interesting creature combinations: six black-and-white species appear as the animals come in six by six, eight types of cat pace in eight by eight, inch worms accompany polar bears, and sloths slink on upside down.

This well-produced, colourful picture-book is a "must have" addition to any collection. Young ones will enjoy and quickly learn the rhyme when it is sung, and older children will enjoy the chance to read the verses by themselves. The wide age range to which this book appeals makes it an excellent choice for any home, school or library collection.

Publishers Weekly

SOURCE: A review of *Two by Two,* in *Publishers Weekly,* Vol. 240, No. 7, February 15, 1993, p. 238.

Three-dimensional artwork of extraordinary richness highlights this verse retelling of the Noah story by the illustrator of *The New Baby Calf.* Reid's vibrantly colored, sculpted Plasticine illustrations give her pictures the illusion of depth seldom achieved with conventional techniques. The intricate spreads teem with activity rendered in real-as-life tactile detail: characters wear robes trimmed with textured embroidery; Noah's long beard descends in whorls like white icing on a cake; every painstakingly molded fin, feather and strand of fur on the arkful of animals begs to be touched. The palette is equally impressive, as the cloud-filled sky darkens and lightens again with the passing of the storm, and the deep blues of the sea offset the pinks and oranges of the sun-drenched landscape. There are cleverly crafted shifts in perspective, too, notably a bird's-eye-view of the animals boarding the ark. Only the text, consisting of original lyrics to a traditional tune, fails to match the art's sparkle: Reid tells the familiar tale in (occasionally limp) iambic tetrameter that sometimes sacrifices scansion for rhyme. Readers will nonetheless enjoy counting along as the animals—from the tiniest mice to the biggest elephants—clamber aboard this beguiling ark.

Kathy Piehl

SOURCE: A review of *Two by Two,* in *School Library Journal,* March, 1993, pp. 193-94.

Noah and his animal companions appear in another rhymed voyage. Reid retells the familiar Bible story in her own verses for the traditional tune, "Who Built the Ark?" The score is appended. What stands out about this version is the masterful use of Plasticine to create engaging images. From the delicate lines of the ark during construction to the panoramas of animals as they board, Reid's marvelous pictures deserve more than one viewing. Young children will appreciate them as an appealing visual accompaniment to a bouncy story, while older readers can find in them encouragement for their own artistic efforts.

Kirkus Reviews

SOURCE: A review of *Two by Two*, in *Kirkus Reviews*, March 15, 1993, p. 378.

Adopting the verse scheme of the traditional song, Reid recounts the building of Noah's Ark and writes a new couplet for each number up to ten ("And in came the animals six by six,/Pandas and penguins, all in a mix"). The animals aren't all named, but they're all countable in Reid's illustrations, formed in Plasticene on board for a vibrant, three-dimensional effect remarkable for its textures, lively expressions (Noah is saintly and benevolent, his wife a smiling babushka), and the subtlety, imagination, and wit of the art—the six pairs of animals are a study in black and white (Holsteins, skunks, zebras); tiny creatures (mice, spiders) challenge sharp eyes; the Ark a-building is an airy frame against the sky. The neatly scanning verse has nice touches of humor ("Even the boas felt constricted") and takes the story on to the rainbow. A delightful presentation of this old favorite. Music included.

Ellen Mandel

SOURCE: A review of *Two by Two*, in *Booklist*, Vol. 89, No. 19-20, June 1&15, 1993, p. 1834.

Yes, the story of Noah and the flood has been told and retold through the ages—but never before by Barbara Reid. Her rhymed verses playfully telescope the ark's construction and the family's preparations before rhythmically counting the pairs of animals coming aboard. But it is Reid's boldly original illustrations that amuse, delight, and demand attention. Sculpted from Plasticine pressed onto illustration board, Reid's pictures, which have a depth of texture and dimension, are alive with human expression and colorful action. It is impossible to pick a favorite depiction—Mrs. Noah clambering aboard, her pockets and aprons laden with the seeds of every plant; old Noah's soulful blue eyes imploring the clay-clouded heavens; the diverse animals cozily tucked into every cranny of the rocking ship; the serene silhouette of the ark resting on the finally quiet sea at sunset; the jubilant cascading of creatures from the boat's belly when the waters recede, or the family resuming their farming

life against a rainbow-brightened sky. Each page offers visual treasures to attract a new generation to the enduring biblical tale.

Janet Summer

SOURCE: A review of *Two by Two*, in *School Librarian*, Vol. 41, No. 4, November, 1993, p. 148.

Two by two, told in rhyme (occasionally a little strained), is great fun. The crowded illustrations are of dough models of scenes from the story. Some scenes, especially the bustling interior of the ark, are intricate with many details and visual jokes to discover. It must have been written for infants, but readers of all ages were held by it. As an added extra, the last page has the tune to 'Who built the ark?,' with the original chorus and Barbara Reid's own rhymes as the verses. A useful book for a versatile teacher.

GIFTS (1994)

Kirkus Reviews

SOURCE: A review of *Gifts*, in *Kirkus Reviews*, January 1, 1996, pp. 64-65.

Lively Plasticine bas-reliefs depict scenes of [a] traveling grandmother and the gifts she brings to her granddaughter from around the world. Bogart offers rhyming questions and answers: "My grandma went to Switzerland,/ said: 'What would you have me bring?' 'Just a chunk of cheese/and a mountain, please,/and a bell that goes ding-a-ling-ling.'" As the grandmother proceeds through her journeys, she grows older while her granddaughter grows up; the exotic settings include India, Africa, Australia, Mexico, and the Arctic. Reid's now-familiar technique has grown steadily more inventive and these illustrations are astonishing. Whether in large, detailed landscapes or dramatic close-ups, the book contains a wealth of plastic effects, from the soft folds and textures of the grandmother's clothes to the sparkling bubbles of a foamy sea. The lyrical and lighthearted rhymes never convey the exuberance of the art but advance the story nicely by providing a sequence of cues for the pictures.

Jody McCoy

SOURCE: A review of *Gifts*, in *School Library Journal*, March, 1996, p. 166.

Another glorious, globetrotting grannie joins the ranks of elderly travelers. Unlike Jill Paton Walsh's *When Grandma Came*, Bogart's Grandma is a happy soul who offers to bring back "gifts." As she heads off to nine very different locales, she asks, "What would you have me bring?" Her granddaughter's exquisitely fanciful replies presented in rhyme celebrate the imagination: a piece of sky, a roar, billabong goo, a memory, a rainbow to wear as a ring, etc. Reid's wonderful Plasticine illustrations, with touches of acrylic for shine, seem so three-dimensional that they beg to be touched. The wealth of texture, depth, and detail is sure to mesmerize even the most jaded eye. The colors are scrumptious. The loving relationship between grandma and granddaughter as each ages is tenderly captured in hugs, smiles, and subtle physical changes. Perhaps this traveler doesn't carpet a town with lupines like Barbara Cooney's *Miss Rumphius,* nor is she as rambunctiously silly as the character in Grahame Base's *My Grandma Lived in Gooligulch,* but *Gifts* is a treasure to read alone, aloud, to a group, or to give to anyone who loves the unique.

THE PARTY (1997)

Gwyneth Evans

SOURCE: A review of *The Party,* in *Quill & Quire,* November, 1997, p. 46.

Barbara Reid's amazing ways with Plasticine are familiar to readers from her imaginative illustrations for a number of books such as *Have You Seen Birds?* and *The New Baby Calf,* but in this new book her invention and creativity seem as fresh as ever. Slices of ham with pineapple rings, expressive faces of different ages, party hats, lawn chairs and a shaggy dog—Reid manages to give them all a convincing texture and vitality on the page. As well as shaping Plasticine into pictures, Reid also composed the verse of the text here. In bouncing rhyme, a little girl gives a present-tense account of being taken with her younger sister to a family party. After some initial feelings of shyness and discomfort, the girls soon plunge into the pleasures of unstructured fun with the other children—running, spinning, laughing 'til it hurts, and eating lots of party food. The focus of most of the book is on movement, and both text and pictures give a vivid sense of physical experience of the moment, as the narrator suffers Aunt Joan's welcoming kiss, zips through the crowd of adults, and hides under the table to lick icing off candles.

We learn that this is Grandma's 90th birthday party, and the mixture of ages of the family party-goers, the huge fenced backyard where the event takes place, and the often-repeated refrain "at the party" combine to evoke a feeling of security and warmth. The pictures are full of amusing details, such as the many different kinds of shoes—all convincingly evoked in Plasticine—and the fat uncle finishing up leftovers as the table is cleared. Personalities and little dramas are suggested in the background: an early tableau of romping children is framed by a pair of droopy adolescents, caught between the generations and feeling too old to join in the fun, but a few pages later we see that they have found each other and are enjoying themselves. Reid skillfully presents the pictures from different angles and always suggests a strong

tactile awareness of the everyday world. Perhaps one of the most appealing qualities of her work, finally, is the way her own creativity with her medium tempts readers to find some modelling clay and try it too!

Jeanne Clancy Watkins

SOURCE: A review of *The Party,* in *School Library Journal,* May, 1999, pp. 95-6.

Polished, combed, and dressed in best bib and tucker, a young girl and her sister are dragged to a family gathering. The party gets off to a rough start with unavoidable kisses from icky Aunt Joan and initial shyness among the children, but the ice soon thaws during a lively game of sharks. Before long, all of the kids are having too much fun to even think about eating, but the buffet calls and then there's Gran's 90th birthday cake. Finally, they all join in a game of twilight hide-and-seek, hoping to postpone the inevitable because now they don't want to go home. Reid's rollicking verses, teamed with her signature Plasticine illustrations, capture the universal joys of a large extended family. The text rolls along at breathtaking pace as the children leap and laugh and their party clothes are reduced to grass-stained rumples. The artwork explodes with the energy used in playing, eating, and celebrating. Personalities burst from the pages and readers will enjoy seeing the mood of the narrator move from resentment and nervousness to happiness and eventually exhaustion. Storyhour participants will join in on the variable refrain—"We laugh till it hurts at the party" or "Leave room for dessert at the party" and, finally, "Oh, what a great time,/what a wonderful time,/such a very late time/at the party." Definitely an event to revisit and remember.

Ilene Cooper

SOURCE: A review of *The Party,* in *Booklist,* Vol. 95, No. 17, May 1, 1999, p. 1600.

Reid captures the experience of a family gathering; but before the fun starts, there are a few anxious moments. The narrator and her younger sister, "squirmy and shy," take the long ride to the relatives' house. There's too much kissing from the older folks and a bit of standoffishness from the cousins, but then the games start, and along with them comes the laughter. Reid uses Plasticine shaped into illustration boards for her art, and the three-dimensional effect is fresh and fetching. All the spreads demand second and third looks, but there are two that are quite remarkable. In the first, the cousins spin in circles, and by blurring the picture, Reid makes sure readers will get the full effect of the dizziness the characters feel. The other picture portrays a table laden with food. Everything from mashed potatoes and a jello mold to deviled eggs and a three-bean salad are meticulously detailed and look good enough to eat. The rhyming text scans well and tells its story, but it's the pictures that make this reunion one where readers will feel right at home.

Publishers Weekly

SOURCE: A review of *The Party,* in *Publishers Weekly,* Vol. 246, No. 18, May 3, 1999, p. 75.

"We are stuffed in the car with a cooler, some chairs,/ a bowl full of dip,/ and a tin full of squares." So goes the lament of two sisters who are dreading their grandmother's 90th birthday party. By day's end, however, they are singing a different tune: "We can't go right now!" "One more game!" "Can't we stay?" Reid's (*Two by Two*) keen awareness of a child's perspective informs both words and pictures; for instance, as the sisters arrive, the text "There's no way to miss being kissed by Aunt Joan" accompanies a picture of the aunt looming large, popping out of the spread with arms outstretched and lips puckered. Reid effectively shows the party evolving into a giddy free-for-all: one spread is deliberately blurred to capture the delicious dizziness that comes from spinning in circles. The Plasticine illustrations at times give the characters' facial expressions an unsettling, almost eerie quality, but overall this is visually enticing.

FUN WITH MODELING CLAY (1998)

Mary Beaty

SOURCE: A review of *Fun with Modeling Clay,* in *Quill & Quire,* March, 1998 p. 72.

Barbara Reid remains the undisputed doyenne of Plasticine illustration. In *Have You Seen Birds?* and *Effie,* she uses not just the medium, but perspective in remarkable ways. In 1997, she won the Governor General's Award for her illustrations in *The Party, Fun With Modeling Clay* is her most recent how-to book, and it's wonderful to have such a gifted artist share her skill with children in this way. Reid's techniques are intended for use with oil-based compounds such as Plasticine and Klean Klay. However, they also work with potter's clay or Fimo, synthetic clay that can be baked to permanent hardness.

For this book, Kids Can has taken selections from Reid's 1988 book, *Playing With Plasticine,* added colour illustrations and photos, and redesigned the whole. It's for children eight and up. This is a crucial stage, when most kids begin to feel their artwork is "no good." The vast majority of children stop creating visual art forever in the middle school years, so it is important to have books that encourage them to develop technique and continue to create work they can be proud of. *Fun With Modeling Clay* is such a book. Reid's simple, illustrated, step-by-step instructions introduce basic tools (all household items) and describe how to make 10 basic shapes. Then, with the same easy-to-follow instructions, she combines these 10 shapes to make animals, people, objects, and landscapes.

The creative details that are the hallmark of Reid's illustrations are present here. The results should please even the most self-critical child and help to build a growing sense of artistic competence.

Ellen Mandel

SOURCE: A review of *Fun with Modeling Clay,* in *Booklist,* Vol. 95, No. 1, September 1, 1998, p. 123.

After assembling everyday household items to use as tools, children can roll modeling clay into balls, pancakes, and snakes. From such basic beginning, youngsters are guided in step-by-step progression to create bugs, birds, cats, dogs, humans, and more. Just as Ed Emberley's drawing books lead novice artists on to ever more complex combinations of simple lines and circles, so Reid builds on the fundamentals until young sculptors are fashioning hockey players, fruit baskets, cars and trains, underwater and outer space scenes, and limitless other creations from lumps of clay. Colorful photographs of finished clay projects combine with inviting art that simulates clay's colors and texture as it demonstrates the lucidly outlined procedures. Aptly titled, this guide is sure to lead children into much fun with modeling clay.

Additional coverage of Reid's life and career is contained in the following source published by The Gale Group: *Something about the Author,* Vol. 93.

Harriette Gillem Robinet

1931 -

American author of historical novels for young adults.

Major works include *Children of the Fire* (1991), *Mississippi Chariot* (1994), *Washington City Is Burning* (1996), *The Twins, the Pirates, and the Battle of New Orleans* (1997), *Forty Acres and Maybe a Mule* (1998).

INTRODUCTION

Although Harriette Robinet began her career writing books for elementary graders about handicapped children, in *Jay and the Marigold* (1976) and *Ride the Red Cycle* (1980), she is known primarily for her young adult novels depicting the experiences of African Americans during the course of United States history. Based on historical fact and acclaimed for their complex characters and realism, Robinet's work has received consistent praise such as that conferred by Susan Dove Lempke in *Booklist*: "Robinet skillfully balances her in-depth historical knowledge with the feelings of her characters."

Her first entry into historical fiction, *Children of the Fire*, set in the time of the Great Fire in Chicago in 1871, has as its protagonist the orphaned daughter of runaway slaves who grows in sympathy and understanding through her experiences during and directly after the fire. As Robinet gained writing experience, her novels became less didactic and more clearly focused on the complexity of her characters and the difficulties of the situations they encounter. The majority of Robinet's protagonists are African American children who face the challenges of both tumultuous historic events and the difficulties imposed upon them because of their skin color. Seen through a child's eye, this double influence of political chaos and race give a new, little explored perspective on historic events such as the Great Depression in *Mississippi Chariot*, the South immediately after Civil War in *If You Please, President Lincoln* (1995) and *Forty Acres and Maybe a Mule*, and the War of 1812 in *Washington City Is Burning* and *The Twins, the Pirates, and the Battle of New Orleans*. Robinet has made valuable contributions to the genre of historic fiction about African Americans. She has been praised by one critic as frequently demonstrating "her ability to create a fictionalized yet credible slave/free black community whose members pursue highly individualized agendas against the backdrop of a larger historical movement."

Biographical Information

Robinet was born and raised in Washington D.C., spending her childhood summers in nearby Arlington, Virginia,

where her ancestors had been slaves. Educated as a bacteriologist, she had a full career in that field working for Children's Hospital in Washington, D.C., Walter Reed Army Medical Center, and the U.S. Army in the Quartermaster Corps. Her literary career was inspired by one of her sons, born with cerebral palsy, and her experiences meeting other handicapped children and adults who, according to an interview with *Something About the Author*, "have shared some of their anger, dreams, and victories" with her. Her interests later grew to encompass the history of African Americans, and her well-researched books have been a welcome and much needed addition to that genre.

Major Works

Robinet's first venture into historical fiction was *Children of the Fire*, set during the Great Fire in Chicago in 1871. Eleven-year-old Hallelujah, the orphaned daughter of escaped slaves, talks her kind guardians into letting her go to look at the fire. She becomes involved with other children who have been caught up in the chaos of the event and its aftermath. As she meets and helps the other children, her experiences begin to change her from a selfish and callous child to a sympathetic and thoughtful young woman. Although critics applauded Robinet's historical accuracy and the refreshing viewpoint of an African American protagonist in a vividly told story, there was general consensus that the writing was too didactic and heavy-handed in its moral lessons.

The title of Robinet's next book, *Mississippi Chariot*, is old slave code for racial violence. The story takes place in the Mississippi Delta during the Great Depression of the 1930s and follows events in the life of 12-year-old Abraham Lincoln Jackson, known as "Shortning Bread." His father, a poor sharecropper, has been convicted of a crime he did not commit and is working on a chain gang. Jackson carries out a plan to help his father escape, but the circumstances of life for African Americans defeat any hope of a return to normal life. In the grim ending, Jackson and his family escape a lynch mob, with the help of a white family, by changing their clothes—white townspeople cannot recognize African Americans who change their clothing—and escape to Chicago. Hazel Rochman writing for *Booklist* commented, "[T]he drama is compelling, the trickery both tense and funny. The sense of the sharecropper's struggle is an integral part of the story."

Washington City Is Burning takes place during the War of 1812 when the British bombarded and burned the capitol city. It is the story of Virginia, a 12-year-old house slave to President James Madison and his wife, Dolley. Virginia is surprised to learn that she has been chosen to serve in the White House by an older house slave because, as a child, she can engage in activities that would be too suspicious for an adult to undertake. In this way she becomes instrumental in aiding escaped slaves, but her need for affection and her conflicted emotions about her status as a slave in the White House lead her to a foolish, if inadvertent, betrayal of her trust. Critic Marie T. Wright, in her review for the *School Library Journal*, wrote, "the slaves' strengths and weaknesses, the hardships and triumphs they endure, and their interactions unfold as readers get information about important events and people in Washington City during the early 1800s."

The Twins, the Pirates, and the Battle of New Orleans also takes place during the War of 1812, but in a very different locale, the back country around New Orleans. Rescued by their father from slavery, twins Andrew and Pierre are left alone in a swamp while their father returns to free his wife and daughter. As indicated by the title, the boys must cope with alligators, pirates, bounty hunters, and various soldiers from the Battle of New Orleans roaming through the swamp. In the end, their father returns and pirate treasure buys freedom for their mother and sister. *Booklist*'s Kay Weisman called this book, "an ambitious novel—full of high adventure, natural detail, and historical particulars that will surprise many young readers."

Robinet explores the post–Civil War South in *Forty Acres and Maybe a Mule*. Winner of the Scott O'Dell Award for Historical Fiction, it tells the story of 12-year-old orphaned slave Pascal. Hearing that President Lincoln

has freed the slaves and that General Sherman has promised 40 acres and maybe a mule for every person, he sets off with his friends Nelly and Gideon to find a Freedmen's Bureau and obtain his share. Along the way they meet other former slaves, poor white farmers, night riders, and politicians. On their new farm in Georgia, they create a community, go to school, and raise a good crop of cotton, only to have it snatched away when President Johnson reverses the Land Act to include only whites. Despite the harshness of the outcome, Pascal remains hopeful in his sense of accomplishment as he and his friends set out to buy land on the Georgia Sea Islands. Hazel Rochman commented in *Booklist*, "The research is accurate but unobtrusive; the personal story dramatizes the hope, anguish, and bitter disappointment of slavery's aftermath."

Awards

Forty Acres and Maybe a Mule earned the Scott O'Dell Award for Historical Fiction in 1998.

TITLE COMMENTARY

JAY AND THE MARIGOLD (1976)

Children's Book Review Service, Inc.

SOURCE: A review of *Jay and the Marigold*, in *Children's Book Review Service, Inc.,* Vol. 5, No. 2, October, 1976, p. 16.

Jay is a severe cerebral palsy who is confined to a wheel chair and cannot speak understandably. As the book so amply states: "Jay's dreams and hopes and yearnings were locked up inside him." The book centers around the summer that Jay finally finds a friend, Pedro, who recognizes his abilities, not just his disabilities and Jay's observance of a marigold struggling to grow in a crack. (It is this that makes him determined to reach his fullest potential.) The story is beautifully told without playing on the reader's sympathies or pity.

School Library Journal

SOURCE: A review of *Jay and the Marigold*, in *School Library Journal,* Vol. 43, No. 1, January, 1977, p. 84.

Jay is so severely limited by cerebral palsy that at eight years old he can neither speak intelligibly nor control his motor behavior. He has no friends until Pedro, a new boy, who is an outsider himself at first, accepts Jay and draws him into the activities of the neighborhood children. Sentimental and didactic, the story likens Jay to a marigold which manages to bloom under the most unfavorable conditions. Although the illustrations depict cerebral palsy postures accurately neither Jay's personality or character come across. Stein's *About Handicaps,* which presents solid knowledge in a straightforward, unmanipulative fashion, remains the best treatment of the subject.

Bulletin of the Center for Children's Books

SOURCE: A review of *Jay and the Marigold,* in *Bulletin of the Center for Children's Books,* Vol. 30, No. 7, March, 1977, p. 113.

Eight-year-old Jay had cerebral palsy; he had been ignored or patronized by other children until his new friend Pedro, who understood how people can hurt you, brought him into the other children's activities. Jay, who had watched baseball on television, made a good umpire, the others discovered. When a stray marigold that grew in a crack of the concrete steps bloomed, Jay was so excited that he said a word, just as the therapist had taught him: "boom" for "bloom." He was sure, the story ends, that "one day—in spite of limitations, in spite of handicaps, in his own way, in his own time—he, too, would bloom." While the story, written by the mother of a child with cerebral palsy, makes it clear that such handicapped children are more intelligent than their peers realize, it is written in pedestrian style. The illustrations are often-awkward drawings, some chopped at the edges of pages.

Dorothy Fischer

SOURCE: A review of *Jay and the Marigold,* in *Curriculum Review,* Vol. 17, No. 4, October, 1978, pp. 269-70.

This is an overly long story about an eight-year-old boy with cerebral palsy. Jay's angry attitude about his limitations is changed after he notices a tender green shoot trying to grow in some concrete steps. His empathy for Pedro, a boy of another race, his acceptance by the neighborhood kids as a baseball umpire, along with his care for the tiny marigold give him faith in his own future. This book is too long for a lower level child to read alone, yet not stimulating enough for an older one. Teachers in grades 1-2 may want to read the book to their classes.

RIDE THE RED CYCLE (1980)

Karen M. Klockner

SOURCE: A review of *Ride the Red Cycle,* in *The Horn Book Magazine,* Vol. LVI, No. 3, June, 1980, p. 303.

Stricken at the age of two with an illness which damaged his brain and affected his entire body, Jerome, at eleven, feels dependent on others and lives with a mixture of emotions, often causing him to lash out at people. He dreams of owning a tricycle—but he isn't even able to walk. The book tells of his struggle to learn to ride the tricycle his father buys and adjusts for him. All summer long he works to make the pedals move but his "dream of success was becoming a nightmare. He felt foolish and silly, not being able to depend on his rotten old legs." When he finally displays his accomplishments on Labor Day, the whole neighborhood looks on and applauds. The simply written story conveys not only Jerome's physical struggle, but his emotional one to achieve individuality and self-respect. Moreover, tensions inherent in the family's situation are made clear. Among the countless recent books about handicapped children, the book stands out for its psychological acuity and compassion without sentimentality.

Booklist

SOURCE: A review of *Ride the Red Cycle,* in *Booklist,* Vol. 76, No. 20, June 15, 1980, p. 1534.

Jerome Johnson's eyes light up when he sees the oversized red tricycle at the bike shop: "Papa, Uh wannn-n tha' un," he calls out. Papa buys it, and Jerome starts working toward his biggest wish—to be able to ride it. Brain-damaged by a childhood virus, Jerome uses a wheelchair and has difficulty speaking. The cycle is his impetus to improve, and over the summer he masters it enough to triumphantly go public at a block party talent show—a success that also holds the promise that Jerome will one day walk. Robinet's simply written story of personal determination is burdened by some overdrawn characterizations and didactic intent: Mama's skeptical, complaining behavior may be accurate in concept, but as executed here seems stiff and artificial; ditto for some of Jerome's lashing out. On the plus side is the story's ultimate effectiveness in drawing readers in. Once past the bumpy exposition, they will be as moved as the crowd at Jerome's herculean bid to prove his ability.

Kirkus Reviews

SOURCE: A review of *Ride the Red Cycle,* in *Kirkus Reviews,* Vol. XLVIII, No. 14, July 15, 1980, pp. 911-2.

Jerome Johnson is eleven; he's confined to a wheelchair by a brain-injury suffered at age two; he's tired of being beholden to everyone (and expected to be grateful); and he desperately wants—as a step toward independence— a big red tricycle, the kind he once saw an old man riding. Presented just that way—baldly—the story still works. Jerome gets his cycle, then can't make his weak legs turn the wheels. He sits in front of the house, immobilized, until it seems he'll never be able to ride. Then he gets his sympathetic oldest sister to take him to a secret spot with a slight slope. While she reads, he struggles: "Soon Jerome could shake the cycle enough on the slope so that his right leg got down fast enough for the left leg to reach the top of its pedal. Then he could grunt the stiff leg down. He pedaled, but not always. He never could be sure." The day comes when he is sure, when his pedaling is the surprise hit of the block party, when—having practiced at night on his strengthened legs—he can actually walk a few steps; and now he can also, willingly, thank everyone who somehow helped. But such clutch-at-the-throat climaxes are relatively commonplace; what's notable here is the sheer concentration conveyed, and the self-faith. And, for some, the effort will seem all the more rewarding because Jerome—affectingly but never sentimentally pictured—is black.

Zena Sutherland

SOURCE: A review of *Ride the Red Cycle*, in *Bulletin of the Center for Children's Books,* Vol. 34 No. 3 November, 1980 p. 63.

Crippled by a virus infection when he was two, Jerome (age eleven, black, in fifth grade) was confined to a wheelchair and had a slow, slurred way of speaking, conveyed in the text by remarks like "Here muhhh cycle. Papa gonna fit it for to rrride!" Jerome's mother thinks it dangerous for the boy to have a tricycle, but his father feels that Jerome can learn. He not only learns, but he asks an older sister to help him in secret practice sessions; he astounds his parents by taking part in a Labor Day parade, and even walks a few steps from his cycle to his wheelchair. Written by the mother of a handicapped child, this is realistic in its details of Jerome's problems and his progress, but the writing style is rather stiff and the dialogue awkward in its use of phonetic spelling; "Boy don't havta be . . ." and "Hope yuh told yuh Papa . . ."

Sharon Wigutoff

SOURCE: "Junior Fiction: A Feminist Critique," in *The Lion and the Unicorn,* Vol. 5, 1981, pp. 4-18.

Ride the Red Cycle by Harriette Gillem Robinet [is], the story of Jerome, a black boy with cerebral palsy who learns with great difficulty to ride a tricycle. Anyone who has looked for good books about Third World children with disabilities knows that they are almost nonexistent. How disappointing, therefore, to see the mother in this book portrayed as unsympathetic and unsupportive, and to have Jerome refuse to be called Jerry because it sounded like a girl's name.

CHILDREN OF THE FIRE (1991)

The Bulletin of the Center for Children's Books

SOURCE: A review of *Children of the Fire*, in *The Bulletin of the Center for Children's Books,* The University of Chicago Press, Vol. 45, No. 1, September 1991, p. 20.

In a story about the Chicago fire of 1871, the protagonist is Hallelujah, who is black and orphaned. She lives with a kind couple, and feels guilty when she tricks them into promising her that she can go watch the next fire in that dry autumn when there were so many. The author has clearly done a great deal of research, and many of the historical details are of interest; unfortunately, such details crowd the story line so that the narrative is drawn-out and repetitive. Hallelujah meets other children, bringing a white child (separated from her parents in the confusion) home; several children join in selling fused glass and pieces of metal as souvenirs. Selfish and callous at first, Hallelujah gains sympathetic insight during the course of the fire and the start of rebuilding, but the character change seems imposed by authorial decision rather than emanating naturally in response to events.

Lucinda Snyder

SOURCE: A review of *Children of the Fire*, in *School Library Journal,* Vol. 37, No. 10, October, 1991, pp. 127-28

The Chicago fire of 1871 is seen as an adventure by 11-year-old Hallelujah. However, as she wanders the streets meeting the rich and poor of all races and religions dispossessed by the fire, she realizes that people's similarities are stronger than their differences. Hallelujah's maturation comes slowly and believably. Her mother was an escaped slave who brought her children safely to Chicago before dying, but Hallelujah is accustomed to an easier life with her foster parents. They have a house and give food to their unemployed Irish Catholic neighbors. Instead of being grateful, Hallelujah is often bossy and inconsiderate toward others. The night of the fire she becomes separated from her family and seeks excitement on her own. Moving around the city, she meets several "children of the fire," and gets to know Rachael, a poor Jewish girl, and wealthy, snobbish Elizabeth. Hallelujah ends up helping Elizabeth and the girls stay together for several days. They become friends, but the message gets heavy-handed when they vow to remember that "we're always free to be ourselves," and "we're all equally special." Although the persistent resurgence of the racial/economic tolerance theme can be distracting, the story is vividly told and full of interesting historical details. Robinet evokes a real sense of the destruction the fire caused and the residents' quick determination to rebuild. The well-realized setting and unusual characters counterbalance the story's didacticism, making the book an uneven but worthwhile effort.

Kirkus Reviews

SOURCE: A review of *Children of the Fire*, in *Kirkus Reviews,* Vol. LIX, No. 19, October 1, 1991, p. 1292.

In search of adventure, feisty 11-year-old Hallelujah escapes the watchful eye of her guardian and watches

Chicago burn down around her during one memorable October week.

Meticulously, Robinet re-creates the events of the 1871 fire. Hallelujah wanders about, witnessing behavior both brave and cowardly; performing some brave deeds of her own; alternating between excitement, horror at the destruction, and guilt that she is enjoying the experience; and meeting a succession of people—including Elizabeth, a wealthy, newly homeless white girl who lives with Hallelujah until her snooty parents track her down.

The characters here are less well developed than the themes; adults can sound childlike ("Lordy, Mr. Joseph, what have you done did?") while children sound like adults ("We're both children. We have the same feelings and needs . . ."), but Hallelujah sees many people put aside their racial prejudices and pitch in to begin rebuilding. The message sits a bit heavily, and there are some careless repetitions; still, this child's-eye view of a great event should appeal to readers with a historical bent.

Sheilamae O'Hara

SOURCE: A review of *Children of the Fire*, in *Booklist*, Vol. 88, No. 4, October 15, 1991, p. 441.

She was named Hallelujah by her father because she was born at sunrise on Easter morning. She was born into slavery in Mississippi but escaped with her parents and sister. Though her father died before reaching freedom, her mother guided her children to Chicago, where they were taken in by the La Salles, who raised the sisters after their mother died. At age 11, Hallelujah is a feisty scapegrace, practicing assertiveness a whole century before it became a feminist ideal. She resents being an orphan and hates being reminded of her dependent position. On October 8, 1871, she deliberately evades her stepbrother and spends the entire night following the path of the Great Chicago Fire. Robinet demonstrates a thorough knowledge of Chicago history, geography, and demographics, and, with minor exceptions—such as calling Adams Street, Adam Street and Desplaines St., Des Plains Street—her information is accurate. Sometimes, though, she seems to spread historical data with a trowel. Her writing is least effective when she has children interacting. After the fire, Hallelujah and a friend talk about the changes in their outlooks like a couple of sanctimonious 80-year-olds. However, Robinet is very effective in describing the beauty and the horror of the conflagration and the reactions of the people caught up in it. Her prose captures the heat, smells, and feel of the night when people struggled to save their most valuable possessions and then abandoned them to save their lives. For these fine descriptions and for the characterization of the indomitable Hallelujah, the novel deserves a place on historical fiction shelves.

Publishers Weekly

SOURCE: A review of *Children of the Fire*, in *Publishers Weekly*, Vol. 238, No. 46, October 18, 1991, p. 62.

Robinet makes history come alive in this riveting account of the Great Chicago Fire as witnessed by an orphaned African American girl. Eager for adventure, Hallelujah, a former slave, follows her foster brother through city streets to watch the conflagration that has started in Chicago's West Division. Excitement turns to fear when the 11-year-old girl sees rows of buildings engulfed in flames and realizes how many people have lost their homes. During the next few hours, as she weaves her way through crowds, experiences the chaos that is the aftermath of destruction and shares the pain of loss with strangers, Hallelujah learns how all people become equals in times of crisis. Hallelujah emerges as a likeable, spunky heroine who discovers her self-worth during the course of events. Readers will feel the intensity of her emotions and will applaud her ability to cling to hope in the midst of disaster.

Voice of Youth Advocates

SOURCE: A review of *Children of the Fire*, in *Voice of Youth Advocates*, Vol. 14, No. 5, December, 1991, p. 318.

Eleven year old Hallelujah, born a slave, is now living in Chicago as the foster child of the La Salles, Miss Tilly and Mr. Joseph. Hallelujah is used to getting what she wants, and what she wants is to see for herself one of the fires plaguing the drought-stricken city this October of 1871. So, when Miss Tilly says "no," she tricks Mr. Joseph into giving permission. Entrusted to the safekeeping of her grown-up foster brother Joseph Edward, Hallelujah soon breaks free, and is on her own for the Great Chicago Fire.

What follows is a young person's view of a Chicago hard for the modern reader to imagine, a Chicago of wooden sidewalks, pig sties, hen houses, stables, corn cribs, and sheds. The rich ethnic mix that is the city today is just being established with the then-recent immigrants from western Europe, Scandinavia, and the Slavic countries, as well as a growing black population: many, like Hallelujah, escaped from slavery. Like any city in any time, there are the rich and the poor; but, in this instance, they are all in equal jeopardy from a disaster that acknowledges no social boundaries. Like lots of folks, my sense of history is perhaps not as well developed as it should be—I had never thought of people who had escaped from slavery and the Great Chicago Fire as being in the same time frame, and I found that juxtaposition fascinating, a whole different slant on what began with Mrs. O'Leary's barn. The concept of the fire as a social equalizer is a good one. My only disappointment is that the author is a trifle heavy-handed sometimes in making her point—for instance, there are passages of dialogue between Hallelujah and the little rich white girl, Elizabeth, which are decidedly un-childlike and didactic. I think most readers, including the young middle school audience I recommend this for, are capable of appreciating a degree of subtlety, and respond more positively to it. It's a promising first effort, however, just the right length and reading level for many sixth and seventh graders, and a welcome, as well as needed, addition to historical fiction with black characters for this age group. Recommend also the *Once Upon America* series begun last year by Viking (*Hero Over Here,* Kathleen V. Kudlinski and *A Long Way to Go,* Zibby O'Neal), and the popular *American Girls* series from Pleasant Co.

Joanne Schott

SOURCE: A review of *Children of the Fire,* in *Quill and Quire,* January, 1992, pp. 33-4.

Hallelujah's status as an orphan defines her perception of herself, though she and her sister have been lovingly cared for by the family who sheltered them and their runaway slave mother, dead several years when the story begins. Fires have plagued Chicago in the fall of 1871 and when Hallelujah at last gets to watch one, she thinks of it merely as a spectacle. It is the destruction of the beautiful courthouse which first moves her to shame at her enjoyment. Looking in a new way at the fire's effects on people's lives gives her insight. Befriending and helping a girl separated from her family and performing an important service for the city give her a sense of worth.

Hallelujah's meetings with people of many backgrounds seem dictated by the need for her to draw particular conclusions, and her ruminations about equality have a rhetoric that is not quite natural. No reader will doubt, however, that Hallelujah's experiences in the Chicago fire are great enough to work changes in her. The recreation of these scenes is one of the book's strengths and the memory of them will remain with the reader.

Mary Harris Veeder

SOURCE: A review of *Children of the Fire,* in *Chicago Tribune Books,* February 9, 1992, p. 7.

Orphaned Hallelujah, named for her Easter Sunday birth in slavery, is living in Chicago by October 1871, a Chicago vigorous, thriving and filled with different and differing racial and ethnic groups. The events of the Chicago Fire are brought to life as they would have been experienced by the children of 1871, in streets and places Chicagoans will recognize. Young readers will recognize as well Hallelujah's need for friends and a sense of herself. This book provides a good way to get past Mrs. O'Leary's cow.

MISSISSIPPI CHARIOT (1994)

Booklist

SOURCE: A review of *Mississippi Chariot,* in *Booklist,* Vol. 91, No. 6, November 15, 1994, p. 591.

Life in the Mississippi Delta in the 1930s is vividly evoked in this story of 12-year-old Shortning Bread Jackson, whose father has been wrongfully accused and sent to the chain gang. Using every trick and disguise and false rumor he can, the boy plots to get his father released, and in the last few chapters, the family escapes the lynch mob and leaves for Chicago. There's some awkward contrivance in the plot—Shortning conveniently saves a white boy from drowning, and the grateful parents help the Jacksons escape—but the drama is compelling, the trickery both tense and funny. The sense of the sharecroppers' struggle is an integral part of the story. The book title refers to the old hymn "Chariot Coming for to Carry Me Home," a code from slavery days to warn of danger. Daily life is desperate, and white power and bigotry seem overwhelming, but one smart boy's determination sets his family free.

Kirkus Reviews

SOURCE: A review of *Mississippi Chariot,* in *Kirkus Reviews,* Vol. LXII, No. 22, November 15, 1994, p. 1541.

It's 1936 in rural Mississippi, and Abraham Lincoln Jackson, or Shortning Bread, as everyone calls him, is on a mission. On his 12th birthday he takes the afternoon off from picking cotton with his brothers to set in motion a plan that will free his father from the chain gang. Everyone in town, black and white, knows that good, kind Rufus Jackson didn't steal John Putnam's car. John's son confessed to having taken the car himself. Still, Sheriff Titus Clark sent Rufus away as a warning to the black community. That was two years ago, and Shortning realizes that nobody will help his father but him. He concocts a story about the FBI investigating his father's case and arranges it so that a white stranger drives into town and seems to talk to the sheriff about Rufus. (He's doing nothing of the kind, but everyone—even Shortning's sister, Peanuts—is convinced that the stranger is really from the FBI.) With the help of Hawk Baker, a white boy whom Shortning saved from drowning, and Hawk's father, Rufus is released from the chain gang. But the family must flee before Rufus is lynched by the sheriff and his men. Shortning dresses the whole family up in clothes from the church charity box—the white townspeople don't recognize blacks when they change clothing—and the family sneaks away to Chicago.

Robinet's (***Children of the Fire,*** 1991, etc.) character, Shortning, is ingenious and endearing.

Ann W. Moore

SOURCE: A review of *If You Please, President Lincoln,* in *School Library Journal,* Vol. 41, No. 6, June, 1995, p. 132.

Depression-era rural Mississippi is a good time and place for blacks to keep their heads down and their mouths shut, but Rufus Jackson has been two years working on the chain gang for a car theft he didn't commit, and on his 12th birthday, Abraham Lincoln "Shortning Bread" Jackson decides to get his father back, somehow. One of a large, hard-working sharecropper family, Shortning Bread is enterprising and intelligent, an appreciative butterfly watcher who chews over the ethics of trickery v. open confrontation. Against his better judgment, he develops a secret friendship with Hawk Baker, son of the (white) postmaster. In the end, although Shortning Bread creates a stir by starting a rumor that the FBI is coming to town, it's Hawk's father who actually brings Rufus home. Knowing that his return will inevitably spark "Mississippi chariot"—the old slave code for racial violence—the Jackson family quickly and quietly departs for Chicago. Robinet gives readers a good, long look at how the deck was stacked against African Americans, but she only sketches most of her characters, and the glimmer of light she places at the end of the tunnel is faint indeed.

IF YOU PLEASE, PRESIDENT LINCOLN (1995)

John Peters

SOURCE: A review of *Mississippi Chariot,* in *School Library Journal,* Vol. 40, No. 12, December, 1994, pp. 112-3.

In December 1863 Moses, a 14-year-old slave, runs away from his Maryland master rather than be sold South. He befriends Goshen, a blind free black, and the two are enticed onto a ship with promises of work. The voyage, however, takes them—and 400 others—to an uninhabited island off Haiti, as part of an ill-conceived colonization scheme. Weeks of hunger, sickness, hardship, struggle, and death follow. Moses—educated, energetic, and healthy—becomes the group's leader. By the time the captives are rescued and returned to the United States, Moses has acquired a "family," established an identity, and come to appreciate his race. While Robinet's story is interesting and unusual, it doesn't entirely succeed. Moses's confused feelings about slavery are inconsistently presented and inadequately discussed. His voice in this first-person narrative borders on quaintness. His rapid rise to leadership is unrealistic (and the cover doesn't help by showing a much younger boy). Finally, Robinet is both overly moralistic and incredibly optimistic (nary a harsh act among 400 people on a miserable island?). *If You Please, President Lincoln* may be worth purchasing for the new insight it provides about white attitudes toward, and projects involving, blacks. Nevertheless, it fails to reach the high quality of books such as Gary Paulsen's *Nightjohn* and Mary Stolz's *Cezanne Pinto.*

Publishers Weekly

SOURCE: A review of *If You Please, President Lincoln,* in *Publishers Weekly,* Vol. 242, No. 26, June 26, 1995, p. 107.

Freedom is not a purely political state, as is amply demonstrated in this powerful novel. Moses, an enslaved youth on Maryland's Eastern Shore, is not emancipated by Lincoln's proclamation in 1863—because he lives in Union territory. Learning that he is to be sold, he escapes and fends briefly for himself in Washington, D.C. There he begins to grow out of the dependent patterns of childhood and to reject the self-serving preaching of his former owner, a priest: "My mind knew right from wrong at last." But he is entrapped by an ill-planned scheme to export freed slaves—this development is based on a historical incident—and with 400 other African Americans he is shipped to a small, barren island off the coast of Haiti. As a leader of what proves to be a cohesive, hard-working group, he finally sheds his last psychological shackles. Back in the States, he begins to plan for a college education. And he begins to tell his story himself, in a slightly formal style and vocabulary that evoke the 19th century without slowing the reader. Robinet (*Mississippi Chariot*) combines desert-island drama with an insightful story of a mind gradually freeing itself.

Carolyn Phelan

SOURCE: A review of *If You Please, President Lincoln,* in *Booklist,* Vol. 91, No. 22, August, 1995, p. 1947.

A historical novel with an exciting plot, convincing characters, and a most original setting. When the first-person story begins, the year is 1863 and narrator Moses is the 14-year-old house slave of a Jesuit priest in Maryland. Escaping to freedom, Moses tries to find work on a ship, but he is shanghaied by Bernard Kock, a man who plans to colonize a Haitian island with emancipated slaves. Conditions on board are wretched, and when the ship reaches desolate Isle a Vache, the enormity of Kock's madness and his passengers' danger becomes all too clear. Through courage and resourcefulness, Moses delivers his fellow colonists from certain death. In the appended Author's Note, Robinet details her research into the history of the actual Isle a Vache expedition. Readers may well conclude that historical research can be more fascinating than writing fiction, even fiction as dramatic as this novel.

Elizabeth Bush

SOURCE: A review of *If You Please, President Lincoln,* in *The Bulletin of the Center for Children's Books,* Vol. 49, No. 1, September, 1995, p. 27.

Free land, free transportation, free tools, and cotton seed. It seems irresistible to some four hundred recently emancipated blacks who don't recognize the offer for what it really is—a plan to remove them to foreign soil, where they won't compete with white American laborers. As they wait, unfed, aboard a cramped ship for the promoters to negotiate fees and contracts, the hapless passengers realize this is only a foretaste of the miseries that await them in their promised land of Isle à Vache, Haiti. Moses of Father Fitzpatrick, a well-educated house slave who has run away from his Jesuit master to avoid being sold South, organizes his fellow "colonists" after they are virtually marooned on an island with barren soil and no fresh water. The tale is based on an actual colonization scheme which Robinet discusses in a concluding note; although details of island life cannot be verified, fictionalized characters are well-developed and the imagined sequence of events from landing to rescue is credibly delineated. Moses' lapses into platitude ("Hardships challenge people to rise or to fall in the virtues of patience and industry and sharing") and bursts of indignation ("How dare some people keep others as slaves? What injustice!") interject a tone of preaching and pedantry that seriously undermines his otherwise warmly personal narration. Still, Moses is a complex protagonist, whose struggle to control his own arrogance toward his less gifted and educated comrades lends insight into a legacy of slavery that threatened solidarity within new free black communities.

Voice of Youth Advocates

SOURCE: A review of *If You Please, President Lincoln,* in *Voice Of Youth Advocates,* Vol. 18, No. 4, October, 1995, pp. 223-4.

An 1864 attempt to colonize slaves is related by fourteen-year-old Moses. After his "Aunt" Rebekah dies, Moses escapes from the home of Father Fitzpatrick where he is a house slave, meets a blind man named Goshen and together they get on a ship in Annapolis full of former slaves going to an island off Haiti. Moses becomes the leader because he can read and has gumption. The passengers face many hardships from starvation and disease on the ship and the island. Finally, Moses goes to Haiti on a barrel boat in shark infested water. He asks that the Haitians tell President Lincoln to send a boat for them. Two weeks later a boat comes and they go back. Moses and Goshen live in a Washington, DC, boardinghouse and eventually Moses's wish for schooling and Goshen's desire for a career and wife are met. The book ends with an author's note that explains the historical background of the story.

This is involving historical fiction from a little-known time. The book would work well as a read-aloud. Moses is a good role model because of his sense of responsibility and emotional and physical strength. The author writes from her experience of living in Washington, DC, and having slave relatives. One of the author's other juvenile books is *Children of the Fire* (1991) about a black girl who lives through the Chicago fire.

WASHINGTON CITY IS BURNING (1996)

Kirkus Reviews

SOURCE: A review of *Washington City is Burning,* in *Kirkus Reviews,* Vol. LXIV, No. 14, July 15, 1996, p. 1055.

Virginia is a slave in the house of President James Madison and his wife, Dolley; she was brought north from the state of Virginia to serve them at the White House in the month preceding the British invasion of Washington. While there she helps transport numerous runaway slaves to safety, inadvertently betrays 12 of them, and witnesses the British sacking of the city. This backstairs view of a slice of history is riveting for its period detail; Dolley Madison's extravagant parties, the trader slaves being marched past the White House, and the burning of the city are seen through the eyes of this bright and courageous 12-year-old who is both witness to and part of history. The characters—and their actions and ethics—are complex, especially Rosetta Bell, a slave who betrays her own people out of bitterness over the loss of her daughter and her own longing for freedom, and Dolley, who was brought up to believe slavery was wrong, yet keeps slaves out of political expediency. A fine, multilayered novel.

School Library Journal

SOURCE: A review of *Washington City is Burning,* in *School Library Journal,* Vol. 42, No. 11, November, 1996, p. 110.

Robinet has used some events of the War of 1812 and other historical facts as the background for this first-person fictionalized narrative. Virginia, or Virgie as Dolley Madison insists on calling her, recounts her life as a young slave of James and Dolley Madison. The strengths of this story are the author's use of the personal-journal style, the incorporation of real facts and people from the African-American community, and the attitudes of the British during that period of our history. Robinet evokes both empathy and dislike for her young heroine as Virginia recounts how she foolishly reveals secret information about slave escapes while trying to get some affection from a traitorous, hateful female slave. The slaves' strengths and weaknesses, the hardships and triumphs they endure, and their interactions unfold as readers get information about important events and people in Washington City during the early 1800s. The author's note will help readers get a better perspective about the truths in this work of fiction. This book could be introduced along with Patricia and Frederick McKissack's *Christmas in the Big House, Christmas in the Quarters.* The dialogue has the nuance of slave speech, but it will not deter readers. An above-average choice for historical-fiction shelves.

Children's Book Review Service, Inc.

SOURCE: A review of *Washington City is Burning,* in *Children's Book Review Service, Inc.,* Vol. 25, No. 3, November, 1996, pp. 35-6.

Virginia isn't an average child of 1814, nor an average slave. She works in President Madison's house and is part of a group helping slaves escape to freedom. The reader will get a good feel for life as a slave in a wealthy household, conditions for those less fortunate, basic relations between the races, the running of the President's home, and Washington life during the War of 1812. Customs, food and dress are carefully portrayed. Parts of the exciting story may seem far-fetched, but it's based on fact, and Robinet explains where fact and fiction meet. An interesting story with an engaging, plucky heroine.

Ilene Cooper

SOURCE: A review of *Washington City is Burning,* in *Booklist,* Vol. 93, No. 5, November 1, 1996, p. 501.

As the story begins, a thrilled Virginia is on her way from James Madison's country home to Washington City, where the president and his wife, Dolley, now reside. She is surprised to learn that another house slave, Tobias, chose her to work at the White House. Virginia will have the opportunity to help slaves escape—because she is a child she can do things that would be too suspicious for an adult to undertake. Set in August 1814, as the war with the British comes to the door of the White House, this historical novel neatly incorporates many interesting details of the era. Equally well drawn is the character of Virginia. Robinet captures Virginia's conflicting feelings about her status. On the one hand, she is proud to be at the White House and flattered when Miss Dolley takes an interest in her, but on the other hand, she is angry at the condition of her people. The decisions she makes, not all good ones, stem from these mixed emotions A good adjunct to history units or just a good read.

Elizabeth Bush

SOURCE: A review of *Washington City is Burning,* in *The Bulletin of the Center for Children's Books,* Vol. 50, No. 4, December, 1996, p. 151.

It's August of 1814, and as the British advance on the young nation's capitol, members of the city's slave and free black community, and particularly those attached to the Madison family at the White House, use the turmoil and confusion as a cover to spirit slaves out of the auction pens (known as "trader slaves") and off to freedom. Tobias, one of President Madison's slaves, has recruited the help of Virginia (who narrates the tale), a teenaged house slave who once proved her bravery before an overseer at Montpelier. But Virginia's need for affection and approval causes her to leak information about the clandestine activities and jeopardize the lives of other slaves. Robinet again demonstrates her ability to create a fictionalized yet credible slave/free black community whose members pursue highly individualized agendas against the backdrop of a larger historical movement. Too often, however, Virginia indulges in "What will happen next?" outbursts, creating melodrama where more subtly deployed tension is required. Robinet clearly states in her end notes that "as far as I know, there were no trader slaves held or clothed at the White House." It is therefore a bit of a stretch to construct a tale which so closely involves major historical figures upon the premise that "on the other hand, I have no proof that they did not assist escapes, either." Those who are not concerned with historiographical quibble, however, will find much to enjoy in this speculation on slave resistance in the ultimate upper-crust household. A bibliography is included.

THE TWINS, THE PIRATES, AND THE BATTLE OF NEW ORLEANS (1997)

Kay Weisman

SOURCE: A review of *The Twins, the Pirates, and the Battle of New Orleans,* in *Booklist,* Vol. 94, No. 6, November 15, 1997, p. 561.

After their rescue from slavery by their father, Jacques, twins Andrew and Pierre are left alone in a swamp southeast of New Orleans while Jacques tries to liberate his wife and daughter. When he fails to return, the boys must fend for themselves, coping with alligators, pirates, limestone caves, bounty hunters, and myriad assorted soldiers on hand for the Battle of New Orleans. The twins manage to survive and, with the help of their father's pirate treasure, purchase the release of their mother and sister. This is an ambitious novel—full of high adventure, natural detail, and historical particulars that will surprise many young readers (for instance, General Andrew Jackson enlisted the help of Jean Lafitte and his Pirate Brotherhood at the Battle of New Orleans). Filled with believable characters spun from thorough research, Robinet's portrayal of Louisiana in 1814, as seen through the eyes of African American children makes this a welcome addition to the historical fiction shelves. Her *Washington City Is Burning* (1996) offers another perspective on this time period.

School Library Journal

SOURCE: A review of *The Twins, the Pirates, and the Battle of New Orleans,* in *School Library Journal,* Vol. 43, No. 12, December, 1997, p. 130.

This watery adventure begins with escaped slave twins, Pierre and Andrew, happening upon a pirate island while exploring the Gulf Coast swampland where their father has left them. The boys have been deliberately set against one another by their master, and are in the awkward process of getting acquainted. Pierre is more outwardly cautious than Andrew, although he eventually realizes that there are many types of bravery. It is December 1814, and the events leading up to the Battle of New Orleans take shape around the brothers as they explore and wait for their father's return. As time passes, the boys realize that something has gone wrong, and they must devise their own plan for freeing their mother and younger sister, who were sold several years before. Unfortunately, the characterization of the twins is slight, with readers usually being told rather than shown how they feel. The third-person narrative is related mainly from Pierre's viewpoint and seems stilted at times. The title may attract readers, but the pacing may not be enough to sustain them. Though not a first purchase, the book provides a new perspective on the Battle of New Orleans, and could be useful in conjunction with historical study of the period, for Robinet's weaving of fact with fiction is accurate and informed.

Mary M. Burns

SOURCE: A review of *The Twins, the Pirates, and the Battle of New Orleans*, in *The Horn Book Guide to Children's and Young Adult Books*, Vol. IX, No. 1, Spring, 1998, p. 80.

Used to dancing in tandem to entertain their master but raised separately, Pierre and Andrew, twelve-year-old twins and fugitive slaves, must not only survive in the swamps near New Orleans but also elude capture and work together to rescue their mother and sister. Action occasionally bogs down in description in this book that features cameo appearances by Jean Lafitte and Andrew Jackson.

Annette Thibodeaux

SOURCE: A review of *The Twins, the Pirates, and the Battle of New Orleans*, in *The Book Report*, Vol. 16, No. 5, March/April, 1998, p. 36.

The essence of Louisiana swamp life in the early 1800s is captured in this tale of twin 12-year-old slaves. Andrew and Pierre are taken from the slave owner, Marquis De Ville, by their father to a swamp hideout. They encounter Jean Lafitte and his band of pirate outlaws, as well as forces of the American and British troops prior to their confrontation at the Battle of New Orleans. Andrew and Pierre prove to be quite resourceful in their attempts to remain free and survive in the swamp while they make preparations to free their mother and sister who are awaiting the auction block in New Orleans. This novel represents the best in historical fiction and will capture the interest of middle schoolers as they study American history. This would also be an excellent read-aloud for social studies classes. *Recommended.*

FORTY ACRES AND MAYBE A MULE (1998)

Publishers Weekly

SOURCE: A review of *Forty Acres and Maybe a Mule*, in *Publishers Weekly*, Vol. 245, No. 44, November 2, 1998, p. 83.

In this novel set in April through September of 1865, Robinet's *(The Twins, the Pirates, and the Battle of New Orleans)* resilient characters lend immediacy to the early events of Reconstruction. Orphaned 12-year-old Pascal is a slave at the Big House on a South Carolina plantation when his runaway brother Gideon, a Union soldier, returns, proclaiming that Lincoln has freed the slaves and General Sherman has promised 40 acres and maybe a mule for both blacks and whites. Pascal, his friend Nelly and Gideon set off in search of a Freedmen's Bureau (where land is deeded) and finally find one in Georgia. Along the way they encounter other former slaves, two of whom they "adopt" as family; poor white farmers (among them the Bibbs family who become neighbors, and with whom they begin a moving friendship); night riders and Republican operatives eager to recruit new voters. Robinet compellingly demonstrates how the courage and determination of Pascal and Gideon's small band transform their 40 acres into a model farm. But there's no sugar-coating here: just as their perfect cotton crop matures, President Johnson reverses his land acts to declare that only white families can own the 40-acre plots of free land. Even this devastating development doesn't attenuate Pascal's sense of accomplishment ("Maybe nobody gave freedom, and nobody could take it away like they could take away a family farm. Maybe freedom was something you claimed yourself"). A stirring story of self-determination.

Susan Dove Lempke

SOURCE: A review of *Forty Acres and Maybe a Mule*, in *Booklist*, Vol. 95, No. 9/10, January 1, 1999, p. 879.

Two years after the Emancipation Proclamation, Pascal's older brother Gideon returns to the plantation where the slaves still work, not realizing they have been freed. Pascal, Gideon, and another child, Nelly, set out to claim the 40 acres Gideon hears have been promised to freed slaves. Throughout the story the tension between the joy of freedom and the dangers of the enraged white southerners tugs at the characters as they farm their new land, attend school, and hear terrible stories. Robinet skillfully balances her in-depth historical knowledge with the feelings of her characters, creating a story that moves along rapidly and comes to a bittersweet conclusion. A fine historical novel that explores the immediate postwar period for African Americans and their white friends and neighbors.

Hazel Rochman

SOURCE: A review of *Forty Acres and Maybe a Mule*, in *Booklist*, Vol. 95, No. 12, February 15, 1999, p. 1068.

In this landmark novel, the attempt of the newly freed slaves to build a home of their own is told through the eyes of a child who remembers the cruelty and separation done to his family in bondage. The research is accurate but unobtrusive; the personal story dramatizes the hope, anguish, and bitter disappointment of slavery's aftermath. Winner of the 1998 Scott O'Dell Award for Historical Fiction.

Additional coverage of Robinet's life and career is contained in the following sources published by The Gale Group: *Black Writers,* **Vol. 2;** *Contemporary Authors,* **Vols. 69-72;** *Contemporary Authors New Revision Series,* **Vol. 42; and** *Something about the Author,* **Vols. 27, 104.**

The Time Machine

H. G. Wells

(Full name Herbert George Wells; also wrote under the pseudonyms Sosthenes Smith, Walter Glockenhammer, and Reginald Bliss) English novelist, short story writer, historian, essayist, nonfiction writer, critic, and autobiographer.

Major works include *The Time Machine* (1895), *The Island of Dr. Moreau* (1896), *The Invisible Man* (1897), *The War of the Worlds* (1898), *The War in the Air* (1908).

The following entry presents criticism on *The Time Machine*.

INTRODUCTION

Wells is best known today as one of the progenitors of modern science fiction who foretold an era of chemical warfare, atomic weaponry, and world wars. *The Time Machine, The Invisible Man, The War of the Worlds, The Island of Dr. Moreau,* and several other works in Wells's canon are classics in the field of science fiction that have profoundly influenced the course of the genre. Although his science fiction works are predominantly informed by a pessimistic, apocalyptic vision that proved the major shaping force on the classic dystopian fiction of the twentieth century, in later speculative works such as *The World Set Free, The Shape of Things to Come,* and *Guide to the New World* Wells developed an ideal of a potential utopian millennium that he believed to be attainable by humankind. As a polemicist, Wells's strident advocacy of free love and socialism, as well as his attacks on what he considered the stifling moral constraints of society, are credited with contributing to the liberalization of modern Western culture. Wells's first book-length scientific romance, *The Time Machine* is now one of his most admired novels. While there had been many time-travel narratives before *The Time Machine,* Wells revolutionized the genre by explaining that time travel might be possible using scientific means rather than fantastic means. The protagonist in Mark Twain's *A Connecticut Yankee in King Arthur's Court* (1889), for example, travels to the Middle Ages from the nineteenth century as a result of a blow on the head. In contrast, Well's protagonist visits the year A.D. 802,701 using the time machine he has built. Thus Wells created a distinction that led to the evolution of the modern science fiction genre in the twentieth century.

Biographical Information

Wells was born into a lower-middle-class Cockney family in Bromley, Kent, a suburb of London, in 1866. Struggling to escape the unrewarding existence that had

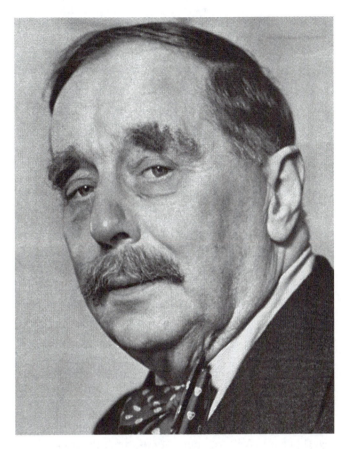

defeated his parents, Wells attended London University and the Royal College of Science, where he studied zoology. One of his professors, the noted biologist T. H. Huxley, instilled in Wells a belief in social as well as biological evolution, which Wells later cited as the single most important and influential aspect of his education. After graduation from London University, Wells wrote a biology textbook and tried his hand at writing fiction, contributing short stories to several magazines. The serialization of his short novel *The Time Machine* brought him his first substantial critical notice—he was hailed as a literary genius by a critic for the *Review of Reviews*— and launched his career. The writing of science fiction and science fantasies occupied the earliest part of his career and brought him great popular and critical attention. As his popularity grew, Wells was enabled by his burgeoning fame to meet Arnold Bennett, Joseph Conrad, and other prominent authors of the day, with whom he exchanged criticism and opinions on the art of writing. His own theory and style of writing was basically journalistic and was acquired while serving under editor Frank Harris as literary critic at the *Saturday Review*. Wells gradually turned from writing entertaining fiction to works that addressed the social and political problems of England and the world. Several socially concerned, comedic novels followed the science fiction works. In such works as *The Wheels of Chance, Kipps: The Story of a Simple Soul,* and *The History of Mr. Polly,* lower-middle-class characters are depicted living at odds with the downtrodden society in which Wells himself had been raised. A socialist, Wells joined the Fabian Society in 1903, but he left the group after fighting a long, unsuccessful battle of wit and rhetoric over some of the group's policies with his friend, the prominent Fabian and man of letters Bernard Shaw. Wells's socialist thought, combined with a belief in the gradual perfection of humanity through evolution and scientific innovation, is expressed in the serious fiction and prognostications that gradually succeeded the humorous character novels during the first decade of the twentieth century. By 1914, through such works as *Anticipations of the Reaction of Mechanical and Scientific Progress upon Human Life and Thought, A Modern Utopia,* and *The New Machiavelli,* Wells was established in the public mind as a leading proponent of socialism, world government, free thought, and free love, and as an enemy of many elements of Edwardian thought and morality.

Before World War I, Wells's name was commonly linked with that of Shaw as an advocate of the new, the iconoclastic, and the daring. But the war and its aftermath of widespread disillusionment upset his optimistic vision of humankind. During the war, as evidenced by the essay *God the Invisible King* and the novel *Mr. Britling Sees It Through,* Wells turned temporarily to belief in God—a belief that he later vigorously repudiated. His postwar ideas on humanity's perfectibility were modified to stress the preeminent importance of education in bringing about progress. In his ambitious two-volume work *The Outline of History,* a composition written to further the cause of world peace, Wells attempted to illustrate the commonality of the origins and histories of the world's peoples. The subject of much critical discussion, *The Outline of History* sparked one of the most celebrated literary debates of the 1920s, between Wells and his long-time antagonist, the Catholic polemicist Hilaire Belloc. Objecting to Wells's naturalistic, Darwinian view of world history, Belloc attacked the *Outline* as a simpleminded, non-scientific, anti-Catholic document. A war of mutual refutation was fought by both writers in the pages of several books and essays. Although much of the scientific community now affirms Wells's biological theses as presented in the *Outline,* during the mid-1920s the preponderance of scientific evidence supported the biological theories of Belloc, who, in the minds of many critics, bested Wells in their exchange of polemical broadsides. Throughout the 1920s and 1930s, Wells's works became progressively less optimistic about the future of humanity and increasingly bitter, as is evident in such satiric novels as *The Croquet Player* and *The Holy Terror.* The advent of World War II increased Wells's despondency about the future, and his last book, *Mind at the End of Its Tether,* predicted the destruction of civilization and degeneration of humanity. Wells died in London in 1946.

Plot and Major Characters

The Time Machine begins with a description of a dinner party at which the protagonist, called simply the Time Traveler, introduces the idea of time travel, as well as his invention of a time machine, to the other dinner guests. The novel then tells the story, narrated by the protagonist's friend, of the Time Traveler's first attempt to use his marvelous machine, which takes him to the year A.D. 802,701. Here he finds an apparently idyllic human race, whom he calls the Eloi. Though the remnants of industrial civilization are to be found only in a deserted museum, the life of the Eloi is seemingly paradisiacal, free of disease and the need to work. But the Time Traveler soon learns otherwise when he discovers another human race, the brutal underground Morlocks, who feed upon the Eloi. The Morlocks are afraid of fire, but the Eloi are so degenerate that they do not know how to make fire. The Time Traveler hypothesizes that, after thousands of years of social and genetic evolution, the human race has become two separate species. Moreover, he speculates that the division between the graceful but stupid Eloi and the violent but resourceful Morlocks has its origins in the division between owners and laborers of his own time. Ironically, it is the Morlocks, not the Eloi, who are the true masters of this point in human development.

Reflecting his scientific education, especially the influence of Huxley, Wells repeatedly employs evolution as a motif in his scientific romances. Just as Charles Darwin and other scientists had demonstrated that, in biological terms, there was nothing particularly special about human beings and that species could and had become extinct, so in his early science fiction Wells does not treat the human race as the end of the evolutionary development of life on Earth. This is apparent in the Time Traveler's voyage into the future after his trip to the year 802,701. In this effort he goes even further into the future, only to find no traces of human life and only the most basic of life forms. Apparently in this far future humanity has become extinct. He pushes even further, thirty million years into the future, and finds no sign of life and the sun cooling. Despite these depressing scenarios, after his return again to his own time, the Traveler resolves to go even further into the future. After his final departure, according to the narrator, the Time Traveler has not returned in three years, leaving the story's listeners to wonder if he himself has become extinct in some future world.

Critical Reception

Even during its first publication in serial form in the journal *New Review, The Time Machine* was recognized as a work of genius. In 1946, the year of Wells's death, V. S. Pritchett wrote of the novel, "Without question *The Time Machine* is the best piece of writing. It will take its place among the great stories of our language." Critics have interpreted the novel in several different ways: as a metaphor for Victorian class wars, a pro-socialist document dramatizing the tension between laborers and employers, and a pessimistic commentary on Darwin's theory of evolution. Critics do agree, however, that *The Time Machine* is a classic not only of science fiction but of English literature as a whole, having entered as it has into contemporary mythology by ushering in the science fiction genre in the twentieth century. In his introduction to the critical edition of *The Time Machine,* published in 1996, editor Leon Stover wrote, "*The Time Machine* is perhaps the most important political novel in modern literature," because of its dramatic illustration of Wells's now famous observation in 1920 that "History is more and more a race between education and catastrophe." The 1960 film version of the novel brought yet another interpretation of *The Time Machine* to a new audience, examining the book's relevance to an age caught in the terror of potential atomic holocaust and the Cold War.

COMMENTARY

R. H. Hutton

SOURCE: An unsigned review in *Spectator,* July, 1895, reprinted in *H. G. Wells: The Critical Heritage,* edited by Patrick Parrinder, Routledge & Kegan Paul, 1972, pp. 34-7.

Mr. H. G. Wells has written a very clever story as to the condition of this planet in the year 802,701 A.D., though the two letters A.D. appear to have lost their meaning in that distant date, as indeed they have lost their meaning for not a few even in the comparatively early date at which we all live. The story is one based on that rather favourite speculation of modern metaphysicians which supposes *time* to be at once the most important of the conditions of organic evolution, and the most misleading of subjective illusions. It is, we are told, by the efflux of time that all the modifications of species arise on the one hand, and yet Time is so purely subjective a mode of thought, that a man of searching intellect is supposed to be able to devise the means of travelling in time as well as in space, and visiting, so as to be contemporary with, any age of the world, past or future, so as to become as it were a true 'pilgrim of eternity.' This is the dream on which Mr. H. G. Wells has built up his amusing story of **The Time Machine.** A speculative mechanician is supposed to have discovered that the 'fourth dimension,' concerning which mathematicians have speculated, is Time, and that with a little ingenuity a man may travel in Time as well as in Space. The Time-traveller of this story invents some hocus-pocus of a machine by the help of which all that belongs or is affixed to that machine may pass into the Future by pressing down one lever, and into the Past by pressing down another. In other words, he can make himself at home with the society of hundreds of thousands of centuries hence, or with the chaos of hundreds of thousands of centuries past, at his pleasure. As a matter of choice, the novelist very judiciously chooses

the Future only in which to disport himself. And as we have no means of testing his conceptions of the Future, he is of course at liberty to imagine what he pleases. And he is rather ingenious in his choice of what to imagine. Mr. Wells supposes his Time-traveller to travel forward from A.D. 1895 to A.D. 802,701, and to make acquaintance with the people inhabiting the valley of the Thames (which has, of course, somewhat changed its channel) at that date. He finds a race of pretty and gentle creatures of silken organisations, as it were, and no particular interests or aims, except the love of amusement, inhabiting the surface of the earth, almost all evil passions dead, almost all natural or physical evils overcome, with a serener atmosphere, a brighter sun, lovelier flowers and fruits, no dangerous animals or poisonous vegetables, no angry passions or tumultuous and grasping selfishness, and only one object of fear. While the race of the surface of the earth has improved away all its dangers and embarrassments (including, apparently, every trace of a religion), the race of the underworld,—the race which has originally sprung from the mining population,—has developed a great dread of light, and a power of vision which can work and carry on all its great engineering operations with a minimum of light. At the same time, by inheriting a state of servitude it has also inherited a cruel contempt for its former masters, who can now resist its attacks only by congregating in crowds during the hours of darkness, for in the daylight, or even in the bright moonlight, they are safe from the attacks of their former serfs. This beautiful superior race of faint and delicate beauty is wholly vegetarian. But the inferior world of industrious dwellers in the darkness has retained its desire for flesh, and in the absence of all other animal life has returned to cannibalism; and is eager to catch unwary members of the soft surface race in order to feed on their flesh. Moreover, this is the one source of fear which disturbs the gentle pastimes of the otherwise successful subduers of natural evils. Here is Mr. Wells's dream of the two branches into which the race of men, under the laws of evolution, had diverged:—

[Quotes ch. 10 'I grieved to think' to 'I give it to you.']

The central idea of this dream is, then, the unnerving effect of a too great success in conquering the natural resistance which the physical constitution of the world presents to our love of ease and pleasure. Let a race which has learned to serve, and to serve efficiently, and has lost its physical equality with its masters by the conditions of its servitude, coexist with a race that has secured all the advantages of superior organisation, and the former will gradually recover, by its energetic habits, at least some of the advantages which it has lost, and will unite with them the cruel and selfish spirit which servitude breeds. This is, we take it, the warning which Mr. Wells intends to give:—'Above all things avoid sinking into a condition of satisfied ease; avoid a soft and languid serenity; even evil passions which involve continuous effort, are not so absolutely deadly as the temperament of languid and harmless playfulness.' We have no doubt that, so far as Mr. Wells goes, his warning is wise. But we have little fear that the languid, ease-loving, and serene temperament will ever paralyse the human race after the manner he supposes, even though there may be at present some temporary signs of the growth of the appetite for mere amusement.

In the first place, Mr. Wells assumes, what is well-nigh impossible, that the growth of the pleasure-loving temperament would not itself prevent that victory over physical obstacles to enjoyment on which he founds his dream. The pleasure-loving temperament soon becomes both selfish and fretful. And selfishness no less than fretfulness poisons all enjoyment. Before our race had reached anything like the languid grace and frivolity of the Eloi (the surface population), it would have fallen a prey to the many competing and conflicting energies of Nature which are always on the watch to crush out weak and languid organisations, to say nothing of the uncanny Morlocks (the envious subterranean population), who would soon have invented spectacles shutting out from their sensitive eyes the glare of either moon or sun. If the doctrines as to evolution have any truth in them at all, nothing is more certain than that the superiority of man to Nature will never endure beyond the endurance of his fighting strength. The physical condition of the Eloi is supposed, for instance, so to have accommodated itself to external circumstances as to extinguish that continual growth of population which renders the mere competition for food so serious a factor in the history of the globe. But even supposing such a change to have taken place, of which we see no trace at all in history or civilisation, what is there in the nature of frivolity and love of ease, to diminish, and not rather to increase, that craving to accumulate sources of enjoyment at the expense of others, which seems to be *most* visible in the nations whose populations are of the slowest growth, and which so reintroduces rivalries and war. Let any race find the pressure of population on its energies diminishing, and the mutual jealousy amongst those who are thus placed in a position of advantage for securing wealth and ease, will advance with giant strides. The hardest-pressed populations are not the most, but on the whole the least, selfish.

In the next place Mr. Wells's fancy ignores the conspicuous fact that man's nature needs a great deal of hard work to keep it in order at all, and that no class of men or women are so dissatisfied with their own internal condition as those who are least disciplined by the necessity for industry. Find the idlest class of a nation and you certainly find the most miserable class. There would be no tranquillity or serenity at all in any population for which there were not hard tasks and great duties. The Eloi of this fanciful story would have become even more eager for the satisfaction of selfish desires than the Morlocks themselves. The nature of man must have altered not merely accidentally, but essentially, if the devotion to ease and amusement had left it sweet and serene. Matthew Arnold wrote in his unreal mood of agnosticism:—

> We, in some unknown Power's employ,
> Move on a rigorous line;

Can neither, when we will, enjoy,
Nor, when we will, resign.

But it is not in some 'unknown Power's employ' that we move on this 'rigorous line.' On the contrary, it is in the employ of a Power which has revealed itself in the Incarnation and the Cross. And we may expect with the utmost confidence that if the earth is still in existence in the year 802,701 A.D., either the A.D. will mean a great deal more than it means now, or else its inhabitants will be neither Eloi nor Morlocks. For in that case evil passions will by that time have led to the extinction of races spurred and pricked on by conscience and yet so frivolous or so malignant. Yet Mr. Wells's fanciful and lively dream is well worth reading, if only because it will draw attention to the great moral and religious factors in human nature which he appears to ignore.

Israel Zangwell

SOURCE: "Without Prejudice," in *The Pall Mall Magazine,* Vol. VII, No. 29, September, 1895, pp. 153-55.

Countless are the romances that deal with other times, other manners; endless have been the attempts to picture the time to come. Sometimes the future is grey with evolutionary perspectives, with previsions of a post-historic man, bald, toothless and fallen into his second infancy; sometimes it is gay with ingenuous fore-glimpses of a renewed golden age of socialism and sentimentality. In his brilliant little romance *The Time Machine,* Mr. Wells has inclined to the severer and more scientific form of prophecy—to the notion of a humanity degenerating inevitably from sheer pressure of physical comfort; but this not very novel conception, which was the theme of Mr. Besant's *Inner House,* and even partly of Pearson's *National Life and Character,* Mr. Wells has enriched by the invention of the Morlocks, a differentiated type of humanity which lives underground and preys upon the softer, prettier species that lives luxuriously in the sun, a fine imaginative creation worthy of Swift, and possibly not devoid of satirical reference to "the present discontents." There is a good deal of what Tyndall would have called "scientific imagination" in Mr. Wells' further vision of the latter end of all things, a vision far more sombre and impressive than the ancient imaginings of the Biblical seers. The only criticism I have to offer is that his Time Traveller, a cool scientific thinker, behaves exactly like the hero of a commonplace sensational novel, with his frenzies of despair and his appeals to fate, when he finds himself in danger of having to remain in the year eight hundred and two thousand seven hundred and one, into which he has recklessly travelled; nor does it ever occur to him that in the aforesaid year he will have to repeat these painful experiences of his, else his vision of the future will have falsified itself—though how the long dispersed dust is to be vivified again does not appear. Moreover, had he travelled backwards, he would have reproduced a Past which, in so far as his own appearance in it with his newly invented machine was concerned, would have been *ex hypothesi* unveracious. Had he recurred to his own earlier life, he would have had to exist in two forms simultaneously, of varying ages—a feat which even Sir Boyle Roche would have found difficult. These absurdities illustrate the absurdity of any attempt to grapple with the notion of Time; and, despite some ingenious metaphysics, worthy of the inventor of the Eleatic paradoxes, Mr. Wells' *Time Machine,* which traverses time (viewed as the Fourth Dimension of Space) backwards or forwards, much as the magic carpet of *The Arabian Nights* traversed space, remains an amusing fantasy. That Time is an illusion is one of the earliest lessons of metaphysics; but, even if we could realise Time as self-complete and immovable, a vast *continuum* holding all that has happened and all that will happen, an eternal Present, even so to introduce a man travelling through this sleeping ocean is to re-introduce the notion of Time which has just been expelled. There is really more difficulty in understanding the Present than the Past or the Future into which it is always slipping; and those old Oriental languages which omitted the Present altogether displayed the keen metaphysical instinct of the East. And yet there is a sense in which the continued and continuous existence of all past time, at least, can be grasped by the human intellect without the intervention of metaphysics. The star whose light reaches us to-night may have perished and become extinct a thousand years ago, the rays of light from it having so many millions of miles to travel that they have only just impinged upon our planet. Could we perceive clearly the incidents on its surface, we should be beholding the Past in the Present, and we could travel to any given year by travelling actually through space to the point at which the rays of that year would first strike upon our consciousness. In like manner the whole Past of the earth is still playing itself out—to an eye conceived as stationed to-day in space, and moving now forwards to catch the Middle Ages, now backwards to watch Nero fiddling over the burning of Rome. The sounds of his fiddle are still vibrating somewhere in the infinite spaces, for this is the only "music of the spheres," these voices of vanished generations, still troubling the undulatory æther. It is all there—every plea of prayer, or cry of pain, or clamour of mad multitudes; every stave of lewd song, every lullaby in every tongue in which mothers have rocked their babes to sleep, every sob of joy or passion; Egypt, Babylon, Assyria, are vocal yet, the sunrise still touches Memnon to music, and still vibrate in the interstellar spaces

> "The glory that was Greece
> And the grandeur that was Rome;"

the bulls of Bashan roar on, the vowelled Greek of the Sophists resounds yet in the lonely vast, the *Mermaid* still rings with the jests of Shakespeare, the chant of the priests ascends with the incense from the Temple of Jerusalem, and the crack of the slave-dealer's whip is no more silent than the passionate trill of the nightingale that Keats heard or the never-fading sweetness of Nell Gwynn's voice. In verity, there is no Time Traveller, Mr. Wells, save Old Father Time himself. Instead of

being a Fourth Dimension of Space, Time is perpetually travelling through Space, repeating itself in vibrations farther and farther from the original point of incidence; a vocal panorama moving through the universe across the infinities, a succession of sounds and visions that, having once been, can never pass away, but only on and on from point to point, permanently enregistered in the sum of things, preserved from annihilation by the endlessness of Space, and ever visible and audible to eye or ear that should travel in a parallel movement. It is true the scientists allege that only light can thus travel through the infinities, sound-waves being confined to a material medium and being quickly dissipated into heat. But light alone is sufficient to sustain my fantasy, and in any case the sounds would be æons behind the sights. Terrible, solemn thought that the Past can never die, and that for each of us Heaven or Hell may consist in our being placed at the point of vantage in Space where we may witness the spectacle of our past lives, and find bliss or bale in the panorama. How much ghastlier than the pains of the pit, for the wicked to be perpetually "moved on" by some Satanic policeman to the mathematical point at which their autobiography becomes visible, a point that moves backwards in the infinite universe each time the green curtain of the grave falls over the final episode, so that the sordid show may commence all over again, and so *ad infinitum.* Pascal defined Space as a sphere whose centre is everywhere and whose circumference is nowhere. This brilliant figure helps us to conceive God as always at the centre of vision, receiving all vibrations simultaneously, and thus beholding all Past time simultaneously with the Present. We can also conceive of Future incidents being visible to a spectator, who should be moved forward to receive the impressions of them æons earlier than they would otherwise have reached him. But these "futures" would only be relative; in reality they would already have happened, and the absolute Future, the universe of things that have *not* happened, would still elude our vision, though we can very faintly imagine the Future, interwoven inevitably with the Past, visible to an omniscient Being somewhat as the evolution of a story is to the man of genius upon whom past and future flash in one conception. Mr. Wells might have been plausibly scientific in engineering his Time Machine through Space and stopping at the points where particular periods of the world's past history became visible: he would then have avoided the fallacy of mingling personally in the panorama. But this would not have suited his design of "dealing in futures." For there is no getting into the Future, except by waiting. You can only sit down and see it come by, as the drunken man thought he might wait for his house to come round in the circulation of the earth; and if you lived for an eternity, the show would only be "just about to begin."

Mr. Wells' other book, published simultaneously, as if by the aid of the Time Machine, and entitled *Select Conversations with an Uncle,* confirms the impression of his powers, though it would not have produced it. It comprises about a dozen articles which appeared in the *Pall Mall Gazette,* and scintillate with the sort of humour which that organ is wont to "slate." There is wisdom as well as fantasy in some of these trifles, though others are too trifling. The best of all is "A Misunderstood Artist," a gentleman who interrupts with an explosive and overwhelming "Bah" a colloquy in a railway carriage respecting art and morality. Art for anything but art's sake, indeed! It transpires that he is a cook—an artist in the plastic! His is the art most misunderstood, most degraded to utilitarian ends, tested by impossible standards, as when he is asked to render oily food palatable to a delicate patient. "Here, in your kitchen," says he, outraged, "I am inspired with beautiful dinners, and I produce them. It is your place to gather together, from this place one, and from that, one, the few precious souls who can appreciate that rare and wonderful thing, a dinner, graceful, harmonious, exquisite, perfect." He reads Poe, and is possessed of an imitative ambition to introduce a new development—the grotesque—into the culinary art. "In my search for the bizarre," says he, "I made some curious arrangements in pork and strawberries, with a sauce containing beer. Quite by accident I mentioned my design to him on the evening of the festival. All the Philistine was aroused in him: 'It will ruin my digestion.' 'My friend,' said I, 'I am not your doctor; I have nothing to do with your digestion. Only here is a beautiful Japanese thing, a quaint, queer, almost eerie dinner, that is in my humble opinion worth many digestions.'" He resigned and took his genius elsewhere, and produced some Nocturnes in imitation of Mr. Whistler, with mushrooms, truffles, grilled meat, pickled walnuts, black pudding, French plums, porter—a dinner in soft velvety black, eaten in a starlight of small scattered candles. That, too, led to a resignation: Art will ever demand its martyrs. Perhaps Mr. Wells is unaware that such colour-symphonies of the stomach are not altogether unknown, and that Suppers in Pink and Breakfasts in Brown are the last resort of novelty-mongering hostesses, to be followed, let us hope, by Indigestions in Green and Yellow.

Bernard Bergonzi

SOURCE: "'*The Time Machine*': An Ironic Myth," in *The Critical Quarterly*, Vol. 2, No. 4, Winter, 1960, pp. 293-305.

H. G. Wells seems so essentially a writer of the first half of the twentieth century that we tend to forget that if he had died in 1900 at the age of thirty-four he would already have had a dozen books to his credit. He first established his reputation by the scientific romances written during these early years of his literary career, and they have remained popular. Historically considered, they are of interest as the forerunners of much latter-day science fiction. Yet, in my opinion, more substantial claims can be made for them. They are often compared with the work of Jules Verne, but this is a misleading comparison even if a plausible one. Wells himself wrote in 1933, "there is no resemblance whatever between the anticipatory inventions of the great Frenchman and these fantasies." His early romances, in fact, despite their air of

scientific plausibility, are much more works of pure imagination. They are, in short, *fantasies,* and the emphasis should be on 'romance' rather than 'scientific.' And like other kinds of literary romance they are distinguished by a quality which may reasonably be called symbolic, even if not specifically allegorical. Indeed, I would claim that Wells's early fiction is closer to the symbolic romances of Hawthorne or Melville, or to a complex fantasy like *Dr. Jekyll and Mr. Hyde,* or even to the fables of Kafka, than it is to the more strictly scientific speculations of Verne. This at least, is the assumption on which I base the following examination of *The Time Machine,* Wells's first novel, which appeared in 1895. This approach has already been hinted at by one of the best of Wells's modern critics, V. S. Pritchett, who has written:

> Without question *The Time Machine* is the best piece of writing. It will take its place among the great stories of our language. Like all excellent works it has meanings within its meaning . . . [1]

An earlier writer on Wells, Edward Shanks, remarked:

> If I were to say that many of Mr. Wells's early books have a poetic quality I should run the risk of conveying a false impression. Luckily they have a peculiar quality which enables them to bear a special description. They are, in their degree, myths; and Mr. Wells is a mythmaker.[2]

Shanks expanded his remarks with particular reference to *The Island of Dr. Moreau,* though they apply equally to *The Time Machine:*

> These passages suggest one interpretation of the book. But it is a myth, not an allegory; and whereas an allegory bears a single and definite interpretation, a myth does not, but can be interpreted in many ways, none of them quite consistent, all of them more alive and fruitful than the rigid allegorical correspondence.

Pritchett has referred to *The Time Machine* as a 'poetic social allegory.' But this narrows the effective range of the work too much; though on one level the 'allegory,' or in Shanks's more appropriate term, the 'myth,' does operate in social terms, its further significance is biological and even cosmological. Structurally, *The Time Machine* belongs to the class of story which includes James's *Turn of the Screw,* and which Northrop Frye has called "the tale told in quotation marks, where we have an opening setting with a small group of congenial people, and then the real story told by one of the members." As Frye observes:

> The effect of such devices is to present the story through a relaxed and contemplative haze as something that entertains us without, so to speak, confronting us, as direct tragedy confronts us.[3]

The aesthetic distancing of the central narrative of *The Time Machine,* 'the time traveller's story,' is carefully carried out. At the end of the book, the traveller says:

"No, I cannot expect you to believe it. Take it as a lie—or a prophecy. Say I dreamed it in the workshop. Consider I have been speculating upon the destinies of our race, until I have hatched this fiction. Treat my assertion of its truth as a mere stroke of art to enhance its interest. And taking it as a story, what do you think of it?"

The manifest disbelief of all his friends other than the story-teller—one of them 'thought the tale a "gaudy lie"'—is balanced by the apparent evidence of his sojourn in the future, the 'two strange white flowers' of an unknown species. In fact, Wells demands assent by apparently discouraging it.

The opening chapters of the novel show us the inventor entertaining his friends, a group of professional men, in the solid comfort of his home at Richmond. They recall the 'club-man' atmosphere with which several of Kipling's short stories open, and their function in the narrative is to give it a basis in contemporary life at its most ordinary and pedestrian: this atmosphere makes the completest possible contrast with what is to come: an account of a wholly imaginative world of dominantly paradisal and demonic imagery, lying far outside the possible experience of the late Victorian bourgeoisie. These chapters are essential to Wells's purpose, since they prevent the central narrative from seeming a piece of pure fantasy, or a fairy story, and no more. The character of the time traveller himself—cheerful, erratic, and somewhat absurd, faintly suggestive of a hero of Jerome K. Jerome's—has a similar function. In the work of other popular writers of fantastic romance in the nineties, such as Arthur Machen and M. P. Shiel (both clearly deriving from Stevenson), a 'weird' atmosphere is striven after from the very beginning and the dramatic power is correspondingly less.

Once the reader has been initiated into the group of friends, he is prepared for whatever is to come next. First the model time machine is produced—"a glittering metallic framework, scarcely larger than a small clock, and very delicately made. . . . there was ivory in it, and some crystalline substance"—and sent off into time, never to be seen again. Then we are shown the full scale machine, and the account of it is a brilliant example of Wells's impressionistic method:

"I remember vividly the flickering light, his queer, broad head in silhouette, the dance of the shadows, how we all followed him, puzzled but incredulous, and how there in the laboratory we beheld a larger edition of the little mechanism which we had seen vanish from before our eyes. Parts were of nickel, parts of ivory, parts had certainly been filed or sawn out of rock crystal. The thing was generally complete, but the twisted crystalline bars lay unfinished upon the bench besides some sheets of drawings, and I took one up for a better look at it. Quartz it seemed to be."

The assemblage of details is strictly speaking meaningless but nevertheless conveys very effectively a sense of the machine without putting the author to the taxing necessity of giving a direct description.

The central narrative of *The Time Machine* is of a kind common to several of Wells's early romances: a central character is transferred to or marooned in a wholly alien environment, and the story arises from his efforts to deal with the situation. This is the case with the time traveller, with the angel in *The Wonderful Visit* and with Prendick in *The Island of Dr. Moreau,* while Griffin in *The Invisible Man* becomes the victim of his environment in attempting to control it. Though Wells is a writer of symbolic fiction—or a myth-maker—the symbolism is not of the specifically heraldic kind that we associate, for instance, with Hawthorne's scarlet letter, Melville's white whale, or James's golden bowl. In Wells the symbolic element is inherent in the total fictional situation, rather more in the manner of Kafka. When, for instance, we are shown in *The Time Machine* a paradisal world on the surface of the earth inhabited by beautiful carefree beings leading a wholly aesthetic existence, and a diabolic or demonic world beneath the surface inhabited by brutish creatures who spend most of their time in darkness in underground machine shops, and only appear on the surface at night, and when we are told that these two races are the descendants respectively of the present-day bourgeoisie and proletariat, and that the latter live by cannibalistically preying on the former—then clearly we are faced with a symbolic situation of considerable complexity, where several different 'mythical' interpretations are possible.

The time traveller—unlike his predecessor, Nebogipfel (hero of *The Chronic Argonauts*, Wells's first version of *The Time Machine,* published in a student magazine in 1888), and his successors, Moreau and Griffin—is not a solitary eccentric on the Frankenstein model, but an amiable and gregarious bourgeois. Like Wells himself, he appears to be informed and interested in the dominant intellectual movements of his age, Marxism and Darwinism. Wells had come across Marx at South Kensington, and though in later years he was to become extremely anti-Marxist, in his immediate post-student days he was prepared to uphold Marxian socialism as 'a new thing based on Darwinism.' However doubtfully historical this may be, the juxtaposition of the two names is very important for Wells's early imaginative and speculative writing. The time traveller, immediately after he has arrived in the world of 802701, is full of forebodings about the kind of humanity he may discover:

What might not have happened to men? What if cruelty had grown into a common passion? What if in this interval the race had lost its manliness, and had developed into something inhuman, unsympathetic, and overwhelmingly powerful? I might seem some old-world savage animal, only the more dreadful and disgusting for our common likeness—a foul creature to be incontinently slain.

At first, however, his more fearful speculations are not fulfilled. Instead of what he had feared, he discovers the Eloi, who are small, frail and beautiful. He is rather shocked and then amused by their child-like ways and manifest lack of intellectual powers—"the memory of my confident anticipations of a profoundly grave and intellectual posterity came, with irresistible merriment, to my mind." Such a 'grave and intellectual posterity' had in fact been postulated by Bulwer Lytton in *The Coming Race*, 1871, a work, which it has been suggested had some influence on *The Time Machine,* though the resemblances are very slight. But it is quite possible that Wells was here alluding to Bulwer Lytton's romance, as well as to the wider implications of optimistic evolutionary theory.

Subsequently the traveller becomes charmed with the Eloi and the relaxed communism of their way of life. They live, not in separate houses, but in large semi-ruinous buildings of considerable architectural splendour, sleeping and eating there communally. Their only food is fruit, which abounds in great richness and variety, and they are described in a way which suggests the figures of traditional pastoral poetry: "They spent all their time in playing gently, in bathing in the river, in making love in a half-playful fashion, in eating fruit and sleeping." Later the traveller takes stock of their world:

> I have already spoken of the great palaces dotted about among the variegated greenery, some in ruins and some still occupied. Here and there rose a white silvery figure in the waste garden of the earth, here and there came the sharp vertical line of some cupola or obelisk. There were no hedges, no signs of proprietary rights, no evidences of agriculture; the whole earth had become a garden.

There appear to be no animals, wild or domestic, left in the world, and such forms of life as remain have clearly been subject to a radical process of selection:

> The air was free from gnats, the earth from weeds or fungi; everywhere were fruits and sweet and delightful flowers; brilliant butterflies flew hither and thither. The ideal of preventive medicine was attained. Disease had been stamped out. I saw no evidence of any contagious diseases during all my stay. And I shall have to tell you later that even the processes of putrefaction and decay had been profoundly affected by these changes.

Man has, in short, at some period long past obtained complete control of his environment, and has been able to manipulate the conditions of life to his absolute satisfaction. The 'struggle for existence' has been eliminated, and as a result of this manipulation the nature of the species has undergone profound modification. Not only have the apparent physical differences between male and female disappeared, but their mental powers have declined as well as their physical. The human race, as it presents itself to the traveller, is plainly in its final decadence. The Eloi, with their childlike and sexually ambiguous appearance, and their consumptive type of beauty, are clearly reflections of *fin de siècle* visual taste. *The Time Machine* is in several respects a book of its time, for speculations about decadence and degeneration were much in the air in the eighties and early nineties, reaching their peak in Max Nordau's massive work of destructive criticism, *Degeneration*.

Wells certainly knew the English edition of this book, which appeared in March 1895, when *The Time Machine* was already completed, for he makes a satirical reference to it in his second novel, *The Wonderful Visit,* published the following October.

In the world that the traveller surveys, aesthetic motives have evidently long been dominant as humanity has settled down to its decline. "This has ever been the fate of energy in security; it takes to art and to eroticism, and then comes languor and decay." But in the age of the Eloi even artistic motives seem almost extinct. "To adorn themselves with flowers, to dance, to sing in the sunlight; so much was left of the artistic spirit, and no more." The implied comment on *fin de siècle* aestheticism is, again, unmistakable. The first chapter of the time traveller's narrative is called 'In the Golden Age,' and the following chapter, 'The Sunset of Mankind': there is an ironic effect, not only in the juxtaposition, but in the very reference to a 'golden age.' Such an age, the *Saturnia regna*, when men were imagined as living a simple, uncomplicated and happy existence, before in some way falling from grace, was always an object of literary nostalgia, and traditionally thought of as being at the very beginning of man's history. Wells, however, places it in the remotest future, and associates it not with dawn but with sunset. The time traveller sees the Eloi as leading a paradisal existence, and his sense of this is imparted to the reader by the imagery of the first part of his narrative. They are thoroughly assimilated to their environment, where "the whole earth had become a garden", and "everywhere were fruits and sweet and delicious flowers; brilliant butterflies flew hither and thither." Their appearance and mode of life makes a pointed contrast to the drab and earnest figure of the traveller:

> Several more brightly-clad people met me in the doorway, and so we entered, I, dressed in dingy nineteenth-century garments, looking grotesque enough, garlanded with flowers, and surrounded by an eddying mass of bright, soft-coloured robes and shining white limbs, in a melodious whirl of laughter and laughing speech.

The writing here suggests that Wells was getting a little out of his depth, but the intention is clearly to present the Eloi as in some sense heirs to Pre-Raphaelite convention. This implicit contrast between the aesthetic and the utilitarian, the beautiful and idle set against the ugly and active, shows how *The Time Machine* embodies another profound late-Victorian preoccupation, recalling, for instance, the aesthetic anti-industrialism of Ruskin and Morris. The world of the Eloi is presented as not only a golden age, but as something of a lotus land, and it begins to exercise its spell on the traveller. After his immediate panic on discovering the loss of his machine, he settles down to a philosophic resignation:

> Suppose the worst? I said. Suppose the machine altogether lost—perhaps destroyed? It behoves me to be calm and patient, to learn the way of the people, to get a clear idea of the method of my

> loss, and the means of getting materials and tools; so that in the end, perhaps, I may make another. That would be my only hope, a poor hope, perhaps, but better than despair. And, after all, it was a beautiful and curious world.

The traveller's potential attachment to the Eloi and their world is strengthened when he rescues the little female, Weena, from drowning, and begins a prolonged flirtation with her. This relationship is the biggest flaw in the narrative, for it is totally unconvincing, and tends to embarrass the reader (Pritchett has referred to the "faint squirms of idyllic petting"). But though the traveller feels the attraction of the kind of life she represents, he is still too much a man of his own age, resourceful, curious and active, to succumb to it. As he says of himself, "I am too Occidental for a long vigil. I could work at a problem for years, but to wait inactive for twenty-four hours—that is another matter."

But it is not long before he becomes aware that the Eloi are not the only forms of animal life left in the world, and his curiosity is once more aroused. He realises that Weena and the Eloi generally have a great fear of darkness: "But she dreaded the dark, dreaded shadows, dreaded black things." Here we have the first hint of the dominant imagery of the second half of the narrative, the darkness characteristic of the Morlocks, and the ugly, shapeless forms associated with it, contrasting with the light and the brilliant colours of the Eloi and their world. Looking into the darkness one night just before dawn the traveller imagines that he can see vague figures running across the landscape, but cannot be certain whether or not his eyes have deceived him. And a little later, when he is exploring one of the ruined palaces, he comes across a strange creature—"a queer little ape-like figure" that runs away from him and disappears down one of the well-like shafts that are scattered across the country, and whose purpose and nature had puzzled the traveller on his arrival: "My impression of it is, of course, imperfect; but I know it was a dull white, and had strange large greyish-red eyes; also that there was flaxen hair on its head and down its back." The traveller now has to reformulate his ideas about the way the evolutionary development of man has proceeded: 'Man had not remained one species, but had differentiated into two distinct animals.' He has to modify his previous 'Darwinian' explanation by a 'Marxist' one: "it seemed clear as daylight to me that the gradual widening of the merely temporary and social difference between the Capitalist and the Labourer was the key to the whole position." Even in his own day, he reflects, men tend to spend more and more time underground: "There is a tendency to utilise underground space for the less ornamental purposes of civilisation." "Even now, does not an East-end worker live in such artificial conditions as practically to be cut off from the natural surface of the earth?" Similarly the rich have tended to preserve themselves more and more as an exclusive and self-contained group, with fewer and fewer social contacts with the workers, until society has stratified rigidly into a two-class system. "So, in the end,

above ground, you must have the Haves, pursuing pleasure and comfort and beauty, and below ground the Havenots; the workers getting continually adapted to the conditions of their labour." The analysis represents, it will be seen, a romantic and pessimistic variant of orthodox Marxist thought: the implications of the class-war are accepted, but the possibility of the successful proletarian revolution establishing a classless society is rigidly excluded. Thus, the traveller concludes, the social tendencies of nineteenth century industrialism have become rigidified and then built in, as it were, to the evolutionary development of the race. Nevertheless, he is still orthodox enough in his analysis to assume that the Eloi, despite their physical and mental decline, are still the masters and the Morlocks—as he finds the underground creatures are called—are their slaves. It is not long before he discovers that this, too, is a false conclusion.

Soon enough, despite his dalliance with Weena, and her obvious reluctance to let him go, the traveller decides that he must find out more about the Morlocks, and resolves to descend into their underworld. It is at this point that, in Pritchett's phrase, "the story alters its key, and the Time Traveller reveals the foundation of slime and horror on which the pretty life of his Arcadians is precariously and fearfully resting." The descent of the traveller into the underworld has, in fact, an almost undisplaced mythical significance: it suggests a parody of the Harrowing of Hell, where it is not the souls of the just that are released, but the demonic Morlocks, for it is they who dominate the subsequent narrative. During his 'descent into hell' the traveller is seized by the Morlocks, but he keeps them at bay by striking matches, for they recoil from light in any form, which is why they do not normally appear on the surface of the earth by day. During his brief and confused visit to their world he sees and hears great machines at work, and notices a table spread for a meal. He observes that the Morlocks are carnivorous, but does not, for a time, draw the obvious conclusion about the nature of the meat they are eating. However, it is readily apparent to the reader. The Morlocks have a complex symbolic function, for they not only represent an exaggerated fear of the nineteenth century proletariat, but also embody many of the traditional mythical images of a demonic world. This will soon be apparent if one compares Well's account of them and their environment with the chapter on 'Demonic Imagery' in Northrop Frye's *Anatomy of Criticism*. As Frye writes:

> Images of perverted work belong here too: engines of torture, weapons of war, armour, and images of a dead mechanism which, because it does not humanise nature, is unnatural as well as inhuman. Corresponding to the temple or One Building of the Apocalypse, we have the prison or dungeon, the sealed furnace of heat without light, like the city of Dis in Dante.[4]

Indeed nothing is more remarkable about *The Time Machine* than the way in which its central narrative is polarised between opposed groups of imagery, the paradisal (or, in Frye's phrase, the apocalyptic) and the demonic, representing extreme forms of human desire and repulsion.

A further significance of the Morlocks can be seen in the fact that they are frequently referred to in terms of unpleasant animal life: thus they are described as, or compared with, 'apes,' 'lemurs,' 'worms,' 'spiders,' and 'rats.' One must compare these images with the traveller's original discovery that all forms of non-human animal life—with the apparent exception of butterflies—had been banished from the upper world, whether noxious or not. There is a powerful irony in his subsequent discovery that the one remaining form of animal life, and the most noxious of all, is a branch of humanity. Furthermore this confusion of human and animal—with its origin in some kind of imaginative perturbation over the deeper implications of Darwinism—was to provide the central theme of *The Island of Dr. Moreau.*

The traveller narrowly escapes with his life from the Morlocks and returns to the surface to make another reappraisal of the world of 802701. The image of the 'golden age' as it has presented itself to him on his arrival has been destroyed: "there was an altogether new element in the sickening quality of the Morlocks—a something inhuman and malign." He has to reject his subsequent hypothesis that the Eloi were the masters, and the Morlocks their slaves. A new relationship has clearly evolved between the two races; the Eloi, who are in terror of dark and moonless nights, are in some way victims of the Morlocks, though he is still not certain precisely how. His experience underground has shattered his previous euphoria (symbolically perhaps an end of the paradisal innocence in which he has been participating), and his natural inventiveness and curiosity reassert themselves. He makes his way with Weena to a large green building that he has seen in the distance many miles off, which he later calls 'the Palace of Green Porcelain.' On their way they spend a night in the open: the traveller looks at the stars in their now unfamiliar arrangements and reflects on his present isolation.

> Looking at these stars suddenly dwarfed my own troubles and all the gravities of terrestial life. I thought of their unfathomable distance and the slow inevitable drift of their movements out of the unknown past into the unknown future. I thought of the great precessional cycle that the pole of the earth describes. Only forty times had that silent revolution occurred during all the years that I had traversed. And during these few revolutions all the activity, all the traditions, the complex organisations, the nations, languages, literatures, aspirations, even the mere memory of Man as I knew him, had been swept out of existence. Instead were these frail creatures who had forgotten their high ancestry, and the white Things of which I went in terror. Then I thought of the Great Fear that was between the two species, and for the first time, with a sudden shiver, came the clear knowledge of what the meat I had seen might be. Yet it was too horrible! I looked at little Weena sleeping beside me, her face white and star-like under the stars, and forthwith dismissed the thought.

The traveller's knowledge of the world of the Eloi and the Morlocks, and the relation between them, is almost complete. When they reach the Palace of Green Porcelain, he finds, as if to belie his reflections on the disappearance of all traces of the past, that it is a vast museum: "Clearly we stood among the ruins of some latter-day South Kensington!" The museum, with its semi-ruinous remains of earlier phases of human achievement, puts the traveller once more in a direct emotional relation with the past, and, by implication, with his own age. Here, the Arcadian spell is finally cast off. He remembers that he is, after all, a late-Victorian scientist with a keen interest in technology. He is intrigued by various great machines, some half destroyed, and others in quite good condition:

> You know I have a certain weakness for mechanism, and I was inclined to linger among these: the more so as for the most part they had the interest of puzzles, and I could make only the vaguest guesses at what they were for. I fancied that if I could solve their puzzles I should find myself in possession of powers that might be of use against the Morlocks.

The Morlocks, after all, are a technological race, and if he is to defend himself against them—as he has decided he must—he must match himself against their mechanical prowess. The images of machinery in this part of the narrative are sufficient to suggest to the reader the presence of the Morlocks, and before long the traveller sees footprints in the dust around him, and hears noises coming from one end of a long gallery, which mean that the Morlocks are not far away. He breaks an iron lever off one of the machines to use as a mace. By now, his feelings for the Morlocks are those of passionate loathing: "I longed very much to kill a Morlock or so. Very inhuman, you may think, to want to go killing one's own descendants! But it was impossible, somehow, to feel any humanity in the things." Since the Morlocks on one level stand for the late nineteenth century proletariat, the traveller's attitude towards them clearly symbolises a contemporary bourgeois fear of the working class, and it is not fanciful to impute something of this attitude to Wells himself. From his schooldays in Bromley he had disliked and feared the working class in a way wholly appropriate to the son of a small tradesman—as various Marxist critics have not been slow to remark. The traveller's gradual identification with the beautiful and aristocratic—if decadent—Eloi against the brutish Morlocks is indicative of Wells' own attitudes, or one aspect of them, and links up with a common theme in his realistic fiction: the hypergamous aspirations of a low-born hero towards genteel heroines: Jessica Milton in *The Wheels of Chance*, Helen Walsingham in *Kipps,* Beatrice Normandy in *Tono-Bungay*, and Christabel in *Mr. Polly*.

Wells's imagination was easily given to producing images of mutilation and violence, and the traveller's hatred of the Morlocks gives them free rein. The reader is further prepared for the scenes of violence and destruction which end the traveller's expedition to the museum by his discovery of "a long gallery of rusting stands of arms", where he "hesitated between my crowbar and a hatchet or a sword." But he could not carry both and kept the crowbar. He contented himself with a jar of camphor from another part of the museum, since this was inflammable and would make a useful weapon against the Morlocks. By now we have wholly moved from the dominantly paradisal imagery of the first half of the narrative to the demonic imagery of the second. Instead of a golden age, or lotus land, we are back in the familiar world of inventiveness and struggle.

When Weena and the traveller are once more outside the museum and are making their way homeward through the woods, he decides to keep the lurking Morlocks at bay during the coming night by lighting a fire. He succeeds only too well, and before long discovers that he has set the whole forest ablaze. Several Morlocks try to attack him, but he fights them off with his iron bar. He then discovers the creatures all fleeing in panic before the advancing fire: in the confusion Weena is lost. There are some powerful descriptions of the Morlocks' plight:

> And now I was to see the most weird and horrible thing, I think, of all that I beheld in that future age. This whole space was as bright as day with the reflection of the fire. In the centre was a hillock or tumulus, surmounted by a scorched hawthorn. Beyond this was another arm of the burning forest, with yellow tongues already writhing from it, completely encircling the space with a fence of fire. Upon the hillside were some thirty or forty Morlocks, dazzled by the light and heat and blundering hither and thither against each other in their bewilderment. At first I did not realise their blindness, and struck furiously at them with my bar, in a frenzy of fear, as they approached me, killing one and crippling several more. But when I watched the gestures of one of them groping under the hawthorn against the red sky, and heard their moans, I was assured of their absolute helplessness and misery in the glare, and I struck no more of them.

Eventually, on the following morning, the traveller gets back to the neighbourhood of the White Sphinx, whence he had started. Everything is as it was when he left. The beautiful Eloi are still moving across the landscape in their gay robes, or bathing in the river. But now his disillusion with their Arcadian world and his realisation of the true nature of their lives is complete.

> I understood now what all the beauty of the overworld people covered. Very pleasant was their day, as pleasant as the day of the cattle in the field. Like the cattle they knew of no enemies, and provided against no needs. And their end was the same.

Here we have the solution to a riddle that was implicitly posed at the beginning of the traveller's narrative. Soon after his arrival among the Eloi he had found that there were no domestic animals in their world: "horses, cattle, sheep, dogs, had followed the Ichthyosaurus into extinction." Yet the life led by the Eloi is clearly that contained in conventional literary pastoral, and the first part of the traveller's narrative partakes of the nature of pastoral—

but it is a pastoral world without sheep or cattle. And a little later, during his speculations on the possibilities of eugenic development, he had reflected:

> We improve our favourite plants and animals— and how few they are—gradually by selective breeding; now a new and better peach, now a seedless grape, now a sweeter and larger flower, now a more convenient breed of cattle.

Something of the sort, he concludes, has brought about the world of 802701. But the paradox latent in the observation is only made manifest in his return from the museum, now possessing a complete knowledge of this world. There are no sheep or cattle in the pastoral world of the Eloi because they are themselves the cattle, fattened and fed by their underground masters. They are *both* a "sweeter and larger flower" and "a more convenient breed of cattle." Thus the complex symbolism of the central narrative of *The Time Machine* is ingeniously completed on this note of diabolical irony. Such knowledge has made the Arcadian world intolerable to the traveller. He is now able to escape from it: the Morlocks have produced his machine and placed it as a trap for him, but he is able to elude them, and travels off into the still more remote future.

The final part of the time traveller's narrative, the chapter called 'The Further Vision,' is an extended epilogue to the story of the Eloi and the Morlocks. The traveller moves further and further into the future, until he reaches an age when all traces of humanity have vanished and the world is given over to giant crabs. The earth has ceased to rotate, and has come to rest with one face always turned to the sun:

> I stopped very gently and sat upon the Time Machine, looking round. The sky was no longer blue. North-eastward it was inky black, and out of the darkness shone brightly and steadily the pale while stars. Overhead it was a deep Indian red and starless, and south-eastward it grew brighter to a growing scarlet where, cut by the horizon, lay the huge hull of the sun, red and motionless. The rocks about me were of a harsh, reddish colour, and all the trace of life that I could see at first was the intensely green vegetation that covered every projecting point on their south-eastern face. It was the same rich green that one sees on forest moss or on lichen in caves: plants which like these grow in a perpetual twilight.

The whole of this vision of a dying world is conveyed with a poetic intensity which Wells was never to recapture. The transition from the social and biological interest of the '802701' episode to the cosmological note of these final pages is extremely well done: the previous account of the decline of humanity is echoed and amplified by the description of the gradual death of the whole physical world. The traveller moves on and on, seeking to discover the ultimate mystery of the world's fate.

> At last, more than thirty million years hence, the huge red-hot dome of the sun had come to obscure

nearly a tenth part of the darkling heavens. Then I stopped once more, for the crawling multitude of crabs had disappeared, and the red beach, save for its livid green liverworts and lichens, seemed lifeless. And now it was flecked with white. A bitter cold assailed me. Rare white flakes ever and again came eddying down. To the north-eastward, the glare of snow lay under the starlight of the sable sky, and I could see an undulating crest of hillocks pinkish-white. There were fringes of ice along the sea margin, with drifting masses further out; but the main expanse of that salt ocean, all bloody under the eternal sunset, was still unfrozen.

Finally, after an eclipse of the sun has reduced this desolate world to total darkness, the traveller returns to his own time, and the waiting circle of friends in his house at Richmond.

A contemporary reviewer paid special tribute to these final pages, and referred to 'that last *fin de siècle,* when earth is moribund and man has ceased to be.'[5] This reference to the *fin de siècle* is appropriate both in its immediate context and in a larger sense, for, as I have already suggested, **The Time Machine** is pre-eminently a book of its time, giving imaginative form to many of the fears and preoccupations of the final years of the nineteenth century. Max Nordau, in fact, had attacked these preoccupations and attitudes in a passage which curiously anticipates the themes and dominant images of **The Time Machine**:

> *Fin de siècle* is at once a confession and a complaint. The old Northern faith contained the fearsome doctrine of the Dusk of the Gods. In our days there have arisen in more highly developed minds vague qualms of a Dusk of the Nations, in which all suns and all stars are gradually waning, and mankind with all its institutions and creations is perishing in the midst of a dying world.[6]

Since **The Time Machine** is a romance and not a piece of realistic fiction, it conveys its meaning in poetic fashion through images, rather than by the revelation of character in action. It is, in short, a myth, and in Shanks's words, "can be interpreted in many ways, none of them quite consistent, all of them more alive and fruitful than the rigid allegorical correspondence." I have tried to indicate some of the thematic strands to be found in the work. Some of them are peculiarly of their period, others have a more general and a more fundamental human relevance. The opposition of Eloi and Morlocks can be interpreted in terms of the late nineteenth-century class struggle, but it also reflects an opposition between aestheticism and utilitarianism, pastoralism and technology, contemplation and action, and ultimately, and least specifically, between beauty and ugliness, and light and darkness. The book not only embodies the tensions and dilemmas of its time, but others peculiar to Wells himself, which a few years later were to make him cease to be an artist, and become a propagandist. Since the tensions are imaginatively and not intellectually resolved we find that a note of irony becomes increasingly more pronounced as the traveller persists in his disconcerting exploration of the world where he has found himself. *The Time Machine* is not only a myth, but an ironic myth, like many other considerable works of modern literature. And despite the complexity of its thematic elements, Wells's art is such that the story is a skilfully wrought imaginative whole, a single image.

NOTES

[1]*The Living Novel,* 1946, pp. 119-20.

[2]*First Essays on Literature,* 1923, p. 158.

[3]*Anatomy of Criticism,* Princeton, 1957, p. 202.

[4] *Anatomy of Criticism,* p. 150.

[5] *Daily Chronicle,* 27 July, 1895.

[6] *Degeneration,* 1895, p. 2.

Robert M. Philmus

SOURCE: "*The Time Machine;* or, The Fourth Dimension as Prophecy," in *PMLA,* Vol. 84, No. 3, May, 1969, pp. 530-35.

The statements that H. G. Wells gave out in the twenties and thirties about his early "scientific romances" or "scientific fantasies," as he alternately called them, are not sympathetic to the spirit of these works written before the turn of the century. In general, he makes them out to be slighter in substance or more tendentious in tone than the serious reader coming upon them now would find them. Nevertheless, Wells does not attempt wilfully to mislead or mystify his readers in later assessments of his early romances; and in fact his own criticism is sometimes actively helpful in understanding his fiction.

Of particular importance are his various observations about **The Time Machine** (1895); and his Preface to the **Scientific Romances** especially—an indispensable account of the theory and practice of his science fiction—draws attention to two aspects of this early fantasy essential to interpreting it. The first of these concerns the Time Traveller's vision of the future, a vision which Wells characterizes as running "counter to the placid assumption" of the nineties "that Evolution was a pro-human force making things better and better for mankind." The second point, already implicit in this last remark from the Preface, is that **The Time Machine** is an "assault on human self-satisfaction."[1]

These observations can in effect be taken to summarize the findings of Bernard Bergonzi's study of **The Time Machine** as an "ironic myth" of degeneration and Mark R. Hillegas' analysis of it as "a serious attack on human complacency."[2] Neither of these studies explains, however, the Traveller's compulsion to resume his time-travelling, to return, presumably, to the world of the Eloi and the Morlocks; and it is towards an explanation of this response to the vision or prophecy of *The Time Machine* that my own interpretation is directed. It seems to me that Wells has structured his romance so as to educe the ultimate consequences of both the myth he develops and the several internal points of view towards it. Since the fantasy thus approaches the very postulates of his science fiction, I propose to examine its structure in detail, considering summarily but analytically the components of that structure: the Time Traveller's vision of the future, his interpretation of it, and the reaction of his audience to the prophetic report.[3]

I

To begin then with the Time Traveller's vision, "degeneration" is not, I think, a precise enough description of the backsliding of the human species into the less and less recognizably anthropomorphic descendants that the Traveller comes upon in the world of 802,701 and beyond. It is true that Wells himself used that term as early as 1891 in an essay outlining the abstract idea behind his vision of the future;[4] but in that same essay, entitled **"Zoological Retrogression,"** Wells also calls this process of reversion "degradation,"[5] which suggests the step-by-step decline from man to beast that he was to take up in *The Island of Doctor Moreau* (1896) as well. More accurately still, one can define the vision in *The Time Machine* of Homo sapiens gradually reduced to species lower and lower on the evolutionary scale as a vision of devolution.

The human ancestry of the degenerate species that the Traveller discovers in the "Golden Age" of 802,701 is scarcely discernible. The feeble and "childlike" Eloi (p. 38)[6] are more human than the "ape-like" and predatory Morlocks (p. 77) that emerge nightly from dark catacombs to prey upon the creatures of the "upper-world"; but while "modification of the human type" among the Morlocks has been "far more profound than among the 'Eloi'" (p. 84), the process of devolution has by no means reached an equilibrium. The oppressive, almost Manichean, threat to the sunlit paradise of the Eloi which the dark and demonic "underworld" of the Morlocks imposes becomes finally the impending destruction of the solar system itself,[7] foreshadowed in the total blackness of the solar eclipse which concludes the chapter called "The Further Vision."

The paradise-hell of the Eloi and the Morlocks in fact leads causally as well as temporally to what the Traveller sees as the further vision of devolution tending towards the extinction of all life. In an episode appearing in the *New Review* but deleted subsequently, he comes next upon a species more degraded than the Morlocks. Of this creature, which he likens to "rabbits or some breed of kangaroo," the Traveller reports: "I was surprised to see that the thing had five feeble digits to both its fore and hind feet—the fore feet, indeed, were almost as human as the fore feet of a frog. It had, moreover, a roundish head,

with a projecting forehead and forward-looking eyes." As a result of his examination, he admits that "A disagreeable apprehension crossed my mind"; but he has no opportunity to observe "my grey animal, or grey man, whichever it was" at greater length because he perceives that he is being stalked by a monster similar to a gigantic centipede.[8] It is left for the reader to infer that at this point in the future the Eloi have devolved into creatures with "five feeble digits," in this case the victims of giant centipedes.

At the next stop in the distant future (in both the Heinemann and the *New Review* versions) all anthropomorphic life seems to have disappeared, and the Traveller sees instead "a thing like a huge white butterfly" and "a monstrous crab-like creature" (p. 137). He goes on until, thirty million years hence, it appears as if animal life has devolved out of existence. Plant life has degenerated to "livid green liverworts and lichens" (p. 139). Here he witnesses a solar eclipse which prefigures the end of the world.

> The darkness grew apace; a cold wind began to blow in freshening gusts from the east, and the showering white flakes in the air increased in number. From the edge of the sea came a ripple and whisper. Beyond these lifeless sounds the world was silent. Silent? It would be hard to convey the stillness of it . . . As the darkness thickened, the eddying flakes grew more abundant . . . and the cold of the air more intense. At last, one by one, swiftly, one after the other, the white peaks of the distant hills vanished into blackness. The breeze rose to a moaning wind. I saw the black central shadow of the eclipse sweeping towards me. In another moment the pale stars alone were visible. All else was rayless obscurity. The sky was absolutely black. (pp. 140-141)

In retrospect, it seems that the unbalanced struggle between the Eloi and the Morlocks prepares for this final vision, that a terrible logic compels the conclusion: "The sky was absolutely black." "People unfamiliar with such speculations as those of the younger Darwin," the Time Traveller had remarked earlier, "forget that the planets must ultimately fall back one by one into the parent body" (p. 76). This is a vision hardly in accord with "Excelsior" optimism; on the contrary, it is precisely calculated to "run counter to the placid assumption . . . that Evolution was a pro-human force making things better and better for mankind."[9]

Indeed, the ideas Wells is dealing with are, as he stated in the early essay on **"Zoological Retrogression,"** an "evolutionary antithesis":

> . . . there is almost always associated with the suggestion of advance in biological phenomena an opposite idea, which is its essential complement. The technicality expressing this would, if it obtained sufficient currency in the world of culture, do much to reconcile the naturalist and his traducers. The toneless glare of optimistic evolution would then

be softened by a shadow; the monotonous reiteration of 'Excelsior' by people who did not climb would cease; the too sweet harmony of the spheres would be enhanced by a discord, this evolutionary antithesis—degradation. (**"Retrogression,"** p. 246)

Wells goes on to illustrate "the enormous importance of degeneration as a plastic process in nature" and its "parity with evolution" by giving examples of species which have retrogressed and of vestigial features now observable which perhaps presage future degeneration. His concluding remarks are especially relevant to the vision presented in *The Time Machine*:

> There is, therefore, no guarantee in scientific knowledge of man's permanence or permanent ascendancy . . . The presumption is that before him lies a long future of profound modification, but whether this will be, according to his present ideals, upward or downward, no one can forecast. Still, so far as any scientist can tell us, it may be that, instead of this, Nature is, in unsuspected obscurity, equipping some now humble creature with wider possibilities of appetite, endurance, or destruction, to rise in the fulness of time and sweep *homo* away into the darkness from which his universe arose. The Coming Beast must certainly be reckoned in any anticipatory calculations regarding the Coming Man. (**"Retrogression,"** p. 253)

Clearly this speculation goes beyond the mere softening of the "glare of optimistic evolution" with a "shadow." The "opposite idea" dominates Wells's imagination—the vision of man's being swept away "into the darkness from which his universe arose"—of "life that . . . is slowly and remorselessly annihilated," as he says in **"On Extinction"**[10]—the vision, in other words, of *The Time Machine*. And his prophecy of the "Coming Beast"—in stories like **"The Sea Raiders"** (1896), *The War of the Worlds* (1898), and **"The Empire of the Ants"** (1904), as well as in *The Time Machine*—though more literal than Yeats's vision of the Second Coming—is no less forceful in its dramatic impact.

II

The vision of the future as a devolutionary process, in reversing the expectations of "optimistic evolution," is not isolated in *The Time Machine* as an imaginative possibility for its own sake. The structure of the world of 802,701, for instance, suggests a critique of the pastoral utopia of Morris' *News from Nowhere* (1891) and other pre-Wellsian utopian romances, since the idyllic world of the Eloi is quite literally undermined by the machine-dominated world of the Morlocks. Thus the vision of the future in *The Time Machine* both reflects and evaluates man's "present ideals," a point that the Time Traveller emphasizes by insisting that the theories he has developed to explain the world of the future derive from what he sees in the present state of human affairs.

Although the Traveller revises his theories as he learns about the nature of the Morlocks, he temporarily settles

on an etiological interpretation of the relationship between the effete (and virtually androgynous) Eloi and their more energetic predators. "The great triumph of Humanity I had dreamed of took a different shape in my mind. It had been no such triumph of moral education and general co-operation as I had imagined. Instead, I saw a real aristocracy, armed with perfected science and working to a logical conclusion the industrial system of today. Its triumph had not been simply a triumph over nature, but a triumph over nature and the fellow-man" (p. 84). To be sure, he himself reserves a doubt concerning this account of how the future world had come to be: "My explanation may be absolutely wrong. I still think it is the most plausible one." His ambivalence here reminds one, not accidentally, of his subsequent remark as to how the reader may accept this vision of the future. "Take it as a lie—or a prophecy . . . Consider I have been speculating on the destinies of our race, until I have hatched this fiction" (p. 145). Together, these statements suggest that any explanation of the imaginary world of the Eloi and the Morlocks is important only insofar as it makes it clear that the world projected in the fiction is prophecy; that is, the "working to a logical conclusion" of what can be observed in the world of the present.

The Time Traveller himself says that he has arrived at his explanation by extrapolating (to appropriate a useful word from the jargon of science fiction) from tendencies existing in the present:

> At first, *proceeding from the problems of our own age,* it seemed clear as daylight to me that the gradual widening of the present merely temporary and social difference between the Capitalist and the Labourer, was the key to the whole position. No doubt it will seem grotesque enough to you—and wildly incredible!—and yet *even now there are existing circumstances* to point that way. (pp. 81-82; my emphasis)

What this passage implies is that the procedure for interpreting the vision of *The Time Machine* recapitulates the process by which the fiction was "hatched"; so that the science-fictional method of prophecy is itself "the key to the whole position." Moreover, on the evidence of the Traveller's own theories, the future that Wells has projected does not, precisely speaking, embody only the consequences of "the industrial system of to-day," but also the consequences of the ideal which directs the course and uses of technological advance.

While they summarily describe a world resulting from man's present ideals, the Time Traveller's theories are also evaluative. In saying, for example, that "the great triumph of Humanity . . . had not been simply a triumph over nature" (as T. H. Huxley had urged[11]) "but a triumph over nature and the fellow-man," the Time Traveller makes a negative moral judgment: "moral education and general co-operation" had not been achieved. And condemnation is again entailed in his observation that the human intellect "had set itself steadfastly towards comfort and ease, a balanced society with security as its watchword"; for "Only those animals partake of intelligence that have to meet a huge variety of needs and dangers" (p. 130). The ideal (perfect security) therefore undermines the means of maintaining it (intelligence); and the result, the Traveller continues, is that "the upper-world man had drifted towards his feeble prettiness, and the underworld to mere mechanical industry. But that perfect state had lacked one thing even for mechanical perfection—absolute permanency" (pp. 130-131). This final interpretation, which elaborates on and at the same time supersedes his previous explanations, accounts more fully for the world of the Eloi and the Morlocks as it obviously impugns man's "present ideals." The ideal of subjugating man and nature to realize a state of "comfort and ease" is satirically judged by projecting its consequences as a vision of the future.

Both the Traveller's principle for interpreting the vision and the process by which that vision has been arrived at assume, therefore, that man's ideals do affect the course of evolution, that the world of 802,701 and beyond is the "working to a logical conclusion" of man's striving for comfort and ease. This point is made explicitly in the version of *The Time Machine* published in the *National Observer,* a version inferior in conception and structure to that put out by Heinemann, and one containing more cross-discussion between the Traveller (referred to as the Philosopher) and his fictive audience than Wells finally (and rightly) decided was necessary. In the serialized episode called "The Refinement of Humanity: A.D. 12,203," the Philosopher remarks to a doctor in his audience:

> You believe that the average height, average weight, average longevity will all be increased, that in the future humanity will breed and sanitate itself into human Megatheria . . . But . . . what I saw is just what one might have expected. Man, like other animals, has been moulded, and will be, by the necessities of his environment. What keeps men so large and so strong as they are? The fact that if any drop below a certain level of power and capacity for competition, they die. Remove dangers, render physical exertion no longer a necessity but an excrescence upon life, abolish competition by limiting population . . . [and you get degeneration].
>
> Somewhere between now and then [i.e., 12,203] your sanitary science must have won the battle it is beginning now.[12]

Here and elsewhere in this early draft Wells does not really achieve any degree of detachment from the Philosopher; but at least passages such as this help to clarify how a vision antithetical to "the placid assumption of that time that Evolution was a pro-human force" can also illustrate the consequences of an ideal seemingly inseparable from that assumption—namely, the ideal of evolving towards greater and greater "comfort and ease."

As far as the Time Traveller's theories are necessary for understanding the prophecy, then, it is somewhat misleading to say that "This horrible degeneration [of the Eloi and the Morlocks] has occurred because mankind, as Huxley feared, was ultimately unable to control the cosmic or evolutionary process."[13] Rather, the Traveller implies, mankind apparently controlled the cosmic process too well, according to an ideal the consequences of which no one could foresee. One of those consequences is that by 802,701 no species has the intelligence any more to set limits on the struggle for existence, in which the defenseless Eloi fall victim to the carnivorous Morlocks. Among these descendants of homo sapiens, the struggle for survival—which, engendered by "Necessity," makes the "absolute permanency" of "mechanical perfection" impossible—now resumes the character that struggle takes among other animals. "Man," the Traveller reflects, "had been content to live in ease and delight upon the labours of his fellow-man, had taken Necessity as his watchword and excuse, and in the fulness of time Necessity had come home to him" (pp. 105-106). And once this "Necessity" reasserts itself, once, that is to say, man's descendants begin reverting to beasts, anthropomorphic life, according to the vision of *The Time Machine,* is irrevocably on the downward path of devolution.

III

This vision of social disintegration and devolution as a critique of the ideal of striving towards "ease and delight" can exist only in the dimension of prophecy, that dimension into which the critique can be projected and imaginatively given life—the world, in other words, of science fantasy.[14] The fourth dimension as a dimension in time is thus a metaphor: it is the dimension open to the imagination. "Our mental existences, which are immaterial and have no dimensions, are passing along the Time-Dimension" (p. 6), the Traveller had said in introducing his audience to the concept of this new dimension. As a world wherein the consequences of the accepted ideal can be envisioned, the fourth dimension provides a critical and comprehensive point of view from which to evaluate the present.

That at the beginning of *The Time Machine* no one except the Time Traveller has conceived of—or even can conceive of—this dimension already indicates a lack of imaginative (and critical) awareness on the part of his audience. His argument for a fourth dimension, prefaced by the caveat that "I shall have to controvert one or two ideas that are almost universally accepted" (pp. 1-2), meets with incomprehension and complacent skepticism. Quite predictably, his audience fails to take seriously—if the point is grasped at all—the relevance of the Time Traveller's vision. No one else seems to connect the vision of "The two species that had resulted from the evolution of man . . . sliding down towards, or . . . already arrived at, an altogether new relationship" (p. 97) with his preconception of an "inevitable tendency to higher and better things" (**"Retrogression,"** p. 247). Perhaps no one in the audience takes this vision seriously because, as Wells speculated elsewhere, "It is part of the excessive egotism of the human animal that the bare idea of its extinction seems incredible to it."[15] Certainly there is no sign that anyone among the listeners sees how, or that, this vision implicates his present ideals, which are responsible for the shape of the future. On the contrary, the reactions typifying the attitude of the audience are the skepticism of the Medical Man, who wants to analyze the flowers that the Traveller has brought back with him, and the arrant disbelief of the Editor, who considers the Traveller's account a "gaudy lie" (p. 148). Only the unidentified narrator of the entire *Time Machine* lies "awake most of the night thinking about it."

In fact, the Time Traveller himself does not seem to be wholly cognizant of the implications of his theories. If his etiology is correct, the cause of the degeneration he discovers exists in the present. Therefore, the burden of what he calls "moral education" remains here and now; and his return to the world of 802,701 would appear to be either a romantic evasion and of a piece with the sentimental "squirms of idyllic petting" that V. S. Pritchett finds embarrassing,[16] or a pessimistic retreat from a world "that must inevitably fall back upon and destroy its makers" (p. 152). In any case, the Traveller's point of view, though more comprehensive than that of the other characters, is still limited; and this limitation has its structural correlative in the fact that his narrative is related secondhand, as it were, three years after his disappearance, and comprises only a part—albeit a large part—of the fiction.

That the structure of *The Time Machine* encompasses, and thereby defines the limits of, the Traveller's point of view indicates that the romance follows an inner logic of its own, a logic, like that governing the Time Traveller's vision, which compels ultimate consequences from a given premise. Accordingly, the logic which necessitates the Traveller's vanishing into the world of his vision depends upon how he accepts that vision. His insistence that "The story I told you was true" (p. 148) implies that he takes his prophecy literally, that he allows it the same ontological status that he himself has. Thus to dramatize the assertion that his tale is literally true, he must go back into the world of the future: since he cannot accept it as fiction, as an invented metaphor, he must disappear into the dimension where his vision "exists." The demand that his vision be literally true, in other words, requires that the Traveller be no more real than it is; and his return to that world fulfills this demand.

In being subsumed in his vision, however, he also renders it no less real than any member of the fictive audience; so that one is forced to give the same degree of credibility to the futuristic fantasy as to the contemporary scene in which the Traveller relates his story. What the reader is left with, that is, is the prophecy, the metaphorical truth which mediates between the blind and complacent optimism evidenced by the fictive audience and the resultant devolution envisioned by the Time Traveller.

The Traveller's return to the world of 802,701, far from vitiating the impact of *The Time Machine,* reinforces its claim to integrity: by having the Time Traveller act out

the ultimate consequence of his taking a prophetic myth literally, Wells illustrates the rigor that he has submitted himself to in satirizing certain "present ideals." The romance, as I see it, is thus rigorously self-contained in "working to a logical conclusion" both the myth of devolution that exposes tendencies "of our own age" and the various points of view regarding the truth of that prophetic myth.

According to this interpretation, Wells's experiment in fiction is comparable in the artistry of its narrative to the contemporaneous experiments of, say Joseph Conrad, who also wrote tales "told in quotation marks"[17] and who found in Wells an early admirer; and for the complexity of its structure and point of view, *The Time Machine* deserves the praise that Henry James in fact bestowed on it.[18]

NOTES

[1] *The Scientific Romances of H. G. Wells* (London, 1933), p. ix.

[2] Bergonzi, "*The Time Machine:* An Ironic Myth," *Critical Quarterly,* II (1960), 293-305, and *The Early H. G. Wells: A Study of the Scientific Romances* (Toronto, 1961), pp. 42-61; Hillegas, "Cosmic Pessimism in H. G. Wells' Scientific Romances," *Papers of the Mich. Acad. of Sci., Arts, and Letters,* XLVI (1961), 657-658, and *The Future as Nightmare: H. G. Wells and the Anti-Utopians* (New York, 1967), pp. 24-34.

[3] All published drafts of *The Time Machine* share these components, though the serialized versions appearing in the *National Observer* (1894) and the *New Review* (1895) differ from the first English edition, published by Heinemann, in many respects—not all of them minor. Sometimes these differences give insight into the meaning of Wells's fantasy, though the serialized versions of course count only as outside evidence for any interpretation. Otherwise they are of interest solely to a study of Wells's progress as a literary artist, a subject it is not my intention to discuss explicitly here.

Some evaluation of the merits of the Heinemann version of *The Time Machine* relative to the various previously published drafts, including the first American edition, can be found in Bergonzi's "The Publication of *The Time Machine* 1894-5," *RES.* N.S., IX (1960), 42-51.

[4] The fact that Wells was familiar with the notion of degeneration at this early date would seem to reduce the possible extent of any influence on him of Max Nordau's *Degeneration* (1894), which Bergonzi adduces as a source for the vision of the future in *The Time Machine.*

[5] "Zoological Retrogression," *The Gentleman's Magazine,* 7 Sept. 1891, p. 246.

[6] All quotations from *The Time Machine* refer to the first English edition (London, 1895).

[7] As Bergonzi observes of *The Time Machine*, "its central narrative is polarised between opposed groups of imagery, the paradisal . . . and the demonic" ("An Ironic Myth," p. 300).

[8] *The Time Machine* in the *New Review*, XII (1895), 578-79.

[9] *The Time Machine* is part of a reaction on the part of many writers of the late eighties and nineties to the strident optimism that permeated the official rhetoric of the Victorian age. See Bergonzi's discussion of the *fin du globe* in his *Early H. G. Wells*, pp. 3-14, et passim. Some material may also be found in Hillegas' *Future as Nightmare* (see n. 2 above), relevant to attitudes towards evolution during the period in which Wells was writing *The Time Machine*.

[10] "On Extinction," *Chambers's Journal*, X (30 Sept. 1893), 623.

[11] In "Evolution and Ethics" and other essays, Huxley declares that ethical man can exist only if he modifies the "cosmic process."

[12] "The Refinement of Humanity," *National Observer*, N.S., XI (21 Apr. 1894), 581-582.

[13] Hillegas, "Cosmic Pessimism," p. 658.

[14] As late as *Men Like Gods* (1923), the utopian fantasy that takes place in the "F dimension," Wells has one of his characters say of another (neither has yet been initiated into Utopia): "He has always had too much imagination. He thinks that things that don't exist *can* exist. And now he imagines himself in some sort of scientific romance and out of our world altogether" (*Men Like Gods,* New York, 1923, pp. 21-22).

[15] "The Extinction of Man," *Certain Personal Matters* (London, 1898 [1897]), p. 172. This essay first appeared in the *Pall Mall Gazette* for 23 Sept. 1894.

[16] *The Living Novel* (London, 1946), p. 119.

[17] Northrop Frye, *Anatomy of Criticism* (Princeton, N. J., 1957), pp. 202-203.

[18] On 21 Jan. 1900, James wrote to Wells: "It was very graceful of you to send me your book—I mean the particular masterpiece entitled *The Time Machine*, after I had so *ungracefully* sought it at your hands" (*Henry James and H. G. Wells,* ed. Leon Edel and Gordon N. Ray, Urbana, Ill., 1958, p. 63).

Alex Eisenstein

SOURCE: "Very Early Wells: Origins of Some Major Physical Motifs in '*The Time Machine*' and '*The War of the Worlds*,'" in *Extrapolation*, Vol. 13, No. 2, May, 1972, pp. 119-27.

In *The Early H. G. Wells,*[1] Bernard Bergonzi treats the dualistic future world of *The Time Machine* mainly as an expression of the traditional mythic schism between Paradise and Perdition. To support his interpretation, he cites the contrasting imagery associated with the two distinct human habitats—and species—delineated in the story: descriptions of the upper realm and its people are predominately sunny and idyllic; those of the lower, somber and infernal.

Yet, beyond the demonic role he thus ascribes to the Morlocks, Professor Bergonzi further claims that these creatures "represent an exaggerated fear of the nineteenth century proletariat."[2] Of course, in terms of the tale's quasi-Darwinian rationale, they are literally the biological and social descendants of the working class, but Mr. Bergonzi attributes to them a much closer identity with the toiling masses: "Since the Morlocks on one level stand for the late nineteenth century proletariat, the Traveller's attitude towards them symbolizes a contemporary bourgeois fear of the working class, and it is not fanciful to impute something of this attitude to Wells himself. From his school days in Bromley he had disliked and feared the working class in a way wholly appropriate to the son of a small tradesman—as various Marxist critics have not been slow to remark."[3] A brief quotation from the last third of the narrative, establishing the protagonist's overwhelming desire (by then) to slaughter all Morlocks, immediately precedes the above discussion in its original context. With such a preface, Mr. Bergonzi's commentary strongly implies that a real-life corollary of this homicidal urge became a deep-seated affliction of the Wellsian psyche.

This malign conjecture further suggests that the Morlocks must ultimately derive from that hypothetical antipathy for Victorian Labor. However, despite the ready assertion of "various Marxist critics," the formulation of these bestial hominids and their plutonian abode stems from other and more primary childhood referents.

First among the latter is Atlas House, the birthplace of Wells and home of his infancy and early childhood. Its particular situation and character reflect, to a large degree, the peculiar dichotomy of the world of A.D. 802,701. His father's crockery shop opened onto High Street, and directly behind the shop lay the small parlor of the Wells home. From this parlor, "a murderously narrow staircase with a twist in it led downstairs to a completely subterranean kitchen, lit by a window which derived its light from a grating on the street level, and a bricked scullery, which, since the house was poised on a bank, opened into the yard at the ground level below."[4] These lines from Wells's autobiography firmly establish his own feeling about the cellar rooms; although the lowest floor allowed direct access to level ground and open air, he thought of these rooms as *"completely subterranean."* (The dim illumination from the grate doubtless served as a constant reminder of this subsurface condition.)

A fanciful extension of the underground status to the backyard should have been fairly automatic for any normally imaginative pre-school youngster, and especially for one who played there so long and so often that he "learnt its every detail."[5] Several of these physical details enhanced the subterranean aura. Beginning at the rear wall of the house, a brickwork pavement spread across half the yard,[6] thus linking it, by similarity of texture, to the indoor domain of the scullery. Large "erections in the neighbors' yards on either side" and "a boundary wall"[7] at the far end hemmed in the backyard, isolating it from the outer world—and, perhaps, vaulting upward like the steep sides of a pit. One adjunct of the yard actually simulated some gloomy catacomb: "Between the scullery and the neighbour's wall was a narrow passage covered over,"[8] where his father stored many piles of red earthenware for the shop. The cellar and the yard, in many of their dominant features, recall the industrial character of the Morlock caverns. Together, they functioned as the apparent site of all the necessary work accomplished in the limited universe accessible to Wells as a toddler—the place where everything was produced, cleaned, or otherwise prepared for use above or below. All the fixtures on that level bespoke some form of utilitarian labor: "In the scullery was a small fireplace, a copper boiler for washing, a provision cupboard, a bread pan, a beer cask, a pump delivering water from a well into a stone sink, and space for coal . . . beneath the wooden stairs."[9] In the yard stood "a brick erection, the 'closet,' an earth jakes over a cesspool, . . . and above this closet was a rainwater tank. Behind it was the brick dustbin . . ."[10] and from the house, "an open cement gutter brought the waste waters of the sink to a soak away"[11] in the center of the half-paved yard. (Note the prevalence of metal, stone, and stone-like materials, and the numerous vessels for storage or processing, along with mechanisms and conduits for the conveyance of working fluids and the disposal of wastes.)

Even the plots adjacent to the yard can be identified with basic functions performed by the Morlocks in their underworld, or with the underworld itself. "On one hand was the yard of Mr. Munday, the haberdasher, . . . who had put up a greenhouse and cultivated mushrooms . . . ; and on the other, Mr. Cooper, the tailor, had built out a workroom in which two or three tailors sat and sewed."[12] On one hand, the "greenhouse" nurtured plants that commonly grow in dark, dank caverns; on the other, one of the notable vestigial "duties" remaining to the Morlocks lay in their capacity as clothiers for the Eloi.

But most important, the major occupation of the subsurface dwellers also loomed in the background of Atlas House. Beyond the boundary wall at the end of the yard spread "the much larger yard and sheds of Mr. Covell the butcher, in which pigs, sheep and horned cattle were harboured violently, and protested plaintively through the night before they were slaughtered."[13] This presence surely made an indelible impression on Wells, for it crops up again as the metaphoric essence of a subsequent major work, *The Island of Dr. Moreau.*

The concept of a hidden lower world exercised an even greater fascination for Wells, one that continued throughout his life. *First Men in the Moon,* though possibly somewhat derivative of Kepler's *Somnium,* clearly contains another surface elysium shielding a vast industrial substratum. The idea emerges, for perhaps its last public appearance, in a metaphor from the *Autobiography* that summarizes his early psychosexuality: "So at the age of seven . . . , I had already between me and my bleak protestant God, a wide wide world of snowy mountains, Arctic regions, tropical forests, prairies and deserts and high seas, . . . about which I was prepared to talk freely, and cool and strange below it all a cavernous world of nameless goddess mistresses of which I never breathed a word to any human being."[14]

A unique bibliographic discovery made by Wells in his early life probably accentuated his receptivity to the concept of a hidden world below; it also lends some credibility to the notion that the infernal aspects of the Morlock habitat indicate the real creative roots of this environmental motif. (Bergonzi does not make this claim outright, but he might easily believe as much, if one may judge from his emphasis of these aspects.) In the words of Wells:

> There was a picture in an old illustrated book of devotions, Sturm's *Reflections,* obliterated with stamp paper, and so provoking investigation. What had mother been hiding from me? By holding up the page to the light I discovered the censored illustration represented hell-fire; devil, pitchfork and damned, all complete and drawn with great gusto. But she had anticipated the general trend of Protestant theology at the present time and hidden hell away.[15]

Hell, of course, embodies the idea of an underworld without recourse to stamp-covered illustrations; nevertheless, the obscured drawing in Sturm was a physical metaphor of all such underworlds, and young Wells may have perceived it as such, if only unconsciously. Yet, among Wells's earliest experiences, all reading and even religious training must rank second to his awareness of Atlas House, for it preceded them all.

The quasi-subterranean kitchen of his birthplace pervaded his psyche to such a degree that he recreated it, under fictional circumstances fraught with gross improbability, in one of the most perilous scenes in *The War of the Worlds.* In the second chapter of Book Two, "The Earth Under the Martians," the narrator is trapped in an abandoned house that barely escapes total destruction when a Martian cylinder lands nearby:

> The fifth cylinder must have fallen right into the midst of the house we had first visited. The building had vanished, completely smashed, pulverised, and dispersed by the blow. . . . The earth all round it had splashed under that tremendous impact . . . and lay in heaped piles that hid the masses of the adjacent houses. . . . Our house had collapsed backward; the front portion, even on the ground floor, had been destroyed completely; by a chance the kitchen and scullery had escaped, and stood buried now under soil and ruins, closed in by tons

of earth on every side save towards the cylinder. Over that aspect we hung now on the very edge of the great circular pit . . . [16]

The house is largely decimated, while the *kitchen and scullery* survive, though engulfed by earth on *three sides.* This result occurs despite the fact that the house collapses *backward.* Presumably, the kitchen is to the rear; how does the rear survive when the front is utterly demolished? It does so, of course, because the author contrived it so, by *fiat.* The event is not impossible, perhaps, but to me it seems most unlikely—compounding the coincidence of the landing itself. The *precise* physical situation must have held a fair amount of intrinsic significance for Wells; surely he could have trapped the narrator beside the impact crater in a manner less idiosyncratic or incredible?

If anyone might doubt that an edifice like Atlas House could adequately serve as model for an extensive subterranean world, he should consider the psychological effect of entering such a building on the first floor and then discovering *another* ground level below. Even from an adult observer, the first encounter with this situation may elicit a sense of suddenly penetrating a dimension of existence normally veiled beneath the mundane, surface world.

From infancy, of course, Wells became increasingly familiar with this bi-level arrangement; it could hardly have seemed very strange to him for all his youth, much less the rest of his life. Nevertheless, this condition does not preclude the possibility that the structure of Atlas House retained a powerful grip on his imagination; it merely indicates that such an influence probably developed in a fairly gradual manner. Still, at some early point in his life, there had to be a *first time* for Wells to experience and perceive the "odd" nature of Atlas House. Whether the metaphoric significance occurred to him immediately, or rather seeped slowly into his mental storehouse without conscious realization, cannot be determined by the literary tools and data currently available; indeed, that question may remain forever moot. Even so, the circumstantial evidence for a connection between early environs and fictional setting cannot be summarily dismissed—especially in view of the complementary origin of the Morlock race.

What of these Morlocks, then? What are their prototypes, if not—at least, not entirely—the imps of Satan that once infested Anglican dogma? What is the principal inspiration for this savage race, if not a similarly savage revulsion for the brutish workers of the world? The actual source again involves childhood fantasizing about Atlas House, this time spurred by a natural-science book Wells read at age seven: "There was Wood's *Natural History,* also copiously illustrated and full of exciting and terrifying facts. I conceived a profound fear of the gorilla, of which there was a fearsome picture, which came out of the book at times after dark [the gorilla, of course; not the picture] and followed me noiselessly about the house. The half landing was a favourite lurking place for this terror. I passed it whistling, but wary and then ran for my life up the next flight."[17] The Morlocks share all the insidious, nocturnal habits of the imaginary ape:

like him, they emerge at night to ambush the dawdler from shadowed hideaways; they clamber up from lower levels to chase and terrorize small and youthful innocents.

That the Morlock race is a literary amalgam of apes and several other creatures has never been a great secret; the story itself indicates as much, and Bergonzi duly notes this. Nevertheless, his own investigation of the early H. G. Wells never leads him to suspect (or betray that he does) the true bedrock origins of Wells's creations. The *real* psychological significance of the Morlocks lies not in any apprehensive loathing for the proletariat, but rather in a profound early fear of wild animals in general and specifically of the gorilla, conceived as a personal household nemesis. In conjunction with the metaphoric aura of the house, this fear-fantasy provided the essential basis for the vision of the future contained in *The Time Machine.* All else, even the ostensible, socio-scientific explanation in the story, are mere after-the-fact rationales overlaid on the germinal idea.

As mentioned above, Wells's first knowledge of wild animals soon crystallized into a fear of monumental proportions: " . . . I was glad to think that between the continental land masses of the world, which would have afforded an unbroken land passage for wolves from Russia and tigers from India, and this safe island . . . stretched the impassable moat of the English Channel."[18] Even much later, at age thirteen, he was still prone to bestial nemeses of the night, as in the following description of the terrors attending the weekend journey to his Uncle Tom's riverside inn, Surly Hall: "My imagination peopled the dark fields on either hand with crouching and pursuing foes. Chunks of badly trimmed hedge took on formidable shapes. Sometimes I took to my heels and ran. For a week or so that road was haunted by a rumour of an escaped panther . . . That phantom panther waited for me patiently; it followed me like a noiseless dog, biding its time. And one night on the other side of the hedge a sleeping horse sighed deeply, a gigantic sigh, and almost frightened me out of my wits."[19] The hobgoblin activities recorded here bear an acute resemblance to those executed by the malevolent ape of Atlas House; Wells evidently retained the primary image long after its inception.

A relevant sidelight on Morlock origins—the Wood volume also triggered in Wells inklings of the rigorous Darwinian principles he later acquired in formal sessions with T. H. Huxley: "Turning over the pages of the *Natural History,* I perceived a curious relationship between cats and tigers and lions and so forth, and to a lesser degree between them and hyenas and dogs and bears, and between them again and other quadrupeds, and curious premonitions of evolution crept into my thoughts."[20] This revelation reinforces the impression that this book was an important wellspring for the speculative constructs employed in *The Time Machine.*

In like manner the dominant apparition of *The War of the Worlds* can be traced to Wells's first direct encounter with the wider Universe. In his fourteenth year, while delving into an attic storeroom in Up Park (his second home), he uncovered the following treasure:

. . . There was a box, at first quite mysterious, full of brass objects that clearly might be screwed together. I screwed them together, by the method of trial and error, and presently found a Gregorian telescope on a trip in my hands. I carried off the wonder to my bedroom. . . . I was discovered by my mother in the small hours, my bedroom window wide open, inspecting the craters of the moon. She had heard me open the window. She said I should catch my death of cold. But at the time that seemed a minor consideration.[21]

Here is the inanimate progenitor of the Martian war machine—both are tripodal devices assembled from cylinders. The parts of the telescope screw together, whereas the cylinders from Mars *un*screw to open. Both the telescope and the war machine involve optical systems—the first for concentrating distant radiation, the other for projecting concentrated radiation over considerable distance (the narrator repeatedly calls the heat-ray mechanism a "camera" or "projector").

The war machines are variously described, but most often as metallic and "glittering."[22] Nothing glitters like gold, of course—except, perhaps, the highly polished tube of a brass telescope; the cowled head of one of these monster machines is termed a "brazen hood"[23] soon after their initial appearance in the story.

The notion of three-legged fighting machines could have sprung from contemplation of any tripod-mounted apparatus—for instance a portrait camera, which possesses the same general attributes that qualify the telescope as a prototype. Even a ringstand or a milking stool could be prime suspects; one of the marching engines of holocaust is actually likened to a milking stool, in a passage describing its exotic mode of locomotion.[24] A telescope, of course, figures prominently in the first chapter; yet, somewhat later, British defenders introduce a much more suggestive instrument— the heliograph. But Wells never *built* a heliograph, nor did he handle a camera in his early years; tripod ringstands remained outside his direct experience until he entered the Normal School of Science in 1884, and his childhood acquaintance with milking stools was surely no better than second hand. Furthermore, the telescope—and only the telescope—engaged his mind and spirit with the remarkable vistas and wonders of Space. No other similar artifact affected his outlook to the extent, and in the direction, that this one did. Such examples as these illustrate how Wells's imagination transformed the objects of commonplace experience into the fundamental imagery of his fictions.

NOTES

[1] Bernard Bergonzi, *The Early H. G. Wells* (Manchester: Manchester University Press, 1961).

[2] Bergonzi, p. 53.

[3] Bergonzi, p. 56.

[4] H. G. Wells, *Experiment in Autobiography* (New York: Macmillan, 1934), p. 22.

[5] *Ibid.*, p. 23.

[6] *Ibid.*, p. 23.

[7] *Ibid.*, pp. 23 and 22, respectively.

[8] *Ibid.*, p. 23.

[9] *Ibid.*, p. 22. Elsewhere in the *Autobiography* (p. 48), Wells recaptures a vivid impression of the working ambience of "washing day, when the copper in the scullery was lit and all the nether regions were filled with white steam and the smell of soapsuds."

[10] Wells, p. 22.

[11] *Ibid.*, p. 23.

[12] *Ibid.*, p. 23.

[13] *Ibid.*, p. 22.

[14] *Ibid.*, p. 58.

[15] *Ibid.*, p. 29.

[16] *Seven Science Fiction Novels of H. G. Wells* (New York: Dover), p. 406; *Seven Famous Novels by H. G. Wells* (Garden City: Garden City Publishing Co., 1934), p. 347; *TWOTW* (New York: Popular Library, 1962), p. 128.

[17] Wells, *Autobiography,* p. 54. From the context, the half-landing in question is not clear (there were several, as the house possessed three stories above ground); however, inasmuch as meals were always eaten in the cellar kitchen, this anecdote probably refers to the landing between cellar and parlor, which would be passed on the way to bed after evening meal.

[18] *Ibid.*, p. 95.

[19] *Ibid.*, pp. 54-55.

[20] *Ibid.*, p. 106.

[21] Wells, *The War of the Worlds*, Ch. 10.

[22] *Ibid.*, Ch. 10.

[23] *Ibid.*, Ch. 10, para. 12.

[24] *Ibid.*, Ch. 12, para. 8; Ch. 13, para. 2; Ch. 13, para. 44; *passim.*

Alfred Borrello

SOURCE: "The End of the World: Youth and *The Time Machine*," in *H. G. Wells: Author in Agony*, edited by Harry T. Moore, Southern Illinois University Press, 1972, pp. 1-16.

Few novelists in this century, perhaps more than in any other period, can resist the delectable temptation to tailor their personal lives, thoughts, emotions into the novels they create. Many who cannot resist are relatively capable, nevertheless, of disguising their efforts to some degree. Herbert George Wells (1866-1946), however, by his own admission was capable neither of resistance nor disguise. He could not resist or disguise because he understood the events of his life in a special light. He saw mirrored in his physical and emotional anxieties and frustrations the sufferings of countless millions. He sensed

> humanity scattered over the world, dispersed, conflicting, unawakened . . . this spectacle of futility fills me with a passionate desire to end waste, to create order, to develop understanding. . . . All these people reflect and are part of the waste and discomfort of my life.[1]

As he tells us, he wanted desperately to "end the waste . . . of humanity." He believed as passionately that he was in possession of the means to fulfill his desire. Those tools he believed he had which would help him to achieve his purpose in life were his ability to write convincingly and to write copiously. At first he produced a small trickle, then an even steadier stream, and finally a boiling, onrushing mass of some one hundred and fifty-six separate titles and countless shorter works.[2] Some of his books were excellent—even Henry James praised them—others were indifferent, and most were dull by contemporary standards. But all were Wells himself and not just Wells of the teens and twenties when he was lionized by critics of the world scene, political pundits, and even Stalin; but rather all were Wells of his sickly, sensitive, uncomfortable youth. They were written within the context of the distant but never fading memories of "smelly drains," grubby lodgings, and the frustrated dreams associated with his search for maturity and stability—his personal "spectacle of futility."

He was born in a shabby (the word is his own) home called Atlas House, significantly and appropriately named for one who was to believe that he had to assume the weight of the world. He never left that first home intellectually. Nothing he ever wrote, no success he was to achieve could erase the haunting memories he associated with it. He dwells on its shortcomings at length in his ponderous autobiography (1934), and shadows of it appear in the homes of some of his principal creations: Kipps (1905), George Ponderevo (1909), Polly (1910), and many other characters.

Equally haunting are the memories of his parents which cover many pages in that same autobiography. Though absolutely devoted to them, he viewed them, nevertheless, as willing victims of the society against which he battled all of his long life. He was angry at their complacency and their seeming refusal to take effective measures to improve their "place" in life. Like every new generation, he, in turn, refused to understand their lives or the secret relationships, joys and pains and heartbreaks which marked their marriage. Stirred to anger as he was

by the closed minds of his parents and their distrust and fear of new and fresh ideas, he nevertheless dwells lovingly upon them as he draws their portraits page after page.

Sarah Neal Wells was the daughter of an innkeeper, literally born to serve. Apparently, Wells considered his maternal grandfather's profession ideally suited to develop the intellectually gifted and frustrated, for this is the life with which he rewards Polly's struggles. The innkeeper, however, destined his daughter for a better life. She was sent as a lady's maid to the household of Sir Henry Featherstonahaugh on whose estate, Up Park, her future husband, Joseph Wells, worked as a gardener. After their marriage, Joseph, who had never genuinely cared for the profession his father had trained him for, decided to leave the relative comfort of the estate to strike off on his own. With the financial aid offered him by a relation and a small inheritance, he opened a tiny crockery and china shop. Unfortunately his acumen as a tradesman was not equal to his ability as a cricketer for which he was locally famous.

The senior Wells was essentially a pastel figure. Wells portrays him again and again in his novels as the unsuccessful Polly ground down by the poverty assigned to him by his birth, and in the frustrations of Kipps who is unable to adjust to his wealth because of the social milieu in which he passed his youth. There are even traces of him in Albert Tewler, the antihero of *You Can't be Too Careful* (1941), whose whole being is directed by caution. Though Joseph Wells was notably unsuccessful, his son cherished the belief that were he given the proper chance, he could have made for himself and his family an excellent life. That opportunity Wells affords to many of his protagonists who quickly seize it.

But reality never afforded Joseph Wells the chance to escape the drabness which he shared with most members of the lower class in Victorian England. After his marriage to Sarah, the children came with ever-increasing regularity to the young couple, and the shop which produced little revenue to begin with seemed to produce less and less each year with each addition to the growing family. Soon it became obvious to the senior Wells that no effort on his part, not even the primitive form of birth control husband and wife practiced, could stave off the inevitable failure of the shop nor secure for them a comfortable living. Fortunately, like the denouement of a Dickens novel, help came in the form of a request from Up Park to Sarah. She took with her the young Wells, Bertie as he was called. He was ill and needed his mother's care. It was at Up Park that he was to catch the first concrete glimpse of a world for which, up to that time, he believed only vaguely that he was intended. A large part of this world was discovered when he was given freedom of the library. Sir Featherstonhaugh's collection, like those of many country aristocrats, was gathered over many generations. Rich in the works of philosophers, the books introduced the young Bertie to authors in whose lasting debt he was to remain throughout his career as a writer. There were three, however, who were to prove most influential. He read Voltaire, whose acrid satire flavors all his works and whose bitterness clouds even the most Utopian of his novels; Swift, whose hatred of the follies of the human race darts in and out of his books and whose giants reappear metamorphosed into towers of intelligence in *The Food of the Gods;* and Plato's *Republic* on which Wells was later to model his idealistic "Kingdom of God" and his "World State."[3] So fondly did he remember Up Park and what his stay there meant to him that he was to recreate it as Bladesover in *Tono-Bungay.*

But the happy life at Up Park soon came to an end almost as swiftly as it had begun, when the ever practical Sarah sensed that it was high time for Bertie to be placed, as her two older sons had been, on the road to a profitable and comfortable way of life. She sincerely believed, despite the absolute failure of her husband, that the good life was to be attained only in shopkeeping. She believed just as sincerely that in drapery was success most assured. Consequently, her youngest son was apprenticed, as were his brothers before him, to a draper. Bertie, however, was not as complacent as his brothers. He was bored and chafed at the emptiness of the life. Perhaps it was his brief taste of the better life he had been given during his stay at Up Park which forced him to walk twenty miles one day to the estate to inform his mother that he had irrevocably decided never to become a shopkeeper. His experiences behind a counter were not entirely wasted, however. He dwells on them with loathing in several of his novels.

From the moment when he made his final decision to abandon any attempt at shopkeeping until he achieved his first genuine success, the publication of *The Time Machine* (1895), his life was marked by privation. Never truly well educated—his early schooling barely gave him the rudiments of reading and writing—he chafed at his lack of knowledge. Reading widely filled some of the gaps, but only when he made the decision to move to London for a concerted attack upon his ignorance was he to take the first real step toward the life of a scientist for which he longed.

Living in London was no easier for a member of his class than life in a provincial town. In fact, it was a good deal less palatable.[4] Nevertheless, despite the thousand-and-one annoyances which marked his life, London gave him the opportunity to come into contact with minds which helped to shape the direction he was to take when he finally focused his aspirations on writing. There he seized the chance offered him to meet and eventually study biology and zoology under Thomas H. Huxley. Huxley imparted to Wells an understanding of life which kept alive the fires of pessimism which were to burn strongly even when Wells was hailed as the apostle of optimism. Huxley gave him that fear for man's future which precipitated the despair that darkened his final years.

It was Huxley's contention that Darwin's discoveries were fundamentally sound and applicable. He espoused the cause of Darwinism when to do so was to call down upon one's head a whirlwind of abuse. He had, ultimately, to defend his beliefs against the attacks of Gladstone, the prime minister. Though he fought long and bitter battles in defense of the theories he held, Huxley never claimed that evolution would result in the millennium for mankind as some had. Rather, he foresaw defeat and ultimate annihilation in mankind's future. He held that the species, by the very evolutionary process many hailed as progress and civilization, had developed to the point where it was engaged in a massive battle with its society, the world, and those cosmic forces loose in the universe which cannot be defeated and which will finally destroy it. But far more devastating than those unknown and uncontrollable cosmic forces is man's most powerful enemy—himself. Huxley contended that man is at war with man and, more tragically, he is at war with himself.

But there was yet another equally powerful force at work within Wells. That force was the element he found most irritating in his mother—her faith. She was literally possessed by what he calls a "Low Church Theology" which had at its core a stern, angry God the Father, the source of whose actions could invariably be discovered in a burning, almost jealous resentment of his creatures. This anger was caused by the sin he was able to identify in even the most holy of his ungrateful creatures. This sin was generally vaguely sexual even when not directly connected with the tentative explorations of a growing boy or the more pronounced and obvious actions of adults. For Sarah, this theology was adequate and satisfying, though she could not consciously trace to such transgressions the source of the poverty and pain doled out in heaping measures to herself and her family. Hers was a negative faith—a faith built on prohibition, proscription, hedged with fears not bound in any way with love, the love Wells felt so great a need for even as a child, the love for which he searched in so many of the sordid affairs he was to engage in as success crowned his efforts as a writer.

At first, Bertie was eager to follow his mother's lead in religion, but early in his life he began to suspect the existence of this cantankerous deity, perhaps because he saw that this god was obviously turning a deaf ear to his and his mother's prayers. But more likely, he began to realize, with the rationalization of youth, that angry as this god was, he made no move to punish him for the minor sexual adventures which were occupying his mind and body more and more. Then, Wells tells us, he had a dream.

> I had a dream of Hell so preposterous that it blasted that resort [as a basis for belief] out of my mind forever . . . there was Our Father in a particularly malignant phase . . . I saw no devil in my vision; my mind in its simplicity went straight to the responsible fountainhead. The dream pursued me into the daytime. Never had I hated God so intensely. And then suddenly the light broke through to me and I knew that God was a lie.[5]

Suspect as this "revelation" may be, his recording of it is significant because it represents one of the major preoccupations of his entire career as a writer. He was to pursue all through his long life some fit substitute for the God who "was a lie." He rejected belief in a deity who possessed those qualities which he subconsciously admitted were necessary to end the "spectacle of futility" which was his understanding of the plight of humanity. Sarah's god was all-powerful, cranky though he may be. He held out to his creatures, though he seemingly despised them, the promise of a perfect life which Huxley believed was impossible to achieve. But it was this very level of human perfection for which Wells hungered. He saw perfection as the only answer to the poverty and pain suffered by him and those countless millions whom he believed he represented. In rejecting Sarah's god, he was forced to reject the Heaven he offered. But Wells could not reject the longing for that Heaven which consumed him and directed everything he wrote and every speech he gave. He had only one route which he could take to satisfy that longing. There must exist somewhere in someone or something a force more powerful than his mother's invisible and omnipotent deity which would crown with success his search for human perfection. That search came to focus in his first novel, *The Time Machine* (1895).

But more suffering was to be Well's lot before the publication of that work. After studying under Huxley, he turned to teaching to sustain himself though he always thought of himself as a man of science. Teaching did not prove to be as lucrative as he had hoped. Much of the anguish which was his in this period of his life is reflected in *Love and Mr. Lewisham* (1900). While teaching, he suffered an injury to his kidney which was followed by a siege of tuberculosis. He was forced to return home to convalesce. During this period of inaction, for want of anything better to do, he turned to writing. He produced two scientific textbooks, some short stories and, finally, after much revision, *The Time Machine.* Its unexpected success forced him to turn to writing for his living.

Its appeal was immediate. Though some recognized elements of Jules Verne's method in it, it projected a vitality and youthful hope that Verne never displayed. Its public, though sensing something new in the tale, failed to grasp what Wells was trying to do. Its significance in terms of his life's work, as a consequence, remained clouded for generations. Contributing factors to this lack of clarity were the scientific patina Wells gave it with all the sociological implications arising from it. Despite the problems it presented, it is, even in this day, a stimulating story.

The Time Traveller's device carries him into the future. In his travels he witnesses the rise and fall of civilizations and their rise again to more brilliant heights. The Time Machine comes to rest in A.D. 802, 701, a period when the most exalted of these civilizations is in decline. It is a Huxleyan world. He encounters the humans of the period and discovers the species divided into two groups: the devourers (the Morlocks) and the devoured (the Eloi). The latter are four feet high, seemingly sexless, beautiful, graceful but indescribably frail creatures who have forgotten all art and industry. The Morlocks, monstrous apelike creatures, live in subterranean caves. They are the mechanics of this age who keep the Eloi, but come up out of their holes to feed on them in the moonless nights.

At this point, the Time Traveller clearly assumes the part of Wells commenting upon the society of his time. The Morlocks in their avariciousness suggest the role assigned by Wells to the capitalists in his young mind; and the poor, sexless, supine Eloi—who freely permit themselves to be cannibalized by the Morlocks—suggest the much oppressed class into which he, Wells, was born. What we are presented here, in a sense, is not so much a picture of the future, but rather a representation of the present—the turn of the century.

In this two-class society of Eloi and Morlocks, love plays no part. It is only with the appearance of the Time Traveller upon the scene that love, and the power that Wells believes it possesses, furtively rears its gentle albeit sexless head. Weena, an Eloi woman, becomes attracted to him, first from gratitude—he rescues her from drowning—and then out of affection. Unknown to him, before his departure to his own time, she places a flower in his pocket, a fragile token of her affection. It is what this flower represents, when he discovers it in his pocket, which proves to be the impetus for his desire to journey once again into the future to discover the key which will prevent the extinction of mankind whose last, dying gasp he has so vividly witnessed.

Though there is reference here to a need for some form of salvation, there is no mention of a god who can save his creatures, nor a religious creed postulated as a guide for that salvation. Rather, there is a suggestion that mankind must be saved through the efforts of man himself, through an individual who, though thoroughly human, is motivated by an unselfish love of humanity and who is willing to confront the dangers, horrors, and agony of the unknown in an attempt to effect that salvation. That figure, in the guise of the Time Traveller and the other protagonists he was to create, Wells believed was himself.[6]

Here then in his first novel is the direction, in microcosm, which Wells's creative life was to take. Like the Time Traveller, Wells has his "time machine" which will help him in his ceaseless, never varying search for the answer to mankind's ultimate problem. Unlike the Time Traveller, however, Wells's machine is not made of ivory and chrome but of pen and ink and paper.

When approached from another point of view, *The Time Machine* also suggests the several paradoxes which were constantly to haunt Wells in his search for the salvation of his species in his writing. The attempted solution of these paradoxes was to affect the direction his writing took as well as occupy his attention for the remainder of his life as a writer and was to end in frustration. The first rests squarely upon his firm belief in Huxley's hypothesis that the species is doomed to extinction. He depicts the Time Traveller standing at the edge of an ocean witnessing the death of the world whose only inhabitants are "monstrous crab-like creatures." Yet the scene, depressing as it is, does not drive from his heart the belief that he could save his race. Like his character, Wells clung unflaggingly to the hope throughout most of his life that some concerted action on the part of the individual, notably men like himself, could frustrate mankind's inevitable disappearance from the globe. This hope animates most of his protagonists even when they are confronted, like the Time Traveller, with seemingly impossible situations. With this firm belief in mind, Wells campaigned through his books (*The Idea of a League of Nations,* 1918; *The Way to a League of Nations,* 1918; *The Salvaging of Civilization,* 1921; etc.) and in personal appearances throughout the world for the unity of mankind which would direct the species to its true purpose—its own salvation. Only toward the end of his life, which witnessed the two world wars he had foreseen and the reality of the atom bomb and other horrible weapons his active imagination had invented, was that hope finally killed.

Further, the novel presents us with the paradox of individuality which figures as an important theme in Well's work as throughout the twentieth-century novel. The Morlocks and Eloi are indistinguishable within their own groups. Even their sex lies hidden. All Eloi have long, flowing hair so reminiscent of the youth of our day. Even their very clothing mitigates against individuality. Only the Time Traveller and Weena, for a brief moment, achieve identity. They achieve it because they actively identify themselves with a purpose other than that of the group. But identification of such a nature means involvement. And involvement brings with it danger and pain. The Time Traveller learns this principle only too well as do all of Wells's protagonists. When the Time Traveller proceeds to rescue Weena from drowning, he acts alone without the help of the Eloi who stand about dumbly disinterested in the fate of one of their kind. Weena, in turn, achieves her individuality when she identifies herself with her rescuer and offers him her love such as it is. Her pain comes when he leaves her.

The question must be asked at this point, as Wells most certainly must have asked himself time and time again, why the struggle? Why endure the pain of identification, the heartache of individuality when no struggle, no pain, no heartache can ultimately, as Huxley believed alter the destiny of mankind? After all, though the Time Traveller believes that he can frustrate that destiny, what his eyes see denies that belief.

Wells's reason for the struggle, for the endurance of the pain and the heartache begins with a rejection. This rejection is the chief motivating force of his characters and is the quality which sets them apart from their peers. Essentially, Wells rejects Christianity and its understanding of mankind as he rejected his mother's faith. He rejects it as insufficient motivation for the struggle. To suffer here on earth in a never-ending battle for a vague promise of an even vaguer joy in Heaven, he labels as insanity. Moreover, to believe that this earthly existence is a transitory phase of a greater, more enduring life is to

him a child's dream. The only reality for Wells and for his characters is the "now" of life on this earth. Moreover, he rejects the passivity Christianity preaches. While he does not deny that pain and suffering are part of man's lot, he insists that struggle is also part. Merely to suffer and to "turn the other cheek" is to consign oneself to defeat.[7]

Because Wells believed that only an earthly reality exists, he affirmed that one must probe this earthly life for the reasons why the futile struggle against man's destiny must be waged. In that examination he discovered the source of man's doom, as Huxley did, in man himself. The species, he believed, is cursed with a fundamental yearning for the *status quo,* for a changeless existence in which life proceeds at the same pointless pace as it has always proceeded—witness its desire for a never-ending Heaven. His mother's willing acceptance of her "place" in life was an example of this desire. The Morlocks and the Eloi are additional examples of this yearning. The Eloi never dream of opposing the Morlocks. They are content, like the lower class of Wells's own day, to live out their dreamlike and more than childish lives until required for some Morlock's dinner. Not even the horror of witnessing one of their companions being dragged bodily into their enemies' lair disturbs their composure. They want nothing but the softness of their lives uncomplicated by thoughts of the future. Wells must have seen their equivalents in many a pub and on many a street in London. But the Eloi are not alone in their desire to keep things as they are. The Morlocks, the capitalists of the future, also want nothing to change. Why should they pursue another course when there are sufficient Eloi to satisfy even the most insatiable appetite? Moreover, the Eloi are easy to keep, and the search for a new source of food would divert their attention from the machines to which they are dedicated.

Yet, cursed as mankind is with this yearning for the *status quo* which will be part of it until its end, the species is also blessed in each of its generations with the happy few whose desire for change is so burning, so all consuming that this small band can move the mass to a higher rung on the ladder of progress. The Time Traveller is such a one. Though he identifies with the Eloi, he cannot rest content with their fate. The pages of human history (and indeed Wells's books) are replete, Wells instructs us in his *Outline of History,* with examples of men imbued with the same desires.

All of Wells's novels are based on this twofold concept of humanity. He literally divides his characters into two camps: the minor figures who, like the Morlocks and Eloi, represent the inertia of the masses; and the central figure—the happy individual who, like the Time Traveller and himself, despite the pain of such positive action, determines to alter his social, emotional, economic, or intellectual position. Polly is a member of this group. And the list could go on and on: The Angel (*The Wonderful Visit,* 1895); Dr. Moreau (*The Island of Dr. Moreau,* 1896); Griffin (*The Invisible Man,* 1897); Lewisham (*Love and Mr. Lewisham,* 1900); Ann Veronica (*Ann Veronica,* 1909); Stratton (*The Passionate Friends,* 1913).

In *The War of the Worlds* (1898), the only character who filters through the horrors wrought by the creatures from Mars is the unnamed individual who devises a plan for the continued existence of his species, and by willingly identifying himself with mankind, like the Time Traveller, he accepts the pain and danger-filled future. Paradoxically, he also receives an individuality in the act. Others, however, crumble in the face of impending doom. A clergyman, in a bitter monologue, sums up Christianity's failure to cope with the disaster. Echoing his frustration are the big guns booming away in the distance in an equally futile attempt to destroy the monsters. They are as efficacious as the cockchafers droning in the nearby hedgerow.

A recognition, then, of these two vital yet contradictory forces in the human species; the dynamic and the passive, serves as the basis for the development of Well's characters. Further, they serve as the foundation of his philosophy of struggle which motivates these characters. That philosophy Wells calls his "religion."[8] It is an ironic appellation because he rejected, on the one hand, a faith with an infinite God, a hierarchy, a Heaven and a Hell, only to establish another "faith" with similar attributes. For his faith has a "god." All who are "dissatisfied" with things as they are, all who sense the need for change, all who identify themselves with others and thereby become intimately involved with the struggle that follows, all in short who, like the Time Traveller, the unidentified character in *The War of the Worlds,* and all of the protagonists in Wells's novels "experience" an "idea" of this "god." This deity, however, has none of the marks of the Christian God about him. He is not infinite, omnipresent, nor all-powerful. He does not suffer passively on a cross. Indeed, were Wells's god to be pictured on a cross, he would be portrayed as having ripped one hand from the nail which held it and clenching it in defiance and anger at his tormentors. Wells's god more closely resembles the dynamic aspects of humanity. He is constantly engaged in a painful struggle for identity during the course of which he grows in strength, power, and boldness. Further, he knows that ultimately his efforts must be directed to the salvation of mankind from inevitable extinction.[9]

But who is this "god"? The answer, Wells tells us, lies in identifying the principles which govern his operation-remember, he is a finite god. Wells maintains that he exists in the minds of men but only when those minds, like those of his protagonists, are moved to act by a desire for change evidenced by that sense of "dissatisfaction" Wells maintained is so essential. He operates, therefore, through men, not, however, as a separate entity as does the Christian God. Mankind is not his puppet. Each man who acts to change his way of life in any fashion is god.

What Wells is telling us in his novels and in the philosophy which guides them is that man's supreme accomplishment, the salvation of his species from annihilation, can be effected not through an old, half-understood, outmoded theology with its vision and aspirations locked on another world; but rather salvation can only be effected through a realistic theology based upon man's own

strengths and upon successful examples of what mankind could do were it to martial those strengths and direct them properly. One of these successful examples Wells believed was himself. As he believed that the pain of his early life reflected the anguish of millions, he more firmly believed that the life he had achieved through struggle could be achieved, as he proves in his novels, by anyone who understands that the small voice of dissatisfaction gnawing away at complacency is the voice of god—man the combatant—fighting for his life.

NOTES

[1] *First and Last Things* (New York, 1918), p. 128.

[2] No definitive bibliography of Wells's work exists nor is there any indication that one will be forthcoming in the near future despite the efforts of the Wells Society which has produced what they call *A Comprehensive Bibliography* (London, 1966). Its introduction claims that in no way is it definitive.

[3] *Experiment in Autobiography* (New York, 1934), p. 45.

[4] For a graphic picture of life on a bare subsistence level at this time see the early chapters of Charles Chaplin's *My Autobiography* (New York, 1964).

[5] *First and Last Things,* p. 131.

[6] *God the Invisible King* (New York, 1917), p. 376.

[7] Ibid., p. 138.

[8] Ibid., p. 389.

[9] Ibid., p. 391.

Alex Eisenstein

SOURCE: "*The Time Machine* and the End of Man," in *Science-Fiction Studies,* Vol. 3, No. 9, July, 1976, pp. 161-65.

As many critics have observed, H. G. Wells was preoccupied very early with speculations on evolution, in particular the evolution of Man and the prospects of intelligent life, whatever its origins. *The Time Machine* (1895), *The War of the Worlds* (1898), and *The First Men in the Moon* (1901) are the best known examples of his interest in such matters, but certain of his shorter works also reflect this concern. Frequently, Wells would recapitulate and refine his major ideas, mining old essays for new story material or refashioning the elements of one tale in the context of another; various scholars have explored the interpenetration of these works in some detail.

In **"The Man of the Year Million"** (essay, 1893)[1] and *The War of the Worlds,* Wells outlined one model for the ultimate evolution of humankind. In both works, the culmination of higher intelligence is a globular entity, brought about by the influence of steadily advancing technology. In each case, it mainly consists of a great, bald head, supported on large hands or equivalent appendages, with thorax vestigial or entirely absent. The Martian is a direct analogue of the Man of the Year Million, as Wells himself indicated by citing his own essay in the body of the novel.[2] The Selenite master-race of *First Men* is a kindred expression of this vision of enlarged intellect—especially the Grand Lunar, with its enormous cranium, diminutive face, and shriveled body. Of more special relevance to the Martians are the malignant cephalopods of **"The Sea Raiders"** (1896) and **"The Extinction of Man"** (essay, 1894), and as well the predatory specimen in **"The Flowering of the Strange Orchid"** (1894).

At least one scholar has referred to **"The Man of the Year Million"** as "another version" of *The Time Machine,* apparently because the domeheads take refuge underground from the increasing rigors of a cooling surface.[3] This connection is rather tenuous, at best; by such criteria, *First Men* also might be deemed a variant of *The Time Machine.* In fact, the Further Vision of the latter constitutes a curious inversion of the above essay, but scholars and critics have failed to perceive this relation. Their failure depends on a more primary error, which is this—the notion that Man is extinct at the climax of the novel.

That the progeny of Man is *not* absent from the final moments of the Further Vision should be evident from a passage that appeared (until recently) only in the serial version. This deleted episode is a philosophic bridge, a key to what happens at world's end. It introduces the successors of Eloi and Morlock: a hopping, kangaroo-like semblance of humanity and a monstrous, shambling centipede. According to Robert Philmus, "these two species must have descended in the course of time from the Eloi and the Morlocks; and again the 'grey animal, or grey man, whichever it was' is the victim of the carnivorous giant insects."[4]

Philmus accentuates the elements of degeneration and regression in Wells's Darwinian conjectures; thus he asserts that *The Time Machine* embodies a vision of the hominid line "irrevocably on the downward path of devolution."[5] The general validity of this viewpoint cannot be disputed; nevertheless, the extreme construction he places upon it leads him considerably astray. Though Wells used terms like "retrogression," "degradation," and "degeneration" in his essays, they were for him *relative* terms only. He would hardly have portrayed Man as reverting *literally* into so primitive a creature; such "devolution," I submit, is not in the Wellsian mode.

Philmus may have been encouraged in this faulty genealogy by the Traveller's observations of the Elysian world of the Eloi, which seems devoid of animal life, excepting a few sparrows and butterflies (4b/288; 5a/292).[6] Of course, this stricture need not apply to the murky lower world, which could easily harbor all sorts of vermin. If butterflies prosper above, in a world of flowers, then centipedes should thrive below, in a realm of meaty table scraps and other waste. And at journey's end, "a thing like a huge white butterfly" makes a brief display, as a demonstration of what has survived the English sparrow (11/328).

The Morlocks of Millenium #803, moreover, are not a race destined for perpetual dominance. This much is made clear by numerous facets of their existence—their lack of light, the disrepair of much of their machinery, their crude and inefficient method of harvesting Eloi. Although the Time Traveller refers to the Eloi as "cattle" and supposes that they may even be bred by the Morlocks (7/311), the rest of the book does not show the latter practicing much in the way of husbandry. Indeed the absence of other land animals in the lush upper world may well be the result of earlier predations by the Morlocks. So the best assumption is that the relationship between the two races is unstable—that the Morlocks are depleting their latest dietary resource, which must eventually go the way of its predecessors.

The kangaroo-beast, therefore, can only be a tribe descended from the Morlocks, now scavenging the surface in the long twilight. The irony of the new situation is evident, and quite typical of the many ironic aspects of the novel: the hound is now the hare, the erstwhile predator has become the current prey.

The ancestry of this pathetic creature is confirmed by its morphology. Consider the appearance of the Morlock: "a queer little ape-like figure," "dull white," with "flaxen hair on its head and down its back" (5b/299), and a "chinless" face, with "great, lidless, pinkish-grey eyes" (6/306). Compare that with the Traveller's description of the later species: "It was . . . covered with a straight greyish hair that thickened about the head into a Skye terrier's mane. . . . It had, moreover, a rounded head, with a projecting forehead and forward-looking eyes, obscured by its lank hair" (325). The ape-like brow-ridge is a tell-tale vestige of the Morlocks, as well as the lank hair that now shields the creature's eyes. The shaggy visage identifies the kangaroo-man as a once-nocturnal animal only recently emerged from darkness. Another indicative trait is its rabbit-like feet, which are compatible with the "queer narrow footprints" of the Morlocks (5a/292).

From a close inspection the Traveller surmises the nature of the beast: "A disagreeable apprehension flashed across my mind. . . . I knelt down and seized my capture, intending to examine its teeth and other anatomical points which might show human characteristics . . ." (326). He might also be looking for the signs of yesterday's carnivore.

This Morlock offspring is no longer extant in the climactic scene of the Further Vision, but it is not the Last Man observed by the Traveller. He arrives in the era of the giant land-crabs, then passes on to the time of the great eclipse, where nothing seems to stir—at first:

> I looked about me to see if any traces of animal life remained. . . . But I saw nothing moving, in earth or sky or sea. The green slime alone testified that life was not extinct. . . . I fancied I saw some black object flopping about . . . but it became motionless as I looked at it, and I judged that my eye had been deceived, and that the black object was merely a rock.

A nearby planet encroaches on the bloated sun; the eclipse progresses, becomes total, and then the shadow of heaven recedes:

> I shivered, and a deadly nausea seized me. . . . I felt giddy and incapable of facing the return journey. As I stood sick and confused I saw again the moving thing upon the shoal. . . . It was a round thing, the size of a football perhaps . . . and tentacles trailed down from it; it seemed black against the weltering blood-red water, and it was hopping fitfully about. Then I felt I was fainting. But a terrible dread of lying helpless in that remote and awful twilight sustained me while I clambered into the saddle. (11/329-30)

The kangaroo-men hop about on elongated feet; the men of the year million hop about on great soft hands; the thing on the shoal hops about on a trailing mass of tentacles. This similarity in modes of locomotion is hardly a literary accident. In contrast, the Sea-Raiders never hop, but creep along at a steady pace when traversing solid ground.

In general form the Last Creature resembles a large cephalopod. Is it a primitive survivor from the ocean deeps, like *Haploteuthis* in **"The Sea-Raiders,"** or is it a being like the Martians, the hypertrophic end-product of intelligent life? Most of the evidence points to the latter—a highly specialized and atrophied edition of genus *Homo*. Note particularly the size of the creature; it is about "the size of a football"—which is to say, about the size of a human head.

The Time Traveller contracts a "terrible dread of lying helpless" in the dying world soon after he becomes fully aware of the thing on the shoal. There seems to be a special revulsion attached to this monster, even though it can hardly pose a real threat to the Traveller. Before it commands his attention, he feels "incapable of facing the return journey"; afterward, the "dread of lying helpless" in its presence impels him to turn back forthwith. Consciously, the Traveller does not perceive the human ancestry of this apocalyptic organism, but apparently the unconscious realization of its true nature makes him flee the final wasteland. Not the oppressive conditions, nor the extinction of Man, nor even the approaching oblivion triggers his retreat; rather, he recoils from the knowledge, however submerged, of what Man has become.

And what has Man become? Certainly not the inflated intellect of a Martian, nor that of a Sea-Raider, despite the somatic affinities. In one important respect, the Last Man differs greatly from these other fantastic creations: it is a being without a face. Even *Haploteuthis* has a definite, mock-human visage—"a grotesque suggestion of a face." To be sure, the super-minds in the Wellsian canon—the million-year domeheads, the Martians, the Grand Lunar—all suffer from facial attrition, yet certain features, especially the eyes, always remain. Not so with the fitful creature on the beach; the swollen surface of its body seems utterly blank, devoid of perceptual apparatus, and its aimless, reflexive actions indicate that it is virtually mindless. In the end, then, Man has become little more than a giant polyp.

All these transmuted beings emphasize two primary functions of life: ingestion and cerebration. The intelligent Sea-Raiders, for example, come to earth in seach of a better feed. Both the Martians and the domeheads have actually surrendered their alimentary canals to cortical advances, and the Martians, like the man-eating squids, also come to Earth for new sustenance. The mindless tropism of the Strange Orchid impels it to siphon off human blood, whereas the Martians strive for the same end with a ruthless deliberation.

The ultimate survivor of *The Time Machine* is not a great brain; as with a polyp, therefore, all that is left is a great ravening stomach. (For this, too, its size is appropriate.) Here, in counterpoint to the Martian terror, is the Wellsian image of ultimate horror.

And so we confront a symbolic paradox: the same emblem represents both the zenith and the nadir of mentality; the opposition of head and stomach, of mind and body, is fused in this one corporeal form. In Wells's iconography, it stands for the ultimate degeneration, whether of body or mind. He disapproved less, we may suppose, of the absolute intellect, reserving his greatest dread for the other, the mindless all-devouring. Yet there can be little doubt that, despite sardonic ambiguities, as in **"The Man of the Year Million"** and *The First Men in the Moon,* he truly preferred neither; his best wish was that Man should master himself without ever losing the essence of humanity. To this end Wells devoted most of his long and active life, even unto *Mind at the End of Its Tether* (1945), where a faint hope still lingers that some ultra-human entity will arise to survive the impending decline of *Homo sapiens*. This was Wells's last desperate hope, and a very feeble one it was; nevertheless, near the end of his life, amid sickness and depression, that glimmer remained. As the nameless narrator of *The Time Machine* insists, when faced with the inevitable disintegration of Man: "If that is so, it remains for us to live as though it were not so" (Epilogue/335).

NOTES

[1] First published in *The Pall Mall Gazette,* Nov 9, 1893, this essay, with title changed to "Of a Book Unwritten," appears in *Certain Personal Matters* (UK 1897), as does the other essay mentioned in this paragraph, "The Extinction of Man."

[2] Another avatar appears in "The Plattner Story," against a setting remarkably suggestive of the Further Vision. Plattner, who is blown through a fourth *spatial* dimension, finds himself on a barren landscape of dark *red* shadows, backed by a *green* sky-glow. He watches the *rise* of a giant green sun, which reveals a deep cleft nearby. A multitude of bulbous creatures float upward, like so many bubbles, from this chasm. These are the "Watchers of the Living," literally the souls of the dead: "they were indeed limbless; and they had the appearance of human heads beneath which a tadpole-like body swung" (para. 26). Significantly, Wells had referred to his Men of the Year Million as "human tadpoles."

In many respects, this realm of the afterlife is a striking reversal of *The Time Machine*'s terminal wasteland, yet quite recognizably akin to it.

[3] Gordon S. Haight, "H. G. Wells's 'The Man of the Year Million,'" *Nineteenth-Century Fiction* 12(1958):323-26.

[4] Robert M. Philmus, *Into the Unknown* (US 1970), pp. 70-71.

[5] *Ibid.,* p. 75.

[6] 7/311 = Chapter 7 in the standard form of the text (i.e., as published in the Atlantic Edition, the *Complete Short Stories,* and almost all editions since 1924), or Page 311 of *Three Prophetic Novels of H. G. Wells* (Dover Publications, 1960). The chapterings of the standard and Dover forms (with "a" and "b" added for convenience) collate as follows: 1a = 1; 1b = 2; 2 = 3; 3 = 4; 4a = 5; 4b = 6; 5a = 7; 5b = 8; 6 = 9; 7 = 10; 8 = 11; 9 = 12; 10 = 13; 11 = 14; 12a = 15; 12b = 16; Epilogue = Epilogue. The deleted passage, pages 325-27 of the Dover text, would appear between the first and second paragraphs of Chapter 11 in the standard text.

Patrick Parrinder

SOURCE: "News from Nowhere, *The Time Machine,* and the Break-Up of Classical Realism," in *Science-Fiction Studies,* Vol. 3, No. 10, November, 1976, pp. 265-74.

Critics of SF are understandably concerned with the integrity of the genre they study. Yet it is a commonplace that major works are often the fruit of an interaction of literary genres, brought about by particular historical pressures. Novels such as *Don Quixote, Madame Bovary* and *Ulysses* may be read as symptoms of cultural upheaval, parodying and rejecting whole classes of earlier fiction. My purpose is to suggest how this principle might be applied in the field of utopia and SF. While Morris's *News from Nowhere* and Wells's **The Time Machine** have many generic antecedents, their historical specificity will be revealed as that of conflicting and yet related responses to the break-up of classical realism at the end of the nineteenth century.[1]

Patrick Brantlinger describes *News from Nowhere* in a recent essay[2] as "a conscious anti-novel, hostile to virtually every aspect of the great tradition of Victorian fiction." In a muted sense, such a comment might seem self-evident; Morris's book is an acknowledged masterpiece of the "romance" genre which came to the fore as a conscious reaction against realistic fiction after about 1880. Yet *News from Nowhere* is radically unlike the work of Rider Haggard, R. L. Stevenson or their fellow-romancers in being a near-didactic expression of left-wing political beliefs. William Morris was a Communist, so that it is interesting to consider what might have been his reaction to Engels' letter to Margaret Harkness (1888), with its unfavorable contrast of the "point blank socialist novel" or "Tendenzroman" to the "realism" of Balzac:

> That Balzac thus was compelled to go against his own class sympathies and political prejudices, that he *saw* the necessity of the downfall of his favourite nobles, and described them as people deserving no better fate; and that he *saw* the real men of the future where, for the time being, they alone were to be found—that I consider one of the greatest triumphs of Realism, and one of the grandest features in old Balzac.[3]

It is not clear from the wording (the letter was written in English) whether Engels saw Balzac's farsightedness as a logical or an accidental product of the Realist movement which in his day extended to Flaubert, Zola, Turgenev, Tolstoy and George Eliot. Engels' disparagement of Zola in this letter has led many Marxists to endorse Balzac's technical achievement as a realist at the expense of his successors. Yet the passage might also be read as a tribute to Balzac's social understanding and political integrity, without reference to any of the formal doctrines of realism. What is certain is that the "triumph" Balzac secured for the Realist school was in part a personal, moral triumph, based on his ability to discard his prejudices and see the true facts. Engels's statement seems to draw on two senses of the term "realism," both of which originated in the nineteenth century. Nor, I think, is this coincidence of literary and political valuations accidental. The fiction of Stendhal, Balzac and Flaubert in particular is characterized by the systematic unmasking of bourgeois and romantic attitudes. In their political dimension, these novelists inherit a tradition of analysis going back to Machiavelli, and which is most evident in Stendhal, who was not a professional writer but an ex-administrator and diplomat. Harry Levin defines the realism of these novelists as a critical, negational mode in which "the truth is approximated by means of a satirical technique, by unmasking cant or debunking certain misconceptions."[4] There are two processes suggested here: the writer's own rejection of cant and ideology, and his "satirical technique." Both are common to many SF novels, including **The Time Machine,** although in terms of representational idiom these are the opposite of "realistic" works. *News from Nowhere,* on the other hand, is the utopian masterpiece of a writer who in his life went against his class sympathies and joined the "real men of the future," as Balzac did by implication in his books.

Morris has this in common with Engels (who distrusted him personally). Hostile critics have seen his socialist works as merely a transposition of the longings for beauty, chivalry and vanquished greatness which inform his early poetry. As literary criticism this seems to me shallow. Nor do Morris's political activities provide evidence of poetic escapism or refusal to face the facts. It was not by courtesy that he was eventually mourned as one of the stalwarts of the socialist movement.[5]

On the surface, *News from Nowhere* (1890) was a response to a utopia by a fellow-socialist—Edward Bellamy's *Looking Backward,* published two years earlier. Morris reviewed it in *The Commonweal,* the weekly paper of the Socialist League, on 22 June 1889. He was appalled by the servility of Bellamy's vision of the corporate state, and felt that the book was politically dangerous. He also noticed the subjectivity of the utopian form, its element of self-revelation. Whatever Bellamy's intentions, his book was the expression of a typically Philistine, middle-class outlook. *News from Nowhere* was intended to provide a dynamic alternative to Bellamy's model of socialist aspiration; a dream or vision which was ideologically superior as well as creative, organic and emotionally fulfilling where Bellamy's was industrialized, mechanistic and stereotyped. Morris was strikingly successful in these aims. The conviction and resonance of his "utopian romance" speak, however, of deeper causes than the stimulus provided by Bellamy.

News from Nowhere is constructed around two basic images or *topoi:* the miraculous translation of the narrator into a better future (contrasted with the long historical struggle to build that future, as described in the chapter "How the Change Came"), and the journey up the Thames, which becomes a richly nostalgic passage towards an uncomplicated happiness—a happiness which proves to be a mirage, and which author and reader can only aspire to in the measure in which they take up the burden of the present. Only the first of these *topoi* is paralleled in Bellamy. The second points in a quite different direction. *News from Nowhere* is a dream taking place within a frame of mundane political life—the meeting at which "there were six persons present, and consequently six sections of the party were represented, four of which had strong but divergent Anarchist opinions" (1). The dream is only potentially a symbol of reality, since there is no pseudo-scientific "necessity" that things will evolve in this way. The frame occasions a gentle didacticism (in dreams begin responsibilities), but also a degree of self-consciousness about the narrative art. "Guest," the narrator, is both a third person ("our friend") and Morris himself; the change from third- to first-person narration is made at the end of the opening chapter. Morris's subtitle, furthermore, refers to the story as a "Utopian Romance." Many objections which have been made to the book reflect the reader's discomfiture when asked to seriously imagine a world in which enjoyment and leisure are not paid for in the coin of other people's oppression and suffering. It could be argued that Morris should not have attempted it—any more than Milton in *Paradise Lost*

should have attempted the task of justifying the ways of God to men. Morris, however, held a view of the relation of art to politics which emphatically endorsed the project of imagining Nowhere.

One of his guises is that of a self-proclaimed escapist: "Dreamer of dreams, born out of my due time,/Why should I strive to set the crooked straight?" *News from Nowhere* stands apart from these lines from *The Earthly Paradise* (1868-70), as well as from the majority of Morris's prose romances. Together with *A Dream of John Ball* (1888) it was addressed to a socialist audience and serialized in *The Commonweal. News from Nowhere* retains some of the coloration of *John Ball*'s medieval setting, but, for a Victorian, radical medievalism could serve as an "estranging," subversive technique. Two of the major diagnoses of industrial civilization, Carlyle's *Past and Present* and Ruskin's essay "The Nature of Gothic," bear witness to the power of such medievalist imagination. Morris's own influential lectures on art derive from "The Nature of Gothic," and are strenuous attempts to "set the crooked straight" even at the cost of violent revolution and the destruction of the hierarchical and predominantly "literary" art of the bourgeoisie.[6] It is easy to find gaps between his theory of culture and his practice in literature and the decorative arts.[7] Nonetheless, his attack on middle-class art finds important expression in *News from Nowhere,* which is an attempt to reawaken those aspirations in the working class which have been deadened and stultified under capitalism. Genuine art for Morris does more than merely reflect an impoverished life back to the reader: "It is the province of art to set the true ideal of a full and reasonable life before [the worker], a life to which the perception and creation of beauty, the enjoyment of real pleasure that is, shall be felt to be as necessary to man as his daily bread."[8] *News from Nowhere,* however deficient in political science, is a moving and convincing picture of a community of individuals living full and reasonable lives. The "enjoyment of real pleasure" begins when the narrator wakes on a sunny summer morning, steps out of his Thames-side house and meets the boatman who, refusing payment, takes him for a leisurely trip on the river.

Morris's attack on the shoddiness of Victorian design and the separation of high art from popular art was pressed home in his lectures. In *News from Nowhere* he turns his attention to another product of the same ethos—the Victorian novel. Guest's girl-friend, Ellen, tells him that there is "something loathsome" about nineteenth-century novelists.

> Some of them, indeed, do here and there show some feeling for those whom the history-books call "poor," and of the misery of whose lives we have some inkling; but presently they give it up, and towards the end of the story we must be contented to see the hero and heroine living happily in an island of bliss on other people's troubles; and that after a long series of sham troubles (or mostly sham) of their own making, illustrated by dreary introspective nonsense about their feelings and

aspirations, and all the rest of it; while the world must even then have gone on its way, and dug and sewed and baked and carpentered round about these useless—animals. [22]

Morris introduced his poem *The Earthly Paradise* as the tale of an "isle of bliss" amid the "beating of the steely sea"; but the "hero and heroine" evoked by Ellen are also clearly from Dickens. (The "dreary introspective nonsense" might be George Eliot's.) Guest is seen by the Nowherians as an emissary from the land of Dickens (19). Both Morris and Bellamy shared the general belief that future generations would understand the Victorian period through Dickens's works. In *Looking Backward,* Dr Leete is the spokesman for a more bourgeois posterity:

> Judged by our standard, he [Dickens] overtops all the writers of his age, not because his literary genius was highest, but because his great heart beat for the poor, because he made the cause of the victims of society his own, and devoted his pen to exposing its cruelties and shams. No man of his time did so much as he to turn men's minds to the wrong and wretchedness of the old order of things, and open their eyes to the necessity of the great change that was coming, although he himself did not clearly foresee it. [13]

Not only Morris would have found this "Philistine." But Morris's Ellen and Bellamy's Dr Leete are on opposite sides in the ideological debate about Dickens's value, which continues to this day. One of the earliest critics to register Dickens's ambiguity was Ruskin, who denounced *Bleak House* as an expression of the corruption of industrial society, while praising *Hard Times* for its harshly truthful picture of the same society.[10] Morris, too, was divided in his response. When asked to list the world's hundred best books, he came up with 54 names which included Dickens as the foremost contemporary novelist. The list was dominated by the "folk-bibles"—traditional epics, folktales and fairy tales—which he drew upon in his romances.[11] Dickens's humour and fantasy appealed to the hearty, extrovert side of Morris stressed by his non-socialist friends and biographers.[12] Yet he also reprinted the "Podsnap" chapter of *Our Mutual Friend* in *The Commonweal,*[13] and inveighed against Podsnappery and the "counting-house on the top of a cinder-heap" in his essay "How I Became a Socialist." It is the world of the counting-house on the cinder-heap—the world of *Our Mutual Friend*—whose negation Morris set out to present in *News from Nowhere.*

Not only do the words "our friend" identify Guest on the opening page, but one of the earliest characters Morris introduces is Henry Johnson, nicknamed Boffin or the "Golden Dustman" in honour of a Dickensian forebear. Mr Boffin in *Our Mutual Friend* is a legacy-holder earnestly acquiring some culture at the hands of the unscrupulous Silas Wegg; Morris's Golden Dustman really is both a cultured man and a dustman, and is leading a "full and reasonable life." He has a Dickensian eccentricity, quite frequent among the Nowherians and a token of the individuality their society fosters. This character, I would

suggest, is strategically placed to insinuate the wider relation of Morris's "Utopian Romance" to nineteenth-century fiction.

The tone of *News from Nowhere* is set by Guest's initial outing on the Thames. Going to bed in mid-winter, he wakes to his boat-trip on an early morning in high summer. The water is clear, not muddy, and the bridge beneath which he rows is not of iron construction but a medieval creation resembling the Ponte Vecchio or the twelfth-century London Bridge. The boatman lacks the stigmata of the "working man" and looks amazed when Guest offers him money. This boat-trip is a negative counterpart to the opening chapter of *Our Mutual Friend,* in which Gaffer Hexam, a predatory Thames waterman, and his daughter Lizzie are disclosed rowing on the river at dusk on an autumn evening. Southwark and London Bridges, made of iron and stone respectively, tower above them. The water is slimy and oozy, the boat is caked with mud and the two people are looking for the floating corpses of suicides which provide a regular, indeed a nightly, source of livelihood. Dickens created no more horrifying image of city life. His scavengers inaugurate a tale of murderousness, conspiracy and bitter class-jealousy. Morris's utopian waterman, by contrast, guides his Guest through a classless world in which creativity and a calm Epicureanism flourish.

Two further Dickensian parallels centre upon the setting of the river. The Houses of Parliament in *News from Nowhere* have been turned into the Dung Market, a storage place for manure. Dickens scrupulously avoids the explicitly excremental, but in *Hard Times* he calls Parliament the "national cinder-heap," and a reference to the sinister dust-heaps of *Our Mutual Friend* may also be detected both here and in "How I Became a Socialist." It seems the Nowherians have put the home of windbags and scavengers to its proper purpose. In the second half of *News from Nowhere,* Guest journeys up-river with a party of friends; this again, perhaps recalls the furtive and murderous journey of Bradley Headstone along the same route. Headstone tracks down Eugene Wrayburn, his rival for the love of Lizzie Hexam. Guest's love for Ellen, by contrast, flourishes among friends who are free from sexual jealousy. Yet jealousy has not disappeared altogether, for at Mapledurham the travellers hear of a quarrel in which a jilted lover attacked his rival with an axe (24). Shortly afterwards, we meet the Obstinate Refusers, whose abstention from the haymaking is likened to that of Dickensian characters refusing to celebrate Christmas. Even in the high summer of Nowhere, the dark shadow of Dickens is occasionally present, preparing for the black cloud at the end of the book under which Guest returns to the nineteenth century.

News from Nowhere has a series of deliberate echoes of Dickens's work, and especially of *Our Mutual Friend.* Such echoes sharpen the reader's sense of a miraculous translation into the future. In chapters 17 and 18 the miracle is "explained" by Hammond's narrative of the political genesis of Nowhere—a narrative which recalls the historiographical aims of novelists such as Scott, Disraeli and George Eliot. These elements of future history and Dickensian pastiche show Morris subsuming and rejecting the tradition of Victorian fiction and historiography. The same process guides his depiction of the kinds of individual and social relationships which constitute the ideal of a "full and reasonable life." Raymond Williams has defined the achievement of classical realism in terms of the balance it maintains between social and personal existence: "It offers a valuing of a whole way of life, a society that is larger than any of the individuals composing it, and at the same time valuing creations of human beings who, while belonging to and affected by and helping to define this way of life, are also, in their own terms, absolute ends in themselves. Neither element, neither the society nor the individual, is there as a priority."[14] SF and utopian fiction are notorious for their failure to maintain such a balance. But the achievement that Williams celebrates should be regarded, in my view, not as an artistic unity so much as a *coalition* of divergent interests. Coalitions are produced by the pressures of history; by the same pressures they fall apart. In mid-Victorian fiction, the individual life is repeatedly defined and valued in terms of its antithesis to the *crowd*, or *mass society*. The happiness of Dickens's Little Dorrit and Clennam is finally engulfed by the noise of the streets; characters like George Eliot's Lydgate and Gwendolen Harleth are proud individuals struggling to keep apart from the mass, while their creator sets out to record the "whisper in the roar of hurrying existence."[15] The looming threat of society in these novels is weighed against the possibility of spiritual growth. George Eliot portrays the mental struggles of characters who are, in the worldly sense, failures. She cannot portray them achieving social success commensurate with their gifts, so that even at her greatest her social range remains determinedly "provincial" and she can define her characters' limitations with the finality of an obituarist. She cannot show the source of change, only its effects and the way it is resisted. Dickens's despair at the irreducible face of society led him in his later works to fantasize it, portraying it as throttled by monstrous institutions and presided over by spirits and demons. His heroes and heroines are safe from the monstrous tentacles only in their "island of bliss." One reason why Dickens's domestic scenes are so overloaded with sentimental significance is that here his thwarted utopian instincts were forced to seek outlet. The house as a miniature paradise offsets the hell of a society.

It should not be surprising that a novelist such as Dickens possessed elements of a fantastic and utopian vision.[16] They are distorted and disjointed elements, whereas Morris in *News from Nowhere* takes similar elements and reunites them in a pure and uncomplex whole. Several of his individual characters display a Dickensian eccentricity, and they all have the instant capacity for mutual recognition and trust which Dickens's good characters show. Yet this mutual trust is all-embracing; it no longer defines who you are, since it extends to everybody, even the most casual acquaintances (Hammond, the social philosopher of Nowhere, explains that there are no longer any

criminal classes, since crimes are not the work of fugitive outcasts but the "errors of friends" [12]). Guest's sense of estrangement in Nowhere is most vivid in the early scenes where he is shown round London. Not only has the city become a garden suburb and the crowds thinned out, but the people he meets are instinctively friendly, responding immediately to a stranger's glance. They are the antithesis of Dickens's crowds of the "noisy and the eager and the arrogant and the forward and the vain," which "fretted, and chafed, and made their usual uproar."[17] The friendly crowd is such a paradox that Morris's imagination ultimately fails him slightly, so that he relapses into Wardour Street fustian:

> Therewith he drew rein and jumped down, and I followed. A very handsome woman, splendidly clad in figured silk, was slowly passing by, looking into the windows as she went. To her quoth Dick: "Maiden, would you kindly hold our horse while we go in for a little?" She nodded to us with a kind smile, and fell to patting the horse with her pretty hand.
>
> "What a beautiful creature!" said I to Dick as we entered.
>
> "What, old Greylocks?" said he, with a sly grin.
>
> "No, no," said I; "Goldylocks,—the lady." [6]

Morris here is feeling his way toward the authentically childlike view of sexual relationships which emerges during the journey up-river. Guest begins to enjoy a gathering fulfillment, movingly portrayed but also clearly regressive. Annie at Hammersmith is a mother-figure, Ellen a mixture of sister and childhood sweetheart. Guest, though past his prime of life, feels a recovery of vigour which is, in the event, illustory; his fate is not to be rejuvenated in Nowhere but to return to the nineteenth century, strengthened only in his longing for change. Though he shares his companions' journey to the haymaking, his exclusion from the feast to celebrate their arrival is another inverted Dickensian symbol.[18] The return to the present is doubly upsetting to the "happy ending" convention (seen for example in Bellamy); for it is not a nightmare but a stoical affirmation of political responsibility. Guest's last moments in Nowhere show him rediscovering the forgotten experience of alienation and anonymity.

Dickens and George Eliot were moralists in their fiction and supporters of social and educational reform outside it. Morris worked to improve Victorian taste while coming to believe that there were no "moral" or "reformist" solutions to the social crisis. It was the perspective of the labour movement and the revolutionary "river of fire"[19] which enabled him to reassemble the distorted affirmation of a Dickens novel into a clear, utopian vision. His vision draws strength from its fidelity to socialist ideals and to Morris's own emotional needs. But Morris, for all his narrative self-consciousness, can only register and not transcend what is ultimately an aesthetic impasse. His book is *News from Nowhere, or An Epoch of Rest;* it shows not only the redemption of man's suffering past but his enjoyment of Arcadian quietism. In Nowhere pleasure may be had "without an afterthought of the injustice and miserable toil which made my leisure" (20). Morris omits to describe how in economic terms leisure is produced, and how in political terms a society built by the mass labour movement has dispersed into peaceful anarchism. He stakes everything on the mood of "second childhood":

> "Second childhood," said I in a low voice, and then blushed at my double rudeness, and hoped that he hadn't heard. But he had, and turned to me smiling, and said: "Yes, why not? And for my part, I hope it may last long; and that the world's next period of wise and unhappy manhood, if that should happen, will speedily lead us to a third childhood: if indeed this age be not our third. Meantime, my friend, you must know that we are too happy, both individually and collectively to trouble ourselves about what is to come hereafter." [16]

It is true that the passage hints at further labours of social construction lying in store for man. Morris, however, prefers not to contemplate them. One is forced to conclude that in *News from Nowhere* the ideal of the perfection of labour is developed as an alternative to the dynamism of Western society. We are left with the irresolvable ambiguity of the Morrisian utopia, which peoples an exemplary socialist society with characters who are, in the strict sense in which Walter Pater had used the term, decadents.[20]

H. G. Wells first listened to Morris at socialist meetings at Hammersmith in the 1880s. Even for a penniless South Kensington science student, attending such meetings was an act of social defiance. But, as he later recalled, he soon forgot his "idea of a council of war, and . . . was being vastly entertained by a comedy of picturesque personalities."[21] He saw Morris as trapped in the role of poet and aesthete, yet in *A Modern Utopia* (1905) he readily acknowledged the attractiveness of a Morrisian earthly paradise:

> Were we free to have our untrammelled desire, I suppose we should follow Morris to his Nowhere, we should change the nature of man and the nature of things together; we should make the whole race wise, tolerant, noble, perfect—wave our hands to a splendid anarchy, every man doing as it pleases him, and none pleased to do evil, in a world as good in its essential nature, as ripe and sunny, as the world before the Fall.[22]

Wells, in effect, accuses Morris of lacking intellectual "realism." His response to this appears to far less advantage in *A Modern Utopia,* however, than it does in his dystopian works beginning with *The Time Machine* (1895). *A Modern Utopia* is an over-ambitious piece of system-building, reflecting its author's eclectic search for a "new aristocracy" or administrative elite; *The Time Machine* is a mordantly critical examination of concepts

of evolution and progress and the future state, with particular reference to *News from Nowhere.*

While Guest wakes up in Hammersmith, the Time Traveller climbs down from his machine in the year 802,701 A.D. at a spot about three miles away, in what was formerly Richmond. The gay, brightly-dressed people, the verdant park landscape and the bathing in the river are strongly reminiscent of Morris. The Eloi live in palace-like communal buildings, and are lacking in personal or sexual differentiation. On the evening of his arrival, the Time Traveller walks up to a hilltop and surveys the green landscape, murmuring "Communism" to himself (6). The reference is to Morris rather than to Marx (whose work and ideas Wells never knew well). Wells has already begun his merciless examination of the "second childhood" which Morris blithely accepted in Nowhere.

From the moment of landing we are aware of tension in the Time Traveller's responses. He arrives in a thunderstorm near a sinister colossus, the White Sphinx, and soon he is in a frenzy of fear. The hospitality of the Eloi, who shower him with garlands and fruit, does not cure his anxiety. Unlike most previous travellers in utopia, he is possessed of a human pride, suspicion and highly-strung sensitivity which he cannot get rid of. He reacts with irritability when asked if he has come from the sun in a thunderstorm: "It let loose the judgment I had suspended upon their clothes, their frail light limbs and fragile features. A flow of disappointment rushed across my mind. For a moment I felt that I had built the Time Machine in vain" (5). When they teach him their language, it is he who feels like a "school-master amidst children," and soon he has the Eloi permanently labelled as a class of five-year-olds.

The apparent premise of *The Time Machine* is one of scientific anticipation, the imaginative working-out of the laws of evolution and thermodynamics, with a dash of Marxism added. Critics sometimes stress the primacy of the didactic surface in such writing.[23] But *The Time Machine* is not exhausted once we have paraphrased its explicit message. Like *News from Nowhere,* it is a notably self-conscious work. Wells's story-telling frame is more elaborate than Morris's, and Robert M. Philmus has drawn attention to the studied ambiguity Wells puts in the Time Traveller's mouth: "Take it as a lie—or a prophecy. Say I dreamed it in the workshop" (16).[24] One of his hero's ways of authenticating his story is to expose the fabrications of utopian writers. A "real traveller," he protests, has no access to the "vast amount of detail about building, and social arrangements, and so forth" found in utopian versions (8). He has "no convenient cicerone in the pattern of the Utopian books" (8). He has to work everything out for himself by a process of conjecture and refutation—a crucial feature of *The Time Machine* which does much to convey the sense of intellectual realism and authenticity. The visit to the Palace of Green Porcelain parallels Guest's visit to the British Museum, but instead of a Hammond authoritatively placed to expound

"How the Change Came," the Time Traveller must rely on habits of observation and reasoning which his creator acquired at the Normal School of Science.

In *The Time Machine* Wells uses a hallowed device of realistic fiction—the demonstration of superior authenticity over some other class of fictions—in a "romance" context. His aim is, in Levin's words, to "unmask cant" and debunk misconceptions. The truths he affirms are both of a scientific (or Huxleyan) and a more traditional sort. The world of Eloi and Morlocks is revealed first as devolutionary and then as one of predator and prey, of *homo homini lupus*. This must have a political, not merely a biological significance. No society, Wells is saying, can escape the brutish aspects of human nature defined by classical bourgeois rationalists such as Machiavelli and Hobbes. A society that claims to have abolished these aspects may turn out to be harbouring predatoriness in a peculiarly horrible form. This must become apparent once we can see the *whole* society. In Morris's Nowhere, part of the economic structure is suppressed; there is no way of knowing what it would have been like. In *The Time Machine* it is only necessary to put the Eloi and Morlocks in the picture together—whether they are linked by a class relationship, or a species relationship, or some evolutionary combination of the two—to destroy the mirage of utopian communism. The Dickensian society of scavengers cannot be so lightly dismissed.

In contrast to Morris's mellow Arcadianism, *The Time Machine* is an aggressive book, moving through fear and melodrama to the heights of poetic vision. The story began as a philosophical dialogue and emerged from successive revisions as a gripping adventure-tale which is also a mine of poetic symbolism. To read through the various versions is to trace Wells's personal discovery of the "scientific romance."[25] *The Time Machine* in its final form avoids certain limitations of both the Victorian realist novel and the political utopia. An offshoot of Wells's use of fantasy to explore man's temporal horizons is that he portrays human nature as at once more exalted and more degraded than the conventional realist estimate.

Imagining the future liberates Wells's hero from individual moral constraints; the story reveals a devolved, simian species which engages the Time Traveller in a ruthless, no-holds-barred struggle. The scenario of the future is a repository for symbolism of various kinds. The towers and shafts of the story are recognizably Freudian, while the names of the Eloi and Morlocks allude to Miltonic angels and devils. The Time Traveller himself is a variant of the nineteenth-century romantic hero. Like Frankenstein, he is a modern Prometheus. The identification is sealed in the Palace of Green Porcelain episode, where he steals a matchbox from the museum of earlier humanity, whose massive architectural remains might be those of Titans. But there is no longer a fit recipient for the gift of fire, and the Time Traveller's matches are only lit in self-defence. We see him travel to the end of the world, alone, clasped to his machine on the sea-shore.

When he fails to return from his second journey we might imagine him as condemned to perpetual time-travelling, as Prometheus was condemned to perpetual torture.

There are few unqualified heroes in Victorian realistic fiction (this is a question of generic conventions, not of power of characterization). The zenith of the realist's art appears in characters such as Lydgate, Dorothea, Pip and Clennam, all of whom are shown as failures, and not often very dignified failures. They are people circumscribed and hemmed in by bourgeois existence. Intensity of consciousness alone distinguishes theirs from the average life of the ordinary member of their social class. As against this, Wells offers an epic adventurer who (like Morris's knights and saga-heroes) is close to the supermen of popular romance. His hero is guilty of sexual mawkishness and indulges in Byronic outbursts of temperament. But what distinguishes him from the run-of-the-mill fantasy hero is the epic and public nature of his mission. As Time Traveller he takes up the major cognitive challenge of the Darwinist age. He boasts of coming "out of this age of ours, this ripe prime of the human race, when Fear does not paralyse and mystery has lost its terrors" (10). The retreat of superstition before the sceptical, scientific attitude dictated that the exploit of a modern Prometheus or Faust should be told in a scaled-down, "romance" form. Nonetheless, the Time Traveller shares the pride of the scientists, inventors and explorers of the nineteenth century, and not the weakness or archaism of its literary heroes.

There is a dark side to his pride. The scene where he surveys the burning Morlocks shows Wells failing to distance his hero sufficiently. The Time Traveller is not ashamed of his cruel detachment from the species he studies, nor does he regret having unleashed his superior "firepower." His only remorse is for Weena, the one creature he responded to as "human," and Wells hints that her death provides justification for the slaughter of the Morlocks. This rationalization is a clear example of imperialist psychology; but Wells was both critic and product of the imperialist ethos. Morris, who was so sharp about Bellamy, would surely have spotted his vulnerability here. It is not merely the emotions of scientific curiosity which are satisfied by the portrayal of a Hobbesian, dehumanized world.

News from Nowhere and *The Time Machine* are based on a fusion of propaganda and dream. Their complexity is due in part to the generic interactions which I have traced. Morris turns from the degraded world of Dickens to create its negative image in a Nowhere of mutual trust and mutual fulfilment. Wells writes a visionary satire on the utopian idea which reintroduces the romantic hero as explorer and prophet of a menacing future. Both writers were responding to the break-up of the coalition of interests in mid-Victorian fiction, and their use of fantasy conventions asserted the place of visions and expectations in the understanding of contemporary reality. Schematically, we may see Wells's SF novel as a product of the warring poles of realism and utopianism, as represented by Dickens and Morris. More generally, I would suggest that to study the aetiology of works such as *News from Nowhere* and **The Time Machine** is to ask oneself fundamental questions about the nature and functions of literary "realism."

NOTES

[1] I use "realism" in a broadly Lukacsian sense, to denote the major representational idiom of 19th-century fiction. See e.g. Georg Lukacs, *Studies in European Realism* (US 1964). I also argue that "realism" in literature cannot ultimately be separated from the modern non-literary senses of the term. No sooner is a convention of literary realism established than the inherently dynamic "realistic outlook" starts to turn against that convention.

[2] Patrick Brantlinger, "*News from Nowhere:* Morris's Socialist Anti-Novel," *Victorian Studies* 19(1975):35ff. This article examines Morris's aesthetic in greater depth than was possible here, with conclusions that are close to my own.

[3] Karl Marx and Frederick Engels, *On Literature and Art,* ed. Lee Baxandall and Stefan Morawski (US 1974), p 117.

[4] Harry Levin, *The Gates of Horn* (US 1966), p 55.

[5] The best political biography is E.P. Thompson, *William Morris: Romantic to Revolutionary* (UK 1955).

[6] Morris's published lectures are reprinted in his *Collected Works,* ed. May Morris, vols. 22-23 (UK 1914), and some unpublished ones in *The Unpublished Lectures of William Morris,* ed. Eugene D. LeMire (US 1969). Three recent (but no more than introductory) selections are: *William Morris: Selected Writings and Designs,* ed. Asa Briggs (US-UK 1962); *Political Writings of William Morris,* ed. A. L. Morton (US—UK 1962); and *William Morris, Selected Writings,* ed. G. H. Cole (US 1961).

[7] Morris took up the practice of handicrafts in 1860 and became, in effect, an extremely successful middle-class designer. His theories of the unity of design and execution were often in advance of his workshop practice. See e.g. Peter Floud, "The Inconsistencies of William Morris," *The Listener* 52 (1954):615ff.

[8] Morris, "How I Became a Socialist" (1894).

[9] See note 6.

[10] Ruskin commented on *Bleak House* in "Fiction—Fair and Foul," published in the *Nineteenth Century* (1880-1), and on *Hard Times* in *Unto This Last* (1860).

[11] *Collected Works* 22:xiii ff.

[12] J. W. Mackail records somewhat fatuously that "In the moods when he was not dreaming of himself as Tristram or Sigurd, he identified himself very closely with . . . Joe

Gargery and Mr Boffin."—*The Life of William Morris* (UK 1901), 1:220-21. Cf. Paul Thompson, *The Work of William Morris* (UK 1967), p 149.

[13] See E.P. Thompson (Note 5) pp 165-67. I have not managed to locate this in the files of *The Commonweal.*

[14] Raymond Williams, *The Long Revolution* (UK 1961), p 268.

[15] George Eliot, Introduction to *Felix Holt* (1866).

[16] The fantastic and utopian elements in Dickens are associated with his genius for satire and melodrama: with his vision of the interlocking, institutional character of social evil, and his delight in sharp and magical polarizations between the strongholds of evil and those of beauty and innocence. The elements of traditional romance in Dickens's vision make him an exaggerated, but by no means unique case; a utopian element could, I think, be traced in every great novelist.

[17] Dickens, *Little Dorrit,* 34.

[18] Tom Middlebro' argues that both river and feast are "religious symbols"—"Brief Thoughts on *News from Nowhere,*" *Journal of the William Morris Society* 2 (1970): 8. If so, this was true for Dickens as well, and I would see him as Morris's immediate source. The symbolism of the feast is present in all Dickens's works and has been discussed by Angus Wilson, "Charles Dickens: A Haunting," *Critical Quarterly* 2 (1960): 107-08.

[19] Morris, "The Prospects of Architecture in Civilization" in *Hopes and Fears for Art* (1882).

[20] Pater describes the poetry of the Pleiade as "an aftermath, a wonderful later growth, the products of which have to the full the subtle and delicate sweetness which belong to a refined and comely decadence." Preface to *The Renaissance* (1873). The compatibility of one aspect of Pater's and Morris's sensibility is suggested by the former's review of "Poems by William Morris," *Westminster Review* 34 (1868):300ff.

[21] *Saturday Review* 82(1896):413.

[22] Wells, *A Modern Utopia* 1:1.

[23] See e.g. Joanna Russ's remarks on *The Time Machine,* SFS 2(1975):114-15.

[24] Robert M. Philmus, *Into the Unknown* (US 1970), p 73.

[25] The most telling contrast is with the *National Observer* version (1894). For a reprint of this and an account of Wells's revisions of *The Time Machine* see his *Early Writings in Science and Science Fiction,* ed. Robert M. Philmus and David Y. Hughes (US 1975), pp 47ff.

Mark M. Hennelly, Jr.

SOURCE: "*The Time Machine:* A Romance of 'The Human Heart,'" in *Extrapolation,* Vol. 20, No. 2, Summer, 1979, pp. 154-67.

> I felt I lacked a clue. I felt—how shall I put it? Suppose you found an inscription, with sentences here and there in excellent plain English, and interpolated therewith, others made up of words, of letters even, absolutely unknown to you? Well, on the third day of my visit, that was how the world of Eight Hundred and Two Thousand Seven Hundred and One presented itself to me! (pp. 57-58).[1]

The reader of H. G. Wells's ***The Time Machine*** (1895) shares these insecurities with the Time Traveller since the full meaning of his "strange adventures" (p. 95), and especially the enigmatic conclusion, remain "absolutely unknown" after the book is closed, that is, not wholly intelligible as allegories of either Huxlian devolution or Marxian dialectical materialism. Although both science and sociology inform the tale, Wells's own oxymoronic label for his favorite early genre explicitly identifies ***The Time Machine*** as a "scientific *romance,*" not scientific naturalism or realism. Consequently, the missing "clue" to the meaning of this "unknown" Romance world is not blatantly supplied by either the "excellent plain English" of the nameless Narrator or that of the Time Traveller himself.

In the preface to the Random House edition (1931) of ***The Time Machine,*** Wells describes his style in the ***Chronic Argonauts,*** the first version of his Romance, as "the pseudo-Teutonic, Nathaniel Hawthorne style."[2] Later in ***Experiment In Autobiography*** (1934), he details more fully the genesis of the tale and Hawthorne's influence: "I began a romance, very much under the influence of Hawthorne, which was printed in the *Science Schools Journal,* the ***Chronic Argonauts.*** . . . It was the original draft of what later became ***The Time Machine,*** which won me recognition as an imaginative writer."[3] But as Hawthorne's famous distinction between the Novel and the Romance in his "Preface" to *The House of the Seven Gables* implies, both of Wells's narrative interlocutors, especially the first Narrator, are concerned with "a very minute fidelity" to the "probable" and not the "possible." Both supply answers from the external, scientific, and "ordinary course of man's experience" although, admittedly, the nature of the experience they are attempting to explain is of the "Marvellous." Both fail to understand that often in the scientific Romance, the scientific is simply an externalization of, an extrapolation of, the psychological. In fact, in a 1897 interview, Wells refuses to accept that realism and the psychological Romance could ever be totally separate since "the scientific episode which I am treating insists upon interesting me, and so I have to write about the effect of it upon *the mind of some particular person.*"[4] Both speakers neglect, then, what Hawthorne calls "the truth of the human heart," that is, the balanced and unified psychological experience which must be interpolated from ambiguous, external clues. And as Wells himself admits in **"Bye-Products in Evolution"**

(1895), "the logical student of evolution" is "invariably puzzle[d]" by aesthetics, but "with regard to the subtle mechanism of mind, we are even more in the dark than when we deal with chemical equilibrium."[5] Consequently, Hawthorne's later advice for understanding the dream-world of his story, "the topsy-turvey commonwealth of sleep," suggests the value of the same kind of reading for Wells's Romance, which is repeatedly called a dreamlike adventure: "Modern psychology, it may be, will endeavor to reduce these alleged necromanies [the nightmares of the Maules and Pyncheons] within a system instead of rejecting them as altogether fabulous" (Chapt. 1). In "The Custom House" opening of *The Scarlet Letter,* Hawthorne defines the world of his Romances even more relevantly: "a neutral territory, somewhere between the real world and fairy-land, where the Actual and the Imaginary may meet, and each imbue itself with the nature of the other." The Time Traveller's perplexed imaginings upon return to the actual present suggest the same neutral territory:

> Did I ever make a Time Machine, or a model of a Time Machine? Or is it all only a dream? They say life is a dream, a precious poor dream at times—but I can't stand another that won't fit. It's madness. And where did the dream come from? . . . [*sic*] I must look at that machine. If there is one! (p. 96).

The consequences of exploring this neutral territory to search for the "truth of the human heart" in ***The Time Machine*** illuminate some of those "unknown" words and letters, which puzzle both the Time Traveller and the reader, and consequently demonstrate that attention to morality is as essential as attention to biology for the understanding of the Romance. Thus, this journey forward in time is actually a journey inward and downward in psychological space; the future macrocosm is the present introcosm. Although this thesis precludes a detailed examination of Wells's early essays on science, Robert Philmus and David Hughes's collection of these writings supports this critical *volte-face* by indicating that 1895 is the watershed year when "The view of nature's laws disposing of what man proposes gives way to the idea of 'artificial' evolution, man's consciously taking charge of his future by shaping his sociocultural environment, over which he can exert control" (***Early Writings,*** p. x). At any rate, after taking a brief survey of previous readings, we will discuss Wells' psychologizing with respect to the Narrator, the frame story of the Dinner Guests, the three worlds of the future, and finally the Time Traveller himself.

The Time Machine has not received the critical coverage it deserves; but scholarly response has clearly isolated three major lines of inquiry—scientific, autobiographical, and mythic. Robert Philmus, for example, most cogently explains the anti-Darwinian and Marxian (or anti-Marxian?) issues by discussing the themes of survival of the unfittest or least human in the Eloi and Morlocks and by implying Wells's ambivalent attitude toward the leisure and proletariat classes. For Philmus, consequently, the novel (not Romance) becomes an oracle of devolution:

This vision of social disintegration and devolution as a critique of the ideal of striving towards "ease and delight" can exist only in the dimension of prophecy, that dimension into which the critique can be projected and imaginatively given life—the world, in other words, of science fantasy.[6]

From a different critical vantage point, Alex Eisenstein traces the genesis of Wells's future shock to his past personal history while growing up at Atlas House where the topography approximated the split-levels of 802,701 and where his reading of Strum's *Reflections* and his viewing of the illustration of an ape from Wood's *Natural History* jointly spawned a fear of simian creatures like the Morlocks.[7] Finally, although Bernard Bergonzi also discovers scientific and socialistic allegories in the tale, he alone stresses its *Romance* genre while locating archetypal patterns:

> Since **The Time Machine** is a romance and not a piece of realistic fiction, it conveys its meaning in poetic fashion though images, rather than by the revelation of character in action. It is, in short, a myth. . . . The opposition of Eloi and Morlocks can be interpreted in terms of the late nineteenth-century class struggle, but it also reflects an opposition between aestheticism and utilitarianism, pastoralism and technology, contemplation and action, and ultimately, and least specifically, between beauty and ugliness, and light and darkness.[8]

Agreeing with Bergonzi's premise concerning genre, but strongly disagreeing with his dismissal of "character," we can now abandon sociology and biology for psychology and morality.

The primary Narrator in **The Time Machine** plays a far more significant role than that Eugene D. LeMire credits him with—namely, taking advantage of "the supreme moment of the raconteur . . . the moment of the long cigar and tall tale."[9] That is, he does not simply narrate the tale; but he is also a character in it, one whose point of view naturally colors his narration, whose sensibilities consequently transcend those of the caricatured and wooden Dinner Guests, and who finally serves as a go between, or mediator between the personalities of the Guests and the Time Traveller and between the Time Traveller and the reader. In an important sense, then, the Narrator is a surrogate for the reader in the Romance; and though less well-drawn, he functions much like Marlowe in *Lord Jim,* or better still, lawyer Utterson in *Dr. Jekyll and Mr. Hyde,* a tale whose use of *Doppelgängers* is very similar to **The Time Machine**'s.

Thus, the Narrator's "inadequacy" parallels the Time Traveller's own avowed problems (pp. 94-95) in accurately and credibly describing "strange adventures":

> In writing it down I feel with only too much keenness the inadequacy of pen and ink—and, above all, my own inadequacy—to express its quality. You read, I will suppose, attentively enough; but you cannot see the speaker's white,

sincere face in the bright circle of the little lamp, nor hear the intonation of his voice (pp. 36-37).

At issue here, however, is not only the partial identification between Narrator and Time Traveller, but also the thematic emphasis upon empirical verification, or direct involvement with experience (rather than scientific or aesthetic detachment), and upon the reader's own active role in interpretively filling in many thematic spaces which the narrative leaves blank. While the Narrator, like Coleridge's Wedding-Guest, seems "better than" the other, more sceptical, shallow Dinner Guests because he "lay awake most of the night thinking about" the tale (p. 96), he does more than provide an example for sensitive reader response. Unlike Utterson, who vanishes from the last pages of Stevenson's Romance and thereby fails to register either a normative or ironic moral reaction to Jekyll-Hyde's disintegration, he finally editorializes significantly on the Time Traveller's concluding and pivotal disappearance. His commentary, though, *apparently* fails to accept the moral inferences of the Traveller's quest. Thus, the reader is tempted either to believe the Narrator's own ignorant yet guarded, optimistic prognosis for the future or to accept the Traveller's ambiguous account of the "unknown." In this latter case, suspecting the simplistic moral tag of the Narrator, as he likewise would in "The Rime of the Ancient Mariner," the reader himself must reinterpret the narrative "clues" for a specific psychological and moral message. The Narrator, at any rate, believes that

> the future is still black and blank—is a vast ignorance, lit at a few casual places by the memory of his story. And I have by me, for my comfort, two strange white flowers gifts from Weena— shrivelled now, and brown and flat and brittle— to witness that even when mind and strength had gone, gratitude and mutual tenderness still lived on in the heart of man (p. 98).

Recalling the Time Traveller's earlier caution to the "untravelled" or inexperienced listener of a tale and his anecdote regarding the futility of an African trying to understand an industrial city (pp. 56-57), the reader is certainly invited to side with the Traveller and to dismiss the Narrator as morally naive, a Pollyanna who is neither sadder nor wiser but rather blithefully ignorant of "the heart of man." However, the narrative problem is not so easily resolved and really cannot be simplified into the *either-or* logic argued above, just as the same narrative dislocation cannot be so easily solved in **The Island of Dr. Moreau** where, before his "cure," the Narrator finds "Beast People" alive and unwell in England, while afterward he perceives only "the shining souls of men." However, in **The Time Machine** both commentaries can be accommodated by correctly understanding the Romance-meaning of the Traveller's return journey. And after comparing present and future societies, we will attempt this understanding.

The narrative frame's dramatization of late Victorian society has escaped critical notice entirely, except for

Philmus's brief allusion to Northrop Frye's discussion of "tales 'told in quotation marks,'"[10] LeMire's reference to the "peculiar abstract names of the characters" and the "ironic comment on the stupidities of class-conflict in Wells' own world,"[11] and finally Philmus and Hughes's recognition of "the unimaginative complacency . . . exemplified by his audience" and of the fact that somehow this audience's "narrow scope of consciousness is responsible for cosmic catastrophe" (*Early Writings,* p. 55). However, and again as in *Dr. Jekyll and Mr. Hyde,* this well-ordered wasteland of insecure, repressed, yet self-satisfied bachelors foreshadows the chaotic future with its schizophrenic upper and lower worlds. Thus, with the Narrator caught between, the microcosmic cross section of upper class gentility apparently contrasts with the hard-working discipline of the Time Traveller, much as the warm and leisurely setting of the smoking room contrasts with the cold (p. 96) and mechanical atmosphere of the scientific laboratory, and as finally the tropical, lotus world of the Eloi contrasts with the cooler, subterranean machine-shop of the Morlocks. In fact, as so often occurs in the allegorical Romance, the tale's very first paragraph provides a threshold symbol for this apparent Jekyll-Hyde polarity by pitting Eloi "laziness" against Morlock "earnestness":

> The fire burned brightly, and the soft radiance of the incandescent lights in the lilies of silver caught the bubbles that flashed and passed in our glasses. Our chairs, being his patents, embraced and caressed us rather than submitted to be sat upon, and there was that luxurious after-dinner atmosphere when thought runs gracefully free of the trammels of precision. And he put it [some recondite matter] to us in this way—marking the points with a lean forefinger—as we sat and lazily admired his earnestness over this new paradox (as we thought it) and his fecundity (p. 25).

As in Stevenson's Romance, however, the real point here is not (or not *simply)* an acknowledgement of Victorian duality, both cultural and psychological, but rather as we shall see, a condemnation of such duality and a moral plea for recognizing the essential, paradoxical unity of a well-balanced and whole personality system. Time Traveller and Guests are One; the Hebraic Morlocks must lie down with the Hellenic Eloi to achieve psychological harmony. Put in another way, the Guests need first to realize they are Eloi (who are called a "wretched aristocracy in decay," p. 75) and then actualize the Morlock side of themselves; while the Time Traveller must realize that essentially he has been acting like a Morlock and then also accept his Eloi half. Specifically, what all the character groupings share is the common flaw of *misoneism*—an obsessive hatred and fear of novelty and temporal change. This taboo threat not only reappears throughout *The Time Machine,* but it is constantly enfleshed in the imagery and finally constitutes, of course, the tale's primary subject matter. As the Time Traveller learns, "There is no intelligence where there is no change and no need of change" (p. 87). Wells's scientific essays repeatedly emphasize this same

point with regard to external adaptation or, to use Wells's term, "plasticity." In **"The Rate of Change in Species"** (1894), for instance, he predicts that in the event of "some far-reaching change effected in the conditions of life on this planet," large organisms like mankind "driving on the old course by virtue of the inertia of their too extensive lives, would have scarcely changed in the century, and, being no longer fitted to the conditions around them, would dwindle and—if no line of retreat offered itself—become extinct" (*Early Writings,* p. 130). The results of this "inertia" are personified in the hedonistic Eloi who exist in "indolent serenity" (p. 62) only for the present; they haven't learned from the mistakes of the past, nor do they, believing as they do in "absolute permanency" (p. 88), foresee a changeable future. The Morlocks, conversely, labor only for the future overthrow and domination of the Eloi. The indolent Guests serenely indulge in the immediate and present gratification of their pleasure principles—cigars and sherry forever. When the Time Traveller's narrative disturbs this reverie, they discount it, deem it a "gaudy lie" (p. 96), or compulsively check their watches (p. 95) in order to escape, ironically, from this tale of time and change back to the narcotics of their own smoking rooms or the peaceful sleep of their boudoirs.[12] To complete this pattern, though we anticipate ourselves, the Time Traveller, as his name suggests, has attempted to cheat "the inevitable process of decay" (p. 76) by his ivory-tower existence in the laboratory, and more specifically by his machine which is an unnatural attempt to control time, to escape the present. Thus, none of the characters realize, at least at the beginning of the Romance, that their misoneism has reduced them to "a very splendid array of fossils" (p. 76) like those decaying in the Palace of Green Porcelain.

This museum, or giant time-capsule, brings us to the first world of the future, the divided-self of the Eloi and Morlocks. Ostensibly, these "two species" appear to be separate and distinct, polarized races with antithetical, not complementary, cultures:

> The two species that had resulted from the evolution of man were sliding down towards, or had already arrived at an altogether new relationship from that of master-slave. The Eloi, like the Carlo-vingian kings, had decayed to a mere beautiful futility. They still possessed the earth on sufferance: since the Morlocks, subterranean for innumerable generations, had come at last to find the daylit surfaces intolerable. And the Morlocks made their garments, I inferred, and maintained them in their habitual needs, perhaps through the survival of an old habit of service (p. 70). . . . And so these inhuman sons of men—! I tried to look at the thing in a scientific spirit. After all, they were less human and more remote than our cannibal ancestors of three or four thousand years ago. And the intelligence that would have made this state of things a torment had gone. Why should I trouble myself? These Eloi were mere fatted cattle, which the ant-like Morlocks preserved and preyed upon—probably saw to the breeding of (pp. 74-75).

I quote this description at length not only to indicate the seeming differences between the two races, but more importantly for the sake of comparing it with passages from Robert Lewis Stevenson and Carl Jung, which will be discussed shortly. The point is twofold. First of all, apparent differences cloak an essential unity—both peoples share the same pigmy size, the same whitish color, and the same curious laugh. Secondly, but most important, both share a symbiotic cosmology whose convex towers and concave wells form one balanced and total circle. In fact, while learning to identify with *both* Eloi *and* Morlocks, the Time Traveller discovers this architectural unity: "After a time, too, I came to connect these wells with tall towers standing here and there upon the slopes" (p. 56). Again, as a scientific footnote to the Romance theme, we should recall that in a 1904 essay, **"The Scepticism of the Instrument,"** Wells criticizes "formal logic" for being unable to cope with what he calls the concept of "complementarity," that is, for creating an apparent conflict where there exists essential unity (see *Early Writings,* pp. 6-7). And as Philmus and Hughes indicate, "As early as **'Zoological Retrogression'** (1891), he uses the term 'opposite idea' not as a synonym for 'antithesis' or 'negation,' but in the sense of 'essential complement'" (*Early Writings,* pp. 6-7). In addition, Wells's essays stressed more and more the importance of Cooperation, rather than competition, among species. In **"Ancient Experiments in Cooperation"** (1892), for example, he writes: "the cooperative union of individuals to form higher unities, underlies the whole living creation" (*Early Writings,* p. 191). In this same essay, cooperative unity seems to carry an internal as well as external significance.

> It is as startling and grotesque as it is scientifically true, that man is an aggregate of amoeboid individuals in a higher unity, and that such higher unities as may be reasonably likened to man . . . have united again into yet higher individual unities, and that, therefore, there is no impossibility in science that in the future men should not coalesce into similar unified aggregates (*Early Writings,* p. 192).[13]

In **"Mr. Marshall's Doppelganger"** (1897) and again in the significantly titled *The Secret Places Of The Heart* (1922), Wells blatantly dramatizes this internal theme of the divided self. But, he also implies that the symbiotic macrocosm of the future is actually an image of the ruptured relationship between modes and levels of consciousness. The last chapter of Stevenson's Romance, "Henry Jekyll's Full Statement Of the Case," employs much the same rhetoric but makes the psychological nature of this relationship more clearly than Wells does:

> . . . man is not truly one, but truly two. . . . I learned to recognize the thorough and primitive duality of man; I saw that, of the two natures that contended in the field of my consciousness, even if I could rightly be said to be either, it was only because I was radically both. . . . It was the curse of mankind that these incongruous faggots were thus bound together—that in the agonized womb of consciousness, these polar twins should be continuously struggling. How, then, were they dissociated?[14]

The answer to this pivotal question, which is also central to the meaning of both the Beast People in *The Island of Dr. Moreau* and the Eloi-Morlock division in *The Time Machine,* is that society, epitomized here by high Victorian obsession with order, security, and intelligence and its repressive terror of chaos, impulse, and desire, has "dissociated" these "polar twins." In fact, in **"Morals and Civilization"** (1897), Wells links such repression to static inertia, or misoneism: "It is no inevitable force which changes militant into static civilizations. As much as anything it is the demoralisation due to security,—a disorganization of the forces of moral suggestion" (*Early Writings,* p. 226). And Jung's commentary on "visionary" literature in "Psychology And Literature" addresses this same compulsive "security" and the consequent "primitive duality of man" (which ought ideally to be a unity), thereby helping to explain why the Traveller "had a vague sense of something familiar" (p. 71) from what he "had seen in the Underworld" (p. 71):[15]

> But the primordial experiences rend from top to bottom the curtain upon which is painted the picture of an ordered world, and allow a glimpse into the unfathomable abyss of the unborn and of things yet to be. Is it a vision of other worlds, or of the darknesses of the spirit, or of the primal beginnings of the human psyche? . . . We are reminded of nothing in everyday life, but rather of dreams, night-time fears, and the dark uncanny recesses of the human mind. . . . However dark and unconscious this night-world may be, it is not wholly unfamiliar. Man has known it from time immemorial, and for primitives it is a self-evident part of their cosmos. It is only we who have repudiated it because of our fear of superstition and metaphysics, building up in its place an apparently safer and more manageable world of consciousness in which natural law operates like human law in a society. The poet now and then catches sight of the figures that people the night-world—spirits, demons, and gods; he feels the secret quickening of human fate by a suprahuman design, and has a presentiment of incomprehensible happenings in the pleorama. In short, he catches a glimpse of the psychic world that terrifies the primitive and is at the same time his greatest hope.[16]

Comparing this account with Wells's own tell-tale description of the origin of his Romances, we can certainly see its significance:

> I found that, taking almost anything as a starting point and letting my thoughts play about with it, there would presently come out of the darkness, in a manner quite inexplicable, some absurd or vivid little nucleus. Little men in canoes upon sunlit oceans would come floating out of nothingness, incubating the eggs of prehistoric monsters unawares; violent conflicts would break out amidst the flower beds of suburban gardens. I would discover I was peering into remote and mysterious worlds ruled by an order, logical indeed, but other than our common sanity.[17]

However, by revealing the general danger of *repudiating* darkness for light and the *greatest hope* in reconciling the two in Wells's "mysterious worlds," cited above, Jung's insights only diagnose a portion of the disease of the human heart. The Palace of Green Porcelain and the White Sphinx provide clues to the rest of the mystery. Both symbols deal with time, change, and misoneism. The Palace, "this ancient monument of an intellectual age" (p. 77), is complex. Its fossilized treasures not only warn against the vanity of human wishes and the "futility of all ambition" (p. 79), such as the Time Traveller's and the Morlocks' emphases on future glory, but it also admonishes hedonists like the Dinner Guests and Eloi who live only for the present and thus court no great expectations. Neither response can arrest "the inevitable process of decay" (p. 76); and both sins of wasting time render the sinners into "dessicated mummies in jars" (p. 77), like the "stuffed animals" who are wasted by time in the museum.

The White Sphinx, on the other hand, parallels the temporal dimensions of the Time Machine and the Palace by placing the blighted worlds of the future, and thus the world of the present, in their proper wasteland context as it overlooks "a tangled waste of beautiful bushes and flowers, a long-neglected and yet weedless garden" (p. 44). Although, in a sense, the Time Traveller finally fulfills the redemptive function of Oedipus, the riddle of this Sphinx has not yet been solved by a questing hero; and thus the sought-for answer, which admits change and time in the three ages of man, has not provided renewing, spring rains. The Sphinx's "white leprous face" (p. 51), "weather-worn" condition, and "unpleasant suggestion of disease" (p. 40), all indicate that wasteland sterility has infected even this major symbol of potential health. Finally, the Sphinx, like the "griffins' heads" (p. 47) and the "Faun" (p. 72), implies the unification of a dual nature; and consequently these three sole survivors of past art are all imaginative reminders of the Romance's psychological theme. As Wells indicates in **"Human Evolution, An Artificial Process,"** published the year following *The Time Machine* and vital to its understanding, civilized man is a compound of "an inherited factor, the natural man, . . . the culminating ape" and "an acquired factor, the artificial man, the highly plastic creature of tradition, suggestion, and reasoned thought" *(Early Writings,* p. 217). Such a compound certainly suggests the symbiotic Morlocks and Eloi, as do the following remarks whose moral psychologizing is as true of *The Time Machine* as of *The Island of Dr. Moreau:* "in this view, what we call Morality becomes the padding of suggested emotional habits necessary to keep the round Palaeolithic savage in the square hole of the civilised state. And Sin is the conflict of the two factors—as I have tried to convey in my *Island of Dr. Moreau*" (p. 217). Wells concludes the essay by hoping that men "have the greatness of heart" to create "a social organization . . . cunningly balanced" (p. 218) between savagery and civilization (p. 218).

However, the subsequent future worlds, of the giant butterflies and crabs and finally of the great "Silence," are dramatic condemnations of the wasteland's denial of the "truth of the human heart" and thus seem to refute Wells's dream of balance. The wish-fulfillment of misoneism has already cursed the earth in the next world since stellar motion is "growing slower and slower" (p. 90) and the sun has "halted motionless upon the horizon" (p. 90). Now the changeless wasteland no longer betrays even a semblance of the Eloi's Eden. The "eternal sea" (p. 91) and "perpetual twilight" (p. 90) reflect "the sense of abominable desolation that hung over the world" (p. 91). Finally, the "huge white butterfly" and "monster crab" (p. 91) are the only survivors of psychological devolution; they are the end-products of, and commentaries upon, the anemic Eloi and blood-thirsty Morlocks. Remembering Stein's classification of humanity into butterflies and beetles in *Lord Jim,* we might reinterpret his metaphor to suggest that caterpillars (crabs) and butterflies are, in essence, the same creature; and it is for this reason that the Greeks were so fond of viewing the butterfly as an emblem of the total psyche. Again, dualistic appearances cloak an inner, unified reality. A "thousand years or more" later (p. 92), the "eternal sunset" (p. 92) is replaced by the Silence, or "black central shadow of the eclipse" (p. 93); and this *Gotterdämmerung* leaves the world in "rayless obscurity" (p. 93), totally without solar change. In a startling and haunting last image, which recalls the false dichotomy between spectators and participants in the previous worlds and starkly joins the human and subhuman, the Traveller describes the final mutant form of life as the hybrid of a soccerball (British football) and octopus: "It was a round thing, the size of a football perhaps, or, it may be, bigger, and tentacles trailed down from it . . . it was hopping fitfully about" (p. 93). This, then, is the end-result of fear of change and fear of unifying the contraries of the human heart.

The previous discussions of the Narrator, the Dinner Guests, and the future worlds, however, make most sense when viewed in the light of the Time Traveller's "growing knowledge" (p. 81). This repeated *gnostic* theme, which is rooted in the Romance, branches out into several different but related genres—the *Bildungsroman,* the myth of the hero, and, as I have argued elsewhere,[18] the Victorian novel which focuses upon some major crisis in epistemology. Most generally, the Time Traveller's reiterated "pale" but also "animated" (see pp. 25 and 36) personality suggests that he, and by extension his wasted culture, is caught between two worlds: one, of pleasure, is externalized in feeble aristocracy like the Eloi and is all but dead; the other, of labor and thought (see p. 88 for Morlock thought), is personified by the Morlocks and is powerless to be born without the correct kind of ideological conception. Like the mythic questers of old and like each individual personality, the Time Traveller can insure this conception by "boldly penetrating . . . underground mysteries" (p. 65), that is, by harrowing hell, reconciling spirit and sense, discovering the hidden truth of the human heart, and living fully in the present.

Specifically, as indicated before, the Time Traveller must admit the Morlock side of himself and integrate this with his more deeply suppressed Eloi side. However, at the tale's outset in London, he is blithefully ignorant of both halves of his heart; and so once in the future, he immediately feels "naked in a strange world" (p. 41). This stripping away of his old personality masks prepares him for his inevitable identity crisis—"my mind was already in revolution" (p. 62) he admits in 802,701. The Time Traveller verbalizes it on the scientific level as "Man had not remained one species, but had differentiated into two distinct animals" (p. 61). After feeling initial disgust for the Morlocks (machinists and meta-eaters like himself) and condescension toward the Eloi (whose enervated spontaneity still highlights his own emotional sterility), the Traveller identifies with both in order to reintegrate these now "distinct animals." Having first struck "in a frenzy of fear" (p. 85) at the Morlocks during the forest fire, he significantly empathizes with their plight: "I was assured of their absolute helplessness and misery in the glare, and I struck no more of them" (p. 85). Previously, in the Palace of Green Porcelain, he had recognized his own "certain weakness for mechanism" (p. 77) and then therapeutically and thematically "felt that *I was wasting my time* in this academic examination of machinery" (p. 78, italics mine). This newly-discovered "knowledge" is put into practice when the Time Traveller, who in previous drafts is called The Philosopher, spontaneously "turned to Weena. 'Dance,' I cried to her in her own tongue" (p. 79). Thus Morlock and Eloi are joined; and, unlike Dr. Moreau's Beast People, their extremes are tempered. Earlier in his quest for the truth of the human heart, the Traveller feels that "my growing knowledge would lead me back" to solve "the mystery of the bronze doors under the sphinx" (p. 55), or implicitly, the mysterious unity of the future world. And even here he anticipates the redeeming solution to the Sphinx's riddle, which would best prepare him and his culture to accept "the wear of time" (p. 79): "To sit among all those unknown things [the mysteries of the Sphinx] before a puzzle like that is hopeless. That way lies monomania. Face this world. Learn its ways, watch it, be careful of too many hasty guesses at its meaning. In the end you will find clues to it all" (p. 55). Thus like any good scientist, but also like any good Romancifier, the Traveller learns in the new world by employing the "experimental method," constantly testing hypotheses against experience, both external and internal.

In **"Human Evolution, An Artificial Process,"** Wells predicts that only in "Education lies the possible salvation of mankind from misery and sin" (***Early Writings***, p. 219). And through his Romance, the Time Traveller certainly tries to dramatize to the Narrator, the Dinner Guests, and, by extension, the Victorian audience at large what Wells means by "Education," that is, that desired balance between savagery and civilization, between past and present. But what of the Victorian wasteland? Does the Time Traveller *educate* and thereby redeem it; or does he reject it? Put another way, is his final role that of a savior, as when he saves Weena from drowning; or is his final role that of a destroyer, as when the forest fires he lights burns her to death? These questions are as complex, but as thematically significant, as the riddle of the

Sphinx since the meaning of his enigmatic return journey back to the future depends upon our answers. If the future is taken realistically, as it would be in a scientific *novel*, then the Traveller's withdrawal from the present merely confirms his sins against time and his escapist obsession with the future. This reading, then, effectively negates the success of his first wonderful visit into the future. If, on the other hand, the future is considered as an allegory of the present, as it should be in the psychological Romance, then the Time Traveller's return journey does not indicate the hero's escape from his destiny but rather suggests a simple redirection of his quest.[19] The Dinner Guests believe the Time Traveller to be either delirious or duplistic, and thus his new-found "knowledge" has not yet saved them. He consequently returns with trusty "kodak" (p. 97) in hand to gather empirical proof for these doubting Thomases. But as the Narrator reports, "he has never returned" (p. 98). Has he failed and been killed by the Morlocks, whom by now he should certainly *know* how to handle? Has he escaped to settle down with the pretty Eloi, perhaps even returning prior to the death of Weena to save her again, before the fact, by committing another sin against time? There is obviously no textual evidence for this reading. Is the future merely a *possible* future, a potential schizophrenia which will only be realized if the current wasteland mentality is not cured; and thus the Time Traveller, attempting to verify this ominous portent to the Guests, is destroyed by his own dualism? Or, following the conditions of the Romance, which the Narrator fails to understand, has he simply returned to he allegorical present to save both the Eloi and the Morlocks and thereby redeem the realistic present of Victorian England?

The Traveller's symbolic identification with Prometheus throughout the tale supports this last hypothesis and thus sustains the Narrator's belief that "gratitude and a mutual tenderness still lived on in the heart of man." As the Traveller explains during the unrelieved darkness of the Eloi's night: "In this decadence, too, the art of fire-making had been forgotten on the earth" (p. 82); and then he begins to educate Weena about the magic of matches. Thus on the realistic level, he brings the gift of fire to the future as Prometheus had brought it from the gods to the human world; on the psychological, or Romance level, he brings back "foreknowledge" (the Greek meaning of *Prometheus*) from the Eloi (*Lord* or *God* in the Bible) and Morlocks to the Dinner Guests in the *educating* form of his Romance. Whether his return journey is intended to help the future or bring help from the future, the meaning is the same; and the Narrator's optimism is implicitly upheld. For the Time Traveller at least, time is no longer out of joint; and his Romance-quest has revealed the unified and balanced truth of the human heart.

In conclusion, as R. H. Hutton's review in the *Spectator* (July 13, 1895) implies, it is indeed a pity that Wells's own Victorian audience, like the Dinner Guests, did not as yet understand this truth and remained wasteland unbelievers:

We have no doubt that, so far as Mr. Wells goes, his warning is wise. But we have little fear that the languid, ease-loving, and serene temperament will ever paralyse the human race after the manner he supposes, even though there may be at present some temporary signs of the growth of the appetite for mere amusement.[20]

NOTES

[1] *The Time Machine/The War of the Worlds,* with an introduction by Isaac Asimov (Greenwich, Connecticut: Fawcett Publications, Inc., 1968); all quotations will be taken from this edition, which is one of the more generally available, and noted within the text.

[2] (New York: Random House, 1931), p. ix.

[3] (London: Victor Gollancz and The Cresset Press, 1934), I, 309.

[4] *To-day,* 2 (Sept., 1897), as quoted in Bernard Bergonzi's *The Early H. G. Wells: A Study Of The Scientific Romances* (Manchester: The University Press, 1961), p. 44, italics mine. The interested reader should consult this book-length study of the genre of the scientific romance, especially Chapter 2 which deals with *The Time Machine.*

[5] *Early Writings In Science And Science Fiction By H. G. Wells,* eds. Robert Philmus and David Y. Hughes (Berkeley and Los Angeles: Univ. of California Press, 1975), pp. 204-05. This collection will subsequently be noted within the text as *Early Writings.*

[6] "'The Time Machine'; or, the Fourth Dimension as Prophecy," *PMLA,* 84 (1969), 534.

[7] "Very Early Wells: Origins of Some Physical Motifs in *The Time Machine* and *The War Of The Worlds,*" *Extrapolation,* 13 (1972), 119-126 *passim.*

[8] "*The Time Machine:* An Ironic Myth," *Critical Quarterly* 2 (1960), 305; this essay later makes up part of Bergonzi's chapter on *The Time Machine* in his study of the scientific romances. See note 4.

[9] "H. G. Wells And The World Of Science Fiction," *Univ. of Windsor Review,* 2 (1967), 60.

[10] Philmus, 535; the reference is to *Anatomy of Criticism,* (Princeton: Princeton Univ. Press, 1957), pp. 202-203.

[11] LeMire, 61-62.

[12] Discussing the tale as a scientific treatise, Alfred Borrello confirms Wells's condemnation of misoneistic tendencies: "The species, he believed, is cursed with a fundamental yearning for the *status quo,* for a changeless existence in which life proceeds at the same pointless pace as it always proceeded—witness its desire for a never-ending Heaven," in *H. G. Wells: Author in Agony* (Carbondale and Edwardsville: Southern Illinois Univ. Press, 1972), p. 13.

[13] See Borrello's discussion of the lack of cultural "individuality" in the Morlocks and Eloi, pp. 11-12.

[14] It is interesting to note here that Wells's Victorian audience saw no relationship between his Romance and Stevenson's—even though it could not help linking the two tales. For example an unsigned review in the *Daily Chronicle* (July 27, 1895) reads: "No two books could well be more unlike than *The Time Machine* and *The Strange Case of Dr. Jekyll and Mr. Hyde,* but since the appearance of Stevenson's creepy romance we have had nothing in the domain of pure fantasy so bizarre as this 'invention' by Mr. H. G. Wells." This review is reprinted in *H. G. Wells: The Critical Heritage,* ed. Patrick Parrinder (London and Boston: Routledge and Kegan Paul, 1972), p. 38.

[15] Here the specific reference is to the resemblance between the meat in the Underworld and the bodies of the Eloi.

[16] Reprinted in *The Spirit in Man, Art, and Literature,* trans. R.F.C. Hull (Princeton: Princeton Univ. Press, 1971), pp. 90-91, 95-96. For the sake of unity, I have combined excerpts from a series of paragraphs dealing with "visionary" literature.

[17] Quoted in Kenneth Young's *H. G. Wells* (Essex: Longman Group Ltd., 1974), pp. 13-14.

[18] "*Dracula:* The Gnostic Quest and Victorian Wasteland," *English Literature in Transition,* 20 (1977), 13-26. This essay also clarifies the relationships between gnosticism, the wasteland theme, and Victorian literature.

[19] See Philmus' relevant description of the future as a fourth dimension, fantasy world, 534-535.

[20] Reprinted in *H. G. Wells: The Critical Heritage,* p. 36.

Barbara Bengels

SOURCE: "Flights into the Unknown: Structural Similarities in Two Works by H. G. Wells and Henry James," in *Extrapolation,* Vol. 21, No. 4, Winter, 1980, pp. 361-66.

Henry James voiced a great admiration for H. G. Wells's 1895 science-fiction gem, **The Time Machine,**[1] and well he might, for his own brilliant chiller, *The Turn of the Screw* (1898), bears a striking resemblance in style and format to the earlier work. That is not to suggest any attempt on James's part to copy from his younger friend; in fact, James states that he first read **The Time Machine** in 1900, five years after its publication, and two years after the publication of *The Turn of the Screw.* There is, nevertheless, an interesting bond between the two men, for while **The Time Machine** fascinated James, Wells seemed equally interested in the Jamesian novel, which he was to satirize in **Boon** several years later when their friendship had gone sour.[2] To gain greater understanding of the fine line between the science fiction of Wells, which focuses on sociological extrapolation, and the gothic mode of James, which centers on psychological implications, it is worthwhile to see how similar the two novels are, and how, when they do diverge, it is always to achieve a greater sense of individual characterization in the one novel and a greater emphasis upon the character of the human race as a whole in the other.

The first, and most obvious, similarity of the two works is in their initial settings. As Bernard Bergonzi points out in his fine essay *"The Time Machine: An Ironic Myth,"* *The Time Machine* "belongs to the class of story which includes James's *Turn of the Screw,* and which Northrop Frye has called 'the tale told in quotation marks, where we have an opening setting with a small group of congenial people, and then the real story told by one of the members.'"[3] In *The Time Machine,* of course, that setting is a skeptical after-dinner discussion of the Time Traveller's latest invention, his time machine, a discussion attended by an assortment of stereotypes—all highly uncharacterized—and the outermost narrator who, while unnamed, nevertheless informs us that he "was one of the Time Traveller's most constant guests" (p. 24).[4] This first chapter establishes the scientific basis for the concept of time travel; in the second chapter, which occurs one week later (on the following Thursday night, with a somewhat different assortment of guests in attendance) the Time Traveller returns late and disheveled, but prepared to unfold his preposterous and astounding tale of future horrors. In *The Turn of the Screw* the single framework chapter immediately establishes the appropriate mood for a ghost story as a generally anonymous group is settled around the fireplace (presumably on Christmas Eve), listening to horror tales. Douglas, the protagonist's erstwhile confidant, promises an even more frightening—because real—story as soon as he can obtain the original manuscript (interestingly enough, also on the following Thursday night), and, while reluctant to unfold a story which has remained untold for forty years, he nevertheless carries on a dialog with the again unnamed outermost narrator, practically imploring him (or her) to help him break the ice. Just as the initial narrator in *The Time Machine* seems to be a special friend of the Time Traveller's, so the outermost narrator in *The Turn of the Screw* seems to bear a special relationship to Douglas, a relationship which allows Douglas to say, "'You'll easily judge,' he repeated: '*you* will.'" (p. 3).[5] Thus, in the opening chapters of both books important groundwork is established: in one, a mood of suspense and tension pervades the scene, preparing the reader for what is to come; in the other, the scientific premise is explained, but, as Bergonzi points out, the "atmosphere makes the completest possible contrast with what is to come: an account of a wholly imaginative world of dominantly paradisal and demonic imagery, lying far outside the possible experience of the late Victorian bourgeoisie."[6] This was all very much in keeping with Wells's style of having the exotic occur in commonplace settings, but James was to follow this pattern too in the main portion of his novel: James "liked the strange and the sinister embroidered on the very type of

the normal and the easy. . . . That is why James preferred daylight ghosts."[7] In both books there also appears an especially attentive listener (akin to the young wedding guest in Coleridge's "Rime of the Ancient Mariner"), who will ultimately retell what he has heard and experienced. Here the two books differ, for we expect that Wells's outermost narrator is an impartial witness to the events in the story—and, in fact, later in the book, a participant in them as he watches the Time Traveller depart on his final journey, thereby ultimately vouching for his veracity. Douglas' friend, however, not only obviously shares some special relationship with Douglas but also reveals that Douglas himself obviously held some very special feelings, feelings in fact of love, for the governess. Therefore, James may very well want us to constantly reassess Douglas' appraisal of the governess's character and of his attestation of her sanity as he recounts the very odd events in which she took part. Finally, in the framework chapters of both books there is an interval of time between the first mention of the extraordinary occurrence and the continuation of the tale—building up tension in the listener and reader alike.

Another area in which both books are strikingly similar is the manner in which their authors try to establish the credibility of their obviously incredible inventions, a machine in the one book and a particularly ambiguous set of ghosts in the other. Wells's Time Traveller first tries to convince his guests of the impossibility of an "instantaneous cube," and once he has established the existence of the Fourth Dimension (this in a pre-Einsteinian world), he leads his guests to see his device:

> "Would you like to see the Time Machine itself?" asked the Time Traveller. And therewith, taking his lamp in his hand, he led the way down the long, draughty corridor to his laboratory. I remember vividly the flickering light, his queer, broad head in silhouette, the dance of the shadows, how we all followed him, puzzled but incredulous, and how there in the laboratory we beheld a larger edition of his little mechanism which we had seen vanish from before our eyes. Parts were of nickel, parts of ivory, parts had certainly been filed or sawn out of rock crystal. The thing was generally complete, but the twisted crystalline bars lay unfinished upon the bench beside some sheets of drawings, and I took one up for a better look at it. Quartz it seemed to be. (p. 22)

The description exhibits a twofold interest: for one thing, it is a fascinating mixture of the gothic with its draughty corridor and flickering lights, and of "early" science fiction with its laboratory and scientific trappings. It is equally fascinating, however, for its imprecision. As Bergonzi points out, "The assemblage of details is strictly speaking meaningless but nevertheless conveys effectively a *sense of the machine* without putting the author to the taxing necessity of giving a direct description."[8] How similar this sounds to James's own description of his technique for creating ghosts "capable of portentous evil."[9] In his "New York Preface" to *Turn of the Screw,* he writes:

What, in the last analysis, had I to give the sense of? Of their being, the haunting pair, capable, as the phrase is, of everything—that is, of exerting, in respect to the children, the very worst action small victims so conditioned might be conceived as subject to. What would *be* then, on reflexion, this utmost conceivability?—a question to which the answer all admirably came. There is for such a case no eligible *absolute* of the wrong; it remains relative to fifty other elements, a matter of appreciation, speculation, imagination—these things moreover quite exactly in the light of the spectator's, the critic's, the reader's experience. Only make the reader's general vision of evil intense enough, I said to myself—and that already is a charming job—and his own experience, his own imagination, his own sympathy (with the children) and horror (of their false friends) will supply him quite sufficiently with all the particulars. Make him *think* the evil, make him think it for himself, and you are released from weak specifications.[10]

Thus he lays the groundwork for ghosts so horrendous that they may very well spring from anyone's fertile imagination, the most imaginative in the tale being the governess herself. (It is especially interesting to note that he speaks in the above paragraph of the children's "false friends" rather than more specifically of the "haunting pair" as he does earlier in the passage, another indication that the "evil" in the book may be even more complicated than the governess can possibly know.)

Finally, it is in the main characters and their experiences that we find some of the most interesting similarities of the two works. Obviously our first need as readers is to be able to believe the fantastic tales the narrators tell. Wells sets himself an easier task in this instance. On the one hand, he warns us through his outermost narrator that his "Time Traveller was one of those men who are too clever to be believed . . . ; you always suspected some subtle reserve, some ingenuity in ambush, behind his lucid frankness" and in fact he had "more than a touch of whim among his elements, and we distrusted him" (p. 23). On the other hand, however, he has the Time Traveller bring back Weena's flowers and then actually vanish into Time in the narrator's presence. Ultimately, because the narrator has the "last word" in the final framework chapter, we are left no alternative but to believe in the Time Traveller's adventures and his version of the dismal future he has visited. Such, however, is not the case with James's governess, for he has carefully failed to return to close his framework chapter at the novel's end. Thus we never hear the remarks and analysis or the credence or disbelief given to the governess's tale of ghostly visitation—for to have openly discussed it would surely have been to spoil James's carefully wrought effect. What we are left with is what Douglas tells us about the governess—and about himself—what she wittingly and unwittingly reveals, and what we make of her actions, and the reactions of those around her. This indeed is far more complex than the Time Traveller's "whimsical" nature. We learn of the governess's instant infatuation with her employer, of her cloistered upbringing, of

her eccentric father, of her need to be in command and worthy of the master, all suggesting the possibility that the ghosts are as much her invention as the machine is the Time Traveller's. But to offset the psychological implications we also learn that after Miles's death she has subsequently gone on to another similar position, in fact in Douglas' own household, certainly a fact that seems to substantiate her reliability and veracity. What we have here, then, is far more difficult to evaluate, James's "*amusette*" to catch those not easily caught."[11]

Regardless of their varying degrees of credibility, however, what is also interesting to note are the initial reactions of both the Time Traveller and the governess (both unnamed) to their new environments and how disturbingly unprepared they are to evaluate their situations. The Time Traveller, for example, informs us that he had "always anticipated that the people of the year Eight Hundred and Two Thousand odd would be incredibly in front of us in knowledge, art, everything" (p. 36). Initially he feels disappointment: "For a moment I felt that I had built the Time Machine in vain" (p. 36). But he is yet far from comprehending the predicament of either the Eloi or of the human race. The governess's initial reactions to Bly are quite the opposite: "I suppose I had expected—or had dreaded, something so dreary that what greeted me was a good surprise. . . . The scene had a greatness that made a different affair from my own scant home, and there immediately appeared at the door, with a little girl in her hand, a civil person who dropped me as decent a curtsy as if I had been the mistress or a distinguished visitor" (p. 7). How unlike the Time Traveller's ego-bruising experience! Thus although their first impressions of their domains are quite opposite (possibly as the result of the way in which they are greeted), they both come to feel similarly about the inhabitants of their new worlds. The Time Traveller speaks of the "very beautiful and graceful creature" (p. 34), of the "something in these pretty little people that inspired confidence—a graceful gentleness, a certain childlike ease" (p. 35). He soon sees himself "like a schoolmaster amidst children" (p. 39) and before long stands in smug judgment of them: "As I stood there in the gathering dark I thought that in this simple explanation I had mastered the problem of the whole secret of these delicious people" (p. 45). So, too, the governess (who, of course, is in fact a schoolmistress amongst her children) sizes them up in the most favorable of terms: Flora is "the most beautiful child I had ever seen" (p. 7), "beatific" (p. 8), "the vision of . . . angelic beauty" (p. 8). "To watch, teach, 'form' little Flora would too evidently be the making of a happy and useful life" (p. 8). When she first sees Miles it is "in the great glow of freshness, the same positive fragrance of purity, in which I had from the first moment seen his little sister. He was incredibly beautiful . . ." (p. 13). And like the Time Traveller, she too begins to feel in command—but of a very different situation: "I had the fancy of our being almost as lost as a handful of passengers in a great drifting ship. Well, I was strangely at the helm!" (p. 10). Therefore, as romantic as is the governess's original appraisal of her situation, she perhaps more rapidly perceives the underlying menace. The Time Traveller had flirted with the idea that the human race might have "developed into something inhuman, unsympathetic, and overwhelmingly powerful" (p. 33), but he continues to survey his Paradise until he discovers the total lack of fellow feeling that allows for Weena's near drowning. His subsequent discovery of the bifurcation of mankind, the inevitable outcome of its earlier worker-aristocrat division, forces him to entirely reevaluate all that he has witnessed both in future and present time. So, too, the governess's increasing awareness of diabolical presences, either real or imagined, forces her to pursue a course of action based upon the assumption that the children are anything but angelic, that they are instead in league with the devilish pair.

To be sure, there are other peculiar correspondences between the two novels, the pervasive and ambivalent use of fire, for example,[12] even the sense of Nathaniel Hawthorne hovering somewhere offstage. (Wells acknowledges that he initially rewrote his earliest draft of **The Time Machine, The Chronic Argonauts,** because it sounded too Hawthornian;[13] James was impressed enough by Hawthorne to write his biography.) But in a larger sense the similarities between the two works appear right from the settings, through the stylistic devices of obscuring the petty details to achieve a sense of the whole, finally in the plight and reactions of the major characters, a young girl whose innocence may be leading her into a hell of her own making, and a scientist who, in his naive optimism, may have to shed his innocence to fully assess the future degeneracy of the human race. They both may hope for the best, but neither science fiction nor human psychology can truly predict what mankind is capable of.

NOTES

[1] Having just read *The Time Machine,* James wrote to Wells in a letter dated January 29, 1900: "You are very magnificent. I am beastly critical—but you are in a still higher degree wonderful. I re-write you, much, as I read—which is the highest tribute my damned impertinence can pay an author." *Henry James and H. G. Wells: A Record of their Friendship, their Debate on the Art of Fiction, and their Quarrel,* ed. Leon Edel and Gordon N. Ray (Urbana: Univ. of Illinois Press, 1958), p. 63.

[2] Edel and Ray, p. 37.

[3] In *H. G. Wells: A Collection of Critical Essays,* Twentieth Century Views, 127 (Englewood Cliffs, N.J.: Spectrum/Prentice-Hall: 1976), p. 40. Henceforth, this will be referred to as "Ironic Myth."

[4] H. G. Wells, *The Time Machine* in *The Time Machine and War of the Worlds: A Critical Edition,* ed. Frank D. McConnell (New York: Oxford Univ. Press, 1977), p. 24. All references to *The Time Machine* are from this edition.

[5] Henry James, *The Turn of the Screw,* ed. Robert Kimbrough (New York: Norton, 1966), p. 3. All references are from this edition.

[6] "Ironic Myth," p. 41.

[7] Leon Edel, *Henry James: 1895-1901—The Treacherous Years* (Philadelphia: Lippincott, 1969), p. 214.

[8] "Ironic Myth," p. 42. Emphasis added.

[9] Henry James, "The New York Preface," in *The Turn of the Screw,* p. 122.

[10] Pp. 122-23.

[11] "The New York Preface," p. 120.

[12] In *The Turn of the Screw,* fire is used throughout as a symbol both of passion and demonic possession; in *The Time Machine* it is both the Time Traveller's mode of escape and ultimately of his loss of Weena.

[13] H. G. Wells, *Experiment in Autobiography* (New York: Macmillan, 1934), p. 253.

John Huntington

SOURCE: "'The Time Machine,'" in *The Logic of Fantasy: H. G. Wells and Science Fiction,* Columbia University Press, 1982, pp. 41-55.

Wells's use of balanced opposition and symbolic mediation as a way of thinking finds its most perfect form in **The Time Machine.** If the novella imagines a future, it does so not as a forecast but as a way of contemplating the structures of our present civilization.[1] At one level **The Time Machine** presents a direct warning about the disastrous potential of class division. But at a deeper level it investigates large questions of difference and domination, and rather than settling the issues, it constructs unresolvable conflicts that return us to the central dilemmas that have characterized the evolutionary debate we looked at in the first chapter [of *The Logic of Fantasy*].

The Time Traveller's insights into the benefits of civilization are paradoxical. In his first interpretation of the meaning and structure of the world of 802,701 he finds a complex pleasure in the union of idyllic ease and evolutionary decline:

> To adorn themselves with flowers, to dance, to sing in the sunlight; so much was left of the artistic spirit, and no more. Even that would fade in the end into a contented inactivity. We are kept keen on the grindstone of pain and necessity, and, it seemed to me, that here was that hateful grindstone broken at last! (p. 43)

If there is regret at lost keenness here, there is also joy at escaped hardship. By the end of the novella, when he realizes that the decline has not conferred quite the benefits he anticipated and that the structure of civilization has degenerated into a primitive horror in which the Morlocks, the slothlike descendents of the laboring class,

Cover illustration by Matt Gabel for The Time Machine, *by H. G. Wells.*

slaughter and eat the Eloi, the species descended from the upper classes, he entertains a different set of conflicting emotions. Now he balances a sense of the ironic justice of this situation with an irrational sympathy for the humanoid Eloi:

> Then I tried to preserve myself from the horror that was coming upon me, by regarding it as a rigorous punishment of human selfishness. Man had been content to live in ease and delight upon the labours of his fellow-man, had taken Necessity as his watchword and excuse, and in the fulness of time Necessity had come home to him. I even tried a Carlyle-like scorn of this wretched aristocracy-in-decay. But this attitude of mind was impossible. However great their intellectual degradation, the Eloi had kept too much of the human form not to claim my sympathy, and to make me perforce a sharer in their degradation and their Fear. (p. 81)

If the moral view, which would find satisfaction in the Eloi enslavement, is not adequate to the situation, it nevertheless works against the sense of pity, which is also, in itself, inadequate. Such nodes of conflicting insights and feelings are the expressions of tensions developed by the brutal oppositions on which the whole novella is built.

We can isolate two large, separate realms of opposition which operate in **The Time Machine.** One, essentially spatial, consists of the conflict between the Eloi and the Morlocks. Though the Time Traveller first views the 802,701 world as free from opposition, the novella traces his discovery of the radical oppositions that actually define that world; what begins as a vision of benign decay and carefree pastoral ends up as a vision of entrapment wherein the economic divisions of the present have become biological and territorial. The other opposition is temporal; it entails the opposition between the civilization of 1895 and a set of increasingly less civilized, more purely natural worlds of the future. Of these, the world of the Eloi-Morlock conflict is of course the most important. Towards the end of the novella the Time Traveller moves further into the future; he sees darkness and cold advance on the earth until life is diminished to huge, sluggish crabs and then finally to a football-sized organism that hops fitfully on the tideless shore.[2]

Because the Time Traveller arrives in 802,701, not by a process of incremental progressions, but by a single leap, the structure of the novella poses a puzzle: what is the relation of the future to the present? The Time Traveller and the reader are engaged in the same activity: they try to understand the nature of the temporal contrast presented and then to discover connections. Like evolutionary biologists, they must first understand what distinguishes two species and then they must reconstruct the evolutionary sequence that links them; the difference between Eohippus and the modern horse is like that between the modern human and the Eloi or the Morlocks. Unlike the biologist, however, the Time Traveller and the reader are engaged in negotiating a pattern more complex than a simple genealogical sequence. We must figure out what bonds exist amidst the differences between the Time Traveller and his and our distant grandchildren. The mental act of reconstructing the evolutionary connection involves more than just taxonomic description; it is not simply a perceiving of a pure two-world system; it entails examining a whole series of ambiguous moral conflicts.

During the course of the novella, as the truth reveals itself and the meanings of the discovered oppositions change, one relation between the present and the future persists: the future is a *reduction* of the present.[3] The future offers a simplification of issues that is much like that which occurs in conventional pastoral: economic and social complexities have disappeared, and the issues of the world are those determined by elementary human nature. But to compare **The Time Machine** to a pastoral is somewhat misleading; though both diminish the importance of civilized forms and conventions, in **The Time Machine** the main agent of change is a biological regression not found in the conventional pastoral. The inhabitants of the future have lost much of the erotic, intellectual, and moral energy that we generally associate with human beings and which it is the purpose of the usual pastoral to liberate. The society of the future is reduced to what in 1895 might be considered childish needs and pleasures, and it is under the terms of this radical diminution that the systems of spatial opposition work.

Such a reduction certainly simplifies social issues, but the first question it raises is how human or how bestial are these distant cousins of present-day humanity. The split between the Eloi and the Morlocks raises this question from opposite directions: the Eloi seem subhumans, the Morlocks superanimals. The Time Traveller certainly considers Weena the most human creature he finds in the future, but as he acknowledges, he tends to think of her as more human than she is.[4] Her humanoid appearance tends to obscure how much she is a pet rather than a human companion. At the other extreme, the Morlocks, though they too are supposedly descended from present-day humanity, because they look like sloths, always seem bestial to the Time Traveller. For much of his time in 802,701 he does not realize their importance; he treats them first as "ghosts," then as lower animals, then as servants to the Eloi. Even at the end when he comprehends their domination of the Eloi he never really conceives of them as human. Thus the novella sets up a symmetrical illusion: the Eloi, because of their appearance, seem more human than they are; the Morlocks, again because of appearance, seem less.

The Time Traveller's relation to the Eloi engages special problems because it involves, not simply identification, but affection across the abyss of species difference. Critics have found the Time Traveller's attention to his "little woman" disturbing and have treated the hints of repressed sexuality, of pedophilia, as a novelistic blunder.[5] I would suggest, however, that the unease generated by this relationship is apt, for at issue is the whole puzzle of human relations to nonhumans. The Time Traveller himself is confused by Weena. He can treat her as an equal and contemplate massacring Morlocks when he loses her, but he also forgets her easily. The tension and the ambiguities of their relationship derive from the impossibility of defining either an identity or a clear difference. To render such a state Wells plays on the inherently ambiguous relationship between adults and children.

The puzzle of Weena's sexuality is reflected and reversed by the Time Traveller's relation to the Morlocks. When he first meets the Eloi he allows them to touch him: "I felt other soft little tentacles upon my back and shoulders. They wanted to make sure I was real. There was nothing in this at all alarming" (p. 30). Similar behavior by the Morlocks, however, leads the Time Traveller to an hysterical smashing of skulls. At first, the touch of the Morlocks is hardly distinguishable from that of the Eloi: it is as if "sea anemones were feeling over my face with their soft palps" (p. 57). But this same intimate approach becomes sinister as the Time Traveller becomes aware of the Morlocks' real intent, and he feels horror later, at night in the forest, when he becomes aware that "Soft little hands, too, were creeping over my coat and back, touching even my neck" (p. 93). The reasons for the different reactions to this intimate approach are obvious; what we need to observe, however, is the area of identity here. If the repressed sexuality of the relation with Weena leads to a passive and childish activity (weaving flowers, dancing to burning matches), the Morlocks' almost

seductive aggression leads to an antipathy which generates violence and ingenious invention.[6]

The central mystery of Eloi and Morlock humanity and of the Time Traveller's relation to it is emblematized by the statue of the sphinx that the Time Traveller sees when he first arrives in 802,701. The symbol works at a number of levels. It stands for the paradox of a progress that is a regression: the future is represented by a monument that we associate with early civilization. Thus, the future is a return to the past, to the childhood, so to speak, of human society. The sphinx herself is also a poser of riddles: when Oedipus met her she asked him the riddle of man who appears in different forms. This connection is clearly in Wells's mind, for no sooner has the Time Traveller seen the statue than he begins speculating about the possibilities of the human form in this distant future. But it is in her own appearance that the sphinx raises the most perplexing puzzle, for she represents a literal combination of human and animal: woman and lion. We ask whether Weena is a woman or not, whether a Morlock is a beast or not; here in the sphinx we have a creature which is both. The sphinx marks the cut; it is a union of a crucial opposition and, like the flying man, points to the possibility of transcending the contradiction. This important mediating symbolism is repeated in a striking but diminished form by the statue of a Faun which the Time Traveller later discovers (p. 77), another literal mixture of human and animal.[7]

Just as the sphinx and the faun render visually the puzzle of the relation of human and beast and offer a union of the supposed dichotomy, they also denote the areas of human and animal activity that have been diminished by the decline into the future. The sphinx, the poser of riddles, is a figure of the very intellectual prowess that the childish creatures of the future lack. Similarly, the faun embodies the sexual energy that is noticeably absent. Thus, while the statues link the human and the animal, they do so ironically; they suggest a potential for accomplishment and for civilization of which the Eloi and the Morlocks are biologically incapable.

While such issues of the relation of present-day humanity to these future creatures pervade the novella, the opposition between the Eloi and the Morlocks themselves, of which the Time Traveller becomes increasingly aware as he learns more about the future's underworld, has an important social meaning. In the split between the two species we see a split intrinsic to technological civilization itself. This is no dark secret of the tale, of course:[8] the Time Traveller's final interpretation of how the split developed refers directly back to the division of labor in contemporary England. But the values that initially caused the split persist in the far future, and, in ways that are not generally recognized, the two species represent and at the same time parody values that belong, not merely to British capitalist civilization, but to all technological cultures. Though the Morlocks are hairy, have an apelike posture, cannot bear light, and live in burrows of a sort, any simple equation of them with the lower animals won't do. They live amidst thudding machines, and their habitat is artificially ventilated. The passage down which the Time Traveller climbs to visit them has a ladder with iron rungs. Unlike the Eloi, the Morlocks function as a group; they are individually weak, but they cooperate. Thus, though their specific intellectual and emotional capacities remain largely unknown, symbolically they subsume one aspect of what we admire in civilization: organized technological mastery. And the Eloi with their trivial, careless aestheticism embody the alternative leisure aspect of civilization, the pure delight in beauty, gaity, play. They live for these and as much as possible avoid even thinking about necessity and pain. The Morlock-Eloi split may be the result of today's class divisions, but in its final form it expresses two high and apparently contradictory values of human civilization: mastery and aesthetic leisure.[9]

The landscape of the future becomes an extension of the contradictions represented in Eloi and Morlock. The surface of the countryside, while much hedged and walled, is devoid of meaningful divisions; the ruined castles of the Eloi hardly differentiate inside and outside; at one time the Time Traveller even gets lost because the field in which he has landed is indistinguishable from any other; only the presence of the statue of the sphinx defines it. But a radically different world exists beneath the Eloi pastoral, and so it is *down* that the Time Traveller must go to find an alternative. Up and down, therefore, become an important expression of the basic Eloi-Morlock opposition. The same opposition is expressed in the opposition between light and dark. The imbalance of the opposition is symbolized by the fact that the Morlocks can intrude on the Eloi above-ground preserve at night.

The cut between the two opposed realms is marked most concretely by the strange palace of green porcelain that the Time Traveller visits when seeking to recover his lost time machine. The building is made of material that reminds the Time Traveller of Chinese porcelain and has an oriental look to it; it seems a special version of the palaces the Eloi inhabit. But within this aestheticized exterior is a museum of technology, a "latter-day South Kensington." It thus partakes of both the worlds of Eloi aesthetics and Morlock technology. But most importantly it blurs the line between up and down. As he walks along one of the galleries, the Time Traveller finds himself unexpectedly underground. He confesses he wasn't even aware of the slope. And then, as if to underline the importance of this transition, but also to offer a new way of treating it, the editor, a person who appears nowhere else in the novella, supplies a curious footnote: "It may be, of course, that the floor did not slope—but that the museum was built into the side of a hill" (p. 85). By translating the up-down division into a lateral one, the museum ingeniously mediates the division's absolute separation. That is not to say that it resolves the split: Weena is still afraid of the dark, and the Time Traveller retreats back to the light. But it is an important symbolic possibility in an otherwise destructive and rigid opposition.

Though a treasury of the present in the future, the museum of green porcelain also stands for the important mediating possibilities of modern technology in the face of the future's natural antithesis. The diminished intelligence of the creatures of the future prevents them from understanding or using the museum; only the Time Traveller is capable of realizing the museum's potential. The Time Traveller thus becomes the main mediator in the future system of static oppositions because by means of his human intelligence, passion, and morality he is able to bridge its dichotomies. He reconciles in himself the masterful and aesthetic aspects of culture that are at war in the future: at the end of the story he displays to his audience a flower, the token of Eloi aestheticism and affection, but he also vigorously demands a piece of meat, a token of Morlock carnivorousness. The future is a horror in part because the divisions that are for us in the present still capable of modification and correction have become a purely natural competition, a predatory antithesis that does not allow for exchange or change. The Time Traveller offers some hope because by using tools and by acting ethically he is able to break down the bounds of the otherwise rigid, hostile evolutionary categories.

It is his mastery of fire that gives the Time Traveller his most distinctive mediating power. That power is complex, however, and as in the cases of the other mediating images, involves contradiction and operates on a number of planes of meaning simultaneously. In *The Time Machine* fire defines civilized humanity. It is an image of both domestic security and war. It has an aesthetic function and a technological one. Finally, it is an emblem of the paradox of degenerative progress that dominates the whole novella.

The Time Traveller himself makes the link between fire and present-day humanity when he observes how rare fire is in nature:

> I don't know if you have ever thought what a rare thing flame must be in the absence of man and in a temperate climate. The sun's heat is rarely strong enough to burn, even when it is focussed by dew drops, as is sometimes the case in more tropical districts. Lightning may blast and blacken, but it rarely gives rise to wide-spread fire. Decaying vegetation may occasionally smoulder with the heat of its fermentation, but this rarely results in flame. In this decadence, too, the art of fire-making had been forgotten on the earth. The red tongues that went licking up my heap of wood were an altogether new and strange thing to Weena. (p. 92).

Implicit in the absence of fire is the question we have looked at earlier of the actual "humanity" of either the Eloi or the Morlocks. In this formulation of the issue, fire is a symbol of human control over nature, a control that the future has lost. Such innocence has ambiguous value; earlier in the story, before the Time Traveller has realized that the Eloi are victims, he approves of such ignorance. It is night; he has lost his time machine; searching for it he blunders into the dilapidated hall of the Eloi and, after striking a match, demands his machine from them. Their confusion conveys two things to him: that "they had forgotten about matches" and that they had forgotten about fear (p. 46). The link between the two forgettings is casual but significant. To forget about matches is to lose as aspect of today's technology, to revert to a primitive state in which tools are unknown. But to forget fear, one would expect, is to live in a world of complete security, to have escaped the primitive natural situation in which fear is necessary for survival. Thus, while the forgetting of matches suggests regression, the forgetting of fear suggests progress. At this early stage in his acquaintance with the future the Time Traveller interprets both forgettings as the privileges of progress, as the evidence of a carefree pastoral idyll. Under these circumstances the paradox that progress has led to regression is not dismaying.

So long as he does not understand the real situation of the future the Time Traveller has no conception of the importance his mastery of fire has, and he uses his matches merely to entertain the Eloi, to make them dance and laugh. The irony of such trivialization is that it actually prevents knowledge, as is clear in the following passage:

> I proceeded, as I have said, to question Weena about this Underworld, but here again I was disappointed. At first she would not understand my questions, and presently she refused to answer them. She shivered as though the topic was unendurable. And when I pressed her, perhaps a little harshly, she burst into tears. They were the only tears, except my own, I ever saw in that Golden Age. When I saw them I ceased abruptly to trouble about the Morlocks, and was only concerned in banishing these signs of her human inheritance from Weena's eyes. And very soon she was smiling and clapping her hands, while I solemnly burned a match. (p. 66)

By using fire as a toy the Time Traveller diverts Weena from exhibiting "signs of her human inheritance." His instinct to avert tears is understandable, but the completeness with which the concern for Weena's innocence overrides the concern with the facts about the Morlocks has signs of panic. The other time that the Time Traveller uses matches to entertain the Eloi is also after they have been "distressed" by his inquiries about the Morlocks (p. 61). In both cases the match is used for entertainment at the expense of further knowledge, to sustain a complacent happiness which is, in fact, an illusion.

Though he is capable of using matches to preserve an innocent decorum, the Time Traveller is not simply a Victorian gentleman intent on preventing children from learning or expressing the grim truth. The match may be a toy, but it is also an instrument for seeing. When he first looks for the time machine the Time Traveller uses a match. When he looks down one of the Morlock wells he uses a match. And when he enters the underworld he uses a match: "The view I had [of the Morlocks' cavern] was as much as one could see in the burning of a match"

(p. 70). When two paragraphs later he chides himself for coming to the future ill-equipped, the Time Traveller emphasizes the importance of matches for his investigation: though he might prefer a "kodak," the match, feeble as it is, is the single "tool" that he has brought. For the Time Traveller to be master of fire is for him to have an intellectual dominance, and the safety match becomes a symbol of that aspect of present-day technology.

Intellectual dominance leads to other kinds of dominance. The ambiguous potential of fire is most forcefully realized when the Time Traveller uses it, not for entertaining or seeing, but as a weapon. The match becomes an important defensive tool which allows the Time Traveller to move across the boundaries of this world. And after he visits the green porcelain palace and comes away with matches and camphor, the Time Traveller begins to use fire as a tool of aggression. With the intention of "amaz[ing] our friends," he sets a pile of wood on fire. Now when Weena wants to dance and play with the light, the Time Traveller prevents her. A little later he is forced to start a second fire.

What is important for our understanding of the symbol is that the fires fail him in diametrically opposite ways. The second, beside which he goes to sleep, goes out and the Morlocks, unhindered by the fire, almost overcome him. But the first, forgotten and left behind, starts a forest fire which threatens to destroy even the Time Traveller himself. We have here an expression of the danger of dependence on the very technology that allows for mastery: it can either fail to perform even its elementary expectations, or it can go wild and overperform. In both cases the human is betrayed by his own technological sophistication. Fire, which up to this point has been a symbol of technology's ability to mediate, here develops its own destructive opposition between too much and too little. The puzzle that a dependence on technology presents is again rendered a little later in the novella when the Time Traveller, mounted on the time machine's saddle, confidently tries to light a match to drive off the assaulting Morlocks and discovers that he has safety matches that won't strike without the box.

Yet it is just at the moments when fire gets out of control that the Time Traveller performs his most radical mediations. When the fire goes out he is forced to lay about with his other tool, a makeshift club, and when he is overtaken by the forest fire he comes to feel pity for the Morlocks. In both cases, though in different ways, he bridges the distance between himself and these alien beings.

In the first instance what starts as an act of self-defence becomes more aggressive until the Time Traveller is enjoying destroying others:

> It was indescribably horrible in the darkness to feel all these soft creatures heaped upon me. I felt as if I was in a monstrous spider's web. I was overpowered, and went down. I felt little teeth nipping at my neck. I rolled over, and as I did so my hand came against my iron lever. It gave me

strength. I struggled up, shaking the human rats from me, and holding the bar short, I thrust where I judged their faces might be. I could feel the succulent giving of flesh and bone under my blows, and for a moment I was free. (p. 95)

The striking word, "succulent," in the last sentence conveys both the pleasure the Time Traveller gets from such battery and the strange similarity between such violent activity and Morlock cannibalism. The Time Traveller here reveals himself as like the Morlocks and quite unlike the passionless and passive Eloi.

A more direct acknowledgment of his union with the Morlocks occurs after the first fire overtakes them all and the Time Traveller stops clubbing the "human rats" and becomes a victim with them. "I followed in the Morlocks' path" (p. 96). In the face of the larger catastrophe of the forest fire, the discriminations and hostilities that have kept the Time Traveller and the Morlocks apart are abandoned, and the Time Traveller, "assured of their absolute helplessness and misery in the glare," refrains from his aggressions. Even when the thought of the "awful fate" of Weena whom he has lost in the confusion moves him "to begin a massacre of the helpless abominations" about him, the Time Traveller "contains" himself.

The logical distinctions to be made at this point are complex. The Time Traveller is both identical with the Morlocks and separate from them. In the morning, exhausted, shoeless, with grass tied to his feet to protect them from the hot soil, he is only remotely the master scientist. He has been reduced to a bare forked thing and forced to acknowledge his bond in suffering with the other creatures of this world. But with the difference between himself and the Morlocks overwhelmed by their common fate as victims of the fire, the Time Traveller reasserts a distinction, not by exhibiting mastery of some sort over the others, but by restraining himself, by mastering his own brutal nature.

The Time Traveller's self-control has a complex symbolic function. It marks his difference from both Morlock and Eloi, since neither species seems capable of such conscious mastery of the self. It is his ability—a distinctly human ability—to bridge distinctions, to recognize an area of identity within a difference, that sets him apart from the other forms of life which will presumably remain locked in opposition. The Time Traveller is able to assert an ethical view in the face of the evolutionary competition that rules the future. He offers the promise of, if not resolving, at least comprehending the problems inherent in the conflict between evolution and ethics. In place of absolute antagonism between classes and between species, he acknowledges momentarily the bonds that extend across those divisions. Such an act of sympathizing with a different creature is an important gesture in Wells; we will explore it more fully in the next chapter. What interests us right now, however, is not the particular thematic issue, but its structural fitness: the act both acknowledges difference and momentarily bridges that

difference. In this way it reflects the central pattern of *The Time Machine* itself: its art is to create emblems of difference and separation and then to meditate on the balances, the antitheses and the identities that are possible.

In saying that reconciling both sides of a conflict is the central act of *The Time Machine,* I do not mean to suggest that the novella is without explicit moral point. The Time Traveller's latest interpretation of the division between Eloi and Morlock foresees and fears the transformation of an economic social division into a biological one, of an ethical issue into an evolutionary one. Clearly, Wells's moral point here is to impress on an audience which tends to accept the economic divisions of civilization as "natural" the horror of what it would mean if that division were truly natural. More narrowly, one may perhaps legitimately examine the novella as a treatise on possible evolutionary directions and study it as a prediction of sorts. But in isolating such moral ideas in the novella, one needs to be aware of the danger of distorting the deepest mechanisms of Wells's imagination: he is not the sort of writer who hides an esoteric meaning which is available only to the painstaking exegete. The difficulty one has deriving a clear reading of the future from *The Time Machine* comes from the large, unresolved oppositions of the tale. Instead of trying to "settle" ambiguities, to find out the one true reading, we should focus on the specific and powerful contradictions the story sets up. To see contradiction clearly in all its appalling and irresolvable conflict, and then to try by whatever imaginative means possible to mediate that disjunction: that is the true and deep moral of *The Time Machine.*

In the last paragraphs of the novella Wells offers us an explicit instance of how to read this way, to accept both sides of a contradiction. The Time Traveller has disappeared on his second journey three years ago, and the narrator speculates about his fate.[10] Wells here enforces ambiguity. And one understands why: any plot resolution would resolve the earlier tensions in such a way as to diminish the complexity of the whole vision. In this final stasis of opposition, not only does the frame distance us, as Robert Philmus has argued,[11] but the narrator proposes an attitude diametrically contrary to that of the Time Traveller. "I, for my own part," the narrator confesses,

> cannot think that these latter days of weak experiment, fragmentary theory, and mutual discord are indeed man's culminating time! I say, for my own part. He, I know—for the question had been discussed among us long before the Time Machine was made—thought but cheerlessly of the Advancement of Mankind, and saw in the growing pile of civilization only a foolish heaping that must inevitably fall back upon and destroy its makers in the end. (p. 117)

Here again we see the two attitudes of promise and hubris implicit in the symbolism of the matches. And then the narrator tries to combine the two in a single stance: if the Time Traveller's vision of bleak decline is the true one, the narrator argues, "it remains for us to live as though it were not so." He finally settles on an image that echoes the more hellish imagery of the novella itself and also alludes to the image of the feeble light shed by the match of science at the end of **"The Rediscovery of the Unique":** "But to me the future is still black and blank—is a vast ignorance, lit at a few casual places by the memory of his story."[12]

We see Wells here balancing pessimism and optimism. But the novella achieves an even more essential balance between a vision of change and a vision of no change. If we recall the two realms of opposition with which we began this essay, we can see that they themselves create an opposition. The horror of the split between the Eloi and the Morlocks lies in the fact that the divisions of modern civilization have not changed but have, by a process of speciation, become intrinsic in nature. But the other opposition, that between the present and the future, is a vision of change, of entropic decline. The first opposition implies that the essential injustice, the conflict of classes, will not change. On the other hand, the second opposition argues that in spite of all humans might do, things will change. The processes of entropy and evolution will continue, and any vision of humanity's place in the universe must take into account these large movements that are outside our control. This conflict between a vision of change and a vision of stasis undermines any simple thematic reading at the deepest level. Viewed as a prediction, the novella contradicts itself: the economic pessimism foresees a grim permanence; the cosmic pessimism sees an equally grim movement. And if the cosmic has the last word, that does not disqualify the economic: in terms of mere hundreds of thousands of years the cosmic process, by dividing the classes into species, merely confirms the continuity of the economic. Only on the scale of millions of years does the division of classes cease to be a controlling factor. So we face a problem as we try to derive a message from *The Time Machine*. But the problem is not a flaw: such unresolved, antithetical conflict is central to the way Wells's imagination works and gives his fiction a profundity, based on the ambiguities of human desire and experience, that is rare in thought about the future.

It may help us see exactly what Wells has achieved in *The Time Machine* if we briefly observe how George Pal in his film of *The Time Machine* (1960) avoids facing the very conflicts that define Wells's work. First of all, Pal erases the issue of evolution and ethics by making the Morlocks monsters and the Eloi simply badly educated humans. Though for a while the film allows us to think there may be a genetic problem, by the end the Eloi, who have spoken English from the beginning, show that they are human in every way: they become social; Weena, a starlet, falls in love; a male Eloi learns to fight; they use records (the talking rings); and in the end the Time Traveller (here H. George Wells) returns with books to repair the educational gap that has prevented the Eloi from succeeding. These people are not involved in any evolutionary or cosmic process; they are simply humans living in a "dark age." And while the Eloi are beautiful humans

who can be reindoctrinated, the Morlocks represent nothing but horror. More than simply a softening of Wells's pessimism has taken place here: the intellectual tensions of the conflicts, both between the present and the future and between the values represented by the Eloi and the Morlocks, have disappeared.

If Pal ignores the biological issue so central to Wells, he evades the economic issue as well. In place of Wells's vision of class difference developing into species difference, Pal gives us a vague history of the first part of our century as it is defined by its wars. We know that the wars went on and that the bombs got more destructive until finally the human race "split." The conflict is not in capitalism itself, but in the opposition of capitalism and communism. The clear hint is that the Morlocks are, loosely, the Russians; the story of the Time Traveller's final return to revive Eloi culture is, thus, an allegory of the liberation of peoples oppressed by totalitarian communism. The sense of catastrophe, individual, social, racial, cosmic, that so darkens Wells's end, is entirely missing from Pal's. Like Nunez in Wells's **"The Country of the Blind,"** the film George seeks a society he can dominate, and this time there seems no chance of the kind of ironic development that keeps Nunez from ruling the country of the blind.

It is important that we understand how Pal has changed the very nature of the story's thought. Wells's myth develops systematically a set of logical oppositions as a way of making us confront contradictions latent in our society and begin to think anew about our civilization, but Pal's myth lacks a logical base; our values and our civilization, except that they have wars, are not questioned. The future need only be returned to the present for all to be well; it can be "cured" by discipline and books. Wells has created a static nightmare which has the virtue of forcing us to reconsider our own world; Pal, by envisioning a change, a restoration, has freed himself from that stasis but has also avoided thought about the need for change in the present or the future. He has robbed Wells's story of the essence of its conflict and replaced intellectual tension with melodramatic conventions that inspire unreflective affirmation.

NOTES

[1] The novella has often been casually lumped with other of Wells's more obviously prophetic novels. The Dover text is entitled, *Three Prophetic Novels of H. G. Wells* and includes along with *The Time Machine,* "A Story of the Days to Come" and *When the Sleeper Wakes.* The urge to see the novella as a serious exercise in extrapolation of the potentials of the human future persists. On the other hand, Robert Philmus, "The Logic of 'Prophecy' in *The Time Machine,*" in Bernard Bergonzi, ed., *H. G. Wells: A Collection of Critical Essays* (Englewood Cliffs, N.J.: Prentice-Hall, 1976), pp. 56-68, despite his title, is not concerned with prediction. What he calls the "dimension of 'prophecy'" (p. 65) is a narrative device common to much fiction.

2 The structure of this decline has been analysed by Darko Suvin in *"The Time Machine* versus *Utopia* as Structural Models for SF," in *Metamorphoses of Science Fiction,* pp. 223-33.

3 The argument of this paragraph owes much to Fredric Jameson's seminal essay, "World Reduction in Le Guin: The Emergence of Utopian Narrative," *Science-Fiction Studies* (1975), 2:221-30.

4 "She always seemed to me, I fancy, more human than she was, perhaps because her affection was so human." *The Time Machine,* p. 82.

5 V. S. Pritchett's distaste for the "Faint squirms of idyllic petting" has found numerous sympathetic readers. See Pritchett's "The Scientific Romances," *The Living Novel,* p. 125.

6 Even when he meets the Eloi, the Time Traveller's first thoughts are violent: "They looked so frail that I could fancy flinging the whole dozen of them about like nine-pins" (p. 30). The obvious but important difference between this "fancy" and his treatment of the Morlocks is that here he is able to resist acting on such fantasies.

7 Mark M. Hennelly, Jr., *"The Time Machine:* A Romance of 'the Human Heart,'" *Extrapolation* (1979), 20:154-67, has observed the Sphinx and the faun as "unification of dual nature" (p. 163).

The Sphinx may have been suggested to Wells by a passage in Huxley: "However shocking to the moral sense this eternal competition of man against man and of nation against nation may be; however revolting may be the accumulation of misery at the negative pole of society, in contrast with that of monstrous wealth at the positive pole; this state of things must abide, and grow continually worse, so long as Istar holds her way unchecked. It is the true riddle of the Sphinx; and every nation which does not solve it will sooner or later be devoured by the monster itself has generated." "The Struggle for Existence in Human Society" (1888), in *Evolution and Ethics and Other Essays,* p. 212.

8 Bergonzi has sketched some basic oppositions: "The opposition of Eloi and Morlocks can be interpreted in terms of the late nineteenth-century class struggle, but it also reflects an opposition between aestheticism and utilitarianism, pastoralism and technology, contemplation and action, and ultimately, and least specifically, between beauty and ugliness, and light and darkness." *The Early H. G. Wells,* p. 61. Contemplation hardly seems appropriate to describe the Eloi.

9 This is a recurrent opposition and puzzle in science fiction of this century. See my "From Man to Overmind: Arthur C. Clarke's Myth of Progress," in Joseph D. Olander and Martin Greenberg, eds., *Arthur C. Clarke* (New York: Taplinger, 1977), pp. 211-22.

10 No hint is given by the Time Traveller of the destination of his second voyage into time. Philmus, perhaps influenced by George Pal's film of 1960 (discussed below), twice suggests he returns to 802,701 ("The Logic of 'Prophecy' in *The Time Machine,*" pp. 57, 67), but that seems doubtful. Such a return is certainly not one of the possibilities the narrator imagines in the "Epilogue."

11 "The Logic of 'Prophecy' in *The Time Machine,*" p. 67.

12 See the last paragraph of "The Rediscovery of the Unique," *Early Writings in Science and Science Fiction,* pp. 30-31.

Robert J. Bebiebing

SOURCE: "The Mythic Hero in H. G. Wells's *'The Time Machine,'"* in *Essays in Literature,* Vol. XI, No. 2, Fall, 1984, pp. 201-210.

In 1915 Van Wyck Brooks hinted at an important quality of H. G. Wells's vision when he said that the author's intelligence is "exuberant" with a "very genuine religious instinct" that Wells "lavished" upon "the social process itself." And in 1922 and 1946 two foreign writers, Evgeny Zamyatin and Jorge Luis Borges, commented on Wells's timeless symbolic processes and mythmaking. But it was in the 1960's that critics began to focus on the archetypal dimensions of Wells's "scientific romances." Bernard Bergonzi argued in 1960 and 1961 that Wells's early fantasies were closer to the fables of Hawthorne, Melville, and Kafka than to science. In support of his argument, Bergonzi quoted both V. S. Pritchett, who saw *The Time Machine* as a "great story . . . that has meanings within meanings," and Edward Shanks, who saw Wells as a "mythmaker." Bergonzi's mythic analysis focused on the "paradisal and demonic" imagery in Wells's first novel and the ironic use of the pastoral myth of the Golden Age. Bergonzi also reminded us that Wells contrasted himself to Jules Verne (whom Wells saw as dealing with "possible things" based on present science) by placing his own work in the class of the *Golden Ass of Apuleius, True Histories of Lucian,* and *Frankenstein.* Since Bergonzi, critics such as Patrick Parrinder and Robert Philmus have written of Wells's "barrier-breaking heroes," "ideological fables," "primordialism," and "mythic mode." And in the later 70s Jean-Pierre Vernier, agreeing with Bergonzi's view of the ironic pastoral myth, argued that *The Time Machine* awakens "archetypal responses in the reader."[1]

Well's biographers Norman and Jeanne MacKenzie also have argued that Wells is distinguished by the "symbolic power" of his stories. The MacKenzies remind us that Wells compared his early creative process to a dreaming in which, the MacKenzies say, "powerful and primitive emotions were translated" into visual images and "patterns of archetypal thought," a pattern of thought Wells himself intimated in his Preface to *The County of the Blind and Other Stories* in 1911:

> I found that, taking almost anything as a starting
> point and letting my thoughts play about it, there

would presently come out of the darkness, in a manner quite inexplicable, some absurd or vivid little nucleus. Little men in canoes upon sunlit oceans . . . , violent conflicts would break out amidst the flowerbeds of suburban gardens; I would discover I was peering into remote and mysterious worlds ruled by an order logical indeed but other than our common sanity.[2]

I am suggesting that if there can be little doubt now about the archetypal dimension of Wells's scientific romances, then clarifying one so far unexamined but central mythic pattern in *The Time Machine* may increase our understanding of that novel's unity and power, and, subordinately, may make one connection, perhaps not adequately recognized, between Wells's first novel and much of his later work. The mythic pattern I refer to is that which Joseph Campbell calls the great "monomyth" of the hero. Wells's otherwise nameless Time Traveller is, to use Wells's own phrase, one of "the active, strong, and subtle." By his violent journey into a mysterious and misunderstood dimension, the hero gains a wisdom that could, but probably will not, be the salvation of his species. And it was just this salvation of his species to which H. G. Wells later devoted his lifework, a devotion for which he was, finally, censured and ridiculed.

Although he wears the face and dress of a late nineteenth-century scientist, the Time Traveller exhibits at least three characteristics of the primordial heroic figure. These characteristics, as they appear in the art and religion of diverse cultures, have been delineated by such students of the mythic hero as Carl Jung, Erich Neumann, Mircea, Eliade, and Joseph Campbell. If the faces, forms, and quests of the hero are as vast and changeable as the hundreds of cultures that have recreated him, the three characteristics I find in Wells's novel are central to the heroic figure generally, as Campbell's work especially makes clear. Indeed, it is Campbell who best summarizes for us the social, psychological, and spiritual qualities of the hero and his quest.

> Beyond the threshold . . . the hero journeys through a world of unfamiliar yet strangely intimate forces, some of which severely threaten him (tests), some of which give magical aid (helpers). When he arrives at the nadir of the mythological round, he undergoes a supreme ordeal and gains his reward . . . represented as . . . sacred marriage . . . father atonement . . . apotheosis, or again—if the powers have remained unfriendly to him—his theft of the boon he came to gain . . . ; intrinsically it is an expansion of consciousness and therewith of being (illumination, transfiguration, freedom). The final work is that of the return. . . . At the return threshold the transcendental powers must remain behind; the hero reemerges from the kingdom of dread (return, resurrection). The boon that he brings restores the world (elixir).[3]

"The changes," Campbell continues, "rung on the simple scale of the monomyth defy description."

The first characteristic of the mythic hero is that he is an extraordinary individual among his fellows—in his powers of perception, his courage and ability to take risks and endure suffering, and his capacity to assert himself and his vision effectively, he is set apart from the mass of humanity. Wells's Time Traveller is certainly an extraordinary man, and the device of the frame story emphasizes this point. By his curiosity, perceptiveness, intelligence, and courage, the first in Wells's series of millennarian heroes stands in sharp contrast to the mundane abilities of his guests—a group of professional and scientific men who serve as foils to the hero. In their dialogue with the Time Traveller, they express only common sense, complacency, positivism, and understood consciousness. If the Traveller's theories are admittedly based on the most advanced thought of "scientific people," he is the kind of scientist who sees the possibilities within the theories as even the scientific people do not. To the physician, the experiment with the model machine has to be "some sleight-of-hand trick or other" that the "common sense of the morning" will settle. To the psychologist it is "an ingenious paradox and trick." And even the "joyous" and "irreverent" editor and journalist, who represent a *fin de siècle* flaccid anarchism, raise objections, resort to caricature, and heap ridicule on the whole "gaudy lie." By their lack of comprehension they reveal the uncommon imagination and power of the hero. He is an eccentric to them, a man whose "earnestness" and "fecundity" they admire if not understand. He is a source of amusement, is "one of those fellows who are too clever to be believed; you never felt that you saw all around him," and is so whimsical that they "distrusted him." Wells's hero is, then, also described as a kind of Trickster figure, a seeming "quack" and magician whose playfulness runs even to Christmas apparitions. "Things that would have made the fame of a less clever man seemed tricks in his hands. It is a mistake to do things too easily."[4]

Not only does the hero see and understand things the guests do not, he has the unusual courage to follow his vision, to chase a theory down dark, rustling corridors at the risk of sanity and life. Indeed, the "full temerity" of his voyage comes to the hero as he slows down his machine and contemplates the most horrible possibilities of the future. But the risk, he assures himself, is unavoidable, "one of the risks a man has got to take." And upon his return, at the threshold of his laboratory, the danger, the suffering, the harrowing test of the voyage is clear:

> He was in an amazing plight. His coat was dusty and dirty, and smeared with green down the sleeves; his hair disordered, and it seemed to me greyer—either with dust or dirt or because its colour had actually faded. His face was ghastly pale; his chin had a brown cut on it—a cut half healed; his expression was haggard and drawn, as by intense suffering. For a moment he hesitated in the doorway, as if he had been dazzled by the light.[5]

The second mythic characteristic of Wells's hero lies in the nature of his quest. The heroic journey—however actual it may in one sense seem or be—is a voyage into self as much as, or more than, a physical journey. Here, deep in the self, he meets the helpful and threatening forces with which he must deal, and through or against whom he must earn his own transformation: the wisdom of expanded consciousness and the means of salvation he imparts to others upon his return.

Wells certainly suggests that the voyage may be read as a journey into deepest self. The Traveller's time theory is above all a theory of a fourth dimension that is attached, in his words, "to our mental existences." The only factor that distinguishes time from the three spatial dimensions is that our bodies move in space, but "our consciousness moves along" time. At many points the voyage is dream-like: "For the most part of that night," he says of the Dark Nights in the woods battling Morlocks, "I was persuaded it was a nightmare." And of Weena's death, he says: "Now, in this old familiar room, it is more like the sorrow of a dream than an actual loss." And he will invite skeptical listeners to interpret his tale as the dream of a man sleeping in his laboratory and, therefore, either a "lie—or a prophecy" (pp. 88-89, 99). The passage to that laboratory is like the passage to the realm of dreams too. It is a "long, draughty corridor" of "flickering light," along which one sees "the dance of shadows" and the "queer, broad head in silhouette" of the Traveller. The imagery of the voyage itself has the hallucinatory quality of a dream. Night follows day "like the flapping of a black wing." The whole "surface of the earth" is "melting and flowing under my eyes" (pp. 22, 30-31).

One's immersion in this realm is a dreadful adventure, a kind of death from one world to be born into another: "I suppose a suicide who holds a pistol to his skull feels much the same wonder at what will come next as I felt then," the Traveller says of the beginning of his voyage. His sensations vary from excessive unpleasantness to "hysterical exhilaration" and a "certain curiosity and therewith a certain dread." And upon his arrival, the conflicting images of the demonic and the paradisal act as threshold symbols of the strangely primordial realm he has entered. Hail stones assault flower blossoms. Colossal stone figures and buildings loom beyond the rhododendrons; a white sphinx suggests mystery and disease. Soon he is "groping among moon-lit ruins and touching strange creatures in the black shadows" (pp. 29-33).

Like Odysseus and a host of heroes before him, the Traveller's survival during the quest and his return depend on, as the Traveller puts it, "force and cunning." Like his predecessors, too, the Traveller meets helpers and threats among the unfamiliar but strangely intimate forces he encounters. Weena, of course, despite her slight consciousness and her diminutive stature, is friend, guide, and object of "a miniature flirtation." She provides "signs of the human inheritance," such as fear, that warn him; she offers flowers that, in the end, become symbols of "gratitude and mutual tenderness," of that human sympathy which, with "mind and strength," threatens to die out in the world. "Nor until it was too late did I clearly understand what she was to me. For by . . . showing in her weak, futile way that she cared for me, the little doll of a creature presently gave my return

to the neighbourhood . . . almost a feeling of coming home" (pp. 55, 63, 104). She is the "child," as even the Traveller repeatedly calls her, the princess, one face of the Nourishing Mother, who deep in the heroic journey, reveals the lost potential, the unconscious source of life in the hero and humanity. Dreading darkness, playfully clapping and dancing before the fire lost to the Upper-worlders, Weena is indeed a child of light, the one whom the hero had hoped to bring back to his own time, yet can do so only metaphorically through his tale.[6]

And like his mythic progenitors, the Traveller is the fire-starter, he who battles the dark, destructive side of world and mind with the creative power in himself. The task of the hero, as Campbell and Jung have argued, is to carry life energy—symbolized by fire—across the "difficult thresholds of transformation" and change the "patterns of consciousness and unconscious life."[7] When he descends to the "Under-world" (to use Wells's own term), the hero battles the destructive human potential, or the bestial insanity, faced at this deepest point of the journey, symbolized by the devouring Terrible Mother in myth and, in Wells's novel, by that "subterranean species of humanity" the cannibal Morlocks—those "bleached, obscene, nocturnal things"—and by the "leprous," mocking, white sphinx, one gateway to this Under-world.[8] Here, in the blackness beneath, the only security against the Morlock is fire: "they did not seem to have any fear of me apart from the light" (p. 66). And when these "damned souls" bring the Under-world to the Upper-world during the "Dark Nights," it is with fire again that the hero—feeling a "strange exultation"—defeats them. Here, in what Campbell calls the nadir of the heroic journey, the Time Traveller knows primitive dread: "I had slept, and my fire had gone out, and the bitterness of death came over my soul. . . . I felt as if I was in a monstrous spider's web" (p. 86).

More important than the particular qualities and unities of the timeless heroic quest itself, however, are the wisdom gained and the message or boon with which the hero returns. Wells's hero returns with a prophecy that he conveys as compulsively as Coleridge's sea voyager. "I want to tell it" he says. "Badly. . . . I've lived eight days as no human being ever lived before!" (p. 28). The message is that which, in a variety of ways and degrees of effectiveness, Wells would speak throughout his life: though humanity as a species has been granted the rare opportunity to do otherwise, it stands to lose all that which its positive potential suggests it can develop—courage, humane assertiveness, perceptiveness, intellect, consciousness, endurance, and wholeness of vision.

> I grieved to think how brief the dream of human intellect had been. It had committed suicide. It had set itself steadfastly towards comfort and ease, a balanced society with security and permanency as its watchword, it had attained its hopes—to come to this at last. . . . No doubt in that perfect world there had been no unemployed problem, no social question left unsolved. And a great quiet had followed. . . .

Nature never appeals to intelligence until habit and instinct are useless. There is no intelligence where there is no change and no need of change. Only those animals partake of intelligence that have to meet a huge variety of needs and dangers. (p. 90)

Stasis and temporary social or technological success lead to psychic, and even physical, decadence, to Eloi and Morlock, to exquisite and fragile children or to soulless beast-men whose only organizing principles are obeisance to machinery and a devouring of humankind.

Wells arrived early at a conception of the degeneration of self and civilization, and he connected the root of all the possibilities and symptoms of degeneracy to that "human selfishness" whose "rigorous punishment" reaches far into the future of the race (p. 75). Such degeneracy is what Erich Neumann called "sclerosis of consciousness" in his own study of the mythic hero's task:

> Typical . . . is the state of affairs in America, though the same holds true for practically the whole Western hemisphere. Every conceivable sort of dominant rules the personality. . . . The grotesque fact that murders, brigands, gangsters, thieves, forgers, tyrants and swindlers, in a guise that deceives nobody, have seized control of collective life is characteristic of our time. . . . Worship of the "beast" is by no means confined to Germany; it prevails wherever . . . the aggravating complexities of civilized behavior are swept away in favor of bestial rapacity. . . . [The] integration of the personality, its wholeness, becomes the supreme ethical goal upon which the fate of humanity depends.[9]

The mindless sensuality of Eloi is no less destructive of self and civilization than the bestial rapacity of the Morlock—both adequately symbolized by Wells's headless faun in the garden. "All traditions, the complex organizations, the nations, languages, aspirations . . . had been swept out of existence," the Time Traveller tells us, and "from the bottom of my heart I pitied this last rill from the great flood of humanity" (pp. 73-74). Neither the "too perfect triumph" of technology, nor the rapacity of vain and selfish power strugglings or wars between classes and nations, nor the comfort and ease that tempt at every turn can be the salvation of the species. Survival must be based not on these attributes of modern civilization but on some other integrating wholeness of vision—which vision Wells would spend the rest of his life struggling to articulate. If at times Wells slipped and turned toward that "too perfect triumph of man" that led toward Eloi and Morlock, as his son Anthony West has suggested, he was nevertheless fighting the old prophetic battle to change patterns of consciousness.[10]

Wells's first fictional hero, then, endures a quest, as we have seen, that traces the traditional patterns of the hero myth central to diverse cultures. Even the return of the hero to the fourth dimension at the end of the novel is not anomalous to the heroic pattern. Frequently, as Campbell points out, the hero may "refuse the responsibility" to return "into the kingdom of humanity" where the boon "redounds to the renewing of humanity," or having returned to mankind, may pass again back into the realm discovered in the quest. Indeed, it is by the freedom to pass back and forth between the world of time and the timeless world of the quest—"permitting the mind to know the one by virtue of the other," that one recognizes the hero as "Master of Two Worlds." For it is in combining the eternal symbols and experience with the historical moment that the myth conveys its truth, not in the lasting physical presence of the hero in his time.[11]

Yet even if we limit our consideration of the heroic journey to Wells's hero specifically, that hero's ultimate return to the dimension of the vision can be seen as an affirmation rather than a denial of his prophetic value for Wells's theme. As Robert Philmus has argued, for example, the Traveller by vanishing into the other world accepts his vision literally and demands that it be not only metaphorically true:

> The Traveller's return . . . far from vitiating the impact of *The Time Machine,* reinforces its claim to integrity: by having the Time Traveller act out the ultimate consequence of his taking the myth literally, Wells illustrates the rigor that he has submitted himself to in satirizing certain "present ideals." The romance, as I see it, is thus rigorously self-contained in "working to a logical conclusion" both the myth of devolution that exposes tendencies "of our own age" and the various points of view regarding the truth of that prophetic myth.[12]

The prophecy, the wisdom gained, is, for the traditional hero as for Wells's first hero, a new pattern of consciousness, a revolutionary vision against entropy and degeneration that may destroy the old canon and build a new.[13] If the wisdom learned from the heroic journey in *The Time Machine* is the awareness of the avenues to human degeneracy, a degeneracy connected in Chapter 11 to the cosmos, it remains for each generation to avoid the fate of "energy in security," to renew for itself—so long as it is a cosmic possibility—its physical power and its positive psychic evolution. If the Traveller "saw in the growing pile of civilization only a foolish heaping that must inevitably fall back upon and destroy its makers in the end," as the narrator tells us, it also "remains for us to live as though it were not so" (p. 104).

As late as 1942 in his D.Sc. thesis at London University, Wells argued that our collective survival lay "in some sort of super-individual, a brave new *persona*" that would integrate the whole human social organism, "the ecology of Homo sapiens." Human ecology Wells defined as the science of working out "biological, intellectual, and economic consequences" to enable us to see the possibilities of the future.[14] What the hero brings to his culture is what Campbell calls the "primitive health" or new consciousness of interrelationships—the ecology if you will—of humanity, nature, and social order.

There is a continuity in much of Wells's work, I am suggesting, that builds upon his first novel's hero and upon that hero's earned wisdom. And perhaps our understanding of Wells will benefit from other critics' still closer examination of that continuity. Let me suggest a few sources of this continuity in closing.

The Invisible Man (1897) presents another visionary scientist among "floundering yokels." Yet he is motivated, even to the point of murder, by pride, vanity, and paranoiac dreams of power. This time it is through a flawed or false hero and his "evil experiment" that Wells defines human degeneracy-through-selfishness by depicting again the death of human sympathy and by warning of the dangers of uncontrolled rational intellect. And this novel and its theme were directly preceded and initially developed by *The Island of Dr. Moreau* (1896) in which an earlier Rappaccini-like scientist dreams of Godlike power and argues for the uselessness of concepts such as pleasure and pain while extolling the delights of "intellectual desires." The theme of responsibility for one's actions and for others (even other creatures) is suggested through the vivisectionist, who is unaware of his victims' agonies and of his responsibilities for his grotesque creations. Yet when the narrator Pendrick returns to London, he sees the beast in all humanity and wonders if God, too, had blundered, if progress or evolution is even possible.

The War of the Worlds (1898) then carries forward Wells's program for the total reform of humanity and social order by warning, as his first hero did, of the dangers of becoming over-specialized prisoners of technology, like the Martians, or of becoming prisoners of the decadence born of the naive yet supreme confidence in the future as progress. And from this point onward to the end of his life, in fiction and nonfiction, Wells will frequently focus on the possible avenues of salvation for the species. *Anticipations* (1901), which Wells accurately called the "keystone to the main arch of my work," more emphatically focuses his concern for secular salvation through revolutionary change: "I'm going to write, talk, preach revolution for the next five years," he promised. It is at this point that Wells approaches a "new synthesis" through his search for a group of heroic individuals, a search that moves from the **"New Republicans"** to the **"Open Conspiracy,"** to the **"Samuari"** of *A Modern Utopia* (1905), and beyond. Wells searches for offshoots, if at times terminal branches, of the heroic personality of the Time Traveller.

In 1933-34 Wells looked back on *Utopia* in his autobiography and continued to argue that through the creation of a heroic class we may attain the knowledge to outrun catastrophe. And widest knowledge he continues to attach, as in *Utopia,* to the best in humanity: to individual uniqueness and liberty, to dynamic society and state, to pluralism of morality, to originality of mind, to courage, self-sufficiency, renunciation, and to endurance. Even economics, Wells argues, like all social theories or institutions, must be attached to human psychology or forever flounder dangerously.

To the end of his life, Wells maintained the thread of continuity that reached back to the Time Traveller's

prophecy. In *Mind at the End of Its Tether* (1945), it is ordinary man who is at the end, and only an extraordinary minority of the highly adaptable (or "Over-Man") may survive. We have come so far, Wells said, outside the order of Nature, have become so much the evolutionary objects of some new, implacable, universal hostility, that we perch on the brink of extinction, perch quite beyond "quantitative adjustments," so that we will have to move so steeply up or steeply down the evolutionary chain that few indeed, if any, may now adapt. Wells concludes his final prophetic warning with two points that return us to the message of his earliest hero. First, the only fight worth the effort is the heroic battle for human advancement, however great the odds now, as if even Hiroshima "were not so." Better, Wells reminds us, to end as a species in "dignity, kindliness and generosity, and not like drunken cowards in a daze or poisoned rats in a sack." And second, the chief form of human adaptability for survival will be a revolutionary change of consciousness, that "mental adaptability" which the mythic hero has always earned and prophesied to humankind.[15]

As Wells's first hero said, and as so many of Wells's later works echoed, "What, unless biological science is a mass of errors, is the cause of human intelligence and vigour? Hardship and freedom: conditions under which the active, strong, and subtle survive and the weaker go to the wall; conditions that put a premium upon the loyal alliance of capable men, upon self-restraint, patience, and decision" (p. 44). If the first part of these words sounds like mere Social Darwinism, and in one sense it does, the second part has new significance for the post-Hiroshima generation.

NOTES

[1]Van Wyck Brooks, *The World of H. G. Wells* (New York: Kennerley, 1915), pp. 168-71; Evgeny Zamyatin, "Herbert Wells," *A Soviet Heretic: Essays of Yevgeny Zamyatin,* trans. Mirra Ginsburg (Chicago: Univ. of Chicago Press, 1970), pp. 259-90; Jorge Luis Borges, "The First Wells," *Other Inquisitions: 1937-1952,* trans. Ruth L. C. Simms (Austin: Univ. of Texas Press, 1964), pp. 81-88. Bernard Bergonzi, "*The Time Machine:* An Ironic Myth," in *H. G. Wells: A Collection of Critical Essays,* ed. Bernard Bergonzi (Englewood Cliffs, NJ: Prentice-Hall, 1976), pp. 39-53, hereafter cited as *Critical Essays,* and Bernard Bergonzi, *The Early H. G. Wells* (Manchester: Manchester Univ. Press, 1961), pp. 16-20, 42-43, 49-61. See also Patrick Parrinder, *H. G. Wells* (Edinburgh: Oliver & Boyd, 1970), and Robert M. Philmus, *Into the Unknown: The Evolution of Science Fiction from Francis Godwin to H. G. Wells* (Berkeley: Univ. of California Press, 1970). Jean-Pierre Vernier, "*The Time Machine* and Its Context," in *The Time Machine, The War of the Worlds: A Critical Edition,* trans. and ed. Frank D. McConnell (New York: Oxford Univ. Press, 1977), pp. 314-320, hereafter cited as *Critical Edition.*

[2]Norman and Jeanne MacKenzie, *H. G. Wells* (New York: Simon and Schuster, 1973), pp. 118-19.

[3]*The Hero with a Thousand Faces* (New Jersey: Princeton Univ. Press, 1968), pp. 245-46. Hereafter cited as *Hero.*

[4]The Trickster is one face of the mythic hero, see esp. *Critical Edition,* pp. 18-20, 22-24. And cf. *Hero,* pp. 44-45, 90, 184.

On the subject of the guests' response to Wells's hero's tale, Campbell again is helpful. Upon returning from his journey the hero always meets the "return blow of reasonable queries, hard resentment, and good people at a loss to comprehend." How to "communicate to people who insist on the exclusive evidence of their senses the message of the all-generating void"—that is the problem the hero faces "throughout the millenniums of mankind's prudent folly," *Hero,* pp. 216, 218. Erich Neumann, in *The Origins and History of Consciousness* (New Jersey: Princeton Univ. Press, 1973), adds that the hero is ever the "outsider" who brings into conflict his "new images" and values (from an inner compelling voice) with the collective, the old order, thereby sacrificing friendship and normal living. See esp. pp. 375, 378.

[5]*Critical Edition,* p. 25. Future references are cited in parentheses.

[6]Carl Jung, *Symbols of Transformation,* trans. R.F.C. Hull. Vol. 5 (New Jersey: Princeton Univ. Press, 1956), pp. 242, 272, 292-93, 300-01. Hereafter cited as *Symbols.* Cf. Neumann's discussion of the "mythological goal of the dragon fight" for the captive woman in *Consciousness,* pp. 105, 201; and the *Critical Edition,* pp. 54-56, 63, 71.

[7]*Symbols,* pp. 121, 149, 170, 212, and *Hero,* pp. 8, 10. When Wells and Jung met in 1923, Wells found Jung's collective unconscious similar to his own concept of the "Mind of the Race"; see MacKenzie, pp. 338, 346.

[8]To the Traveller the Sphinx represents disease and the mysteries "which I could not face" of the Under-world (p. 64). She seems to hover, to watch him, to smile in mockery, and the Traveller finally realizes that he cannot defeat her or open her mysteries by force so much as, like Oedipus, by craft and cunning (pp. 36, 50). And somehow this "crouching white shape" seems to him connected to the riddles of how mankind has evolved (pp. 33, 36, 50). The Sphinx is the traditional symbol of the dragon devourer, the Terrible Mother, the guardian of the mysteries of destruction and regeneration or creative evolution. It is her defeat that allows for the enthronement or prophecy of the Good Mother. See *Consciousness,* pp. 161-62, 324.

[9]Neumann, *Consciousness,* pp. 391-92.

[10]Anthony West, "H. G. Wells," in *Critical Essays,* pp. 10, 12-13, 20. West suggests that Wells strayed from his "deeper intuitions" during his "middle period" of scientific utopianism beginning around 1901 with *Anticipations.* But, West argues, Wells returned in later years to his belief that virtue does not reside in intellect alone. The idea of revolutionary change, West reminds us, was the *sine qua non* of Wells's utopias. West is on this point in considerable contrast to Frederick Karl in "Conrad, Wells and the Two Voices," *PMLA,* 88 (1973), 1049-65. Karl argues that after the scientific romances especially, Wells, unlike Conrad, was an "ahistorical" ameliorist in the liberal, utilitarian, scientific tradition.

[11]See *Hero,* esp. pp. 193, 229, 356, 358. Campbell's examples range from Buddha, the Hindu Muchukunda, saints dying in supernal ecstasy, and to numerous heroes "fabled to have taken up residence forever" in the realm discovered in the journey. "The last act in the biography of the hero is that of the death or departure"; yet he remains a "synthesizing image" of the historical and the timeless worlds.

[12]Robert Philmus, "*The Time Machine;* or, the Fourth Dimension as Prophecy," *PMLA,* 84 (1969), 530-35.

[13]Campbell argues that the mythic hero is always connected to larger cosmic forces and that he is therefore an "evolutionary" hero leading humanity to further stages of development in social, artistic, and spiritual realms. He is the "creative power" of things becoming; see *Hero,* esp. 315, 336-37. Compare Neumann, *Consciousness,* p. 131. Both Neumann and Mircea Eliade have argued equally emphatically for the hero as "revolutionary" figure who "brings to birth those forms the age is most lacking," who restores a balance to his age, and who "regenerates time" as a representative of eternal powers and truths. See *Consciousness,* pp. 376-77, 381, and Eliade, *The Myth of the Eternal Return* (New York: Pantheon Books, 1954), esp. pp. 35-47, 55-57, 69, 87-88.

[14]See MacKenzie, pp. 163, 437.

[15]See Wells, *Mind at the End of Its Tether* (London: William Heinemann, 1945), esp. pp. 4, 18, 30, 34. Campbell's and Neumann's argument for the significance of the timeless heroic quest in the mid- and late-twentieth century world is remarkably similar to Wells's, but especially as the argument culminates in *Tether.* Campbell, to take one instance, also emphasizes the delicate ecology of planetary community now as a new, dangerous stage in human evolution as much in need as preceding stages of some new heroic consciousness. The whole thing is being worked out, Campbell argues, on a level deeper than the boundaries of nationalism or ego-consciousness; it is being worked out, toward success or failure, in the collective unconscious and on the "titanic battlefields" of the planet, and it is bound to be a "long and very frightening process." It is man who has become the "alien presence" and "mystery" whose "image of society is to be reformed" toward non-nationalistic and non-egocentric systems. The "whole destiny" of a species is to be, or not, atoned. See *Hero,* esp. pp. 388-90. Neumann similarly argues, in his appendices most clearly, that the global revolution of modern times is an evolutionary storm-center. The regeneration of the species toward some new

stage of advancement must go beyond mere re-collectivization as well as beyond mere nationalism and egocentricity or selfishness. See *Consciousness,* pp. 422, 436, 441.

Robert A. Berger

SOURCE: "'Ask What You Can Do for Your Country': The Film Version of H. G. Wells's *'The Time Machine'* and 'The Cold War,'" in *Literature/Film Quarterly,* Vol. 17, No. 3, 1989, pp. 177-87.

The major themes of H. G. Wells's novel, **The Time Machine,** have been clearly established. In the novel, Wells combines an essentially common-sense parable about the potential dangers of class society devolving (to use Robert Philmus's idea) into two separate species—the well-known Eloi and Morlocks, or bourgeoisie and proletariat of the 1890s—with a bleak prophecy, a Huxleyan or "cosmic pessimism," about the future of the human species on a planet doomed to extinction.[2] Though the novel is indebted to what Bernard Bergonzi terms "a romantic and pessimistic variant of orthodox Marxist thought," which recognizes social classes but denies the possibility of proletariat revolution, the 1895 version of the often revised text of **The Time Machine,** as several critics of the novel have pointed out, represents Wells's ultimate rejection of his early Marxist positions (Bergonzi 52). Indeed, as Wayne Connely argues, **The Time Machine** parodies Marxist dialectic through the Time Traveller's evolving series of discoveries about the nature of the seemingly Edenic world into which he stumbles. Nevertheless, despite its pessimistic theme, Wells's novel at least recognizes the political problematics of the class situation of his times, utterly unlike the 1960 George Pal film version of **The Time Machine.**

While the film retains many contradictory traces of the original novel, it nonetheless replaces the novel's major themes with a political allegory calling for strong leadership to contend with two major problems of late 50s/early 60s America: first, how to contend with and ultimately defeat the Soviet Union without risking (or being afraid of) the horrifying and seemingly unavoidable possibility of a nuclear holocaust, and second, how to persuade an increasingly rebellious Youth, perceived by the nation as essentially hedonistic, to temper their consumerism and join the task of fighting Communism. The film's specific solution to these problems is an idealistic John F. Kennedy look-a-like (Rod Taylor), who emerges in essence magically to marshal the dormant California surfer Youth of the film (the Eloi) into a vigilant force opposing the Morlock Underground Evil (undoubtedly the spector of Communism) threatening to devour them. The changes that Pal and his screenwriter, David Duncan, make—indeed, their very use of the book—tell us much about the disguised ideology of the film and about the relationship between 1950s science-fiction films and the Cold War. That is, the film's insidious ideological mission becomes clear after examining how the film changes—not just "updates" as a summary of the film in *Magill's Cinema*

Annual (Mitchell 585) would have us believe—the Wells's novel. First, however, we need briefly to situate the film in the historical and cinematic context of the 1950s, as well as in the context of George Pal's career as a producer and director of science-fiction films. Then we shall return to the specifics of how *The Time Machine,* the film, attempts to conscript its intended audience into a larger ideological force.

I

The 1950s was a time of intense anti-communist fervor, coupled with a gigantic move into the suburbs and apparent materialistic prosperity by millions of Americans. The anti-communism of the period, fueled by an intense fear of the Other, helped institute the national security state—as well as the creation of a "military-industrial complex"—while the move into the suburbs first underwrote and then reinforced the overwhelming conformity that characterized the decade. It would be a mistake, however, to view the 1950s as monolithic. Indeed, Douglas T. Miller and Marion Nowak identify three distinct periods within the Fifties—"The Age of Fear." "The Era of Conservative Consensus," and "The Time of National Reassessment"—each of which signaled a shift in the focus of national attention during the decade (Miller 13-18).[3] The 1950 decade begins with an obsessive interest in supposed Communist internal subversion (triggered by Truman's security checks, capitalized on by McCarthy, and culminated by the end of the Korean War and the Rosenberg's execution). It then shifts its attention in 1953 to an abiding interest in material comfort (represented by the spectacular growth of the suburbs and parallelled by the growth of multinational corporations, advertising and television). Finally, it stumbles towards an end around 1958 with underground doubts emerging about "the American Century" (sparked by Sputnik, Little Rock, the Beats, and fears of juvenile delinquency). Thus, in the 1950s, there exists a *double structure*. On one level, one can see certain recurring themes—anti-communism, conformity, and conservatism. On another level, though, one can note subtle shifts in the national sensibility.

Not surprisingly, the intellectual and popular culture of the decade often took the lead in reproducing the then dominant conformist ideology. Large circulation magazines and television, of course, were two of the major conduits of this ideology, but movies, despite their losses at the box office, also shared in the task (Miller 314-344).[4] Though it is clear that movie producers were primarily or consciously interested in making money, one can still note the underlying ideology that pervades their products, and film historians such as Nora Sayre, Peter Biskind, and Michael Rogin have begun, from various perspectives, to interpret politically the films of the 1950s.[5] Nora Sayre, for example, argues that "the tenor of the films of the fifties was that ours was a splendid society, and that one ought to cooperate with it rather than criticize it" (99). She points to Elia Kazan's *On the Waterfront* (1954) as the decade's best and as a key for understanding the central ideology that runs through most fifties' films. Peter Biskind concurs with Sayre, though he argues that Sidney Lumet's *Twelve Angry Men* (1957) represents the "seminal" film of the decade as it promotes a "pluralist" ideology designed to bring people (in this case Henry Fonda's fellow jurors) into a "corporate-liberal" consensus (16-20). Once again, though, we must view these overall characterizations of 1950s films with a sense of the shifting national concerns. This perspective accounts, clearly, for the preponderant number of avowedly anti-communist films—for example, *I was a Communist for the FBI* or *My Son John*—near the beginning of the decade. And it also explains how other films—less clearly anti-communist and more focused on conformity, consumerism, and their subsequent problems—came to dominate Hollywood. In particular, Youth—the site of much ideological hand-wringing during the 1950s—was an important subject. In films like *Rebel Without a Cause* or *Blackboard Jungle*—designed to recapture the then dwindling movie audiences—teenagers, created by society solely to consume and then blamed for their conspicuous consumption, were reconciled to authority and family or school. Hedonistic youth consumers—their brains decaying with rock and roll or TV—blurred into juvenile delinquents, and after Sputnik they became the focus of national attention in the ideological battle against Communism. If Johnny couldn't read and Ivan could—what was the future of the country? The typical 1950s film, then, generally tends to reflect both the overall ideology of the decade (anti-communism conformity, conservatism) *and* the shifting national concern (communism, complacency, and kids).

Allowing for some obvious exceptions, 1950s science-fiction films—one of the most significant genres of the decade—also reflect this double structure. Overall, many fifties' science-fiction films, as Susan Sontag notes, concern the widespread fear of science and technology. The scientist—generally a stand-in for the 50s "egghead"—is often the villain of these pictures, and science-fiction films frequently try to capitalize on the fear of what scientists arrogantly had unleashed—the Bomb. But science fiction films of the 1950s also emphasized in general conformity and anti-communism—the threat to a small community (a metynomic figure for America) often coming from some alien "invasion."[6] As Michael Rogin states, "The aliens of cold war science fiction are deliberate stand-ins for Communists."[7]

But science-fiction films, as might be expected, also shifted their concerns as the decade progressed. Several early science-fiction films—*Red Planet Mars, Invasion U.S.A.,* or *The Next Voice You Hear*—were self-conscious anti-communist fantasies, while other early films, particularly several "invasion" SF movies (like *War of the Worlds* or *Invaders from Mars*), thinly disguised their ideological messages. Some exceptions, of course, exist: as Peter Biskind suggests, two early films, *The Day the Earth Stood Still* and *It Came from Outer Space,* both offered more left-wing, or at least more cosmic, visions of aliens (145-159). And clearly, in one form or another, anti-communism—for example, in *Invasion of the Body*

Snatchers 1956)—still dominates the genre after the decade's early years. But other concerns, like juvenile delinquency or fear of nuclear war, began to appear. 1950s science-fiction movies, then, both reflected the dominant concerns of the decade and often offered solutions—sometimes disguised, sometimes not—for the problems that faced America. If a complacent United States were threatened by Communists (symbolized by giant ants, deadly mantises, grasshoppers, and the like—many of which were created by the Bomb), then as many of these films showed, we needed to turn to our experts (military and scientific) to save us. And as many commentators have pointed out, the well-known line in *Them!* ("Your personal safety depends upon your cooperation with the military authorities") epitomizes the weird, contradictory faith that many of these films express in the State and ironically in Science—whose inventions supposedly caused all of the problems in the first place.

George Pal's 1950s films—some of which he produced, others of which he produced and directed—may well be among the most right-wing of the decade and possibly, if one speaks generally, fall into the three periods I have outlined. In essence, he began the interest in postwar science-fiction film with his pseudo-documentary, *Destination Moon,* (1950) a paean to American technological know-how and to American business, which defies the government and sends a mission to the moon. His next two films, *When Worlds Collide* (1951) and *War of the Worlds* (1953), seem to reflect the Great Fear that overtook the United States in the early 1950s. In particular, *War of the Worlds,* Pal's first attempt at remaking a Wells novel, remarkably undermines the original novel. As in its source, biology, not human endeavor, saves humanity from the Martian invasion, but in the movie, this miracle occurs after a worldwide prayer session, which suggests that divine intervention was ultimately responsible for rescuing the Earth. The novel, of course, parodies religion in its portrait of the cowardly curate.[8] In the mid-1950s, Pal turns away in general from such science-fiction epics and makes films like *Houdini* (1953), *The Naked Jungle* (1955), *The Conquest of Space* (1955), and *Tom Thumb* (1958). Perhaps *Houdini*—a film in which its escape-artist protagonist, the victim of appendicitis, drowns—best exemplifies (undoubtedly unconsciously) the suffocating and trapping nature of the 1950s. But an attack by mad red ants on a South American plantation in *The Naked Jungle* returns Pal to his obsessive fear of the Other. In 1960, Pal, who began his film career with fantasy puppet shorts, finally returns to science-fiction and to H. G. Wells and directs a remake of ***The Time Machine.***

II

George Pal's *The Time Machine,* an immensely popular film, is both a fifties and a late-fifties science-fiction film. It addresses many of the problems of the 1950s SF movie—nuclear war, communism, indifferent youth—but it does so with a new urgency, reflecting the sense that the "consensus" solution of the mid-fifties no longer adequately answered these problems. What is needed, the film suggests, is a new leader—a combination of Prometheus, Faust, and Twain's Connecticut Yankee—to lead the California surfer youth (read hedonistic, indifferent or rebellious teenagers) into a "new world" that transcends the fear of nuclear holocaust.[9] This is the encoded political message of the film, and we can see how this message unfolds, as I have suggested, both by analyzing the film and by describing those parts that deviate from the novel.

After an opening sequence of clocks, which includes the apparent destruction of Big Ben—a symbol, I suppose, of civilization under the gun—we are first introduced to this new leader, when the Time Traveller, now named George, returns from the future to a dinner with his Victorian friends. Looking rather beat-up, George narrates his journey to the future, beginning with a demonstration of a small-scale time machine to his friends on December 31, 1899. As in the book, the other people in the room, who are astounded by George's demonstration, represent the self-satisfied middle-class. Wells implicitly criticizes these other characters in the book as being ignorant about the realities of Evolution and social classes. The movie also reprimands George's guests, though it focuses on their interest in using science for military purposes. They are "practical men, business men," as they call themselves, interested in the "commercial" and military "possibilities" of a time machine. As Dr. Hillyer (Sebastian Cabot) tells George, "there's a war on in South Africa. The Boers are putting up a pretty stiff fight. George, the country needs inventors like you. Now I can put you in touch with the war office, if you wish." George, though, opposes this attempt to conscript science for war and later tells his best friend, businessman David Filby (played by Alan Young), "I don't care about the time I was born into. It seems people aren't dying fast enough these days. They call upon science to invent new, more efficient weapons to depopulate the earth." Such sentiments echo other war-is-hell movies of the late Fifties—such as *Bridge on the River Kwai* or *The Naked and the Dead.* Yet George expresses an attitude that is more scientific and utopian than pacifistic. He wants to know "Can man control his destiny? Can he change the shape of things to come?" George's "Wellsian" attitude valorizes the position of the scientist philosopher-king who seeks to create—*á la* B. F. Skinner—a brave new world dominated by rationality.

The choice of a name for the Time Traveller reinforces this interpretation of George's position. In the book, he is known only as "The Time Traveller," but in the movie he is called "George." Such an unnecessary change calls for some speculation. The name, of course, alludes to H. G. Wells's middle name, *George,* and on the Time Machine itself, Pal amusingly includes a plate, "Manufactured by H. George Wells." The name also jokingly refers to *George* Pal. But the name may well suggest another well-known national persona, *George* Washington, who also led his people—if we accept the conventional mythology—into a "new world."

In any event, George, disgusted with his own time, begins travelling into the future. Pal indicates this time travelling with some interesting photographic tricks—among them the sun and moon speeding across the sky, a snail racing across the floor, flowers rapidly opening and closing, and most important, the changing fashions on a female mannequin in the window of Filby's store across the street.[10] As George says, "I began to grow very fond of that mannequin, maybe because like me she didn't age." During this journey, which utterly deviates from the novel, George makes three main stops—in 1917, in 1940, and prophetically for the movie, in 1966—and learns about World Wars One, Two, and depressingly, Three. In the last war George sees images of our consumer society—Jaguars, electric shavers, skyscrapers: "the labor of centuries," as George terms it—obliterated "in an instant" first by "atomic satellites zeroing in" and then by "Mother Earth" who "aroused by man's violence, responded with a violence of her own." Interestingly, the nuclear attack comes from "atomic satellites"—Sputniks—the very symbol of our failed educational system and of Soviet domination in the world. The movie thus obliquely criticizes the United States' military deficiencies—what was erroneously termed at the time a "missle gap." Scrambling back into his machine, George himself escapes from what we have come to see as the standard apocalyptic lava flow, and then has to wait for centuries for the mountain that has formed around him to wear down. This is how the movie "updates" the novel. On the surface, then, *The Time Machine* resembles any number of "nuclear films," which attempted, according to Joe Kane, "to exploit technologically-induced fears instilled by the new instability of world existence" (9). Up to this point with its depiction of the world's destruction, the film could be read, even admiringly, as one more nuclear warning movie. But the film continues and explores the "post-holocaust" society, which I understand as an allegory for our own society, and it is here that Pal's solution to nuclear war—or really to the paralysis of will caused by the fear of nuclear war—can be seen.

When the mountain wears away, George arrives in the future under a sphinx—brown colored, not white as Wells stresses.[11] Also unlike the book, no one is there to meet him. He first marvels at what seems a perfect world, but complains that it would not be much of a paradise if no one was there to share it with him. After searching, he finally comes upon the Eloi playing along a river; and it is here that, as in the book, he saves Weena (played by Yvette Mimeux) from drowning after no one else does anything to save her. At first glance, the Eloi, with their blond hair and vacuous manners, anticipate the seemingly infinite beach movies of the early 1960s. They lounge along a river, frolic in the gardens, and stroll hand-in-hand without any cares—a perfect portrait of the leisure/consumer society. They also call to mind the widely disseminated image of 1950s hedonistic youth in their indifference to books, the origins of food and clothes, and strangers.[12] Their actions prompt George to criticize them: "What have you done?" George asks. "Thousands of years of building and rebuilding, creating and recreating so that you can let it all crumble to dust. A million years of sensitive men dying for their dreams. For what? So you can swim and dance and play." The absurdity of such sentiments, given the horrific wars he has experienced while time travelling, suggest that the antiwar message that we heard earlier in the film is rather superficial. Here George is actually speaking to the 1950s's youth. Support for this reading comes from the fact that, if one looks closely, one can see that the crumbling dining hall (or dormitory cafeteria) where the Eloi munch on oversized fruit is built, oddly enough, on what looks like—or at least suggests—a *parking lot.* Pal obliquely evokes here the 1950s's car/consumer culture—the parking lot supporting a decaying facade, Pal's symbol of the shopping mall, suburban world. These youths, whom George later terms "living vegetables," originate in the novel, but we read them as 1950s's teenagers when they all—zombie-like—march toward the sphinx when the Morlock controlled air-raid sirens sound.

In the novel, the Time Traveller, like Wells, prefers the Eloi over the Morlocks, but ultimately he realizes that neither group can be salvaged. In the movie, however, George clearly sides with the Eloi, and after Weena comes out to warn him about the dark and the Morlocks, he begins to see in her some possibility for reawakening the Eloi and thus humanity. As he tells her,

> You were safe inside your great house, and yet you came out into the night to warn me. The one characteristic which distinguished man from the animal kingdom was the spirit of self-sacrifice. And you have that quality. I think all your people have it, really. It just needs someone to reawaken it. I should like to try, if you'll let me.

While Wells suggests that curiosity or reason are the major human-distinguishing characteristics, George designates "self-sacrifice" as the single most important trait that distinguishes human beings from animals. And his valorization of self-sacrifice sounds familiar. For me, it anticipates Kennedy's charge, given in his inaugural address, "Ask not what your country can do for you, ask what you can do for your country." I don't want to accuse Kennedy or his speechwriters of having watched *The Time Machine,* nor do I want to suggest a Pynchonesque version of history in which cause and effect are reversed. Rather, in that speech, Kennedy was just echoing, according to Miller and Nowak, the dominant sensibility of the late 1950s, and *The Time Machine* reproduces the general trend towards self-sacrifice and submission to larger national goals as a response to the later Cold War crises. As Miller and Nowak write,

> "The anxious late-fifties mood of critical national and self-reappraisal brought about a great search for new goals. . . . Unfortunately, most thinkers saw the need for goals only within the rigid context of fifties thinking: a domestic policy aimed at accelerating economic growth and a foreign policy based on containing and ultimately triumphing over communism. John F. Kennedy exemplified this

with his call for national self-sacrifice, a faster growth rate for the GNP, and putting a man on the moon" (242-243).

George's next speech to Weena further discloses both the central ideology informing the film, as well as the film's main solution to what he sees as the Eloi's—and the American's—problems. After asking Weena about the past and the future and being told that "there is no past" and "there is no future," George sets out to explain to her the meaning of history:

> The past, man's past, is mainly a grim struggle for survival. But there have been moments when a few voices have spoken up and these rare moments have made the history of man—man's past—a glorious thing. I refuse to believe it's dead and gone. We've had our dark ages before and this is just another one of them. All it needs is for someone to show you the way out. I'm only a tinkering mechanic, (but) I'm sure there must be this hidden spark in one of you. If only I can kindle that spark, my coming here will have some meaning.

Here is George at his most Promethean—and reactionary. What we need, this Carlylean philosophy of history suggests, is a leader who can reawaken the slumbering youth of America.

Needless to say, George's call-to-arms to the Eloi is not found in the novel. Wells clearly establishes, as many commentators have pointed out, that both the Eloi and the Morlocks were degenerate forms of humanity.[13] Wells's position in the English middle-class perhaps underlies his physical distaste for his Morlocks, but he makes it clear that the human race had devolved into separate *species* and that both groups were responsible for what had happened. As the Time Traveller tells us:

> I grieved to think how brief the dream of the human intellect had been. It had committed suicide. It had set itself steadfastly toward comfort and ease, a balanced society with security and permanency as its watchword, it had attained its hopes—to come to this at last. Once, life and property must have reached almost absolute safety. The rich had been assured of his wealth and comfort, the toiler assured of his life and work. No doubt in that perfect world there had been no unemployment problem, no social question left unsolved. And a great quiet had followed. (Wells 90)

In the end the Time Traveller expresses a pity for both the Eloi and the Morlocks, because they forgot Huxley's admonition "that we cast aside the notion that escape from pain and sorrow is the proper object of life" (86):

> It is a law of nature we overlook, that intellectual versatility is the compensation for change, danger, and trouble. An animal perfectly in harmony with its environment is a perfect mechanism. Nature never appeals to intelligence until habit and instinct are useless. There is no intelligence where there is no change and no need of change. Only those

animals partake of intelligence that have to meet a huge variety of needs and dangers. So, as I see it, the Upper-world man had drifted towards his feeble pettiness, and the Under-world to mere mechanical industry. (Wells 90)

In Pal's remaking of the book, however, the Eloi clearly remain human, while the Morlocks have inexplicably become monsters. Just how this came about is explained to us through a set of talking rings which Weena shows George. A voice in one of the rings tells us that

> The war between the east and the west, which was in its three-hundred and twenty-sixth year, has at last come to an end. There is nothing left to fight with, and few of us left to fight. The atmosphere has become so polluted with deadly germs that it can no longer be breathed. There is no place on this planet that is immune. The last surviving factory for the manufacture of oxygen has been destroyed.

Another ring tells George about how the Morlocks and Eloi came into existence:

> I am the last to remember how each of us—man and woman—made his own decision. Some chose to take refuge in the great caverns and find a new way of life far below the Earth's surface. The rest of us decided to take our chances in the sunlight, small as those chances might be.

Exactly how the Eloi—or anyone else—could survive on the Earth's surface without any oxygen is unclear. But this passage demonstrates how the movie utterly abandons Wells's consciously implausible, though within the context of this time, politically conscious explanation for the creation of the Eloi and the Morlocks. The movie's abandonment of Wells's explanation for the development of classes into species—however ludicrous that seems—indicates how Pal reproduces (consciously or unconsciously) the notion of "an end of ideology," classless society promulgated by many fifties' intellectuals.[14] Any talk of social classes—or class struggle—would have seemed at best irrelevant, if not subversive, in the 1950s. Just what happened to the underclasses is not clear, but as George, as a voice-over narrator, speculates, "So that was the true history of the Eloi and the Morlocks. . . . By some awful quirk of fate, the Morlocks had become the masters and the Eloi, their servants." So much for Wells's version of class struggle.

Instead, after the Eloi and, most importantly, Weena—like "fatted cattle"—are drawn into the sphinx by the air-raid sirens, George attempts to save them. He descends into the underground in ventilator wells (which look interestingly enough like missile silos), and after discovering that the Morlocks have degenerated into the "lowest form of human life—cannibalism," George attacks the monsters. The Morlocks represent, of course, the Other—and within the context of 1950s cold-war science fiction, Communists. They continue to embody the proletariat as in the novel, but here they are clearly below the threshold of humanity, while the Eloi remain above. As George,

astonished to hear of the Morlocks, says to Weena, "You mean those *animals* run the machines!" (my italics). At first, George battles the Morlocks alone, but, after watching George, one of the Eloi males finally makes a fist—a significant first step away from hedonism and towards anti-communism—and helps George kill one of the Morlocks. After that, several Eloi males, having shaken their heads free of the cobwebs of hedonism and fear, help fight the Morlocks. Finally, as George torches the underground, all of the Eloi escape up through the well leading to the surface. There, George, taking charge, orders them to throw all of the "deadwood"—symbolically perhaps all those who won't join the new crusade—down the venting wells, and the Morlock empire of evil is destroyed.

Significantly, George is helped by a male Eloi—rather than Weena—as much of the movie reproduces the sexism of the 1950s. Women in the film carry two contradictory burdens. On the one hand, the film implicitly blames women for the Spenglerian "Decline of the West" into a nuclear holocaust by using the everchanging fashion on the female mannequin to signify George's movement in time. Just after he first begins to time travel, George stops the machine, and shocked by the changes in fashion, says "Good Heavens! That's a dress. . . . I wonder just how far women would permit this to go." The viewer subconsciously associates this shock with the madness of endless war and eventually with nuclear conflict. In this guise, women in the film recall Philip Wylie's vicious attack on "Momism" in his bestselling book of essays, *A Generation of Vipers*. Somehow, Wylie and the film concur, women are to blame for all that has happened. On the other hand, women also are associated with passivity and lack of change. The mannequin is reassuring to George: "The years rolled by, everything unfamiliar," says George, looking at the mannequin, "except the smile of my never-aging friend." Symbolically, the mannequin becomes Weena, who, as played by Yvette Mimeux, seems little more than a dummy. The only other significant woman figure in the movie—George's housekeeper, Mrs. Watchett (unheard of in the novel: Wells's time Traveller has a manservant)—serves as George's seemingly mindless, sexless "mother." Indeed, at one point, just when George is flirting with Weena, he calls Mrs. Watchett old and useless. Such gratuitous attacks on women simply underscore the reflex sexism of the movie. The Eloi differentiate little, if at all, between men and women. (No Morlock women—if they even exist—are seen.) But at the end of the film, as we have seen, it is the male Eloi who help George, while Weena's reawakening consists of an interest in the hair styles of the past. Flirting with George, she asks him, "Would I be pretty?"

At the end of the movie, George recovers his time machine (though Weena is lost to him outside the metal doors of the sphinx), mistakenly goes forward in time to escape the last band of dying Morlocks, and then, realizing his error, reverses the machine and returns to his own time. His mistake perhaps betrays the film's own unease with its source, because in Wells's novel, at the end, the Time Traveller loses Weena, recovers the time machine, and travels forward into the future. We first find him stopped on a desolate beach where he sees only "a huge white butterfly" and "a monstrous crab-like creature" (94-95)—possible symbols for the Eloi and Morlocks. Then he travels still further—thirty million years into the future—when life has been reduced to a round "football"-sized thing, "hopping fitfully about" (97). Such is Wells's bleak vision of the future—with a dying sun and the earth slowly falling towards it. The movie, however, utterly ignores this vision. George comes back to his own time, tells his story, and then, depressed by the doubts of his friends, returns to the future, armed with three unidentified books, so that he can, in the words of Filby, "build a *new world* for the Eloi, build a *new world* for himself" (my italics). That phrase—"new world"—interestingly echoes the ending of *Them!* when Edmund Gwenn, the omniscient scientist, tells us that we have inescapably entered an "atomic age," a "new world." George's "new world," though, much like President Reagan's fantasy "star wars" program, magically banishes, as it were, fear of this nuclear age. His "new world"/new frontier country—a country based on self-sacrifice particularly by its Youth—can ultimately defeat the threat of Communism. In the United States, this "new world" eventually assumed two guises: the liberal one found in the Peace Corps and the anti-communist one found in a failed war in Vietnam. In this project, *The Time Machine*, like much of the cultural practice of that time, had its part.

To conclude, by ignoring Wells's vision of a devolving human race—and above all, by abandoning his cosmic pessimism—Pal essentially *domesticates* the novel and makes safe such threatening ideas for his late Fifties/early Sixties' audience. The movie contains traces of the original novel—and thus capitalizes on Wells's popularity or name-recognition—but it avoids using any dangerous or threatening material found in the novel, hence rendering Wells's terrible vision harmless. Domesticating terrible visions is, of course, typical of much 1950s science-fiction, as Vivian Sobchack asserts. But perhaps what makes Pal's *The Time Machine* even more depressing is how the movie has usurped for the popular consciousness the message of the novel. Many of my friends and colleagues, who remember seeing the film, assumed Wells also had elevated the Eloi over the Morlocks. Their image of the book attests to Pal's disservice to Wells. Above all, though, it is the film's cold war/new frontier message that is the most disturbing. It criticizes the admittedly materialistic Youth rebellion of the 1950s, while pointing towards a remilitarization of the young in the upcoming global struggle against Communism.

NOTES

[1] I want to thank my student assistant, Greg Castanias, for his excellent help on this paper, as well as Wabash College for providing funds for his assistance.

[2] See West, Bergonzi, Hilleagas, Costa, Suvin, Huntington, and McConnell and Hynes; though see Caudwell for a Marxist rebuttal.

[3] See also Oakley for a similar historical scheme.

[4] For a discussion about the decline of Hollywood in the 1950s, see also Sklar 269-285.

[5] For other histories of fifties film, see Gow and Dowdy.

[6] For discussion, see Sayre 191-204; Biskind 102-159; Chapman; Kane; Murphy; Baxter; and Sobchack 43-55.

[7] See also Biskind, who writes, the giant ants in *Them!* act like "those humans that Americans regarded as ant-like, which is to say, behaved like a mass, loved war, and made slaves . . . (that is) communists, both the Yellow Hordes that had just swamped GIs with their human waves in Korea, and the Soviets, with their notorious slave-labor camps" (132).

[8] See Grant, who makes a similar point (157).

[9] See Wasson who suggests that Pal's "George is a cautious Prometheus bringing a new technology, a spirit of self-sacrifice, and the right to overthrow an oppressor" (194). Wasson, however, incorrectly notes a "remarkable continuity" (196) between the novel and the film.

[10] For a technical discussion concerning the film's special effects, see Scot. The special camera effects draw attention, of course, to the camera itself—perhaps the "real" time machine. Pal's joke of naming the Time Traveller after himself perhaps suggests the central role that filmmakers have in conscripting their audience.

[11] The significance of a *white* sphinx has generated some critical attention. See Lake, who argues that it suggests the evolutionary death of humankind (79), and Scafella, who more generally contends that the sphinx helps allegorize the situation of the modern scientist. Pal's decision to make the sphinx *brown* may reflect consciously a "pragmatic" *mise-en-scene* choice but unconsciously a thorough rejection of Wells's message about both devolution and the ideology of science.

[12] For a discussion about youth in the 1950s, see Miller, "Growing Up," 269-290. See also Fine.

[13] See, for example, Bengonzi.

[14] See, for example, Bell. For a discussion of intellectual life in the 1950s, see Miller, "Intellectuals: The Conservative Contraction" 220-247.

WORKS CITED

Baxter, John. *Science Fiction in the Cinema.* New York: A. S. Barnes, 1976.

Bell, Daniel. *The End of Ideology.* New York: Collier, 1962.

Bengonzi, Bernard. *The Early H. G. Wells: A Study of the Scientific Romances.* Toronto: University of Toronto, 1961.

Biskind, Peter. *Seeing is Believing: How Hollywood Taught Us to Stop Worrying and Love the Fifties.* New York: Pantheon, 1983.

Caudwell, Christopher. "H. G. Wells: A Study in Utopianism." *Studies in a Dying Culture.* London: Bodley Head, 1938. 73-95.

Chapman, Robert S. "Science Fiction of the 1950s: Billy Graham, McCarthy and the Bomb." *Foundation,* 1-8. Boston: Gregg, 1978. 38-53.

Connely, Wayne C. "H. G. Well's [sic] The Time Machine: It's [sic] Neglected Mythos," *Riverside Quarterly* 5 (1972): 178-191.

Costa, Richard Haven. *H. G. Wells.* New York: Twayne, 1967.

Dowdy, Andrew. *Films of the Fifties.* New York: Morrow, 1973.

Fine, Benjamin. *1,000,000 Delinquents.* New York, 1957.

Grant, Barry K. "Looking Upward: H. G. Wells, Science Fiction and Cinema." *Literature/Film Quarterly.* 14 (1986): 154-163.

Gow, Gordon. *Hollywood in the Fifties.* New York: A. S. Barnes, 1971.

Hillegas, Mark R. *The Future as Nightmare: H. G. Wells and the Anti-Utopians.* New York: Oxford, 1967.

Huntington, John. "The Science Fiction of H. G. Wells." *Science Fiction: A Critical Guide.* Ed. Patrick Parrinder. London: Longmans, 1979. 34-50.

Huxley, Thomas H. "Evolution and Ethics," *Evolution and Ethics and Other Essays.* London, 1894.

Kane, Joe. "Nuclear Films." *Take One* 2 (1969): 9-11.

Lake, David J. "The Whitened Sphinx and the Whitened Lemur: Images of Death in *The Time Machine.*" *Science-Fiction Studies* 6 (1979): 77-84.

Miller, Douglas T. and Marion Nowak. *The Fifties: The Way We Really Were.* Garden City, N.Y.: Doubleday, 1977.

Mitchell, Ronald. "The Time Machine." *Magill's Cinema Annual 1984.* New York, 1985.

Murphy, Brian. "Monster Movies: They Came from Beneath the Fifties." *Journal of Popular Film* 1 (1972): 31-44.

Oakely, J. Ronald. *God's Country: America in the Fifties.* New York, December, 1986.

Philmus, Robert. "The Logic of 'Prophecy' in *The Time Machine.*" *H. G. Wells: A Collection of Critical Essays.* Ed. Bernard Bengonzi. Englewood Cliffs, N.J.: Prentice-Hall, 1976. 56-68.

Rogin, Michael. "Kiss Me Deadly: Communism, Motherhood, and Cold War Movies." *Representations* 6 (Spring 1984): 1-36.

Sayre, Nora. *Running Time: Films of the Cold War.* New York: Dial, 1982.

Scarfella, Frank. "The White Sphinx and The Time Machine." *Science-Fiction Studies* 8 (1981): 255-265.

Scot, Darrin. "Unique Lighting and Cinematographic Innovations Mark the Photography of M-G-M's 'The Time Machine,'" *American Cinematographer* 41.8 (1960): 490-491, 497-498.

Seton, Marie. "George Pal." *Sight and Sound* 5 (Summer 1936): 13.

Sklar, Robert. *Movie-Made America: A Cultural History of American Movies.* New York: Vintage, 1975.

Sobchack, Vivian C. *The Limits of Infinity: The American Science Fiction Film, 1950-1975.* South Brunswick, N.J.: A. S. Barnes, 1980.

Sontag, Susan. "The Imagination of Disaster (1967)." *Awake in the Dark: An Anthology of American Film Criticism, 1915 to the Present.* New York: Vintage, 1977. 263-278.

Suvin, Darko. "A Grammar of Form and a Criticism of Fact: *The Time Machine as a Structural Model for Science Fiction.*" Eds. Darko Suvin and Robert M. Philmus. Lewisburg: Bucknell, 1977. 90-115.

Wasson, Richard. "Myths of the Future." *The English Novel and the Movies.* Eds. Michael Klein and Gilliam Parker. New York: Ungar, 1981. 187-196.

Wells, H. G. *The Time Machine* and *The War of the Worlds.* Ed. Frank McConnell. New York: Oxford, 1977.

West, Anthony. "H. G. Wells." *H. G. Wells: A Collection of Critical Essays.* Ed. Bernard Bergonzi. Englewood Cliffs, N.J.: Prentice-Hall, 1976. 8-23.

Wylie, Philip. "Momism." *A Generation of Vipers.* New York, 1942.

Kathryn Hume

SOURCE: "Eat or be Eaten: H. G. Wells's 'Time Machine,'" in *Philological Quarterly,* Vol. 69, No. 2, Spring, 1990, pp. 233-57.

"It is very remarkable that this is so extensively overlooked," says the Time Traveller, speaking of time as the fourth dimension.[1] Similarly remarkable is the way we have overlooked the comprehensive functions of oral fantasies in *The Time Machine.* They play a fourth dimension to the other three of entropy, devolution, and utopian satire. They ramify, by regular transformations, into those other three; into the social and economic worlds of consumption and exploitation; and into the realm of gender anxieties. They transform the ideological commonplaces from which the text constructs its reality. They create a network of emotional tensions that subliminally unites the three time frames: Victorian England, the Realm of the Sphinx, and the Terminal Beach. At the same time, this nexus of related images undercuts and fragments the logical, scientific arguments being carried out on the surface of the tale.

The Time Machine is the first of Wells's scientific romances to achieve canonical status.[2] In their eagerness to elevate and assimilate this text, however, critics have lost awareness that some of its parts are not explained by their normal critical strategies. One such feature to disappear from critical discourse is the failure of any coherent social message to emerge from the world of the Eloi and Morlocks. Another partly repressed feature is the disparity between the Time Traveller's violent emotions and the experiences that evoke them.[3] A third feature lost to view is the dubious logic that binds the two futuristic scenarios.

I would like to approach the text with both the oral image complex and these elided mysteries in mind. What emerges will not fill the gaps in the narrative logic; the text resists such treatment, for reasons that will be shown. Rather, I wish to explore the hidden dynamics of emotion and logic. Since the semes attached to eating, consumption, and engulfment point in so many directions, I shall start instead with the public ideologies of power, size and gender. Then we can explore their symbolic manifestations as fantasies of being eaten or engulfed; as equations involving body size, intelligence, and physical energy; and as gender attributes projected on the world. Once sensitized to these concerns, we can examine the two future scenarios and their relationship to the Victorian frame. By exploring the interplay of ideology with its symbolic distortions, we will better sense what the text represses, and why despite (or even because of) this hidden material, the book has such disturbing power.

IDEOLOGICAL ASSUMPTIONS

Ideology, used here in Roland Barthes' sense, means the unexamined assumptions as to what is natural and inevitable and hence unchangeable. One realizes these "inevitabilities" to be historical and contingent most readily by comparing cultures, for within a culture, the ideological is taken to be "real."

The part of the general ideology relevant here consists of a nexus of values that include power, body size, and gender. Separating the values even to this extent is artificial; they intertwine tightly, and in turn link to other values such as dominance, exploitation, race, physical height, and bodily strength. They also merge with political and social and military power. The form taken by this family of assumptions in England made the British Empire possible.

Let us assume you are a nineteenth-century Briton—white, male, and a member of the politically powerful classes. You are also nominally Christian and equipped with the latest weaponry. You could expect to march into any country not blessed with most of these characteristics and expropriate what you wanted, be it raw material, cheap labor, land, or valuables. Such power gives the ability to exploit and consume. The so-called inferior races had no choice, since their technology was insufficient to resist British force. The Traveller's outlook is very much that of the nineteenth-century Briton among the aliens. His strength, technological know-how, and culture elevate him in his own mind. He scribbles his name on a statue, much as other nineteenth-century Britons carved theirs on Roman and Greek temples. To the empire builders, killing Africans or Indians was not "really" murder; they were Other and hence less than truly human. While the Traveller controls his impulse to massacre Morlocks (and is even praised for his restraint by one critic),[4] he smashes at their skulls in a way he would never dream of doing in Oxford Street. He is outraged (as well as frightened) when his trespassing machine is impounded. In the "kangaroo" and "centipede" episode found in the *New Review* serialization of the novel, his immediate impulse is to hit one of the kangaroo-like creatures on the skull with a rock. When examination of the body suggests that it is of human descent, he feels only a flash of "disagreeable apprehension," evidently directed toward this proof of Man's degeneration, not at his own murderous action. His regret at leaving the body (possibly just unconscious) to the monstrous "centipede" appears to be regret at the loss of a scientific specimen, not guilt at leaving this "grey animal . . . or grey man" to be devoured.[5] He protects himself from any acknowledgment of this self-centeredness by viewing his urges as scientific, but ultimately he sees himself as having the right to whatever he wants, and cherishes himself for being the only "real" human and therefore the only creature with rights.

Part of this superiority stems from physical size, the second element in the ideology and one closely linked to power. Size generally permits a man to feel superior to women, and a British man to feel superior to members of shorter races. In English, size is a metaphor used to indicate that which is valuable, good, desirable. "Great," "high," and "large" are normally positive markers.[6]

In the two paragraphs that encompass the narrator's first language lesson and his response to it, we find the word "little" used eight times. Attached in his mind to the littleness of the Eloi is their "chatter," their tiring easily, their being "indolent" and "easily fatigued," and their "lack of interest" (p. 35). Littleness and its associated debilities are so grotesquely prominent that one cannot help note this obsession with the inferiority attaching to bodies of small size. What the narrator thinks will shape and limit what he hears and sees. When he first hears the Eloi (p. 29), they look and sound like "men" running. Later, his senses register "children": "I heard cries of terror and their little feet running" (p. 46).

The ideological inferiority of littleness is reinforced for readers by the Traveller's reactions to artifacts of the prior civilization. He admires and wonders at the "ruinous splendor" consisting of "a great heap of granite, bound together by masses of aluminium, a vast labyrinth of precipitous walls" (p. 36). He cannot describe such a building without expressing this admiration for sheer size: the buildings are "splendid," "colossal," "tall," "big," "magnificent," "vast," "great," and "huge." He never wonders whether the size was functional and if so, how. Nor does he speculate on whether it was achieved through slave labor, as were the colossal monuments of antiquity which it resembles, with its "suggestions of old Phoenician decorations" (p. 33). He simply extends automatic admiration to such remains because of their impressive size.

The third element in the common ideology, besides power and size, is gender. Power and size support the superior status of maleness. Wells extends this prejudice to the point of defining humanity as male. Early in his narrative, the Time Traveller recounts his fear that "the race had lost its manliness" (p. 28). No sooner does he identify the Eloi as shorter than himself than they become "creatures" and are quickly feminized with such terms as "graceful," "frail," "hectic beauty," "Dresden china type of prettiness." All later descriptions use codes normally applied to women or children: mouths small and bright red, eyes large and mild, a language that sounds sweet and liquid and cooing and melodious. Ultimately, he equates loss of manliness with loss of humanity.

To sum up the ideological assumptions: the text shows as natural and inevitable the interconnection of power, size and male gender. Wells was to prove capable of challenging the politics of power in later scientific romances. He questions the might-makes-right outlook of Empire in his reference to the Tasmanians in *The War of the Worlds* (1898), and in Dr. Moreau's parodic imposition of The Law on inferior beings (1896). Callousness towards non-British sentients is rebuked by Cavor, who is shocked by Bedford's slaughter of Selenites in *The First Men in the Moon* (1901). However, though power may be somewhat negotiable to Wells, size and maleness remain positively marked throughout the scientific romances. In *The Food of the Gods* (1904), size automatically conveys nobility of purpose, and this idealized race of giants consists so exclusively of men that it will have trouble propagating.

If this text merely echoed the ideology of its times, *The Time Machine* (1895) would be drab and predictable. The symbolic enlargements and distortions of these values are what create the images and tensions that make it interesting, so let us turn to them.

SYMBOLIC TRANSFORMATIONS OF IDEOLOGY

Power belongs to the same family of values as "exploitation" and "consumption." These terms from the political and economic spheres take on added resonances when they emerge as oral fantasies about eating and being eaten. As Patrick A. McCarthy points out, cannibalism lies at the heart of this darkness, or so at least the Traveller asseverates.[7] Actually, the evidence for cannibalism is far from complete, as David Lake observes, and the narrator may be jumping to totally unwarranted conclusions. However the notion of humans as fatted kine for a technologically superior group will reappear in *The War of the Worlds,* so it evidently held some fascination for Wells. The latter book certainly makes the connection between eating people and economic exploitation,[8] a parallel made famous by Swift's "Modest Proposal."

The putative cuisine of the Morlocks is only the most obvious of the oral fantasies. "Eat or be eaten" is a way of characterizing some social systems, but in Wells's futures, the words are literally applicable, and the text regales us with variations upon the theme of eating. The Time Traveller fears that the Morlocks will feed upon him as well as on Eloi. In the extra time-frame of the *New Review* version, the centipede appears to be hungry. The crabs make clear their intentions to consume the Traveller. The Sphinx traditionally devoured those who could not guess her riddle; the Traveller's entering her pedestal constitutes but a slight displacement of entering her maw. The Victorian frame features a prominent display of after-dinner satisfactions (including drinks, cigars, and feminized chairs that embrace and support the men) and a meal at which the Traveller urgently gobbles his food. Oral fantasies also take the forms of engulfment: one can be overwhelmed, drowned, swallowed by darkness, or rendered unconscious. Both in the narrator's dreams and in his physical adventures, we find several such threats of dissolution.

Norman Holland observes that "the single most common fantasy-structure in literature is phallic assertiveness balanced against oral engulfment,"[9] exactly the pattern of *The Time Machine.* Typical of the phallic stage anxieties is the exploration of dark, dangerous, and congested places. Time travel and other magic forms of travel are common omnipotence fantasies at this stage of development. So is the pre-oedipal polarization of agents into threatening and non-threatening, and the focus on a single figure. Opposing this phallic quest are oral anxieties. One such wave of anxiety oozes forth as the engulfing embraces of night (e.g., "dreaming . . . that I was drowned, and that sea-anemones were feeling over my face with their soft palps"—p. 57). Another such anxiety grips the narrator when he faces the yawning underworld; indeed, upon escaping from below, he collapses in a dead faint. The threat of being eaten, and the enfolding gloom of the Terminal Beach are two others.

The protagonist faces engulfment of body and mind. When he returns to his own time, he responds with typical defenses against oral anxieties; he eats something ("Save me some of that mutton. I'm starving for a bit of meat"— p. 18), and he tells his tale. Holland observes that "a common defense against oral fusion and merger is putting something out of the mouth . . . usually speech" (p. 37).

This fantasy content forecloses many options for plot development. Within the economy of oral anxieties, the subject eats or is eaten; there is no third way. When the Time Traveller finds himself on the Terminal Beach, where nothing appears edible or consumable or exploitable, he cannot assert his status as eater. Evidently, he subliminally accepts power relationships in terms of this binary fantasy, and thus dooms himself to being devoured through sheer default of cultural imagination. His technological magic may permit him to withdraw physically, but psychically, he is more defeated than triumphant at the end. Like his strategic withdrawal from the underworld, his departure is a rout. We note that although he returns home, he does not long remain. He is swallowed up by past or future.[10]

The commonplace assumptions in this text about bodily size undergo equivalent amplifications and distortions that affect the plot. We find elaborate equations between bodily size, intelligence, and bodily energy. Some of these simply reflect the science of the day. Researchers were establishing averages for sizes and weights of male and female brains, and followed many dead-end theories as they tried to prove what they were looking for: superiority of men over women and of whites over darker races. Furthermore, many scientists were convinced that the First Law of Thermodynamics, conservation of energy, applied to mental "energy" as well as physical.

> Food was taken in, energy (including thought) emerged, and the energy was "an exact equivalent of the amount of food assumed and assimilated." In Hardaker's crudely quantitative universe bigger was definitely better, and men were bigger.[11]

If the human race dwindles in size, so will its brain size, so will intelligence, and so will physical energy. Thus much is good science of the day. The text moves from science to symbolism, however, in linking the First and Second Laws of Thermodynamics and implying that energy loss in the universe will directly diminish the mental and physical energy of humanity. Although Wells does not state this explicitly, he apparently accepted it. The loss of culture and security would otherwise have reversed the devolutionary decline as the descendants of humans had once more to struggle for existence. This reason for species degeneration remains implicit, but it clearly follows the fantastic elaboration of ideology and science.

The explicit reason given for degeneration is Darwinian. The Traveller decides that strength and size must have declined because they were no longer needed for survival: "Under the new conditions of perfect comfort and security, that restless energy, that with us is strength, would become weakness. . . . And in a state of physical balance and security, power, intellectual as well as

physical, would be out of place" (p. 42). Such a safe society dismays him. He relishes swashbuckling physical action, and is loath to consider a world that would exclude it. Indeed the Morlocks provide him with a welcome excuse to exercise powers not wanted in London. "I struggled up, shaking the human rats from me, and, holding the bar short, I thrust where I judged their faces might be. I could feel the succulent giving of flesh and bone under my blows, and for a moment I was free" (p. 95). "Succulent" is highly suggestive, relating as it does to the realm of the edible.

The equivalence of body, mind, and energy determines major features of the futuristic scenarios. We find something like medieval planes of correspondence. As the cosmos runs down, men will lose energy individually—a linkage no more logical than the Fisher-King's thigh wound causing sterility to fall upon the crops of his realm. Given this as a textual assumption about reality, however, we can see that clever, efficient and adaptive beings are impossible, although a setting like the Terminal Beach would call forth precisely such a humanity in the hands of other writers.

Gender, the third ideological element, undergoes a different kind of symbolic transformation. The traditional semes of "masculine" and "feminine"—whether culturally derived or natural—are widely familiar and even transcend cultural boundaries. Semes of the masculine include such constellated values as culture, light, the Sun, law, reason, consciousness, the right hand, land, and rulership. The feminine merges with chaos, darkness, the Moon, intuition, feeling, the left hand, water, and the unconscious.[12] The dialogue between them in some cultures involves balance; in the West, however, we find masculine consciousness fighting off or being overwhelmed by the feminine powers associated with unconsciousness. Thus the eat-consume-overwhelm nexus also enters the story as an attribute of gender.

Much of what troubles us in the realm of the Sphinx derives its power from the text's manipulation of these values. The grotesque is frequently formed from the mingling of characteristics from two "naturally" separate sets, man and beast, for instance. Despite cultural changes since the turn of the century, the traditional assumptions about gender are well enough ingrained in us by reading, if nothing else, to give the story's grotesques most of their original power. Wells attaches but also denies "feminine" and "masculine" attributes to both Eloi and Morlocks. The resulting contradictions prevent us from resolving the tensions roused by these grotesques into the kinds of reality that we are culturally conditioned to find comfortable.

The Eloi at first appear to be the only race, and then the superior of the two. Their life consists of a pastoral idyll, sunlight, and apparent rulership. Thanks to happiness; beauty, absence of poverty, and uninterrupted leisure, their life better fits our notion of Haves than Havenots. However, closer inspection shows them to be small, lacking in reason, deficient in strength, passively fearful, ineffectual, and ultimately just not "masculine" enough to be plausible patriarchal rulers, the standard against which they are implicitly held. In the *National Observer* version the Eloi have personal flying machines, but Wells ultimately deprived them of anything so technical. For all that they are feminized, however, they lack positive identity with the feminine, so we cannot reconcile them to our sense of the real by means of that pattern.

The Morlocks, by virtue of living in the dark and underground, seem first of all sinister, but secondarily are marked with symbolism of the unconscious and hence the feminine. Their access to the innards of the Sphinx reinforces the latter. Confusing our judgment, however, is their possible control of the machines, a power linked in Western eyes with the masculine rather than the feminine. Likewise, their apparently predatory aggression, their hunting parties (if such they be) fit "masculine" patterns. However, they seem deficient in strength and size to the Traveller, and their inability to tolerate light makes them obviously vulnerable in ways not befitting a "master" race. When comparing the two races, we find that both have traits associated with ruling and exploiting. The Eloi apparently live off the labor of the Morlocks while the latter apparently live off the flesh of the former. However, both are "feminized" in ways that render them less than masterful. These ambiguities in the cultural symbol system cannot be resolved. The traits associated with each race remain in uneasy tension, and contribute to the difficulty that critics have had in putting labels to the two races.

Power, size, and gender; oral fantasies, the laws of thermodynamics as applied to bodies and thought, and the grotesque: this peculiar mixture propels the story and gives it much of its intensity, its disturbing power. However, these concepts are not entirely consistent and harmonious. The conflicts they generate undermine the narrative logic and thereby dissolve the coherence of the ideas Wells was exploring. As we move to the future scenarios, we will note the gaps in the logic.

IN THE RIDDLING REALM OF THE SPHINX

Almost any way we approach this addled utopia, we find irreducible ambiguity. Does *The Time Machine* seriously concern a possible—albeit distant—future, or is futurity only a metaphoric disguise for the present? Darko Suvin focuses on the biological elements of the story, so he views the futurity as substantial and important. Others who focus on entropy or time travel likewise assume the significance of the futurity.[13] After all, without a real time lapse, anatomical evolution would be impossible. Alternatively, the "future" settings may be read as versions of Wells's present. "If the novella imagines a future, it does so not as a forecast but as a way of contemplating the structures of our present civilization."[14] Social warnings of danger 800,000 years away will inevitably fail to grip. Hence, the reality of time in this text—Wells's cherished fourth dimensional time—depends upon whether readers are focusing on biological or social systems.

Even if the critic ruthlessly simplifies to one or the other, interpretations go fuzzy at the edges or lead to contradiction. The biological reading appears at first to be straightforward. Wells asks, "what if progress is not inevitable and devolution can happen as well as evolution?" The Traveller decides that the Eloi degenerate because they no longer need to fight for survival—an interesting argument to present to the increasingly nonphysical Victorian society. The need for serious, bodily rivalry makes utopia a dangerous goal, and social restraint unhealthy. Wells thus raises a genuine problem, but does not develop it.

The social reading is yet more disturbing in its inability to satisfy the expectation of coherence. Oppressing the working class is dangerous as well as inhumane, and if we continue along such lines, the Haves will fall prey to the Havenots. At first glance, this seems like an unexceptionable social warning about mistreating the Workers. Somewhat unexpectedly, Wells treats the situation not as a revolution devoutly to be desired, but as a nightmarish terror. He evidently could not work up much sense of identification with the exploited. Hence the dilemma: not improving conditions leads to nightmare, but improving them in the direction of equality gets us back to utopia and its degeneration. If one accepts the biological message—physical competition—one must ignore the social message; if one accepts the social—improved conditions—one must ignore the biological. Wells offers us no way to accept both.

Since these two approaches lead to contradiction, one might try to escape the ambiguity by generalizing the referents of Eloi and Morlocks. Then one can read this as a parable about human nature,[15] or opt for Bergonzi's approach, and see the struggle between Eloi and Morlocks as polysemous. They are Pre-Raphaelite aesthetes and proletarians, and their struggle variously resonates with "aestheticism and utilitarianism, pastoralism and technology, contemplation and action, and ultimately . . . beauty and ugliness, and light and darkness" (Bergonzi, p. 305). If you are content, with Bergonzi, to call the tale "myth" and agree that meaning in myth is always multiple, you have one solution to the problem of interpretation. Otherwise, you must accept that the Eloi and Morlocks do not form coherent portraits. Their unstable identities—e.g., Morlocks as underclass or rulers—seem better likened to the duck/rabbit optical illusion, which has two embedded forms but which we are compelled to see as only one at a given time. The Eloi are an upper class in terms of pleasant material living conditions and freedom from toil, but they are an exploited class if they are being kept as cattle. The same double-identity obscures any explanation of the Morlocks. I have argued elsewhere that another possibility is that the two represent a dual assessment of the middle class alone: on the surface, we find an idealized and ineffectual claim to sweetness and light and vague aestheticism, but the vicious, exploitive side of bourgeois power, which preys upon the helpless, is hidden (Hume, pp. 286-87). We can (and will) make many other such equations because each reader's assumptions will activate different voices within the text. Resolution, though, is unlikely. The two races have been rendered permanently ambiguous through their clashing qualities.

They also resist interpretation because of the disparity between the Traveller's emotions and what he actually experiences. The Morlocks are only guilty of touching him and of trying to keep him from leaving them. They use no weapons, and they attempt to capture rather than kill him. They may be interested in studying him or in trying to establish communication. After all, as Lake points out, the Morlocks apparently visit the museum out of curiosity. The Traveller is as ready to jump to dire conclusions as Bedford is in *The First Men in the Moon.* What pushes him to such extremes of fear and loathing may be his deep uneasiness over code violations. The grotesque mixing of masculine and feminine and of human and animal seem to produce in him much the sort of panic and hostility as that felt by some people towards transvestites and physical freaks.

Even the Sphinx plays her part in such confusions. "The State" and its powers are conventionally symbolized by the masculine, the father, the lawgiver. Well's symbols for government are patriarchal in other romances, and his heroes either rebel against this oedipal oppressor or make their way into patriarchal power and identify with it. Dr. Moreau is such a threatening father, indeed a not-very-displaced castrating father. Almost all the clashes over authority in *The Food of the Gods* are put in terms of fathers and sons. The Invisible Man's hatred for established authority causes him to act in a way that literally kills his father. The Martians allow the protagonist to project his dissatisfactions with the social system onto an enemy, and with the defeat of the enemy, take up a patriarchal role and uphold the status quo.

The Sphinx, though, is female, the spawn of chaos.[16] She looms over the landscape, evidently the symbol of a ruling power, present or past, but also a grotesque yoking of beast and woman. (The other ornaments in her realm—a griffin and a faun—are also hybrids.) Bram Dijkstra has explored the Sphinx in late nineteenth-century art. He sees her renditions there as embodying tensions between the sexes that reflect male fears of

> a struggle between woman's atavistic hunger for blood—which she regarded as the vital fluid of man's seminal energies and hence the source of that material strength she craved—and man's need to conserve the nourishment that would allow his brain to evolve. Woman was a perverse instrument of the vampire of reversion, and by giving in to her draining embrace, men thought, they must needs bleed to death. (Dijkstra, p. 332)

In the art of this era, then, we find the same configuration of man being consumed, that consumption being carried out in such a way as to diminish not only his manly strength but also his intelligence. Oral fantasies here merge with the peculiarly end-of-the-century way of construing conservation of energy in physical and mental terms. Wells's world ruled by the Sphinx is indeed one bled of its masculinity and mental power, a world of reversion.

Wells's susceptibility to such oral anxieties is underlined by another gap in the logic. The oral fears emerge in a curiously skewed form. Haves normally exploit, "eat," or consume Havenots in a capitalist system; that is how the image usually enters socio-economic discourse. In *The Time Machine,* however, the cannibalistic urges are instead projected onto the Havenots. One finds a similar reversed logic in the material fiction of America and England in the period of 1870 to the 1920s. Those white, Anglo-American populations who were spreading empire and invading the Philippines or carrying out wars in India and Africa entertained themselves with invasion tales in which they themselves were the victims. *The War of the Worlds* is just such an invasion tale, probably the greatest to emerge out of this literary type in England. Wells likens Martian treatment of Britons to British treatment of Tasmanians. America battened on fictions about the Black Menace, the Yellow Menace, the Red Menace, not to mention fears that England, Canada, or Mexico would invade America. Throughout the same period, America was stripping Native Americans of land and lynching Blacks, and sending armies to the Philippines and Haiti.[17] Whether Wells is using this trick of mind to characterize his protagonist, or whether Wells himself is denying political guilt and replacing it with self-justifying political fears simply is not clear. The application of the cannibalistic fantasy to the exploited group remains a notable gap in the logical fabric of the whole.

What are we to make of this adventure in the realm of the Sphinx, then? A rather mixed message, at best. Utopias by most definitions eliminate competition. This proves a dangerous ideal, because so safe an environment would encourage bodily weakness, and then degeneration of mind and feminization. In other words, beware Socialism! However, the paradise of capitalists is a world in which the Great Unwashed lives underground, its misery unseen and ignored. This too leads to degeneration, as we see, because it also abolishes real struggle. Without the chance or need to compete—literally to destroy or exploit or "consume"—man devolves, according to Wells's ideology. The importance of competition comes out when we realize its relevance to power, size, and masculine behavior patterns, and its status as guarantor of intelligence. This competitive violence appears to be the most consistently upheld value in the first adventure, but even such struggle is undermined by the arguments in the second adventure, the excursion to the Terminal Beach. There entropy, by means of the planes of correspondence, cancels the energizing effect of struggling for existence.

THE TERMINAL BEACH: A JOURNEY TO THE INTERIOR

"Journey to the interior" nicely condenses what happens here. *The Time Machine* as a totality consists of a trip to the interior of some unknown land, as found in *She, Henderson the Rain King, Heart of Darkness,* and *The Lost Steps.* The foray from 800,000 to thirty million years into the future is an embedded journey to the interior, a *mise en abîme* repetition. Call the Terminal Beach a mindscape reached by being eaten. The Traveller enters the Sphinx much as Jonah or Lucian enter their respective whales.[18] Entropy may supply the logic that links the two scenarios, but the emotional unity derives from oral fantasies.

The Terminal Beach actually consists of two scenes and several fractional visions. The crab-infested litoral comes first, then the world in which life lingers in the form of a black, flapping, tentacled "football." The eclipse and snowflakes both belong to the second scene, increasing its inhospitability. However, both form a continuum of desolation and an invitation to despair.

That the Traveller's responses need not be quite so bleak becomes clear if we contrast Wells's handling this situation with what might be called the Germinal Beach in Arthur C. Clarke's *2010.* There, new life is discovered, but the physical conditions are much the same as in Wells, and Clarke clearly had both of Wells's beaches in mind. Clarke's setting consists of ice and water, where Wells has water, pebbles, and ice. Clarke's tragic snow-flakes result from the ruptured space ship. Clarke offers a huge, slow-moving, semi-vegetative creature. Both authors suggest the frailty of life through flickering, flapping, flopping, intermittent movement. In *The Time Machine,* day and night "flap" as the Traveller zooms into the future; the black creature on the strand flops, a screaming butterfly flutters, crab mouths flicker, the sea surface ripples. The larval stages of Clarke's life-form remind the speaker of flowers and then butterflies, and then flop about like stranded fish. Wells eclipses the sun to squeeze the last drop of symbolic value out of the light and darkness; Clarke has his observer break their artificial light so that the phototropic life-form will return to the sea. The Time Traveller sees "a curved pale line like a vast new moon" (p. 107) and as the eclipse passes off, notes "a red-hot bow in the sky" (p. 109); Clarke's Dr. Chang notes that "Jupiter was a huge, thin crescent" (p. 81),[19] and a few pages after this scene, another character stares at a picture of Earth as a thin crescent looming above the Lunar horizon.

Even in the most distant future, the Time Traveller can breathe the atmosphere and can escape any immediate danger by pulling a lever, yet he despairs. Clarke's Chinese astronaut will die as soon as his oxygen runs out, yet he remains scientifically alert and basically excited and pleased, although the level of life visible in each scene is roughly the same: non-human, non-intelligent, and prob-ably scarce. Clearly the two authors perceive the land-scapes from different vantages. To Clarke, Europa is the key to hegemony of the outer planets, the source of "the most valuable substance in the Universe" (p. 66). With Europa's water and cold fusion, settlers would enjoy vir-tually unlimited power for themselves plus fuel for their spaceships. By contrast, the Time Traveller sees nothing worth colonizing in either scene, nothing to exploit or

utilize, nothing to consume. Wells and Clarke are at one in valuing worlds for what we can exploit.

Again, Wells disturbs his Traveller by violating his codes for normal reality. Instead of finding light and dark, he finds all liminal and borderline colors and values: palpi-tating greyness, steady twilight (p. 104), a sun that glows dully, and a beach on which there are no waves, only an oily swell. An eclipse is suitably liminal as well, a state that produces neither true day nor true night. In addition to being in a permanently transitional phase, his world is also liminal with regards to land and water. The ocean has approached over the millennia; what was high land in Victorian London and 800,000 years later is about to be overwhelmed by the advancing ocean. Light and land, often mind-scape equivalents to mind and body, are threatened by the encroaching, engulfing forces of darkness and water. Insofar as sea and darkness have symbolic associations with the unconscious and the feminine, this threat repeats both the gender and oral anxieties seen in the earlier adventure.

One's first instinct upon reading the Terminal Beach chap-ter is to interpret it solely as a funereal rhapsody on entropy, as a look at the inevitable death of the sun and the ramifi-cations of this eventuality for mankind. George H. Darwin provided Wells with ideas about tidal friction and slowed rotation. The Book of Revelation contributes water-turned-blood. These simple transformations, plus the narrator's depression at what he finds, make the bleakness and hope-lessness seem natural and inevitable. I would argue that to some degree they are actually cultural and ideological.

One has only to look at *The War of the Worlds* or even *The First Men in the Moon* to see very different fic-tional responses to apparently dead-end situations. The protagonists in those stories, or various lesser characters, face new situations with the same sort of scientific curi-osity and engagement shown by Clarke's Dr. Chang. They are not foolish optimists, but a bleak and threaten-ing situation is cause for intellectual stimulation, for forming and confirming theories, for taking pride in observing new phenomena, for striving against the envi-ronment. The Time Traveller, though, seemingly suffers an entropic loss of his own energy as he observes that life in general has lost the struggle. The point of failure, however, actually came where Wells's thermodynamic fantasy overcame his Darwinian science. When the social system eventually disintegrated, the descendents of Eloi and Morlocks should have improved through survival of the fittest. His assumptions about mind, energy, and body, though, render his fictional creations helpless long before the final scenes. That helplessness was dictated by a fantastic distortion of the laws of thermodynamics, not by the laws themselves, so here again, we find the ampli-fications and elaborations of basic ideologies affecting plot. Mankind disappears because of one such fantasy; the Traveller's panic takes its form from another.

In superficial regards, *The Time Machine* is obviously enough a social satire to justify our expecting a reasonably coherent warning. The doubled identities of both Eloi and Morlocks turns them into the literary equivalent of an optical illusion. Coherence can no more emerge from them than from Escher's drawing of water flowing downhill in a circle. Scientifically, **The Time Machine** explores entropic decline, but refuses to give us ingenious humanity striving ever more ferociously to put off the inevitable. Humanity has already degenerated irreversibly through the exercise of what is generally considered its higher impulses. Even that would be a warning, but Wells undercuts it with his thermodynamic fantasies, which would bring about similar degeneration in any case through the links he posits among body and mind and energy. Thus do some of the rather fierce undercurrents in this romance break up its arguments, leaving them as stimulating fragments rather than logical structures. The powerful emotions both expressed by the Traveller and generated in readers are tribute to the subsurface currents, especially the oral-stage anxieties. The torment they represent is most clearly seen in the blind, defensive, totally illogical projection of savagery and cannibalism upon the group most apparently exploited. Like the imperialistic nations fantasizing their own humiliation at the hands of invaders, Wells's Traveller, and possibly Wells himself, are projecting behavior upon others in ways that suggest considerable repressed social guilt.

The return of the repressed is important to the dynamics of this tale. I will finish my arguments with one further variant on that theme. When the Time Traveller seeks the ruler of the pastoral realm, he seeks an Absent Father, and finds instead the Sphinx, avatar of threatening femininity. Within the classical Greek world view, "man" is the proud answer to the Sphinx's riddle, and man as Oedipus vanquishes the feminine and chaotic forces from Western civilization. In **The Time Machine,** "man" is no longer as proud an answer, and man has no power to prevent the lapse from order towards entropy. One might even argue that this time-travelling Oedipus is to some degree the criminal responsible for the status quo, for the ideologies he embodies have limited his culture's vision and rendered alternatives invisible. The Greeks and their civilization based on patriarchal structures banished the Sphinx. Here, she returns, and she succeeds in swallowing humanity after all.

NOTES

[1] The Atlantic edition of *The Works of H. G. Wells,* 1 (New York: Charles Scribner's Sons, 1924): 4-5.

[2] Bernard Bergonzi rendered *The Time Machine* orthodox by bestowing upon it two charismatic labels: "ironic" and "myth." See *"The Time Machine:* An Ironic Myth," *Critical Quarterly* 2 (1960): 293-305.

[3] See David J. Lake, "Wells's Time Traveller: An Unreliable Narrator?" *Extrapolation* 22, no. 2 (1981): 117-26.

[4] John Huntington sees this mastery of his actions as index to the protagonist's superiority over both Eloi and Morlocks, since they lack such self-control. See *The*

Logic of Fantasy: H. G. Wells and Science Fiction (Columbia U. Press, 1982), p. 51.

[5] For details of this and many other variants, including a previously unpublished draft of an excursion into the past, see *The Definitive Time Machine: A Critical Edition of H. G. Wells's Scientific Romance,* with introduction and notes by Harry M. Geduld (Indiana U. Press, 1987), quotations from p. 179.

[6] In her utopian novel, *The Dispossessed,* Ursula Le Guin calls our attention to this unthinking esteem for height by replacing commendatory terms based on size with those based on centrality.

[7] See McCarthy's *"Heart of Darkness* and the Early Novels of H. G. Wells: Evolution, Anarchy, Entropy," *Journal of Modern Literature* 13, no. 1 (1986): 37-60.

[8] See Kathryn Hume, "The Hidden Dynamics of *The War of the Worlds,"* *PQ* 62 (1983): 279-92; Wells developed the connection more forcefully in the serialized version.

[9] Norman N. Holland, *The Dynamics of Literary Response* (New York: W. W. Norton, 1975), p. 43.

[10] For an argument in favor of the Traveller's being a traditional monomyth hero, and hence triumphant, see Robert J. Begiebing, "The Mythic Hero in H. G. Wells's *The Time Machine,"* *Essays in Literature,* 11 (1984): 201-10. Wells's many escape endings are analyzed by Robert P. Weeks in "Disentanglement as a Theme in H. G. Wells's Fiction," originally published in *Papers of the Michigan Academy of Science, Arts, and Letters* 39 (1954), reprinted in *H. G. Wells: A Collection of Critical Essays,* edited by Bernard Bergonzi (Englewood Cliffs, New Jersey: Prentice-Hall, 1976), pp. 25-31. Interestingly, Wells considered another kind of ending, at least in response to editorial pressures. In the version of this story serialized in *The National Observer,* the story ends with the Traveller referring to hearing his child crying upstairs because frightened by the dark. This *ad hoc* family man, however, may result from hasty termination of the serial. Henley, as editor, liked Wells's work while his replacement, Vincent, did not. See Geduld for such variants.

[11] For the nineteenth-century science behind all the assumptions about body size and energy, see Cynthia Eagle Russett, *Sexual Science: The Victorian Construction of Womanhood* (Harvard U. Press, 1989), p. 105.

[12] In other words, Yin, Yang, and Jung. These symbolic clusters of values are discussed and illustrated throughout both the following Jungian studies by Erich Neumann: *The Origins and History of Consciousness,* Bollingen Series 42 (Princeton U. Press, 1970) and *The Great Mother: An Analysis of the Archetype,* Bollingen Series 47 (Princeton U. Press, 1972).

[13] Darko Suvin, *Metamorphoses of Science Fiction: On the Poetics and History of a Literary Genre* (Yale U.

Press, 1979), chapter 10. For an analysis of time travel, see Veronica Hollinger, "Deconstructing the Time Machine," *Science-Fiction Studies* 14 (1987): 201-21.

[14] Huntington, p. 41. Others focusing on social issues include Patrick Parrinder, "*News from Nowhere, The Time Machine* and the Break-UP of Classical Realism," *Science-Fiction Studies* 3, no. 3 (1976): 265-74, and Wayne C. Connely, "H. G. Well's [sic] *The Time Machine:* It's [sic] Neglected Mythos," *Riverside Quarterly* 5, no. 3 (1972): 178-91.

[15] Stephen Gill sees the Morlocks as "the bestial nature of human beings." Hennelly sees it about the failure to reconcile the contraries in the human heart, and Lake explores it as a protest against death. See Gill, *Scientific Romances of H. G. Wells: A Critical Study* (Cornwall, Ontario: Vesta Publications, 1975), p. 38, and Mark M. Hennelly, Jr., "*The Time Machine:* A Romance of 'The Human Heart,'" *Extrapolation* 20, no. 2 (1979): 154-67; and David J. Lake, "The White Sphinx and the Whitened Lemur: Images of Death in *The Time Machine*," *Science-Fiction Studies* 6, no. 1 (1979): 77-84.

[16] See Frank Scafella, "The White Sphinx and *The Time Machine*," *Science-Fiction Studies* 8, no. 3 (1981): 255-65, p. 259. Bram Dijkstra explores the *fin de siècle* fascination with sphinxes in art in *Idols of Perversity: Fantasies of Feminine Evil in Fin-de-Siècle Culture* (Oxford U. Press, 1986), pp. 325-32.

[17] For an analysis of the British version of such invasion jitters, see Cecil Degrotte Eby, *The Road to Armageddon: The Martial Spirit in English Popular Literature, 1870-1914* (Duke U. Press, 1987). For the American version, see H. Bruce Franklin, *War Stars: The Superweapon and the American Imagination* (Oxford U. Press, 1988).

[18] Two mindscapes similarly reached in a physical interior are Harlan Ellison's "Adrift Just Off the Islets of Langerhans: Latitude 38° 54' N, Longitude 77° 00' 13" W," and Norman Spinrad's "Carcinoma Angels." In the latter, the protagonist psychically descends into his own body to kill cancer cells. He "finally found himself knee-deep in the sea of his digestive juices lapping against the walls of the dank, moist cave that was his stomach. And scuttling towards him on chitinous legs, a monstrous black crab with blood-red eyes, gross, squat, primeval." The Wellsian intertext enriches the cancer/crab wordplay. "Carcinoma Angels" is found in *Dangerous Visions,* ed. Harlan Ellison (London: Victor Gollancz, 1987), 513-21, quotation, p. 521.

[19] The "Germinal Beach" occurs on pp. 77-82 of Arthur C. Clarke, *2010* (London: Granada, 1983).

David C. Cody

SOURCE: "Faulkner, Wells, and the 'End of Man,'" in *Journal of Modern Literature,* Vol. 18, No. 4, Fall, 1993, pp. 465-74.

We finish thus; and all our wretched race
Shall finish with its cycle, and give place
To other beings, with their own time-doom;
Infinite eons ere our kind began;
Infinite eons after the last man
Has joined the mammoth in earth's tomb and
    womb.
      —James Thomson, "The City of
              Dreadful Night" (1874)

Why should we bear with an hour of torture, a
    moment of pain,
If every man die for ever, if all his griefs are in vain,
And the homeless planet at length will be wheel'd
    thro' the silence of space,
Motherless evermore of an ever-vanishing race,
When the worm shall have writhed its last, and its
    last brother-worm will have fled
From the dead fossil skull that is left in the rocks
    of an earth that is dead?. . . .
Have I crazed myself over their horrible infidel
    writings? O yes,
For these are the new dark ages, you see, of the
    popular press,
When the bat comes out of his cave, and the owls
    are whooping at noon,
And Doubt is lord of this dunghill and crows to
    the sun and the moon,
sTill the Sun and the Moon of our science are
    both of them turn'd into blood
And Hope will have broken her heart, running
    after a shadow of good. . . .
      —Alfred, Lord Tennyson, "Despair:
              A Dramatic Monologue" (1881)

One must err to grow and the writer feels no remorse for this youthful effort. Indeed he hugs his vanity very pleasantly at times when his dear old Time Machine crops up once more in essays and speeches, still a practical and convenient way to retrospect or prophecy.
      —H. G. Wells, Preface (1931) to
              The Time Machine (1895)

In his 1950 Nobel Prize speech, William Faulkner contemplates the ultimate fate of mankind in a nuclear age and considers the role that the writer might play in helping to determine that fate. In one of the most famous passages he would ever write, he suggests that the young writer of his day, although living in the debilitating shadow of "a general and universal fear so long sustained by now that we can even bear it," must "teach himself that the basest of all things is to be afraid; and, teaching himself that, forget it forever, leaving no room in his workshop for anything but the old verities and truths of the heart, the old universal truths lacking which any story is ephemeral and doomed—love and honor and pity and pride and compassion and sacrifice."[1] "Until he relearns these things," Faulkner insists, "he will write as though he stood among and watched the end of man. I decline to accept the end of man. It is easy enough to say that man is immortal simply because he will endure: that when the last ding-dong of doom has clanged and faded from the last worthless rock hanging tideless in the last red and dying evening, that even then there will still be one more sound: that of his puny inexhaustible voice, still talking. I refuse to accept this. I believe that man will not merely endure: he will prevail" (p. 4).[2] Although the Nobel Speech is addressed to "the young man or woman writing today" and although it concerns itself with "our tragedy today" ("There are no longer questions of the spirit," Faulkner writes, " . . . There is only the question: when will I be blown up?"), it has as one of its central themes the crucial importance of remembering or re-learning the "old universal truths" which mankind is in danger of forgetting. Faulkner insists that man is immortal not merely because he will "endure," but because he is possessed of a soul, "a spirit capable of compassion and sacrifice and endurance" which will permit him, in the end, to "prevail," and he makes the point too that "the poet's voice" is one of the "props" or "pillars" that will help man to do so: "The poet's, the writer's duty," he informs us, "is to write about these things. It is his privilege to help man endure by lifting his heart, by reminding him of the courage and honor and hope and pride and compassion and pity and sacrifice which have been the glory of his past" (p. 4).[3]

The Speech, then, is emphatic in its defence of the "old verities and truths of the heart." Whether Faulkner's life's work is in fact "uplifting" in this sense—whether he really did believe, that is, that his own work signified an affirmative belief—is a complex question that is not easily resolved. In the Speech, however, Faulkner contrasts his own efforts on behalf of mankind with the work of other writers who have failed in their duty because they have written as though they "stood among and watched the end of man." He does not identify such writers by name, but that oddly detailed reference to a "last worthless rock hanging tideless in the last red and dying evening" gives us some sense of what he had in mind—for although it has been plausibly suggested that in the Speech as a whole he disparages the pessimistic view of man's future that had been expressed by Joseph Conrad in his essay "Henry James: An Appreciation," the very specificity of that apocalyptic reference makes it clear that Faulkner is in fact recalling the climacteric scene in H. G. Wells's *The Time Machine: An Invention* (1895).[4]

We do not know when Faulkner first encountered Wells's "scientific romance"—which purports, of course, to be the narrative of a traveller who has quite literally "stood among and watched the end of man"—but we do know that his personal library at Rowan Oak contained a copy of a special limited edition published in 1931, with a preface by the elderly Wells and remarkable "designs" in color by W.A. Dwiggins.[5] In the penultimate chapter of *The Time Machine,* the Time Traveller moves forward into the distant future, watching as the earth's rotation upon its axis gradually slows, the planet eventually coming to rest "with one face to the sun, even as in our own time the moon faces the earth" (77). As he begins to slow his motion through time, "the dim outlines of a desolate beach" gradually become visible, and when he comes to rest he finds himself in a world very different from the one he has left behind:

> The sky was no longer blue. North-eastward it was inky black, and out of the blackness shone brightly and steadily the pale white stars. Overhead it was a deep Indian red and starless, and south-eastward it grew brighter to a glowing scarlet where, cut by the horizon, lay the huge hull of the sun, red and motionless. The rocks about me were of a harsh reddish colour. . . . [T]he machine was standing on a sloping beach. The sea stretched away to the south-west, to rise into a sharp bright horizon against the wan sky. There were no breakers and no waves, for not a breath of wind was stirring. (p. 77)

It was on this desolate beach, clearly, with its tideless sea brooding beneath a red and dying sun, that Faulkner first stumbled over his "last worthless rock." It is not a pleasant place, and the Time Traveller—appalled by the "abominable desolation," but "drawn on by the mystery of the earth's fate"—decides to venture still further into the future. When he halts once more, "more than thirty million years hence," he finds himself upon the same stretch of beach, now lying cold and apparently lifeless in a dying world in which "the huge red-hot dome of the sun had come to obscure nearly a tenth part of the darkling heavens." Here, troubled by "a certain indefinable apprehension," he watches as "an inner planet passing very near to the earth" gradually eclipses the sun—a scene which Dwiggins depicts in an illustration entitled "MORE THAN THIRTY MILLION YEARS HENCE." . . . As the eclipse becomes total, the silence, cold, and darkness grow overwhelming, but one final epiphany awaits him:

> A horror of this great darkness came on me. The cold, that smote to my marrow, and the pain I felt in breathing, overcame me. I shivered, and a deadly nausea seized me. Then like a red-hot bow in the sky appeared the edge of the sun. . . . As I stood sick and confused I saw again the moving thing upon the shoal—there was no mistake now that it was a moving thing—against the red water of the sea. It was a round thing, the size of a football perhaps, or, it may be, bigger, and tentacles trailed down from it; it seemed black against the weltering blood-red water, and it was hopping fitfully about. Then I felt that I was fainting. But a terrible dread of lying helpless in that remote and awful twilight sustained me while I clambered upon the saddle." (p. 80)

In much of the horror literature produced in the late Victorian and Edwardian periods, characters experience symptoms such as nausea, sickness, and confusion after an encounter with the "uncanny"—Freud's *unheimlich*—or with what we have more recently come to refer to as the "abject." In her *Powers of Horror* (1982), Julia Kristeva defines "abjection" as that which "disturbs identity, system, order. What does not respect borders, positions, rules. The in-between, the ambiguous, the composite."[6] Such encounters appear so frequently in the horror literature of the *fin de siècle* that they might almost be called a defining characteristic of the genre, just as the literature itself was a symptom of the intense anxiety which existed in the culture that engendered it. In Kipling's "The

Strange Ride of Morrowbie Jukes" (1885), for example, the protagonist, caught up in his Imperialist nightmare, compares his "inexplicable terror" to "the overpowering nausea of the Channel passage—only my agony was of the spirit and infinitely more terrible."[7] We might also recall the "horror and revolting nausea" experienced by the doctor who witnesses the ghastly demise of Helen Vaughn in Arthur Machen's "The Great God Pan" (1890); the "horror" and "loathing" with which Basil Hallward views the infamous portrait in Wilde's *The Picture of Dorian Gray* (1891); and the "horrible feeling of nausea" that overcomes Jonathan Harker when he meets the Count in Bram Stoker's *Dracula* (1897): in all such descriptions, the response is triggered by the realization that an ontological border (between the normal and the abnormal, the safe and the unsafe) has been violated.[8] In this sense, the Time Traveller's nausea is due not merely to the cold and the thin atmosphere which he encounters in the future, but also to his realization—not as mere theory or hypothesis, but as fact—that mankind has no place there. Faulkner's young writers, attempting to create in a time when not the century, but the world itself seemed about to come to an end, were similarly distressed—and so, if the speech is any indication, was Faulkner himself.

To appreciate the relevance of Faulkner's reference to *The Time Machine,* then, we must be cognizant, as Faulkner himself obviously was, of the various implications of that final moment of horror, which is given particular emphasis in Wells's narrative not merely because the encounter itself marks the culmination of the Time Traveller's adventuring (the round object the size of a football is the last sight he sees before he flees back to the relative safety of the late-nineteenth century) and not merely because it provides us with a glimpse of the end of life on earth. In his preface to the 1931 edition of *The Time Machine,* the elderly Wells noted that although his romance "seems a very undergraduate performance to its now mature writer, as he looks it over once more," it nevertheless "goes as far as his philosophy about human evolution went in those days" (p. ix). During the Victorian period as a whole, of course, and during the *fin de siècle* in particular, the prevailing "philosophy about human evolution" underwent a remarkable transformation. For many years, many more or less eminent Victorians, equating technological advances with moral ones, had attempted to reconcile the moral values of Christianity with what was (ostensibly, at least) morally neutral Darwinian thought: their tendency, inevitably, was to distort the latter so that in various ways it could be made to reinforce belief in human "Progress," both spiritual and material. By 1895, however, the great age of Victorian optimism was already over, and in this sense *The Time Machine* reflects an ongoing ideological crisis within late-Victorian culture itself, as the heirs of Darwin asserted the primacy (and the purity) of their own vision, which was much less overtly anthropocentric. It is only a slight exaggeration to suggest, as two recent critics have done, that by 1895 "the conventional pieties of romantic Christianity seemed on the verge of being finally destroyed by the overwhelming evidence for Darwinian materialism."[9]

The groundwork for such destruction, however, had been laid much earlier. In 1834, for example, William Whewell had noted in his Bridgewater Treatise on *Astronomy and General Physics Considered with Reference to Natural Theology* that all planets orbiting the sun were gradually losing velocity because of the resistance offered by an "ethereal medium":

> It may be millions of millions of years before the earth's retardation may perceptibly affect the apparent motion of the sun; but still the day will come (if the same Providence which formed the system, should permit it to continue so long) when this cause will entirely change the length of our year and the course of our seasons, and finally stop the earth's motion round the sun altogether. The smallness of the resistance, however small we choose to suppose it, does not allow us to escape this certainty.[10]

By 1852, seven years before the first publication of Darwin's *The Origin of Species*, Lord Kelvin and others had already formulated the Second Law of Thermodynamics, and Kelvin himself had stated that "Within a finite period of time past, the earth must have been, and within a finite period to come, the earth must again be, unfit for the habitation of man as at present constituted."[11] In his *The Conservation of Energy* (1873), Balfour Stewart would note that "We are led to look to an end in which the whole universe will be one equally heated inert mass, and from which everything like life or motion or beauty will have utterly gone away."[12] In his *Degeneration* (1893), the eccentric Max Nordau would suggest that even the "degenerate" art and music and literature of the day betokened doom: "The old Northern faith contained the fearsome doctrine of the Dusk of the Gods. In our days there have arisen in more highly-developed minds vague qualms of a Dusk of the Nations in which all suns and all stars are gradually waning and mankind with all its institutions and creations is perishing in the midst of a dying world."[13] Many of the most prominent scientists of the period agreed that in the long term at least, the prospects for continued human existence were grim; this view is also reflected in such dark and anxiety-ridden poems as James Thomson's "The City of Dreadful Night" (1874) and the elderly Tennyson's "Despair: A Dramatic Monologue" (1881).

The same premise, of course, shaped *The Time Machine.* Looking back in 1931 on the *weltanschauung* that had prevailed during his youth, Wells would note that "the geologists and astronomers of that time told us dreadful lies about the 'inevitable' freezing up of the world—and of life and mankind with it. There was no escape, it seemed. The whole game of life would be over in a million years or less. They impressed this upon us with the full weight of their authority . . ." (ix-x). That Darwin himself eventually accepted this pessimistic vision of the future of mankind, and that he too found the idea profoundly disturbing, is made clear in one of his letters to J. D. Hooker, dating from Feb. 9, 1865:

I quite agree how humiliating the slow progress of man is, but everyone has his own pet horror, and this slow progress or even personal annihilation sinks in my mind into insignificance compared with the idea or rather I presume certainty of the sun some day cooling and we all freezing. To think of the progress of millions of years, with every continent swarming with good and enlightened men, all ending in this, and with probably no fresh start until this our planetary system has been again converted into red-hot gas. Sic transit gloria mundi, with a vengeance. . . . [14]

The same point would later recur in William James's *The Varieties of Religious Experience* (1902), although James inverted the central metaphor:

The lustre of the present hour is always borrowed from the background of possibilities it goes with. Let our common experiences be enveloped in an eternal moral order; let our suffering have an immortal significance; let Heaven smile upon the earth, and deities pay their visits; let faith and hope be the atmosphere which man breathes in;—and his days pass by with zest; they stir with prospects, they thrill with remoter values. Place round them on the contrary the curdling cold and gloom and absence of all permanent meaning which for pure naturalism and the popular scientific evolutionism of our time are all that is visible ultimately, and the thrill stops short, or turns rather to an anxious trembling.

For naturalism, fed on recent cosmological speculations, mankind is in a position similar to that of a set of people living on a frozen lake, surrounded by cliffs over which there is no escape, yet knowing that little by little the ice is melting, and the inevitable day drawing near when the last film of it will disappear, and to be drowned ignominiously will be the human creature's portion. The merrier the skating, the warmer and more sparkling the sun by day, and the ruddier the bonfires at night, the more poignant the sadness with which one must take in the meaning of the total situation. [15]

Wells's "imaginative romance," then, is a dramatization of the views of those "geologists and astronomers" who were proponents of "popular scientific evolutionism" and of their counterparts in physics, biology, and even philosophy. As a literary fantasy, *The Time Machine* owes a great deal to works by Swift, Poe, Stevenson, Twain, and Kipling; as a modern myth, it echoes ancient legends concerning the Twilight of the Gods; but as a presumably scientific Jeremiad, it is most obviously and specifically indebted to the thought of Thomas Henry Huxley, the great rationalist and defender of Darwin whose lectures on Biology and Zoology had greatly impressed Wells during his first year (1884) as a student at the Normal School of Science. [16] In his influential essay "Evolution and Ethics" (first presented as a Romanes lecture, in 1893), Huxley acknowledged that to the popular mind, "evolution" meant "progressive development," but he emphasized that "every theory of evolution must be consistent not merely with progressive development, but with indefinite persistence in the same condition and with

retrogressive modification." [17] It was Huxley's definition of the latter term as "progress from a condition of relative complexity to one of relative uniformity" that provided Wells with the "central idea" for the work that would eventually become *The Time Machine.* "The theory of evolution," Huxley wrote, "encourages no millennial anticipations. If, for millions of years, our globe has taken the upward road, yet, some time, the summit will be reached and the downward route will be commenced. The most daring imagination will hardly venture upon the suggestion that the power and intelligence of man can ever arrest the procession of the great year" (p. 85). Fascinated by the concept of "degeneration following security," Wells would vividly describe its ultimate consequences in the penultimate chapter of *The Time Machine,* in which the "round thing" encountered on the dying beach is, in fact, the last representative of degenerate "man"—man as he would appear after thirty million years of inexorable "progress" on a "downward route" dictated by laws of physics and thermodynamics.

It is this denial of the possibility that man might somehow "prevail," then, that Faulkner condemns in a Speech which implicitly contrasts the uplifting "old verities and truths of the heart" with the deeply pessimistic premise underlying Wells's late-Victorian nightmare. In this sense, Faulkner's Speech, always viewed as a classic affirmation of the values of humanism, is also a profoundly conservative work in which he adopts the traditional stance of the Biblical prophet—or of the Victorian sage. Ignoring his own prolonged flirtation with literary Decadence and with the implicitly nihilistic attitudes of the Lost Generation, Faulkner condemns Wells because in writing *The Time Machine* he had contributed to rather than helped to alleviate the potentially overwhelming anxieties that would eventually begin to cripple modern literature. Hence Faulkner's invocation of implicitly Victorian virtues in the Speech itself, and hence the relevance of the fact that in the midst of an attempt to "uplift the hearts" of the young writers who lived in the shadow of a possible nuclear holocaust, he would invoke—as epitomizing a decadent and enervating sense of imminent and inevitable doom—a work written fifty-five years earlier (and two years before Faulkner himself had been born) in the midst of another period of cultural malaise. [18] Even in this sense, however, his choice of *The Time Machine* as a text to react against was singularly apt, for as Wells informs us, the Time Traveller "thought but cheerlessly of the Advancement of Mankind, and saw in the growing pile of civilization only a foolish heaping that must inevitably fall back upon and destroy its makers in the end" (p. 86). In declining to accept "the end of man," then, Faulkner is rejecting the very premise that haunts the conclusion of *The Time Machine*—the assumption that life itself has no ultimate or transcendent meaning.

The connection between Faulkner's Nobel Prize Speech and Wells's work does not end there, however, for in declining to accept the end of man, Faulkner was also echoing or recapitulating a memorable conversation that

Wells had had in 1906 with Theodore Roosevelt, then President of the United States. Roosevelt, of course, was a staunch advocate of American expansionism—his best-known literary work, *The Winning of the West*, being in effect, as David Wrobel has noted, "a study of American imperialism and its march across the continental mainland."[19] Many years afterwards, in his *Experiment in Autobiography* (1934), Wells recalled the conversation and brooded over its implications:

> It is a curious thing that as I talked with President Roosevelt in the garden of the White House there came back to me quite forcibly that undertone of doubt that has haunted me throughout this journey. After all, does this magnificent appearance of beginnings, which is America, convey any clear and certain promise of permanence and fulfilment whatever? . . . Is America a giant childhood or a gigantic futility, a mere latest phase of that long succession of experiments which has been and may be for interminable years—may be, indeed, altogether until the end—man's social history?
>
> I can't now recall how our discursive talk settled towards this, but it is clear to me that I struck upon a familiar vein of thought in the President's mind. He hadn't, he said, an effectual disproof of a pessimistic interpretation of the future. If one chose to say America must presently lose the impetus of her ascent, that she and all mankind must culminate and pass, he could not conclusively deny that possibility. Only he chose to live as if this were not so.
>
> That remained in his mind. Presently he reverted to it. He made a sort of apology for his life, against the doubts and scepticisms that, I fear, must be in the background of the thoughts of every modern man who is intellectually alive. He mentioned my *Time Machine*. . . . He became gesticulatory, and his straining voice a note higher in denying the pessimism of that book as a credible interpretation of destiny. With one of those sudden movements of his he knelt forward in a garden-chair—we were standing, before our parting, beneath the colonnade—and addressed me very earnestly over the back, clutching it and then thrusting out his familiar gesture, a hand first partly open and then closed.
>
> "Suppose, after all," he said slowly, "that should prove to be right, and it all ends in your butterflies and morlocks. That doesn't matter now. The effort's real. It's worth going on with. It's worth it. It's worth it—even so." . . .
>
> I can see him now and hear his unmusical voice saying, "The effort—the effort's worth it," and see the gesture of his clenched hand and the—how can I describe it?—the friendly peering snarl of his face, like a man with the sun in his eyes. He sticks in my mind at that, as a very symbol of the creative will in man, in its limitations, its doubtful adequacy, its valiant persistence, amidst perplexities and confusions. He kneels out, assertive, against his setting—and his setting is the White House, with a background of all America.[20]

In his Speech, then, Faulkner—himself speaking, as it were, "with a background of all America"—is also rehearsing the role played by Roosevelt when, acknowledging the possibility that it might all end in "butterflies and morlocks," proclaims that he nevertheless "chose to live as if this were not so." Both Roosevelt and Faulkner reject Wells's premise that America itself is a "gigantic futility," just as both refuse to accept the inevitability of "the end of man." Perhaps they do so because to do otherwise would be to admit that their own struggles and sacrifices, their own "anguish and travail"—Faulkner's as an artist, Roosevelt's as a "reformer"—had been in vain. Speaking as a writer, speaking to writers, and for writers, Faulkner also speaks—as sage and prophet—to all mankind, refusing to accept the Time Traveller's testimony that the writer's struggle to uplift the human heart is a pointless one. By implication, he offers himself as a writer who has both uplifted hearts and insisted that human existence is meaningful; in this crucial sense, the Nobel Speech is also an attempt on his part both to find meaning in his own existence and to define a philosophical perspective from which that existence can be judged. His ringing affirmation of humanist values upon the occasion of his receipt of the most prestigious of literary awards, then, may have been at least in part an attempt to respond to or forestall criticism of his own work; criticism grounded on the premise that his own work was not "uplifting." In the Speech, he undertakes both to enhance his status and reputation as an American man of letters and to influence or even to re-define the context within which his audience would receive and react to his own "life's work in the agony and sweat of the human spirit," and in a dramatic sense he uses the Speech to position himself as the very incarnation of what Wells, speaking of Roosevelt, had called the "very symbol of the creative will in man, in its limitations, its doubtful adequacy, its valiant persistence, amidst perplexities and confusions." The general outlines of this effort are readily visible in the portions of the Speech in which he proclaims the continuing importance of certain traditional values in a world which has come to neglect them. Faulkner does so, perhaps, because he feared that without that faith in the meaningfulness of his own life's work he would himself be consumed by the same "general and universal" fear of which he speaks so eloquently in the Nobel Speech and elsewhere—the fear that had preoccupied H. G. Wells as it had preoccupied Shakespeare: the old fear that all our yesterdays have but lighted fools the way to dusty death.

NOTES

[1] William Faulkner, "Speech of Acceptance upon the award of the Nobel Prize for Literature, delivered in Stockholm on the tenth of December, nineteen hundred fifty," in *The Faulkner Reader* (Random House, 1954), pp. 3-4. All citations from the Nobel Speech refer to this edition.

[2] The reference to "the last worthless rock" is, of course, accompanied by a reference to "the last ding-dong of doom," otherwise the world's death-knell—a Faulknerian variation on the traditional Crack of Doom that is to

herald the Day of Judgment. It is tempting to read this phrase as a deliberate echo or redaction of Shakespeare's reference to "the last syllable of recorded time" in the great nihilistic speech from *Macbeth* that had already provided Faulkner with the title for *The Sound and the Fury*. In this sense, the thrust of the Nobel Speech would also refute Macbeth's conclusion that life—the "walking shadow," the "poor player"—will "strut and fret his hour upon the stage" and then "be heard no more." What Faulkner meant by the word "prevail" is an interesting question in itself. One wonders whether he meant more than is implicit in the ambiguous vision, set forth four years afterwards in *A Fable,* of man's progress through the Universe as a sort of interplanetary Mad Hatter's Tea Party: "Oh, yes, he will survive it because he has that in him which will endure even beyond the last ultimate worthless tideless rock freezing slowly in the last red and heatless sunset, because already the next star in the blue immensity of space will be already clamorous with the uproar of his debarkation, his puny and inexhaustible voice still talking, still planning; and there too after the last ding dong of doom has rung and died there will be one sound more: his voice, planning still to build something higher and faster than ever before, yet it too inherent with the same old primordial fault since it too in the end will fail to eradicate him from the earth." [William Faulkner, *A Fable* (New York, 1954), p. 354.]

[3] Joseph Blotner and several other critics have remarked the fact that three years later, in the preface to *The Faulkner Reader,* Faulkner would repeat that the writer's purpose was "to uplift man's heart," even though the source of this "hope and desire" may be "completely selfish, completely personal." [William Faulkner, *The Faulkner Reader* (Random House, 1954). p. x.] On this occasion he suggested that he remembered encountering the phrase as a boy in the preface to an unidentified book by the Polish novel Laureate Henryk Sienkiewicz. (Several commentators have noted that the book was *Pan Michael,* the third volume of a lengthy historical romance typical in its way of the nineteenth-century revival of interest in the medieval cult of chivalry). In fact, the passage appears at the end of the book, not in the preface, but this reference too suggests a connection between Faulkner's speech and his sense of the importance of the values of the past. His hortatory invocation of the "old verities and truths of the heart, the old universal truths lacking which any story is ephemeral and doomed—love and honor and pity and pride and compassion and sacrifice" as the proper study of "the young man or woman writing today" has a characteristically Victorian ring: we might, for example, compare it with the sentiment expressed by the young John Buchan, when in 1896 he reminded his reader that "The old noble commonplaces of love and faith and duty are always with us, since they are needful for the making of any true man or woman." [John Buchan, "Prefatory," in *Scholar-Gypsies* (Bodley Head, 1896).]

[4] In 1967 Eric Solomon suggested that Faulkner owed "much of the rhetoric and many of the key ideas" in the speech to Conrad's essay on James, first published in the *North American Review* in 1905 and later reprinted in Conrad's *Notes on Life and Letters.* Conrad refers to the last day as a moment when some last artist "will formulate, strange as it may appear, some hope now to us utterly inconceivable." Solomon notes that Conrad and Faulkner employ "remarkable similar phrases and attitudes that reflect their essentially hopeful views of man's chances in a doom-ridden world." Christof Wegelin, writing in 1974, agreed that "the final paragraph of Faulkner's speech owed its rhetoric and its key ideas to Conrad," but concluded that "there is nothing in Conrad to match Faulkner's optimism" and went on to suggest that "while Faulkner expressed an essentially hopeful view, Conrad was at best dubious about man's end." Conrad suggests that "When the last aqueduct shall have crumbled to pieces, the last airship fallen to the ground, the last blade of grass have died upon a dying earth," a man "gifted with a power of expression and courageous enough to interpret the ultimate experience of mankind in terms of his temperament, in terms of art" will be "moved to speak on the eve of that day without tomorrow— whether in austere exhortation or in a phrase of sardonic comment, who can guess?" Hence, presumably, Faulkner's sardonic glimpse of post-Doomsday man and his "puny inexhaustible voice, still talking." This stands in stark contrasts, obviously, to the Time Traveller's vision of the overwhelming silence that reigns at the end of things. See Eric Solomon, "Joseph Conrad, William Faulkner, and the Nobel Prize Speech," *Notes and Queries* (New Series XIV, 1967), pp. 247-48, and Christof Wegelin, "'Endure' and 'Prevail'" Faulkner's Modification of Conrad," *Notes and Queries* (New Series XXI, 1974), pp. 375-76. For the relevant passage in Conrad's essay, see his *Notes on Life and Literature* (Doubieday, Page & Company, 1924), pp. 13-14. It may be worth noting that Conrad (a longtime friend who would in 1907 dedicate *The Secret Agent* to Wells, was himself indebted to *The Time Machine* both in the essay on Henry James and in such crucial works as *Heart of Darkness.* In any case the pages of Faulkner's copy of *Notes on Life and Literature* remained uncut, and we might also note that in describing his "last evening" Conrad refers only to the "feeble glow of the sun," and to the "last flicker of light on a black sky": his evening is neither "tideless" nor "red," and there is no reference to any rock, "worthless" or otherwise.

[5] H. G. Wells, *The Time Machine* (Random House, 1931). All citations from *The Time Machine* refer to this edition. See Joseph Blotner's *William Faulkner's Library— A Catalogue* (University Press of Virginia, 1964), p. 75.

[6] Julia Kristeva, *Powers of Horror: An Essay on Abjection* (Columbia University Press, 1982), p. 4.

[7] Rudyard Kipling, *The Portable Kipling,* ed. Irving Howe (Viking, 1982), p. 14.

[8] For relevant citations and insightful commentary see Susan J. Navarette's "The Physiology of Fear: Decadent Style and the *Fin de Siècle* Literature of Horror"

(Doctoral Dissertation, Department of English, The University of Michigan, 1989), pp. 53-54. I am also indebted to Professor Navarette for bringing the relevant passage in Max Nordau's *Degeneration* to my attention.

9 See Samuel L. Hynes and Frank D. McConnell, "*The Time Machine* and *The War of the Worlds:* Parable and Possibility in H. G. Wells," in H. G. Wells, *The Time Machine; The War of the Worlds: A Critical Edition,* edited by Frank D. McConnell (Oxford University Press, 1977), p. 345.

10 William Whewell, *Astronomy and General Physics Considered with Reference to Natural Theology* (William Pickering, 1834), pp. 199-200.

11 Lord Kelvin, quoted in Sir William Thomson's *Mathematical and Physical Papers,* 5 Volumes (Cambridge University Press, 1882-1911), I: p. 514.

12 Balfour Stewart, *The Conservation of Energy* (H. S. King, 1873), p. 153.

13 Max Nordau, *Degeneration* (1893), (D. Appleton and Company, 1895), p. 2.

14 Charles Darwin, *More Letters of Charles Darwin,* 2 Vols. ed. Francis Darwin (D. Appleton and Company, 1903), vol. I, pp. 260-261.

15 William James, *The Varieties of Religious Experience* (1902), (Penguin Books, 1982), p. 141.

16 For information on this relationship, and for an interesting commentary on the genesis of the various versions of *The Time Machine,* see Harry M. Geduld's introduction to *The Definitive Time Machine: A Critical Edition of H. G. Wells's Scientific Romance* (Indiana University Press, 1987).

17 Thomas H. Huxley, "Evolution and Ethics," in *Evolution and Ethics and Other Essays* (AMS Press, 1970), p. 85. We might note in passing that Huxley begins his lecture with a summary of the plot of "Jack and the Bean-Stalk" and that it would appear that Wells also appropriated the basic structure of this fairy tale for *The Time Machine.*

18 Wells in middle age was guardedly optimistic about man's future, but by the time of his death in 1946 he had—as such works as *The Fate of Man* (1939) and *Mind at the End of its Tether* (1946) reveal—become increasingly bleak and pessimistic. As he wrote in *The Fate of Man* (Longmans, Green, & Co., 1939):

> There is no reason whatever to believe that the order of nature has any greater bias in favor of man than it had in favor of the icthyosaur or the pterodactyl. In spite of all my disposition to a brave looking optimism, I perceive that now the universe is bored with him, in [sic] turning a hard face to him, and I see him being carried less less and less

> intelligently and more and more rapidly, suffering as every ill-adapted creature must suffer in gross and detail, along the stream of fate to degradation, suffering, and death. . . . Adapt or perish, that is and always has been the implacable law of life for all its children. Either the human imagination and the human will to live, rises to the plain necessity of our case and a renascent Homo Sapiens struggles on to a new, a harder, and a happier world dominion, or he blunders down the slopes of failure through a series of unhappy phases, in the wake of all the monster reptiles and beasts that have flourished and lorded it on the earth before him, to his ultimate extinction" (pp. 247-48).

It is difficult to determine how familiar Faulkner was with Wells's later works, although Blotner also notes that Faulkner kept a copy of *The Outline of History* (1923) in the bookcase in his bedroom at Rowan Oak.

19 David M. Wrobel, *The End of American Exceptionalism* (University Press of Kansas, 1993), p. 66.

20 H. G. Wells, *Experiment in Autobiography* (The Macmillan Company, 1934), pp. 648-649.

Patrick Parrinder

SOURCE: "Possibilities of Space and Time (*The Time Machine*)," in *Shadows of the Future: H. G. Wells, Science Fiction, and Prophecy,* Syracuse University Press, 1995, pp. 34-48.

I

Towards the end of ***The Time Machine,*** the Traveller finishes the story of his adventures, pauses, and looks around at his listeners. He is like a lecturer waiting for the first question after his talk, and like many nervous lecturers he tries to start the ball rolling by interrogating the audience himself. ' "No. I cannot expect you to believe it" ,' he begins. ' "Take it as a lie—or a prophecy. Say I dreamed it in the workshop. . . . Treat my assertion of its truth as a mere stroke of art to enhance its interest. And taking it as a story, what do you think of it?" '(12). There is another awkward silence, while the Time Traveller fiddles with his pipe, and the audience shift uneasily in their chairs. Then the newspaper editor says that their host ought to be a writer of stories. The narrator, who is not sure what to think, returns to the Traveller's house in Richmond the next day, just in time to speak with him before he departs on the second voyage, from which he never returns. As Robert Philmus has observed, within the narrative framework it is the Traveller's second disappearance and failure to return that proves the reality of time travel, establishing him as a prophet rather than a liar.[1]

For the narrator in the 'Epilogue,' the Time Traveller's tale appears as a brief moment of enlightenment, like the flaring of the match in '**The Rediscovery of the Unique,'** amid the vast ignorance and darkness of the future. The light of prophecy is also the light of science—but it is the extent of the blackness that terrifies. Wells says something very similar in *The Future in America,* when he speaks of the loss of his belief in the imminence of the Christian apocalypse during his adolescence. The study of biology revealed to him an 'endless vista of years ahead' (p. 10). Space, too, appeared as an endless vista, and it is notable that in his early works Wells often uses the word figuratively to indicate a measure of time, as in the phrase 'a space of time.'[2] The complementarity of space and time in the Wellsian universe is summed up in the title of his 1899 volume of stories, *Tales of Space and Time.*

But travel in time with its prophetic associations engages Wells's imagination more intensely than journeys into space. Despite his reputation as the founder of modern science fiction, he took little or no interest in the fiction of spaceships and stellar travel. His rhetorical vision in *The Discovery of the Future* of beings who 'shall laugh and reach out their hands amid the stars' (p. 36) was to inspire other writers, though it corresponds to very little in Wells's own output. Apart from the mystical dream-narrative of his short story **'Under the Knife,'** *The First Men in the Moon* is his only narrative of a journey beyond the earth's atmosphere; and it is notable that Bedford, the narrator, experiences the dissolution of identity in 'infinite space' during the comparatively short return journey from the moon. He recounts this phase of his adventures in a detached, almost serene way, very different from the Time Traveller's 'hysterical exhilaration' (3) as he rushes into the future. There is fear and trembling in Wells's imagination of time travel; in *The First Men in the Moon,* however, the experience of thrilling revelation is reserved not for the journey but for the discoveries that the two explorers make on the moon.

What, then, was the source of the exhilaration of time travel? It reflects the bias of Wells's scientific interests, in evolutionary biology and palaeontology rather than astronomy and physics, but it also has a more personal appeal, reflecting his imaginative 'impatience.' We can hardly avoid relating it both to the religious millennialism of his upbringing,[3] and to his intimations of an early death. The fundamental commonsense objection to time travel is the one put forward by Wells's fellow-novelist Israel Zangwill, writing about *The Time Machine* in his *Pall Mall Magazine* column in September 1895. To travel forward more than a few years in time, Zangwill argued, is to travel through one's own death.[4] (It is also, one might add, to travel through the death of the machine: metal fatigue and corrosion are often swifter processes than the decay of the human body.) Admittedly, the idea of 'travelling through' death is misleading, since what the time machine achieves for its rider is the circumvention and bypassing of the ravages of time. Since he is still alive and has only aged by a few hours when he reaches 802,701, his journey takes place in a different time-frame from the one that he leaves behind and later re-enters.[5] Wells is aware of some at least of the paradoxes that beset all time-travel narratives. These are most obtrusive

at the end of the story, when the narrator returns to Richmond the day after the Traveller's return and sees the Time Machine in the empty laboratory before meeting its inventor in the smoking-room. The Traveller has already passed through this moment in the empty laboratory twice, once on his journey forwards and once on his return journey; on the latter occasion he ' "seemed to see Hillyer . . . but he passed like a flash" ' (12). If Hillyer is the narrator (as Geduld suggests),[6] the Traveller is seeing him either at this moment or on the occasion, somewhat later, when the narrator re-enters the laboratory. On that second occasion, the narrator catches sight of the ghostly figure of the Traveller on the machine, in the act of departure—or arrival—or both. There are further complications that could be teased out from the story's opening-up of such paradoxes.[7]

Before receiving his 'death warrant' after his footballing accident in 1887, Wells had written 'A Vision of the Past.' Immediately after it, he wrote *The Chronic Argonauts,* the first version of *The Time Machine,* which is set in present time. At the end of *The Chronic Argonauts* the Reverend Elijah Cook returns from an involuntary voyage into the future, but we never hear his tale of what happened there. Wells's friends complained about the abrupt ending, but it was many years before he was able to write the promised sequel to his own satisfaction. When it eventually appeared in book form, it had been revised at least half a dozen times.[8] For six years (1888-94), we may say, Wells had hesitated on the brink of a genuinely prophetic narrative. His exultation once he had succeeded in giving the future a body and shape is perhaps mirrored in the pun (supposing it is a pun) in Section 4 of *The Time Machine,* when the Traveller reflects on the 'oddness of wells still existing.'

In *The Chronic Argonauts* there are two narratives, which Wells calls 'exoteric' and 'esoteric.' The exoteric or external story is told by 'the author' (that is, Wells himself), while the esoteric or internal one is told, in an incomplete and fragmentary form, by the Reverend Elijah Cook. The figure who never tells his story is Nebogipfel, the inventor of the time machine or 'Chronic Argo' himself. He only expounds the principles of time-travelling, in conversation with Elijah Cook. In the *National Observer* version of Wells's tale, published between March and June 1894, Nebogipfel, now rechristened or relabelled the Time Traveller, is constantly interrupted by his hearers. His mixture of philosophical argument and adventure narrative is punctuated by commentaries and outbursts of scepticism. The sheer imaginative power of his tale is never given full rein, as if some inhibition still curbed its author. As storytelling, this version is bungled just as 'The Chronic Argonauts' is bungled.[9] But in the final version Wells's inhibitions are overcome, and, once we are with the Traveller on his voyage, the smoking-room setting of the tale is forgotten for very long stretches. The Delphic voice pours forth at last. The Traveller is now more than a mere narrative device. He is a heroic figure within the confines of the story, as well as an avatar of the visionary personality that Wells was discovering, with growing confidence, within himself.

II

When Dr. Nebogipfel's unwilling passenger, the Rev. Elijah Cook, arrives back from his journey in **The Chronic Argonauts** he announces that he has several depositions to make. These concern a murder in the year 1862 (indicating that, unlike the Time Traveller, the Argonauts have gone both ways in time), an abduction in 4003 and a series of ' "assaults on public officials in the years 17,901 and 2" .'[10] In the *National Observer* 'Time Machine,' the world of the Eloi and Morlocks is set in AD 12,203. In the final version, the date, conveniently registered on the Time Machine's instrument panel, is 802,701. There follows the 'Further Vision,' in which the Traveller journeys forward another twenty-nine million years. The reader of the different versions of **The Time Machine** succumbs to the spell of these mysterious numbers themselves—above all, the puzzling figure 802,701—but, beyond that, the meaning of such vast expanses of imaginary time calls out for explanation.

When the Time Traveller's guests encounter the idea of visiting the future, it is plain how limited their (and, by extension, our) horizons are. The Journalist dubs their host 'Our Special Correspondent in the Day after Tomorrow' (2). The Editor wants a tip for next week's horse-racing. The Very Young Man suggests investing some money and travelling forward to collect the profits. Yet even the relatively modest *National Observer* voyage crossed a timespan of more than twice as long as recorded history. Wells's familiarity with the prehistoric vistas opened up by nineteenth-century geology and archaeology had shaped his vision of time travel. As a South Kensington student, he belonged to the first generation of young people to learn as a matter of course about the Stone Age, the era of the dinosaurs, and the formation of the earth. This marvellous new field of knowledge, which rapidly became a staple of popular culture, is evoked in the Epilogue to **The Time Machine** where the narrator imagines the Traveller voyaging into Palaeolithic, Jurassic and Triassic times.

Humanity emerged at a relatively late point in the evolutionary chain, yet our race is still almost unimaginably old. In Wells's next scientific romance, Dr. Moreau reminds the narrator that ' "Man has been a hundred thousand [years] in the making" ' (Ch. 14). Actually, Moreau's figure is a gross underestimate, as the chronological horizon of **The Time Machine** hints. In **The Outline of History,** Wells was to put the emergence of the subhuman *pithecanthropus erectus* at six hundred thousand years ago, though since the advent of radiocarbon dating this has been increased to 1.8 million years.[11] In September 1994 reports appeared of the discovery of a fruit-eating humanoid creature (possibly analogous to the Eloi on the evolutionary scale) said to be 4.4 million years old.

Before **The Time Machine** Wells had implied a possible chronology for future evolution in **'The Man of the Year Million.'** Then, in a discussion of **'The Rate of Change in Species'** (December 1894), he outlined the

considerations that may have led him to lengthen the Time Traveller's journey from the ten thousand years of the *National Observer* version to eighty times as long. Wells claimed it was a little-noticed biological fact that the rate of possible change was governed by the gap between generations, and hence by the average age of maturity in a species. Evolution by natural selection—the strictly Darwinian model to which Wells and Huxley adhered—could not have brought about significant changes within the human species within recorded history, so that any such changes must be cultural, not natural in origin. Wells was determined to show the results of hypothetical natural evolution, not of artificial or eugenic processes in **The Time Machine.** The Traveller's voyage through the best part of a million years thus reflects both the probable age of the human species, in the understanding of Wells's contemporaries, and the minimum time needed for natural selection to produce new degenerate beings descended from present-day humanity.

The time-horizon of Wells's story is also affected by contemporary physical predictions of the future of the solar system. The Traveller reaches a point where not only humanity, but the sun's heat itself is manifestly on the wane. If the story of evolution pointed to the plasticity of biological species, Lord Kelvin's Laws of Thermodynamics portrayed the universe as a finite enclosure in which energy was limited. As a student, Wells had once engaged in a spoof demonstration of a perpetual motion machine (powered by a concealed electromagnet)[12]—a thermodynamic impossibility not unlike a time machine, since both depend on the ability to bypass the normal framework of what, in a lost article, he had called the 'Universe Rigid.'[13] The Second Law of Thermodynamics with its statement that energy always tends to disperse made it clear that the sun and other stars must eventually cool and burn out. **The Time Machine** reflects this entropic process, as well as Sir George Darwin's calculations of the effects of tidal drag on the earth's motion. Later in his life, however, Wells readily admitted that his astronomical predictions had been too gloomy.[14] The study of radioactivity had revealed that the source of the sun's heat was thermonuclear fusion rather than combustion; the sun was not a coal fire, so to speak, but a nuclear reactor. The predicted life of the solar system increased from the implied timescale of the 'Further Vision' to ten thousand million years, or perhaps a million million years.[15]

These are unimaginable and almost meaningless expanses of time, yet paradoxically **The Time Machine** renders a thirty million-year future thinkable. That is the 'virtual reality' effect of the story's mythical, apocalyptic hold over the reader. To ask how Wells manages it is to come up against the truism that our only models for imagining the future derive from our knowledge and understanding of the past. He could write of travelling one million or thirty million years ahead only in the light of the geologists' consensus that the earth was already much older than that, though precisely how much older was a matter of conjecture. Kelvin had estimated that the age of the oldest rocks was as little as twenty-five million years, while T. H. Huxley guessed at four hundred million. Summing up the controversy in *The Outline of History,* Wells is unable to arbitrate between these two. Reusing one of his favourite metaphors, he adds that 'Not only is Space from the point of view of life and humanity empty, but Time is empty also. Life is like a little glow, scarcely kindled yet, in these void immensities' (p. 8). In *The Time Machine* he had slightly prolonged that little glow.

III

Wells's use of geological chronology does not explain how he was able to depict the sub-civilisation of the Eloi and Morlocks at a precise date in the future, given in the final version as 802,701. Readers have often wondered why he settled on this curious figure. We may approach an answer by looking more closely at the sensations of time-travelling described in the story. Riding into the future, the Traveller observes the speeding-up of natural phenomena: the alternation of night and day until the two are indistinguishable, the flickering change of the seasons, the swift growth and disappearance of trees. This part of his narrative, which has the vertiginous effect of a constantly accelerating film, may make us wonder how fast he is travelling and how 'long' his journey takes. At one point he mentions a speed of more than a year a minute, but if this were his average velocity it would take nearly eighteen months to reach 802,701. Travelling more rapidly later in the story, he approaches the 'Further Vision' at a speed of something like fifty years per second; but, in fact, five hundred years per second would be a more plausible average speed.[16] At that rate he could have reached the age of the Eloi and Morlocks in less than half an hour.

During his voyage he sees signs of changing civilisations as well as changing natural phenomena. ' "I saw huge buildings rise up faint and fair, and pass like dreams",' he reports (3). How often did this happen? ' "I saw great and splendid architecture rising about me, more massive than any buildings of our own time, and yet, as it seemed, built of glimmer and mist" .' There would have been no need to go forward three-quarters of a million years in order to see the architecture of successive human civilisations. Our knowledge of past history suggests that 800 years might have been enough. Even given vastly more durable building materials, 8000 years would have been amply sufficient. Assuming some degree of continuity in human civilisation, changes in architecture would normally take place far more frequently than the natural climatic changes that the Traveller also observes—' "I saw a richer green flow up the hillside, and remain there without any wintry intermission" ' (3)— let alone the species modifications that have produced the Eloi and Morlocks.

The order of the figures in 802,701 suggests a suitably entropic and cyclical 'running-down' number.[17] We can explain how Wells may have arrived at it, however, by the supposition that *The Time Machine* embodies not one future time scale but two. The two scales, those of historical time measured by the rise and fall of cultures and civilisations, and of biological time measured by the evolution and devolution of the species, are superimposed upon one another. To begin with, I suggest that Wells must have projected the invention of the Time Machine forward to the beginning of the twentieth century, so that the dinner party at Richmond may be imagined as taking place in 1901. (Analogously, the events of *The War of the Worlds*—which Wells began writing immediately after *The Time Machine* was published— also take place 'early in the twentieth century' (I,1).) He had already used the early twentieth century as baseline in *The Chronic Argonauts,* where the furthest point that we know to have been reached is the years 17,901-02: that is, a voyage of 16,000 years. In *The Time Machine* the world of the Eloi and Morlocks is located not 16,000 but 800,800 years after 1901—a significantly bifurcated number. The 800 years, enough to allow for the rise and fall of a civilisation or two in historical time, take us to 2701. To this figure Wells added a further 800,000 (that is, the best part of a million years) of evolutionary time. Supposing the number 802,701 to have been determined by a process such as this, its poetic appeal as a symbol of entropy would have ensured its adoption. Its significance . . . is that *The Time Machine* is plotted with both time scales, the evolutionary and the historiographic, in mind, though these are incompatible in certain respects. Without the 800-year time scale we cannot easily explain such crucial details as the survival of unmistakably classical forms of architecture into the far future, creating an essentially familiar landscape dominated by the Sphinx and surrounded by ruined palaces and gardens.

IV

The Sphinx and the decaying palaces are central to the symbolism of the story. The Sphinx is the symbol of foreboding and prophecy. The palaces and gardens suggest the landscape of neoclassical paintings and country houses, while alluding to a line of English utopian romances which would have been fresh in the minds of Wells's first readers: Richard Jefferies' *After London* (1885), W. H. Hudson's *A Crystal Age* (1887), and, above all, William Morris's *News from Nowhere* (1890). Morris's death in 1896 drew an affectionate if patronising acknowledgment from Wells in the *Saturday Review*— 'His dreamland was no futurity, but an illuminated past,' Wells wrote[18]—but a more wholehearted tribute, and one which hints at the strong connections between *News from Nowhere* and *The Time Machine,* appears at the beginning of *A Modern Utopia:*

> Were we free to have our untrammelled desire, I suppose we should follow Morris to his Nowhere, we should change the nature of man and the nature of things together; we should make the whole race wise, tolerant, noble, perfect . . . in a world as good in its essential nature, as ripe and sunny, as the world before the Fall. But that golden age, that perfect world, comes out into the possibilities of space and time. In space and

time the pervading Will to Live sustains for evermore a perpetuity of aggressions.[19]

Chapter Five of *The Time Machine* in the first edition is titled 'In the Golden Age.' In Wells's vision, the 'possibilities of space and time' are not unlimited. In space and time what appears to be a Morrisian utopia can only be fatally flawed; no earthly paradise of this sort is possible. The words Eloi and Morlocks signify angels and devils, and the two races, the products of natural selection, are held together in a predatory and symbiotic relationship—a 'perpetuity of aggressions' without which neither could flourish.

The Time Machine is both an explicitly anti-utopian text, and one which deliberately recalls *News from Nowhere* at a number of points. Morris's pastoral, idyllic society is centred on Hammersmith in West London, while the society of the Eloi is centred two or three miles upstream at Richmond. Both are placed in a lush parkland replacing the nineteenth-century industrial and suburban sprawl beside the River Thames. The Eloi, like the inhabitants of Nowhere and of most other contemporary socialist utopias, eat together in communal dining halls. William Guest, Morris's 'time traveller,' learns about the history of twentieth- and twenty-first century England from an old man at the British Museum, while Wells's Traveller journeys to the Palace of Green Porcelain, an abandoned museum of the arts and sciences modelled on the Crystal Palace and the South Kensington Museum.[20] On the evening of his first day with the Eloi, the Traveller climbs to a hilltop, surveys the countryside and exclaims ' "Communism" ' (4) to himself. The Communism he has in mind must be the pastoral utopia of Morris and Thomas More, rather than the revolutionary industrial society of Marx and Saint-Simon.

On two occasions the Time Traveller mocks at the artificiality of utopian narratives, as if to establish the superior authenticity of his own story. A ' "real traveller" ,' he protests, has no access to the vast amount of detail about buildings and social arrangements to be found in these books (5). He has ' "no convenient cicerone in the pattern of the Utopian books" '(5); instead, he has to work everything out for himself by trial and error. The emphasis is not on the exposition of a superior utopian philosophy but on the Traveller's own powers of observation and his habits of deductive and inductive reasoning. In terms of narrative structure as well as of evolutionary possibility, Wells claims to present a less self-indulgent, more realistic vision than Morris and his tradition could offer—as if the world of 802,701 were somehow less of a wish-fulfilment fantasy than Morris's Nowhere. The Time Traveller shows himself in the opening chapters to be a master of several sciences. He is a brilliant inventor and engineer, who is able by his own efforts to test the practical consequences of his theoretical discoveries in four-dimensional geometry.[21] He understands the principles of biology and psychology, and in studying the Eloi and Morlocks without the benefit of a guide he finds himself in the position of an anthropologist and ethnographer. Like an ethnographer in the field, he learns the language of his hosts and attempts to question them about 'taboo' topics such as the mysterious wells dotted across the countryside.' At each stage, but always aware that he may lack some crucial information, he attempts to theorise his findings.[22] In a characteristic Wellsian touch, he reverses the usual relations between a nineteenth-century anthropologist and his subject-matter, comparing his account of the Eloi to the '"tale of London which a negro, fresh from Central Africa, would take back to his tribe"'—though he adds that the negro would find plenty of willing informants, and in any case,' "think how narrow the gap between a negro and a white man of our own times, and how wide the interval between myself and these of the Golden Age!" '(5).

Admittedly, the Traveller often fails to live up to his ideal of scientific detachment. Unlike the utopias against which he is reacting, Wells's tale is a violent adventure story as well as something resembling a fieldwork report. The Traveller's behaviour in moments of crisis is typically hysterical, panic-stricken, negligent and, when he confronts the Morlocks, ruthless and desperate. In all this he embodies what Wells in *A Modern Utopia* was to call the Will to Live. Equally, the bloodthirstiness of Wells's anti-utopian realism invites the rejoinder that William Morris made in his review of Edward Bellamy's urban, collectivist utopia *Looking Backward:* 'The only safe way of reading a utopia is to consider it as the expression of the temperament of its author.'[23] *The Time Machine* debunks the utopian dream (a dream that would be reinstated in many of Wells's later works) en route to the discovery that the human species is engaged in a brutal struggle for survival which, in the long run, it cannot win—since all terrestrial life is doomed to extinction. Wells enables his Time Traveller to circumvent his own natural death—to cheat death, so to speak—only to inflict violent death on some of humanity's remote descendants, before going on to witness the collective death of the species and the environment that has sustained it.

In speaking of authorial temperament, Morris was invoking one of the principal categories of late nineteenth-century literary theory. He would have been aware of the widespread reaction against the claims to scientific objectivity made by the realist and naturalist movements; every work of art, it was argued, betrayed the imprint of its maker's personality.[24] To modern readers, once we have acknowledged the complexity and uniqueness of a text like *The Time Machine,* such appeals to personality and temperament have come to seem tautologous rather than illuminating. Nevertheless, we may say that when Wells's artistic imagination was at its most vivid, in the early scientific romances, it was also at its most violent. Ten years after the searing anti-utopianism of these books, he was ready to present his own, comparatively pacific vision of *A Modern Utopia.* As it happens, this apparent change of heart runs parallel with a dramatic improvement in his medical condition.

The cannibalistic Morlocks, the bloodsucking Martians and the bath of pain in which the vivisectionist Dr.

Moreau transforms wild animals into sham human beings were all conceived during the years in which Wells himself was often bedridden and spitting blood. Since tuberculosis had been (wrongly) diagnosed, it is significant that the first of the Eloi whom the Time Traveller meets face to face has the ' "hectic beauty" ' of a ' "consumptive" ' (3). The Traveller feels intensely for this society of doomed consumptives, and, once he is armed with a rusty iron bar, he does his best to wreak havoc among the species that lives off them. Wells suffered a final serious relapse in 1898, after the completion of his early romances. He moved to the south coast and commissioned the architect Charles Voysey to build him a house on the cliffs at Sandgate, designed to accommodate the wheelchair to which he soon expected to be confined. But this soon became irrelevant to the needs of its resilient and indeed hyperactive owner.

As his self-identification with the consumptive Eloi came to seem groundless, so did the calculations of planetary cooling reflected in both *The Time Machine* and *The War of the Worlds* lose their sway over contemporary scientific opinion. In *The Interpretation of Radium* (1908)—the book which led Wells to envisage the possibility of atomic warfare—Frederick Soddy wrote that 'Our outlook on the physical universe has been permanently altered. We are no longer the inhabitants of a universe slowly dying from the physical exhaustion of its energy, but of a universe which has in the internal energy of its material components the means to rejuvenate itself perennially over immense periods of time.'[25] Wells's switch shortly before the First World War from entropic pessimism to a position much closer to Soddy's thermonuclear optimism followed his discovery of the internal energy and potential for self-renewal of his own body, so that he was doubly removed from the outlook of the author of *The Time Machine.*

v

However anti-utopian its outcome, the Time Traveller's voyage confirms that a kind of utopia had been achieved in the 'nearer ages,' when, for example, disease had been stamped out, the processes of natural decay slowed if not halted, and population growth brought under control. Nature had been subjugated—for a time (4). There emerged the monumental civilisation whose buildings and landscapes still dominated the age of the Eloi and Morlocks. It is the Traveller's fate to chart the seemingly inevitable decline that followed once the human species had reached its zenith, or what the narrator terms the 'manhood of the race' (Epilogue). Pursuing Wells's deterministic hypothesis of a necessary downward curve in human fortunes, he is a symbolic figure embarking on the central quest of the scientific romance, the journey towards, and beyond, the 'last man.'[26]

The Time Traveller is a variant on the heroes of nineteenth-century Gothic and romantic melodrama. He arrives in the future in the midst of a thunderstorm, but when he discovers that the Morlocks have removed his

machine his elation gives way to a frenzy of despair. His violent emotionalism is reminiscent of *Frankenstein*— a literary model which Wells acknowledged[27]—and, since Mary Shelley's romance is subtitled *The Modern Prometheus* in allusion to Prometheus's legendary role as the creator of humanity, it is interesting that the Time Traveller has a still better claim to Promethean ancestry. The name Prometheus means 'forethought.'[28] Just as Prometheus was one of the Titans, the Traveller is identified with the race of 'giants' who preceded the Eloi and Morlocks and built the great palaces. The Eloi recognise his semi-divine status when they ask, at the moment of his arrival, if he has come from the sun (p. 39). He brings a box of matches with him, and when they run out he steals another box from the Palace of Green Porcelain. Prometheus stole fire from Zeus and brought it down to earth as a gift concealed in a stalk of fennel, to show his friendship for suffering humanity. But neither the frugivorous Eloi nor the half-blind Morlocks are fit recipients for the gift of fire. Future humanity has degenerated so much that the Traveller's matches are used only as purposeless toys, or in self-defence against the Morlocks. In the end his playing with fire causes reckless destruction including, it would seem, the death of Weena who is the one friend he has made in the new world.

Pursuing the imaginative logic of the Time Traveller's identification with Prometheus, we can come to a possible solution to the mystery of his disappearance on his second voyage. Can it be that—punished for his daring in setting out to discover the future in defiance of the gods—his fate is to remain bound to his machine, condemned to perpetual time-travelling just as Prometheus was bound to a rock and condemned to perpetual torture? All that we know is that the narrator's question, 'Will he ever return?' must be answered in the negative. A life of torture, too, was the fate of another famous figure of Greek legend, with whom the Traveller must also be identified: Oedipus, who answered the riddle of the Sphinx, which was the riddle of human life. What the Traveller instinctively fears as he looks into the Sphinx's sightless eyes is the death of humanity and his own inability to survive in a post-human world: ' "I might seem some old-world savage animal . . . a foul creature to be incontinently slain" ' (3). But he does not flinch from his self-appointed mission of traversing the valley of the shadow of death and reporting the Shape of Things to Come to the people of his own time: ' "It is how the thing shaped itself to me, and as that I give it to you" ' (10).

[1] Robert M. Philmus, 'The Logic of "Prophecy" in *The Time Machine*' in Bernard Bergonzi, ed., *H. G. Wells: A Collection of Critical Essays* (Englewood Cliffs, N.J.: Prentice-Hall, 1976), pp. 67-68.

[2] See, for example, *The Time Machine,* 3 and 4; 'How I Died,' p. 182.

[3] See Norman and Jeanne Mackenzie, *The Time Traveller: The Life of H. G. Wells* (London: Weidenfeld & Nicolson, 1973), especially pp. 24, 121-24.

4 Israel Zangwill, 'Without Prejudice,' reprinted in Patrick Parrinder, ed., *H. G. Wells: The Critical Heritage,* pp. 40-42.

5 Recent discussions of this question include those by Roslynn D. Haynes in *H. G. Wells: Discoverer of the Future* (London and Basingstoke: Macmillan, 1980), p. 58, and by Harry M. Geduld in *The Definitive 'Time Machine': A Critical Edition of H. G. Wells's Scientific Romance,* ed. Geduld (Bloomington and Indianapolis: Indiana University Press, 1987), pp. 96-97.

6 *The Definitive 'Time Machine,'* p. 118.

7 See ibid., p. 120, n.6.

8 Geoffrey West, *H. G. Wells: A Sketch for a Portrait,* pp. 288-94.

9 'The Chronic Argonauts' and the '*National Observer* Time Machine' are reprinted in *The Definitive 'Time Machine,'* pp. 135-52 and 154-74 respectively.

10 *The Definitive 'Time Machine,'* p. 145.

11 Henry Gee, 'What's our line?,' *London Review of Books,* 16:2 (27 January 1994), p. 19.

12 Geoffrey West, *H. G. Wells: A Sketch for a Portrait,* p. 61.

13 See H. G. Wells, 'Preface,' *The Time Machine* (New York: Random House, 1931), p. ix.

14 Ibid., pp. ix-x.

15 See H. G. Wells, *The Discovery of the Future,* p. 17 n.6.

16 'Fifty years per second,' because the dials of the Time Machine are calibrated in days, thousands of days, millions of days, and thousands of millions, and the Traveler reports that the 'thousands hand was sweeping round as fast as the seconds hands of a watch' (11). If one complete revolution of the 'thousands' dial represents a million days, he is covering a million days a minute, or 46 years per second—but it would still take more than a week to traverse 30 million years. We may, of course, find the references to the dials highly implausible, especially as the time to be measured is not linear. If the dials measure terrestrial days, one must wonder how they cope with or allow for the slowing down of the terrestrial day to the point where a single solar revolution 'seemed to stretch through centuries' (11)!

17 Cf. William Bellamy, *The Novels of Wells, Bennett and Galsworthy 1890-1910* (London: Routledge & Kegan Paul, 1971), p. 221.

18 H. G. Wells, 'The Well at the World's End,' in *H. G. Wells's Literary Criticism,* p. 112.

19 H. G. Wells, *A Modern Utopia* (London: Chapman & Hall, 1905), p. 7. Subsequent page references in text.

20 This was the nineteenth-century name for what are now four separate museums clustered together in South Kensington: the Geological Museum, the Natural History Museum, the Science Museum and the Victoria and Albert Museum. It is to this Museum (not the district of London in which it is located) to which the Time Traveller refers when he describes the Palace of Green Porcelain as a ' "later-day South Kensington" ' (8).

21 The Time Traveller's discovery is that the fourth dimension is *Time.* In this he anticipates Einstein. The widespread popular view of the fourth dimension in the late nineteenth century was of an extra dimension of space, corresponding to the 'spirit world' and frequented by ghosts. See Michio Kaku, *Hyperspace: A Scientific Odyssey Through Parallel Universes, Time Warps, and The Tenth Dimension* (New York and Oxford: Oxford University Press, 1994), especially p. 84.

22 On two occasions his explanations make use of the contemporary anthropological concept of ' "savage survivals" ' (4).

23 William Morris, 'Looking Backward,' *Commonweal* (22 June 1889), p. 194.

24 One influential expression of this view was Henry James's essay 'The Art of Fiction' (1884). See *Henry James, Selected Literary Criticism,* ed. Morris Shapira (London: Heinemann, 1963), p. 66.

25 Frederick Soddy, *The Interpretation of Radium: Being the Substance of Six Free Popular Experimental Lectures Delivered at the University of Glasgow,* 3rd edn. (London: Murray, 1912), p. 248.

26 On 'last man' fictions see Patrick Parrinder, 'From Mary Shelley to *The War of the Worlds;* The Thames Valley Catastrophe,' in David Seed, ed., *Anticipations: Essays on Early Science Fiction and Its Precursors* (Liverpool: Liverpool University Press, 1995), pp. 58-74.

27 See H. G. Wells, preface to *The Scientific Romances of H. G. Wells* (1933), reprinted in *H. G. Wells's Literary Criticism,* pp. 240, 241. Subsequent page references in text.

28 Robert Graves, *The Greek Myths* (Harmondsworth: Penguin, 1955), I, p. 148.

David Hughes

SOURCE: "A Queer Notion of Grants," in *Science-Fiction Studies,* Vol. 25, No. 75, July, 1998, pp. 271-84.

This paper[1] traces a previously neglected allusion in H. G. Wells's **The Time Machine** to a story by Grant Allen, "Pallinghrust Barrow." Allen's is a ghost story, which consequently may seem like an unlikely source of affinities with Wells's scientific romance, especially since the Time Traveller's allusion to it appears to be whimsical.

Yet "Pallinghurst Barrow" turns out to be a full-blown influence: thematic, structural, and generic. Its presence, too, is equally pervasive more than forty years later, in Wells's **The Croquet Player** (1937). Mediating between the latter and **The Time Machine,** "Pallinghurst Barrow" affords grounds for a new look at both.

Surprisingly, Allen has been virtually ignored in the criticism of Wells's science fiction. Although it was as late as 1934, Wells himself confessed to "a certain mental indebtedness" to "that . . . rather too much forgotten writer." He spoke mainly of the bad press ·both he and Allen had aroused for their novels of sexual protest, his own composed years after Allen died in 1899. But he also briefly recalled three of Allen's many initiatives that must have attracted him in Allen's lifetime and while he himself was composing and revising **The Time Machine.** These were Allen's "essays in natural history," his "aggressive Darwinism," and his "very pronounced streak of speculative originality" (**Experiment in Autobiography** 461).[2]

In **The Time Machine** itself, Allen is named precisely for speculative originality. The Time Traveller, not yet knowing of the Morlocks, makes out a string of grey figures in pre-dawn darkness and falls into a literary meditation—for him a rare response—the point of which is that for the moment it strikes him that what he sees might be of Allen's invention:

> "They must have been ghosts," I said; "I wonder whence they dated." For a queer notion of Grant Allen's came into my head, and amused me. If each generation die and leave ghosts, he argued, the world at last will get overcrowded with them. On that theory they would have grown innumerable some Eight Hundred Thousand years hence, and it was no great wonder to see four at once. But the jest was unsatisfying, and I was thinking of these figures all the morning. (5:60)

Today, Allen is forgotten, but some digging reveals here the plot-line of "Pallinghurst Barrow," which, it turns out, resembles that of **The Time Machine** sufficiently to purge any suspicion that the unknown Wells was merely dropping a then-well-known name. The story had appeared in the Christmas 1892 *Illustrated London News* and (minus illustrations) in Allen's *Ivan Greet's Masterpiece* the following May.[3] Wells's allusion to it first occurs in March 1895, in the *New Review* version of **The Time Machine.** If Wells ran across it in the *News,* the illustrations must surely have caught his eye, especially the apparition of a Stone Age chieftain and his cannibal swarm, deep in the barrow.

"Pallinghurst Barrow" is a story of some 7,000 words told in the third person. The following abstract includes, among other key quotations, those that specifically identify it (and to contemporary readers would manifestly advertise it) as Wells's source. It falls naturally into four parts.[4] In the opening, the susceptible Rudolph Reeve stands bemused in a solitary landscape. The date is Michaelmas Eve, close upon the autumnal equinox; the

scene is the Old Long Barrow near Pallinghurst Manor and the heath surrounding it; and the occasion is a peculiarly fiery sunset. Lingering long and ignoring his hostess's injunction to be punctual for dinner, Rudolph by and by discerns, "through no external sense, but by pure internal consciousness," something calling him into the barrow, "something . . . moving and living within." With an effort, he breaks away at top speed, hounded by disembodied voices—or so it seems—until at last he gains the safety of the manor gate, "trembling still from the profundity of his sense that someone was pursuing."

The second part of the story is a framing interlude at the dinner hour featuring stock characters discussing Rudolph's report of the eerie sunset in view of the local belief that "Every year on Michael's night / Pallinghurst barrow burneth bright." The yea-sayers are the hostess's twelve-year-old daughter, sighted with a child's eyes; the mandatory superstitious Scots buffoon, an expert, ironically, in electrical science and the Brush Arc Light;[5] and, foremost among them, the esoteric Buddhist, Mrs. Bruce, who "open[s] the floodgates of her torrent speech with triumphant vehemence," averring that "all the spirits of all that is, or was, or ever will be, people the universe everywhere, unseen, around us." Meanwhile, Rudolph's very modern hostess is volubly contemptuous; the archaeologist twinkles sceptically, with "scientific smile"; the materialist, Dr. Porter, observes "with covert levity" that "millions of ghosts of remote antiquity must swarm about the world"; and Miss Quackenboss, the pretty American, quips that "Europe must be chock full of them!" But Mrs. Bruce, carrying all before her, proclaims the spirits from all the ages to be numberless, although "each of us sees . . . those only he is adapted to seeing." The scene ends when Rudolph, retiring with a headache, takes more than double the medicinal dose of marijuana syrup prescribed by Dr. Porter and nods off over the adventures of Childe Roland in a volume of fairy tales.

Next, Rudolph awakens in the night to a lambent blue light on the heath. Spirit voices call. Drawn to the barrow, he paces three times round it "widershins" [sic] (counterclockwise), crying, "Open door! Open door! / And let me come in," for he recalls it was thus that Childe Roland gained the fairy realm. "[I]nstantly he was aware that the age had gone back upon its steps ten thousand years, as the sun went back upon the dial of Ahaz; he stood face to face with a remote antiquity. . . . [N]ew ideas, yet very old, undulated centrically towards him from the universal flat of time and space and matter and motion."[6] Stone Age wraiths force him below for a sacrifice to their cannibal king. "They were savages, yet they were ghosts. The two most terrible and dreaded foes of civilized experience seemed combined at once in them." Rudolph escapes the hacking flint blades that would offer him up for the blood feast only when a new spirit appears, dressed unexpectedly in 16th-century garb, and advises him: "Show them iron!" At that, he brandishes his pocket-knife, the ghosts quail before it, and escaping the crypt, he passes out on the heath.

Finally, safely in bed back at the manse, he sends the next morning for his hostess's small daughter. When he had wakened in the night, she was at her bedroom window and had pointed him silently towards the barrow; and now she remembers and whispers in his ear a rhyme taught her by an old gypsy woman:

> Pallinghurst Barrow—Pallinghurst Barrow!
> Every year one heart thou'lt harrow!
> Pallinghurst ring—Pallinghurst ring!
> A bloody man is thy ghostly king.
> Men's bones he breaks, and sucks their marrow,
> In Pallinghurst ring on Pallinghurst Barrow.

Thus, it would seem to be Mrs. Bruce's "torrent speech" which the Time Traveller recalls (a wide search of Allen's writings reveals no other candidate), and in accord with Wells's later sweeping admission of a "mental indebtedness" to Allen, even the above brief synopsis is enough to suggest that the entire curiously mutated ghost story which is "Pallinghurst Barrow" taught Wells a good deal.

Darko Suvin finds in *The Time Machine* the structural and thematic model of all later Anglophone science fiction. If so, "Pallinghurst Barrow" is a kind of first sketch. The subject of both stories is "dominant existence or power" as structurally conveyed, with irony, by means of a Darwinian traverse of scenes and actions that invert accepted hierarchical relationships, especially the fundamental relationship of human mastery to time ("Grammar" 110).[7] Thus, in Wells's overall scheme, the biological and physical trajectory of the earth is an arc now near its apex, and the far slope visits the cannibalism of our ancestors on our progeny and ends at last in the nonexistence that was and will be absolute (prefigured by the solar eclipse of the year 30 million).

Allen is not philosophically forthright, but his description of the Hampshire heath functions like Darwin's metaphor of "the tangled bank" as a microcosm of nature's scheme—but without Darwin's sense of gradual ennoblement.[8] The barrow Rudolph sits on is "covered close with short sward of subterranean clover, that curious, cunning plant that buries its own seeds by automatic action," and close by, "innumerable plants of sundew spread their murderous rosettes of sticky red leaves . . . to catch and roll round the struggling insects." The sundew, of course, is notable for inverted predation (it also grows where Wells's Angel of Art falls to earth in *The Wonderful Visit*[9]), and the self-seeding clover's automatic survival imports the same for the savagery of the race buried beneath it.

Like the Social Darwinists, Wells and Allen conjugate evolutionary and historical time together. For that purpose, cannibalism, as a time-collapser, is made to order. It was thought that the barrow people had been black.[10] Thus, the "Pallinghurst" ghosts, "tawny-skinned"—and inky and prognathous in the *News* illustrations—to Allen's readers must have been indistinguishable from the living cannibal "natives" in whom they recognized the white man's peril. Allen's implicit straddling of space and time suggests ongoing reciprocities and transpositions

between savagery and civilization. In Wells, of course, the dichotomy is mapped out along lines of class, not race, but the predatory Morlocks and their helpless Eloi cousins are reciprocally interlocked. Besides, the basic story-line of both Allen and Wells simply pits a Victorian Englishman against his cannibal ancestry/progeny.

Cannibalism, class-based or race-based, connotes at once virility and automatism in the predator, and automatism and effeteness in the prey. The middle term is automatism. At the same time, the prevailing view in cosmology likened the course of the solar system to the running down of a clock,[11] while the triumphs of the Victorian machine civilization rested upon putting nature's laws to work. Accordingly, Wells invented the Time Machine. The heath gives way to a house in Richmond (a "lung" of industrial London), and the barrow-spell gives way to a machine-to-machine survey and exposition of time's progress, biological and astrophysical. By the end, on the beach of the year 30 million, even the bare idea of "tense" is dissolved into a predestinate "universe rigid"; and the Morlock-Eloi automatism—with its inverted Spencerianism and cruel travesty of Marx's laborers as grave-diggers of the bourgeoisie—is merely a part of the mandated decline. Moreover, the Time Machine as vehicle doubles as narrative device which looks back to the future, and this creates the sense of the unitary coherence of all time that lends the book its special sense of absolute closure. True, a possibility remains that telling the Morlock-Eloi story may alter it. It may turn out to be a lie, assuming—perhaps improbably—that its readers do not share the apathy of the Time Traveller's original audience.[12]

To "scope out" civilization's "bragging rights" against a Darwinian backdrop is a ready ticket to thematic irony (which is discussed later in Wells). Rudolph is a sort of Eloi. As the sun drops at the equinox, he might be, as it were, another Time Traveller at the eclipse of the year 30 million[13]—a spokesman for the irony of fate—the irony of time's inevitable conquest of life. But to Rudolph, nature is a mode of feeling (an approach lifted from Keats). Drinking in "the exquisite flush of the dying reflections from the dying sun upon the dying heather, . . . redder and fiercer than anything he ever remembered to have seen since the famous year of the Krakatoa sunsets," he wonders, "with all the artistic pleasure of a poet or a painter," "why death is always so much more beautiful, so much more poetical, so much calmer than life." Meantime, in the midst of these ornamental responses to Krakatoa, the voice of Allen, science journalist, calls attention to the murderous sundew and cunning clover.

The stories also employ structural irony (Allen's in the end is self-cancelling), largely through factoring technology into plot, whether as servant or master. In Wells, the Time Traveller means to head off the Morlocks with the technological marvel of matches, but the fire gets out of hand and pursues him; a second fire disastrously goes out as he dozes.[14] In Allen, the technological convenience is the pocket knife. It works perfectly: the specters quail. A sort of irony obtains in that a weapon trivial in itself, but a synecdoche for the Age of Steel, easily dispels the seeming menace of the Stone Age. The specters fall away, as specters do, confronted by a talisman. The ironies cancel out. Allen has been building what seems today to be a science-fiction predicament to be carried through on its own terms, but then he dodges the issue by saying suddenly, "Well, this is a ghost story."

It is not certain when Allen appeared on Wells's horizon. References by Wells early and late suggest it was in the 1880s.[15] Allen was then a multifarious, highly visible purveyor of popular science and fiction whose evolutionary and philosophical orientation and occasional artistic innovativeness would attract Wells. His stories, novels, and natural science essays appeared in *Belgravia,* the *Cornhill, Longman's,* and later *Tit-Bits* (taking a prize of £1000) and the *Strand;* his more ambitious pieces appeared in the *Contemporary Review* and the *Fortnightly Review;* and he was professionally associated with the *St. James's Gazette* and the *Pall Mall Gazette,* to both of which Wells later contributed. Also, Allen was a Darwinian (author of a perceptive Darwin biography); a Fabian; a religious and sexual free-thinker escaped from pious (Catholic) environs; an outsider (Canadian-born and a past-resident of the United States, France, and the West Indies); and, although an Oxford-trained classicist, also a self-taught botanist, psychologist, and physicist.[16] In sum, he was a facile popularizer. But already by 1888, George Bernard Shaw, in reviewing *The Devil's Die,* shrewdly observed Allen's crypto-thematic allegiance in this novel to the "Spencer-Darwin-Tyndall culture" and its teaching that "struggle for existence" is a "vagary of the energy stored in an earth predestined to . . . tumbl[e] back [into the sun]" (3).[17]

Wells must have noticed Allen's gift of exploiting his factual and speculative science essays in fictional counterparts. Among the best is "Pallinghurst Barrow." Not only is it grounded in the concept of a Stone Age Britain, the anthropology, the folklore studies, and the botany that Allen tirelessly expounded in the 1880s (in essays like "Chippers of Flint," "Cauld Iron," "Who Were the Fairies?" and "Concerning Clover"[18]), but its plot is inscribed already in his 1885 archaeological essay, "Ogbury Barrows." At a dig near Stonehenge, Allen was in on the discovery of "what was once a living cannibal king of the stone age in Britain," a skeleton surrounded by bones of wives and slaves roasted and eaten at the interment. Allen describes the excavation factually, then glides into a "witnessing" of the old bloody rites, which passed, he says, "like a vision before my mind's eye" (519). Here is a harbinger of *fin-de-siècle* fascination with humanity's ancestral savagery. Years before Huxley's "Evolution and Ethics" and Max Nordau's popularizing of Cesare Lombroso's theories of "degeneration," Allen raises the specter of cannibal atavism, later manifested in such diverse fictional modes and imaginative powers as are represented by "Pallinghurst Barrow" itself, *The Time Machine, Dracula,* and *Heart of Darkness.*[19]

Rudolph feels what Allen felt at Ogbury. In his magnum opus, *The Evolution of the Idea of God* (1897)—twice reviewed by Wells, favorably, then less so[20]—Allen argues in the chapter "The Life of the Dead" (earlier, "Immortality and Resurrection" [1893]) that tumuli were meant to keep the dead down, because "it was far less the spirit than the actual corpse itself that early men . . . were really afraid of" (59; "Immortality" 322). Thus, one may think of Rudolph's flight as a direct survival of the old barrow-makers' fear of their own dead in their own time, now colonizing the present. Similarly, the fear of the Eloi for the Morlocks is the fear of the Victorian bourgeoisie that the proletariat will "rise." Is there a hint that neither social nor genetic transmission explains the Eloi's fear? We are told that the Eloi's progenitors forced workers underground and some "starve[d]" or "suffocated for arrears [in rent]" (5:63). But if (as discussed above, in the context of Wells's notion of "the uni-verse rigid") "tense" is an empty category, then the Morlocks *are* the entombed workers, and *The Time Machine* is (vestigially) a ghost story.

Forty years later, Allen turns up in Wells's *The Croquet Player.* In both genre and theme, he is central to this work, which, by virtue of fantastically extending his "queer notion," is a ghost story to end ghost stories. In terms of genre, if ghost-longevity is a whimsy to the Time Traveller, in his counterpart, Dr. Finchatton, it seems risible in the telling but is really terrifying; and as to theme, if *The Time Machine* extends Allen's "notion" that the past cycles into the present practically to the end of time, *The Croquet Player* extends it practically to the beginning of time. Admittedly, Allen is never cited, and the case for the statements just made rests squarely on a single passage which is a remarkable reprise and extension of the words of Allen's Mrs. Bruce. Finchatton is talking to the narrator of the book, George Frobisher, in reference to the obsessive fear that a dream has roused in him, itself associated with a palaeolithic skull dug up in the fens:

> It's bad enough to be haunted by Georgian ghosts, Stuart ghosts, Elizabethan ghosts, ghosts in armor and ghosts in chains. Yet anyhow one has a sort of fellow feeling for them. . . . But souls of a tribe of ape men might be . . . Grisly ghosts. . . . And . . . if cave men, why not apes? Suppose all our ancestors rose against us! Reptiles, fish, amoebae! The idea was so fantastic that . . . I tried to laugh. . . . *I couldn't laugh.* . . . (2:45)

There are other indications of Allen's tracks. Besides Finchatton, others also reportedly believe that all the inhabitants of Cainsmarsh, where he practices, are threatened (in the words of a local vicar) by "something colossally evil" *"underground"* and (in the words of a local archaeologist) by "resurrected savageries" "thrusting" from a "real past" that "our grandfathers never . . . suspected" (2:40, 3:64)—the past opened by Darwin. But in itself the passage above is good presumptive evidence for *The Time Machine's* affinity to the ghost-story genre simply because its origin is in Allen's ghost story, it is transmitted by Wells through *The Time Machine,* and it winds up in this ghost story later written by Wells himself.

It remains to consider some uses of the structural device of framing. In all three works, the protagonist's fantastic tale when it reaches the reader includes the presence of a fictive audience. In general, this framing enables Allen to *subvert* a reader's willing suspension of disbelief, Wells in 1895 to *assist* it, and Wells in 1937 to *pretend* to play this game. That is, in *The Croquet Player* the real aim is to rouse belief of a nonliterary order, leading to action or at least to a disposition towards it. It is only the first step to secure Finchatton's credibility and with it a suspension of disbelief. Finchatton is a sane man who has proved it by engaging a psychiatrist on account of a mental malaise. His seriousness contrasts with the idle snobbery of Frobisher, who takes him up exactly as he had Edgar Allan Poe in boyhood: "it is just because they *are* impossible that I like impossible stories" (3:52).

Then Finchatton's psychiatrist, Dr. Norbert, appears, dismisses Finchatton, takes over (actually as Wells's *raisonneur*), and informs Frobisher that "Cainsmarsh" is a mental construct his client has built up out of the little beastlinesses a doctor suffers in the fens, a construct which is a homeopathic medicine against the overwhelming savageries reported by press and radio, and, as such, the beginning of resistance. Once, says Norbert, we dwelt in "a magic sphere" (3:63), but now "resurrected savageries" "break the Frame of the Present" (2:40, 3:64, 4:88),[21] and we must counter "endemic panic," becoming "giant-minded" (3:56, 65, 4:85, 92, 97) and transcending the Homo sapiens who is still the "fearing, snarling, fighting beast he was a hundred thousand years ago." "These are no metaphors, Sir" (4:89). Frobisher merely records that he heard all this, agreed it might well be "the sunset of civilization" (that solar image again), and left to see his aunt for their usual game "at half-past twelve . . ." (4:98). The book ends so. The snob, as he promised at the beginning, has reported it all from "the background, so to speak—or 'frame' perhaps is better . . ." (1:16). Indeed, the Frobisher-frame—a seaside spa—is exactly the delusory "Frame of the Present" which "resurrected savageries" are breaking, and—if Wells is successful—the reader is disaffected and willingly trades the pleasure expected from esthetic closure for the courage to attack the forces of dissolution beyond the covers of the book.

In "Pallinghurst Barrow," the frame works the other way—as a means of keeping its contents in check. There might be serious irony, for example, in sandwiching the framing function of Mrs. Bouverie-Barton's appointed dinner hour between encounters with cannibals. But the sting is lost amid the trivializing facetiousness of the guests. Such linguistic belittling of a fictional "novum" has been remarked by Suvin as "characteristic for English class snobbery, and as such not without importance for Victorian SF" in insinuating that the status quo is inviolate in the face of whatever fictional novelty (*Victorian* 308).[22] It need hardly be added that inevitably Allen belittles his "novum"—the bare idea of Darwin in a ghost story is an oxymoron—because the ending of his story must renounce the opening: the cannibals must be figments and not the true Darwinian revenants they appeared

for a while to be. Is this a case of artistic timidity or of the demands of Grub Street? Both, no doubt. Soon it would be Wells negotiating these tensions and equivocations.

"Pallinghurst Barrow" in the third person and *The Time Machine* in the first person tell the same archetypal tale. A slightly aberrant protagonist enters a pastoral country in thrall to a mysterious, baleful subterranean power, descends against it, engages in mortal combat, and returns to tell the tale. But the news of the exploit, or even the possibility of it, is greeted by the stay-at-homes with frivolous witticism. Allen's Mrs. Bouverie-Barton ("modern, and disbelieved in everything"), Dr. Porter ("materialist"), and Professor Spence ("scientific smile") are rivalled and emulated by Wells's Psychologist, Doctor, Journalist, and Editor. But there the similarities end. Not only do Allen's bantering characters neutralize each other, not only do Rudolph's neuralgic headaches and poetic transports deprive him of credibility, not only does he need no enemies when his allies are a twelve-year-old, a superstitious Scot, and an esoteric Buddhist; the trouble is that Rudolph never himself speaks his piece. Even his barrow fight looks stagy as Allen omnisciently directs it. But though he is said to be "too clever to be believed" (1:37), the Time Traveller tells his own story, insisting on no interruptions, and at that, the reader falls into his hands.

Also, the reader finds Wells's story and frame—unlike Allen's—creating a "complementarity" of views that complete each other (often ironically).[23] As noted earlier, the after-dinner assemblage of the book's opening paragraph, quizzical but "gracefully free of the trammels of precision," will strike one in hindsight as Eloi-in-gestation, "embraced and caressed" by easy chairs of the Time Traveller's invention. Yet to this same audience, the Time Traveller interrupts himself towards the end of his narrative to pose a question. Taking the opposite tack from the thundering Dr. Norbert's "these are no metaphors, Sir," he proposes a figurative approach. "Take [what I have told you] as a lie—or a prophecy—," he says, and "my assertion of its truth as a mere stroke of art to enhance its interest. And taking it as a story, what do you think of it?" (12:87). He appeals to the esthetic sense, but if his audience were alert enough to exercise it, they must see the reciprocity between themselves and the prey of "802,701." This reflectiveness is rare in the Time Traveller, too. It is more in his character to act out what he thinks of his story by disappearing into time again, as if to find an end to a tale he regards as unfinished. The "what do you think of it?" is Wells's question, rousing the reader to weigh the nearly concluded narrative (and its frame) metaphorically.

The Time Traveller is not immune to irony himself, having one foot in the frame and another in the tale, but the ironies are integral to his role of discovery. He loves a machine like the Morlocks and unwittingly brings them to mind with his exclamation: "What a treat it is to stick a fork into meat again!" (2:40). Yet he would not have adventured had he been otherwise. Likewise, the "atrocious folly" (9:77) of the fire he sets that roars after him and Weena correlates with the "more than a touch of whim" (1:37) that rushed him unprepared into kingdom come in the first place, with real consequences for himself and its inhabitants. His technological mastery is essential yet eludes his control, whether in the fires he lights, the Time Machine stolen by the Morlocks, or his haphazard journey itself.

Yet such accidents may be taken as signs of indeterminacy. Allen's story involves the closed book of the past, but the present may be redeemable by the future. In Wells's Epilogue, Hillyer (the frame narrator) observes that "long before the Time Machine was made," it was clear its inventor saw "in the growing pile of civilisation only a foolish heaping that must inevitably fall back upon and destroy its makers in the end" (90). But, in the absence of the Time Traveller, now departed again on his machine, he adds: "If that is so, it remains for us to live as though it were not so" (90). The tenor of this injunction in relation to the Time Traveller and his tale is open to question, as is Wells's view of it, but a reasonable interpretation is that to live and act as though one is self-determined is to evolve an open future. The sun's death is determinate, but 802,701 may not be. It may lie open to thought, experience, action, questioning, and, in sum, to the human will.

It is curious that **The Time Machine** is the product of basic tensions in the scientific outlook yet displays elements of the ghost story. Perhaps the case of **The Croquet Player** helps, somewhat inversely, to clarify what Wells was up to. To Frobisher, the tag he gives Finchatton's tale of "a sort of ghost story" (1:9) signifies titillation. But the reader discovers a book made not only to void the Frobisher mentality but the "literary" mentality altogether. At the time of its publication, Wells was advocating what he called the "directed thought" of organized science—positivistic thought—as against the older mode he called "experience-checked imagining."[24] That is, his idea of science, in or out of fiction, had done an about-face. "Experience-checked imagining" is as good a description as any of one's exploratory responses (often as a teenager) on first reading Wells's works of the 1890s. Quite the opposite is the effect of **The Croquet Player**'s mission to excise the "cave man who is over us, who is in us, who is indeed *us*" (4:91). In the early Wells, it is a long shot if the cave man who is *us* can transcend himself, though science may furnish the tools.

Yet one must wonder still what Wells found congenial in a literary form so antithetical to open inquiry as, of all others, the ghost story; and "Pallinghurst Barrow" is just that, ancillary Darwinism notwithstanding. If nothing else, its periodical publication at Christmas proves its credentials. Allen's knowledge of science (except in the laboratory) was more than equal to Wells's,[25] but, hack as he was, when he did attempt serious scientific speculation (nonfictional, until well after "Pallinghurst Barrow"), he earned little or nothing and was lucky if he was reviewed less condescendingly than, for example, by the mathematician Karl Pearson on *force and Energy* (1888),

who ended with instructions to "do penance at once by writing us a blood-curdling Christmas ghost story" (422). A conventional sensationalism was Allen's bread and cheese.

But again, why the early Wells's spiritualistic elements—ghosts, invisibility, out-of-body and stolen-body occurrences, and such? The answers are several, none wholly satisfying. Ghosts were a sure-fire commodity. For instance, in 1891 W. T. Stead, a true believer, advertised in the *Review of Reviews,* "Wanted, A Census of Ghosts!," and a flood of testimonials filled his Christmas number of 100,000 copies, "Real Ghost Stories," and a New Year's sequel, "More Ghost Stories."[26] Wells's artistic imagination in any case was pliant and opportunistic. At about the time of final revision of **The Time Machine,** he attacked the methods, results, membership, and reading public of the Psychical Research Society in the influential pages of *Nature* (121). Yet in 1897, asked if he kept up on science, he astonished the reporter when he admitted that he never missed a Psychical Research Society paper and regretted "sneering" in "indiscreeter days"— though he slyly added that he read for the "light . . . thrown on those mental operations that occur beneath the threshold of consciousness" (Anonymous, *Supplement to Pearson's Weekly* ii). A certain waywardness lights up **The Time Machine.** On behalf of sceptical inquiry, the assemblage in Richmond expects a trick, like last year's Christmas ghost (1:37), and the psychologist, prompted by the Time Traveller, gives the nod to "presentation below the threshold" (1:36-37). But on behalf of belief, Hillyer glimpses a "ghostly . . . transparent . . . phantasm" slipping (the Time Traveller says) "like a vapour through the interstices of intervening substances" (12:89, 2:43), and in 802,701 the Time Traveller *is* a ghost—a ghost of the present—and would be that only but for the "dimensional" (science-fictional) logic he earlier affirmed that requires him to rematerialize whenever the machine stops (thereby involuntarily becoming an agent of change).

It is more than 20 years since Darko Suvin observed of the devolutionary themes of **The Time Machine** and **The Croquet Player** that "This inversion of the Darwiman arrow of time seems to have been one of Wells's basic intellectual, morphological, and visionary discoveries" ("Grammar" 112). The perception is just. The devolutionary theme was not Wells's singular fictive discovery, but he made it his own by working out its thematic, formal, and structural potentialities over decades. In contrast, "Pallinghurst Barrow" presented itself and was published as a pure and simple "blood-curdling ghost story." Two final facts in evidence are therefore worth citing to put Wells's debt to Allen beyond doubt. First, **The Time Machine** ends on the note that perhaps the Time Traveller (like Rudolph) was "swept back into the past, and fell among the blood-drinking hairy savages of the Age of Unpolished Stone." But Wells's definitive acknowledgment went by post. On June 11, 1895, Allen wrote (some weeks before they first met) thanking Wells for "a presentation example" of **The Time Machine.** He praised "its brilliant whimsicality, and its underlying philosophic import" (except its pessimism: "my own faith in the future is robust"), and promised, if he had a chance to review it, to "note its originality and freshness." In replying, Wells wrote: "I believe that this field of scientific romance with a philosophical element which I am trying to cultivate, belongs properly to you. Hence the book I sent."[27] Hence, too, in that book, it is a pure literary tribute when Wells, at a moment of potential danger to the Time Traveller, causes him to recall a purely literary allusion and specify its author by name. It powerfully testifies to Allen's presence at large. Moreover, it was no covert avowal recognizable by Allen only. Appearing in the *Illustrated London News*, "Pallinghurst Barrow" joined stories over the years by Rider Haggard, Henry James, Marie Corelli, Wilkie Collins, and Robert Louis Stevenson. Wells expected a wide sampling of his readers to remember Allen's story and to appreciate how closely it bore upon his own.

NOTES

[1] I gave the original version of this paper in London for the 1995 centennial of the *The Time Machine*. It is now fundamentally revised in the light of Robert M. Philmus's "Revisi(tati)ons of *The Time Machine*" (forthcoming in *English Literature in Transition*, Aug. 1998), a groundbreaking study of formal connections of *The Time Machine* to the ghost-story genre.

[2] John Batchelor (in *H. G. Wells* [Cambridge: Cambridge UP, 1985] 80-82) links Wells's novels of sexual emancipation (e.g., *In the Days of the Comet, Ann Veronica*) thematically to Allen's *Woman Who Did* (1895). Sweeping claims of plagiarism made by Ingvald Raknem (in *H. G. Wells and his Critics* [London: George Allen & Unwin, 1962] 417-19) are suspect at best, and his charge that *The Wonderful Visit* pirates Allen's *The British Barbarians* is false. The Wells-Allen correspondence blows this canard to bits (see my "H. G. Wells and the Charge of Plagiarism," *Nineteenth Century Fiction* 21[1966]: 85-89); but it still crops up, for example in *The Critical Response to H. G. Wells*, ed. William J. Scheick (Westport, CT: Greenwood, 1995) 23.

[3] The two texts are identical. Others—e.g., in *The Mammoth Book of Victorian and Edwardian Ghost Stories* (ed. Richard Dalby [NY: Carroll & Graf, 1995] 291-307)—may be abridged or altered. Since the story is short, I cite it without page references.

[4] Allen himself assigns the story five parts by dividing the dinner interlude in two.

[5] Charles F. Brush (1849-1929) invented "Brush lights" (popularly so called), distributed after 1891 by General Electric. Cf. *National Cyclopaedia of American Biography*, vol. 21.

[6] See 2 Kings 20:11 and Isa. 38:8. In the latter, the shadow of the sun falls back "ten steps on the dial of Ahaz," signifying Ahaz's revival of barbaric rites of human sacrifice.

[7] I follow Suvin's scheme of predator-prey hierarchies. Also useful is Robert M. Philmus's "The Logic of Prophecy in *The Time Machine*," in *H. G. Wells: A Collection of Critical Essays*, ed. Bernard Bergonzi (Englewood Cliffs, NJ: Prentice-Hall, 1976) 56-68.

[8] Suvin ("Grammar," 112 n.5) lists critical literature on the "excelsior" thrust of Darwin's and T. H. Huxley's seriations evolving from most humble to most advanced life.

[9] Wells writes: "There is a place on the moor where the black water shines among the succulent moss, and the hairy sundew, eater of careless insects, spreads its redstained hungry hands to the God who gives his creatures—one to feed another" (*The Wonderful Visit* [London: J. M. Dent & Co., 1896] 13).

[10] As Allen elsewhere put it: "we of nineteenth-century England may be largely or even exclusively descended from the crouching, dark-skinned, Australian-like savages who hunted the mammoth beside the banks of some primeval and forgotten Thames . . ." (*Common Sense Science* [Boston: Lothrop & Company, 1886] 168-69).

[11] On Victorian science's view of the solar system as a clock running down, see my "The Garden in Wells's Early Science Fiction," in *H. G. Wells and Modern Science Fiction*, ed. Darko Suvin and Robert M. Philmus (Lewisburg, PA: Bucknell UP; London: Associated University Presses, 1977) 51 and 68n.

[12] On Wells's "The Universe Rigid" (1893), see Philmus and Hughes, 5-6. The discussion includes "The Rediscovery of the Unique" (1893) and how the "complementarity" of the two essays is reflected in *The Time Machine*, giving it some sense of an open future.

[13] In a timescape of Thomas Hardy's, both Allen and Wells are anticipated. In *A Pair of Blue Eyes*, as a geologist clings for his life to a sea-cliff, "time closed up like a fan," "till the lifetime scenes of the fossil[s] confronting him were a present and modern condition of things." Quoted by Leo Justin Henkin, *Darwinism in the English Novel, 1860-1910: The Impact of Evolution on Victorian Fiction* (NY: Corporate Press, 1940) 226.

[14] On matches as representing technology, see John Huntington, *The Logic of Fantasy: H. G. Wells and Science Fiction* (NY: Columbia UP, 1982) 75-78.

[15] H. G. Wells, *Anticipations* (NY: Harper & Brothers, 1901) 43; *Experiment in Autobiography*, 154.

[16] See Edward Clodd's *Grant Allen: A Memoir (with a Bibliography)*. London: Grant Richards, 1900.

[17] This unsigned review is attributed to Shaw by Dan H. Laurence, *Bernard Shaw: A Bibliography* (Oxford: Clarendon Press, 1983, Vol. 2) 548.

[18] "Chippers of Flint," *Cornhill Magazine* (Feb. 1880): 189-200; "Who Were the Fairies?" *ibid.* (Mar. 1881):

335-48; "Cauld Iron," *ibid.* (Nov. 1892): 520-30; "Concerning Clover," *Popular Science Monthly* (Nov. 1885): 73-84.

[19] See Ernest Fontana, "Lombroso's Criminal Man and Stoker's *Dracula,*" in *Dracula: The Vampire and the Critics,* ed. Margaret L. Carter (Ann Arbor: UMI Research Press, 1988) 59-65; and Ian Watt, *"Heart of Darkness* and Nineteenth Century Thought," in *Joseph Conrad's Heart of Darkness,* ed. Peter Angst (NY: Chelsea House, 1987) 77-89.

[20] Wells reviewed Allen at least six times in the 1890s: 1) "An Unemancipated Woman," *Pall Mall Gazette* (20 Feb. 1895): 4 (on *The Woman Who Did;* unsigned, my attribution); 2) "The Woman Who Did," *Saturday Review* (9 Mar. 1895): 319-20 (unsigned; excerpted in *Experiment in Autobiography,* 463-65); 3) "Mr. Grant Allen's New Novel," *Saturday Review* (14 Dec. 1895): 785-86 (on *The British Barbarians,* unsigned), rpt. in *H. G. Wells's Literary Criticism,* ed. Patrick Parrinder and Robert M. Philmus [Sussex: Harvester; N.J.: Barnes & Noble, 1980] 59-62; 4) "Fiction," *Saturday Review* (21 November 1896): 552 (on *A Splendid Sin,* unsigned, attributed by Robert M. Philmus in "Wells as Literary Critic for the *Saturday Review,*" *SFS* 4.2 (July 1977): 166-93; 5) "The Idea of God," *Daily Mail* (27 Nov. 1897) (on *The Evolution of the Idea of God,* signed); 6) "On Comparative Theology," *Saturday Review* (12 Feb. 1898): 211-23 (on *The Evolution of the Idea of God,* signed), rpt. in Philmus and Hughes, 40-46.

[21] In *Experiment in Autobiography,* Wells says, "I suppose for a time [20 years earlier] I was the outstanding instance among writers of fiction in English of the frame getting into the picture" (416). In *The Croquet Player,* however, the picture breaks the frame.

[22] Suvin also quotes Wells's late "Fiction about the Future" (1938) to the same effect: a timid science-fiction author will "pretend that all along he was only making fun" (305). Invaluable though he is on Victorian science-fiction novels, authors, and readers, including Allen's, Suvin hardly touches short stories.

[23] "Complementarity" is a term borrowed from physics, according to which "different approaches ('standpoints' in Wells's terminology) are necessary to reveal all aspects of phenomena and . . . the results of these experimental approaches are 'complementary' rather than mutually exclusive" (Philmus and Hughes, 6). The term may relate to interactions both between Wells's frame and tale and between the determinacy of the year 30 million and the possible indeterminacy of the year 802, 701. (The critical coinage is Philmus's, and he develops it further in "Revisions of the Future: *The Time Machine,*" *Journal of General Education* [Spring 1976]: 23-30.)

[24] Huntington in *The Logic of Fantasy* paraphrases Wells in *The Work, Wealth and Happiness of Mankind* (1931): "'Undirected thought' is 'imaginative play' checked by

experience and thus close to but different from mere dreaming. 'Directed thought' is purposeful and conscious; it arrives at conclusions; it leads to actions and exclusions" (2). For the opposing bent of the early Wells, see him on "inductive reading" in "Popularising Science" (1894), quoted in part in Philmus and Hughes, 3.

[25] Allen's output probably surpassed Wells's in science popularizing (even with the late, collaborative *Science of Life*), and Allen kept more abreast of the literature. Wells, for example, "resisted August Weismann's theory of germ plasm when it first came to his attention late in 1894" (Philmus and Hughes, 9), and *The Time Machine* still reflects Lamarck's view of response to environment as destiny; but Allen, reviewing Weismann in 1890 ("Science," *Academy,* Feb. 1, 83), already accepted the theory of the immortality of the germ plasm.

[26] *Review of Reviews* (Sept., Oct., Dec. 1891): 257, 347, 574.

[27] Undated reply to Allen's letter of June 11 (quoted further in Philmus and Hughes, 89). Wells's first review of *The Woman Who Did* was tolerant; the later review cited here is harsh. See notes 2 and 20.

WORKS CITED

Allen, Grant. *The Evolution of the Idea of God: An Inquiry into the Origins of Religion.* NY: Henry Holt, 1897.

———. "Immortality and Resurrection." *Fortnightly Review* (Sept. 1893): 317-28.

———. "Ogbury Barrows." *Cornhill Magazine* (Nov. 1885): 512-22.

———. "Pallinghurst Barrow." *Illustrated London News* (Christmas Number, 1892): 12-18.

———. "Pallinghurst Barrow." *Ivan Greet's Masterpiece, Etc.* London: Chatto & Windus, 1893. 67-89.

Anonymous. "The Story of a Story, or, How the Invisible Man Was Created." *Supplement to Pearson's Weekly* (20 Nov. 1897): ii.

Philmus, Robert M., & David Y. Hughes, eds. *H. G. Wells: Early Writings in Science and Science Fiction.* Berkeley: University of California Press, 1975.

Pearson, Karl. "Science." *Academy* (29 Dec. 1888): 421-22.

Shaw, George Bernard. "Mr. Grant Allen's New Novel." *Pall Mall Gazette* (24 April 1888): 3.

Suvin, Darko. *Victorian Science Fiction in the UK: The Discourses of Knowledge and of Power.* Boston: G.K. Hall, 1983.

———. "A Grammar of Form and a Criticism of Fact: *The Time Machine* as a Structural Model for Science

Fiction." In *H. G. Wells and Modern Science Fiction,* eds. Darko Suvin & Robert M. Philmus. Lewisburg, PA: Bucknell UP, 1977. 90-115.

Wells, H. G. *The Croquet Player.* NY: Viking Press, 1937.

———. *Experiment in Autobiography.* NY: Macmillan, 1934.

———. "The Peculiarities of Psychical Research." *Nature* (6 Dec. 1894): 121.

———. *The Definitive Time Machine: A Critical Edition of H. G. Wells's Scientific Romance with Introduction and Notes,* ed. Harry M. Geduld. Bloomington: Indiana UP, 1987.

How to Use This Index

> **Calvino, Italo**
> 1923–1985 .... CLC 5, 8, 11, 22, 33, 39,
> 73; SSC 3

list all author entries in the following Gale Literary Criticism series:

BLC = Black Literature Criticism
CLC = Contemporary Literary Criticism
CLR = Children's Literature Review
CMLC = Classical and Medieval Literature Criticism
DA = DISCovering Authors
DAB = DISCovering Authors: British
DAC = DISCovering Authors: Canadian
DAM = DISCovering Authors: Modules
     DRAM: Dramatists Module; MST: Most-Studied Authors Module;
     MULT: Multicultural Authors Module; NOV: Novelists Module;
     POET: Poets Module; POP: Popular Fiction and Genre Authors Module
DC = Drama Criticism
HLC = Hispanic Literature Criticism
LC = Literature Criticism from 1400 to 1800
NCLC = Nineteenth-Century Literature Criticism
PC = Poetry Criticism
SSC = Short Story Criticism
TCLC = Twentieth-Century Literary Criticism
WLC = World Literature Criticism, 1500 to the Present

The cross-references

> See also CANR 23; CA 85-88;
>   obituary CA116

list all author entries in the following Gale biographical and literary sources:

AAYA = Authors & Artists for Young Adults
AITN = Authors in the News
BEST = Bestsellers
BW = Black Writers
CA = Contemporary Authors
CAAS = Contemporary Authors Autobiography Series
CABS = Contemporary Authors Bibliographical Series
CANR = Contemporary Authors New Revision Series
CAP = Contemporary Authors Permanent Series
CDALB = Concise Dictionary of American Literary Biography
CDBLB = Concise Dictionary of British Literary Biography
DLB = Dictionary of Literary Biography
DLBD = Dictionary of Literary Biography Documentary Series
DLBY = Dictionary of Literary Biography Yearbook
HW = Hispanic Writers
JRDA = Junior DISCovering Authors
MAICYA = Major Authors and Illustrators for Children and Young Adults
MTCW = Major 20th-Century Writers
NNAL = Native North American Literature
SAAS = Something about the Author Autobiography Series
SATA = Something about the Author
YABC = Yesterday's Authors of Books for Children

26, 80

Gay, Marie-Louise 1952- **27**
See also CA 135; SAAS 21; SATA 68

Gaze, Gillian
See Barklem, Jill

Gee, Maurice (Gough) 1931- **56**
See also CA 97-100; CANR 67; CLC 29; SATA 46, 101

Geisel, Theodor Seuss 1904-1991 .... **53**
See also Dr. Se uss
See also CA 13-16R; 135; CANR 13, 32; DA3; DLB 61; DLBY 91; MAICYA; MTCW 1, 2; SATA 1, 28, 75, 100; SATA-Obit 67

George, Jean Craighead 1919- **1**
See also AAYA 8; CA 5-8R; CANR 25; CLC 35; DLB 52; JRDA; MAICYA; SATA 2, 68

Gerrard, Roy 1935-1997 .... **23**
See also CA 110; 160; CANR 57; SATA 47, 90; SATA-Brief 45; SATA-Obit 99

Gewe, Raddory
See Gorey, Edward (St. John)

Gibbons, Gail 1944- **8**
See also CA 69-72; CANR 12; MAICYA; SAAS 12; SATA 23, 72, 104

Giblin, James Cross 1933- **29**
See also CA 106; CANR 24; MAICYA; SAAS 12; SATA 33, 75

Ginsburg, Mirra **45**
See also CA 17-20R; CANR 11, 28, 54; SATA 6, 92

Giovanni, Nikki 1943- **6**
See also AAYA 22; AITN 1; BLC 2; BW 2, 3; CA 29-32R; CAAS 6; CANR 18, 41, 60; CDALBS; CLC 2, 4, 19, 64, 117; DA; DAB; DAC; DAM MST, MULT, POET; DA3; DLB 5, 41; INT CANR-18; MAICYA; MTCW 1, 2; PC 19; SATA 24, 107; WLCS

Glenn, Mel 1943- **51**
See also AAYA 25; CA 123; CANR 49, 68; SATA 51, 93; SATA-Brief 45

Glubok, Shirley (Astor) **1**
See also CA 5-8R; CANR 4, 43; MAICYA; SAAS 7; SATA 6, 68

Goble, Paul 1933- **21**
See also CA 93-96; C ANR 16; MAICYA; SATA 25, 69

Godden, (Margaret) Rumer 1907-1998 .... **20**
See also AAYA 6; CA 5-8R; 172; CANR 4, 27, 36, 55, 80; CLC 53; DLB 161; MAICYA; SAAS 12; SATA 3, 36; SATA -Obit 109

Godfrey, Martyn N. 1949- **57**
See also CA 126; CANR 68; SATA 95

Goffstein, (Marilyn) Brooke 1940- **3**
See also CA 21-24R; CANR 9 , 28; DLB 61; MAICYA; SATA 8, 70

Gomi, Taro 1945- **57**
See also CA 162; SATA 64, 103

Goodall, John Strickland 1908-1996 .... **25**
See also CA 33-36R; 1 52; MAICYA; SATA 4, 66; SATA-Obit 91

Gordon, Sheila 1927- **27**
See also CA 132; SATA 88

Gorey, Edward (St. John) 1925-2000 .... **36**
See also CA 5-8R; CANR 9, 30, 78; DLB 61; INT CANR-30; MAICYA; SATA 29, 70; SATA-Brief 27

Goscinny, Rene 1926-1977 .... **37**
See also CA 117; 113; SATA 47; SATA-Brief 39

Graham, Bob 1942- **31**
See also CA 165; SATA 63, 101

Graham, Lorenz (Bell) 1902-1989 .... **10**
See also BW 1; CA 9-12R; 129; CANR 25; DLB 76; MAICYA; SAAS 5; SATA 2, 74; SATA-Obit 63

Grahame, Kenneth 1859-1932 .... **5**
See also CA 108; 136; CANR 80; DAB; DA3;

DLB 34, 141, 178; MAICYA; MTCW 2; SATA 100; TCLC 64; YABC 1

Gramatky, Hardie 1907-1979 .... **22**
See also AITN 1; CA 1-4R; 85 -88; CANR 3; DLB 22; MAICYA; SATA 1, 30; SATA-Obit 23

Greenaway, Kate 1846-1901 .... **6**
See also CA 137; D LB 141; MAICYA; SATA 100; YABC 2

Greene, Bette 1934- **2**
See also AAYA 7; CA 53-56; CANR 4; CLC 30; JRDA; MAICYA; SAAS 16; SATA 8, 102

Greene, Constance C(larke) 1924- **62**
See also AAYA 7; CA 61-64; CANR 8, 38; JRDA; MAICYA; SAAS 11; SATA 11, 72

Greenfield, Eloise 1929- **4, 38**
See also BW 2; CA 49-52; CAN R 1, 19, 43; INT CANR-19; JRDA; MAICYA; SAAS 16; SATA 19, 61, 105

Greer, Richard
See Silverberg, Robert

Gregory, Jean
See Ure, Jean

Grewdead, Roy
See Gorey, Edward (St. John)

Grey Owl **32**
See also Belaney, Archibald Stansfeld
See also DLB 92

Grifalconi, Ann 1929- **35**
See also CA 5-8R; CANR 9, 35; MAICYA; SAAS 16; SATA 2, 66

Grimes, Nikki 1950- **42**
See also CA 77-80; CANR 60; SATA 93

Gripe, Maria (Kristina) 1923- **5**
See also CA 29-32R; CANR 17, 39; MAICYA; SATA 2, 74

Grode, Redway
See Gorey, Edward (St. John)

Gruelle, John (Barton) 1880-1938
See Gruelle, Johnny
See also CA 115; 175; SATA 3 5; SATA-Brief 32

Gruelle, Johnny **34**
See also Gruelle, John (Barton)
See also DLB 22

Guillot, Rene 1900-1969 .... **22**
See also CA 49-52; CANR 39; SATA 7

Guy, Rosa (Cuthbert) 1928- **13**
See also AAYA 4 ; BW 2; CA 17-20R; CANR 14, 34, 83; CLC 26; DLB 33; JRDA; MAICYA; SATA 14, 62

Haar, Jaap ter **15**
See also ter Haar, Jaap

Hadley, Lee 1934-1995 .... **40**
See also Irwin, Hadley
See also CA 101; 149; CANR 19, 36, 83; MAICYA; SATA 47, 8 9; SATA-Brief 38; SATA-Obit 86

Haenel, Wolfram 1956- **64**
See also CA 155; SATA 89

Haertling, Peter 1933-
See Hartling, Peter
See also CA 101; CANR 22, 48; DLB 75; MAICYA; SATA 66

Hagon, Priscilla
See Allan, Mabel Esther

Haig-Brown, Roderick (Langmere) 1908-1976 **31**
See also CA 5-8R; 69-72; CANR 4, 38, 83; CLC 21; DLB 88; MAICYA; SATA 12

Haley, Gail E(inhart) 1939- **21**
See also CA 21-24R; CANR 14, 35, 82; MAICYA; SAAS 13; SATA 43, 78; SATA-Brief 28

Hamilton, Clive
See Lewis, C(live) S(taples)

Hamilton, Franklin

See Silverberg, Robert

Hamilton, Gail
See Corcoran, Barbara

Hamilton, Virginia 1936- **1, 11, 40**
See also AAYA 2, 21; BW 2, 3; CA 25-28R; CANR 20, 37, 73; CLC 26; DAM MULT; DLB 33, 52; INT CANR-20; JRDA; MAICYA; MTCW 1, 2; SATA 4, 56, 79

Hamley, Dennis 1935- **47**
See also CA 57-60; CANR 11, 26; SAAS 22; SATA 39, 69

Handford, Martin (John) 1956- **22**
See also CA 137; MAICYA; SATA 64

Hanel, Wolfram
See Haenel, Wolfram

Hansen, Joyce (Viola) 1942- **21**
See also BW 2; CA 105; CANR 43, 87; JRDA; MAICYA; SAAS 15; SATA 46,101; SATA-Brief 39

Hargrave, Leonie
See Disch, Thomas M(ichael)

Harris, Christie (Lucy) Irwin 1907- **47**
See also CA 5-8R; CANR 6, 83; CLC 12; DLB 88; JRDA; MAICYA; SAAS 10; SATA 6, 74

Harris, Joel Chandler 1848-1908 .... **49**
See also CA 104; 137; CANR 80; DLB 11, 23, 42, 78, 91; MAICYA; SATA 100; SSC 19; TCLC 2; YABC 1

Harris, Lavinia
See St. John, Nicole

Harris, Rosemary (Jeanne) **30**
See also CA 33-36R; CANR 13, 30, 84; SAAS 7; SATA 4, 82

Hartling, Peter **29**
See also Haertling, Peter
See also DLB 75

Haskins, James S. 1941- **3, 39**
See also Haskins, Jim
See also AAYA 14; BW 2, 3; CA 33-36R; CANR 25, 48, 79; JRDA; MAICYA; SATA 9, 69, 105

Haskins, Jim
See Haskins, James S.
See also SAAS 4

Haugaard, Erik Christian 1923- **11**
See also CA 5-8R; CANR 3, 38; JRDA; MAICYA; SAAS 12; SATA 4, 68

Hautzig, Esther Rudomin 1930- **22**
See also CA 1-4R; CANR 5, 20, 46, 85; JRDA; MAICYA; SAAS 15; SATA 4, 68

Hay, Timothy
See Brown, Margaret Wise

Hays, Wilma Pitchford 1909- **59**
See also CA 1-4R; CANR 5, 45; MAICYA; SAAS 3; SATA 1, 28

Haywood, Carolyn 1898-1990 .... **22**
See also CA 5-8R; 130; CANR 5, 20, 83; MAICYA; SATA 1, 29, 75; SATA-Obit 64

Heide, Florence Parry 1919- **60**
See also CA 93-96; CANR 84; JRDA; MAICYA; SAAS 6; SATA 32, 69

Heine, Helme 1941- **18**
See also CA 135; MAICYA; SATA 67

Henkes, Kevin 1960- **23**
See also CA 114; CANR 38; MAICYA; SATA 43, 76, 108

Henry, Marguerite 1902-1997 .... **4**
See also CA 17-20R; 162; CANR 9; DLB 22; JRDA; MAICYA; SAAS 7; SATA 100; SATA-Obit 99

Hentoff, Nat(han Irving) 1925- **1, 52**
See also AAYA 4; CA 1-4R; CAAS 6; CANR 5, 25, 77; CLC 26; INT CANR-25;JRDA; MAICYA; SATA 42, 69; SATA-Brief 27

Herge **6**
See also Remi, Georges

Hesse, Karen 1952- **54**

See also CA 73 -76; CANR 48; MAICYA; SATA 15

Mitchell, Clyde
See Silverberg, Robert

Mohr, Nicholasa 1938- **22**
See also AAYA 8; CA 49-52; CANR 1, 32, 64; CLC 12; DAM MULT; DLB 145; HLC 2; HW 1, 2; JRDA; SAAS 8; SATA 8, 97; SATA-Essay 113

Mole, John 1941- **61**
See also CA 101; CANR 18, 41, 83; SATA 36, 103

Molin, Charles
See Mayne, William (James Carter)

Monjo, F(erdinand) N(icholas III) 1924-1978
2
See also CA 81-84; CAN R 37, 83; MAICYA; SATA 16

Montgomery, L(ucy) M(aud) 1874-1942 .... **8**
See also AAYA 12; CA 108; 137; DAC; DAM MST; DA3; DLB 92; DLBD 14; JRDA; MAICYA; MTCW 2; SATA 100; TCLC 51; YABC 1

Moore, Lilian 1909- **15**
See also CA 103; CANR 38; MAICYA; SATA 52

Mora, Pat(ricia) 1942- **58**
See also CA 129; CANR 57, 81; DAM MULT; DLB 209; HLC 2; HW 1, 2; SATA 92

Mori, Kyoko 1957(?)- **64**
See also AAYA 25; CA 153; SAAS 26

Morpurgo, Michael 1943- **51**
See also CA 158; SATA 93

Moser, Barry 1940- **49**
See also MAICYA; SAAS 15; SATA 56, 79

Mowat, Farley (McGill) 1921- **20**
See also AAYA 1; CA 1-4R; CANR 4, 24, 42, 68; CLC 26; DAC; DAM MST; DLB 68; INT CANR-24; JRDA; MAICYA; MTCW. 1, 2; SATA 3, 55

Mude, O.
See Gorey, Edward (St. John)

Mueller, Joerg 1942- **43**
See also CA 136; SATA 67

Mukerji, Dhan Gopal 1890-1936 .... **10**
See also CA 119; 136; MAICYA; SATA 40

Muller, Jorg
See Mueller, Joerg

Mun
See Leaf, (Wilbur) Munro

Munari, Bruno 1907- **9**
See also CA 73-76; CANR 38; MAICYA; SATA 15

Munsch, Robert (Norman) 1945- **19**
See also CA 121; CANR 37, 87; MAICYA; SATA 50, 83; SATA-Brief 48

Murphy, Jill (Frances) 1949- **39**
See also CA 105 ; CANR 44, 50, 84; MAICYA; SATA 37, 70

Murphy, Jim 1947- **53**
See also AAYA 20; CA 111; SATA 37, 77; SATA-Brief 32

Myers, Walter Dean 1937- **4, 16, 35**
See also AAYA 4, 23; BLC 3; BW 2; CA 33-36R; CANR 20, 42, 67; CLC 35; DAM MULT, NOV; DLB 33; INT CANR-20; JRDA; MAICYA; MTCW 2; SAAS 2; SATA 41, 71, 109; SATA-Brief 27

Myers, Walter M.
See Myers, Walter Dean

Naidoo, Beverley 1943- **29**
See also AAYA 23; CA 160; SATA 63

Nakatani, Chiyoko 1930-1981 .... **30**
See also CA 77-80; SATA 55; SATA-Brief 40

Namioka, Lensey 1929- **48**
See also AAYA 27; CA 69-72; CANR 11, 27, 52, 84; SAAS 24; SATA 27, 89

Napoli, Donna Jo 1948- **51**
See also AAYA 25; CA 156; SAAS 23; SATA 92

Naylor, Phyllis (Reynolds) 1933- **17**
See also AAYA 4, 29; CA 21-24R; CANR 8, 24, 59; JRDA; MAICYA; SAAS 10; SATA 12, 66, 102

Needle, Jan 1943- **43**
See also AAYA 23; CA 106; CANR 28, 84; SAAS 23; SATA 30, 98

Nesbit, E(dith) 1858-1924 .... **3**
See also Bla nd, Edith Nesbit
See also CA 118; 137; DLB 141, 153, 178; MAICYA; MTCW 2; SAT A 100; YABC 1

Ness, Evaline (Michelow) 1911-1986 .... **6**
See also CA 5-8R; 120; CANR 5, 37; DLB 61; MAICYA; SAAS 1; SATA 1, 26; SATA-Obit 49

Neufeld, John (Arthur) 1938- **52**
See also AAYA 11; CA 25-28R; CANR 11, 37, 56; CLC 17; MAICYA; SAAS 3; SATA 6, 81

Nielsen, Kay (Rasmus) 1886-1957 .... **16**
See also CA 177; MAICYA; SATA 16

Nimmo, Jenny 1942- **44**
See also CA 108; CANR 52, 83; SATA 87

Nixon, Joan Lowery 1927- **24**
See also AAYA 12; CA 9-12R; CANR 7, 24, 38; JRDA; MAICYA; SAAS 9; SATA 8, 44, 78, 115

Noestlinger, Christine 1936- **12**
See also CA 115; 123; CANR 38; MAICYA; SATA 64; SATA-Brief 37

North, Andrew
See Norton, Andre

North, Captain George
See Stevenson, Robert Louis (Balfour)

Norton, Alice Mary
See Norton, Andre
See also MAICYA; SATA 1, 43

Norton, Andre 1912- **50**
See also Norton, Alice Mary
See also AAYA 14; CA 1-4R; CANR 68; CLC 12; DLB 8, 52; JRDA; MTCW 1; SATA 91

Norton, Mary 1903-1992 .... **6**
See also CA 97-10 0, 139; DLB 160; MAICYA; SATA 18, 60; SATA-Obit 72

Nourse, Alan E(dward) 1928-1992 .... **33**
See also CA 1-4R; 14 5; CANR 3, 21, 45, 84; DLB 8; SATA 48

Nye, Naomi Shihab 1952- **59**
See also AAYA 27; CA 146; CANR 70; DLB 120; SATA 86

Oakley, Graham 1929- **7**
See also CA 106; CANR 38, 54, 85; MAICYA; SATA 30, 84

Oberman, Sheldon 1949- **54**
See also CA 152; SAA S 26; SATA 85; SATA-Essay 114

O'Brien, Robert C. **2**
See also Conly, Robert Leslie
See also AAYA 6

O'Connor, Patrick
See Wibberley, Leonard (Patrick O'Connor)

O'Dell, Scott 1898-1989 .... **1, 16**
See also AAYA 3; CA 61-64; 129; CANR 12, 30; CLC 30; DLB 52; JRDA; MAICYA; SATA 12, 60

Ofek, Uriel 1926- **28**
See also CA 101; CANR 18; SATA 36

Ogilvy, Gavin
See Barrie, J(ames) M(atthew)

O Mude
See Gorey, Edward (St. John)

Oneal, Elizabeth 1934-
See Oneal, Zibby
See also CA 106; CANR 28, 84; MAICYA;

SATA 30, 82

Oneal, Zibby **13**
See also Oneal, Elizabeth
See also AAYA 5; CLC 30; JRDA

Orgel, Doris 1929- **48**
See also AITN 1; CA 45-48; CANR 2; SAAS 19; SATA 7, 85

Orlev, Uri 1931- **30**
See also AAYA 20; CA 101; CANR 34, 84; SAAS 19; SATA 58

Ormerod, Jan(ette Louise) 1946- **20**
See also CA 113; CANR 35; MAICYA; SATA 55, 70; SATA-Brief 44

Osborne, David
See Silverberg, Robert

Osborne, George
See Silverberg, Robert

O'Shea, (Catherine) Pat(ricia Shiels) 1931-**18**
See also CA 145; CANR 84; SATA 87

Ottley, Reginald Leslie 1909-1985 .... **16**
See also CA 93-96; CANR 34; MAICYA; SATA 26

Owen, Gareth 1936- **31**
See also CA 150; SAAS 14; SATA 83

Oxenbury, Helen 1938- **22**
See also CA 25-28R; CANR 35, 79; MAICYA; SATA 3, 68

Paisley, Tom 1932-
See Bethancourt, T. Ernesto
See also CA 61-64; CANR 15; SATA 78

Parish, Margaret Cecile 1927-1988
See Parish, Peg gy
See also CA 73-76; 127; CANR 18, 38, 81; MAICYA; SATA 73

Parish, Peggy **22**
See also Parish, Margaret Cecile
See also SATA 17 ; SATA-Obit 59

Park, Barbara 1947- **34**
See also CA 113; SATA 40, 78; SATA-Brief 35

Park, (Rosina) Ruth (Lucia) **51**
See also CA 105; CANR 65; SATA 25, 93

Pascal, Francine 1938- **25**
See also AAYA 1; CA 115; 123; CANR 39, 50; JRDA; MAICYA; SATA 51, 80; SATA-Brief 37

Patent, Dorothy Hinshaw 1940- **19**
See also CA 61-64; CANR 9, 24; MAICYA; SAAS 13; SATA 22, 69

Paterson, Katherine (Womeldorf) 1932-**7, 50**
See also AAYA 1, 31; CA 21-24R; CANR 28, 59; CLC 12, 30; DLB 52; JRDA; MAICYA; MTCW 1; SATA 13, 53, 92

Paton Walsh, Gillian 1937-
See Walsh, Jill Paton
See also AAYA 11; CA NR 38, 83; DLB 161; JRDA; MAICYA; SAAS 3; SATA 4, 72, 109

Paulsen, Gary 1939- **19, 54**
See also AAYA 2, 17; CA 73-76; CANR 30, 54, 83; JRDA; MAICYA; SATA 22,50, 54, 79, 111

Pearce, Philippa **9**
See also Christie, (Ann) Philippa
See also CLC 21; DLB 161; MAICYA; SATA 1, 67

Pearson, Kit 1947- **26**
See also AAYA 19; CA 145; CANR 71; JRDA; SATA 77

Peck, Richard (Wayne) 1934- **15**
See also AAYA 1, 24; CA 85-88; CANR 19, 38; CLC 21; INT CANR-19; JRDA; MAICYA; SAAS 2; SATA 18, 55, 97; SATA-Essay 110

Peck, Robert Newton 1928- **45**
See also AAYA 3; CA 81-84, 182; CAAE 182; CANR 31, 63; CLC 17; DA; DAC; DAM MST; JRDA; MAICYA; SAAS 1; SATA 21, 62, 111; SATA-Essay 108

Children's Literature Review
Cumulative Nationality Index

AMERICAN

Aardema, Verna **17**
Aaseng, Nathan **54**
Adkins, Jan **7**
Adler, Irving **27**
Adoff, Arnold **7**
Alcott, Louisa May **1, 38**
Alexander, Lloyd (Chudley) **1, 5, 48**
Aliki **9**
Anderson, Poul (William) **58**
Angelou, Maya **53**
Anglund, Joan Walsh **1**
Armstrong, William H(oward) **1**
Arnold, Caroline **61**
Arnosky, James Edward **15**
Aruego, Jose (Espiritu) **5**
Ashabranner, Brent (Kenneth) **28**
Asimov, Isaac **12**
Atwater, Florence (Hasseltine Carroll) **19**
Atwater, Richard (Tupper) **19**
Avi **24**
Aylesworth, Thomas G(ibbons) **6**
Babbitt, Natalie (Zane Moore) **2, 53**
Bacon, Martha Sherman **3**
Ballard, Robert D(uane) **60**
Bang, Molly Garrett **8**
Baum, L(yman) Frank **15**
Baylor, Byrd **3**
Bellairs, John (A.) **37**
Bemelmans, Ludwig **6**
Benary-Isbert, Margot **12**
Bendick, Jeanne **5**
Berenstain, Jan(ice) **19**
Berenstain, Stan(ley) **19**
Berger, Melvin H. **32**
Bess, Clayton **39**
Bethancourt, T. Ernesto **3**
Block, Francesca (Lia) **33**
Blos, Joan W(insor) **18**
Blumberg, Rhoda **21**
Blume, Judy (Sussman) **2, 15**
Bogart, Jo Ellen **59**
Bond, Nancy (Barbara) **11**
Bontemps, Arna(ud Wendell) **6**
Bova, Ben(jamin William) **3**
Boyd, Candy Dawson **50**
Brancato, Robin F(idler) **32**
Branley, Franklyn M(ansfield) **13**
Brett, Jan (Churchill) **27**
Bridgers, Sue Ellen **18**
Brink, Carol Ryrie **30**
Brooks, Bruce **25**
Brooks, Gwendolyn **27**
Brown, Marcia **12**
Brown, Marc (Tolon) **29**
Brown, Margaret Wise **10**
Bruchac, Joseph III **46**
Bryan, Ashley F. **18**
Bunting, Eve **28, 56**
Burch, Robert J(oseph) **63**
Burnett, Frances (Eliza) Hodgson **24**
Burton, Virginia Lee **11**
Byars, Betsy (Cromer) **1, 16**
Caines, Jeannette (Franklin) **24**

Calhoun, Mary **42**
Cameron, Eleanor (Frances) **1**
Carle, Eric **10**
Carter, Alden R(ichardson) **22**
Cassedy, Sylvia **26**
Charlip, Remy **8**
Childress, Alice **14**
Choi, Sook Nyul **53**
Christopher, Matt(hew Frederick) **33**
Ciardi, John (Anthony) **19**
Clark, Ann Nolan **16**
Cleary, Beverly (Atlee Bunn) **2, 8**
Cleaver, Bill **6**
Cleaver, Vera (Allen) **6**
Clifton, (Thelma) Lucille **5**
Coatsworth, Elizabeth (Jane) **2**
Cobb, Vicki **2**
Cohen, Daniel (E.) **3, 43**
Cole, Brock **18**
Cole, Joanna **5, 40**
Collier, James L(incoln) **3**
Colum, Padraic **36**
Conford, Ellen **10**
Conrad, Pam **18**
Cooney, Barbara **23**
Cooper, Floyd **60**
Corbett, Scott **1**
Corcoran, Barbara **50**
Cormier, Robert (Edmund) **12, 55**
Cox, Palmer **24**
Creech, Sharon **42**
Crews, Donald **7**
Crutcher, Chris(topher C.) **28**
Cummings, Pat (Marie) **48**
Curry, Jane L(ouise) **31**
Cushman, Karen **55**
Dalgliesh, Alice **62**
Danziger, Paula **20**
d'Aulaire, Edgar Parin **21**
d'Aulaire, Ingri (Mortenson Parin) **21**
Davis, Ossie **56**
Day, Alexandra **22**
de Angeli, Marguerite (Lofft) **1**
DeClements, Barthe **23**
DeJong, Meindert **1**
Denslow, W(illiam) W(allace) **15**
dePaola, Tomie **4, 24**
Dillon, Diane (Claire) **44**
Dillon, Leo **44**
Disch, Thomas M(ichael) **18**
Dixon, Franklin W. **61**
Dodge, Mary (Elizabeth) Mapes **62**
Domanska, Janina **40**
Donovan, John **3**
Dorris, Michael (Anthony) **58**
Dorros, Arthur (M.) **42**
Draper, Sharon M(ills) **57**
Dr. Seuss **1, 9, 53**
Duke, Kate **51**
Duncan, Lois **29**
Duvoisin, Roger Antoine **23**
Eager, Edward McMaken **43**
Ehlert, Lois (Jane) **28**
Emberley, Barbara A(nne) **5**

Emberley, Ed(ward Randolph) **5**
Engdahl, Sylvia Louise **2**
L'Engle, Madeleine (Camp Franklin) **1, 14, 57**
Enright, Elizabeth **4**
Epstein, Beryl (M. Williams) **26**
Epstein, Samuel **26**
Estes, Eleanor (Ruth) **2**
Ets, Marie Hall **33**
Feelings, Muriel (Grey) **5**
Feelings, Tom **5, 58**
Ferry, Charles **34**
Field, Rachel (Lyman) **21**
Fisher, Aileen (Lucia) **49**
Fisher, Leonard Everett **18**
Fitzgerald, John D(ennis) **1**
Fitzhugh, Louise **1**
Flack, Marjorie **28**
Fleischman, (Albert) Sid(ney) **1, 15**
Fleischman, Paul **20**
Forbes, Esther **27**
Foster, Genevieve Stump **7**
Fox, Paula **1, 44**
Freedman, Russell (Bruce) **20**
Freeman, Don **30**
Fritz, Jean (Guttery) **2, 14**
Fujikawa, Gyo **25**
Gaberman, Judie Angell **33**
Gag, Wanda (Hazel) **4**
Gaines, Ernest J(ames) **62**
Galdone, Paul **16**
Gallant, Roy A(rthur) **30**
Gantos, Jack **18**
Garden, Nancy **51**
Gauch, Patricia Lee **56**
Geisel, Theodor Seuss **53**
George, Jean Craighead **1**
Gibbons, Gail **8**
Giblin, James Cross **29**
Giovanni, Nikki **6**
Glenn, Mel **51**
Glubok, Shirley (Astor) **1**
Goble, Paul **21**
Goffstein, (Marilyn) Brooke **3**
Gordon, Sheila **27**
Gorey, Edward (St. John) **36**
Graham, Lorenz (Bell) **10**
Gramatky, Hardie **22**
Greene, Bette **2**
Greene, Constance C(larke) **62**
Greenfield, Eloise **4, 38**
Grifalconi, Ann **35**
Grimes, Nikki **42**
Gruelle, Johnny **34**
Guy, Rosa (Cuthbert) **13**
Hadley, Lee **40**
Haley, Gail E(inhart) **21**
Hamilton, Virginia **1, 11, 40**
Hansen, Joyce (Viola) **21**
Harris, Joel Chandler **49**
Haskins, James S. **3, 39**
Hautzig, Esther Rudomin **22**
Hays, Wilma Pitchford **59**
Haywood, Carolyn **22**

Nationality Index

CHILDREN'S LITERATURE REVIEW
Cumulative Title Index

Title Index

Title Index

Title Index

Title Index

Title Index

Title Index

ISBN 0-7876-3229-5

90000